LICENSING STANDARD ESSENTIAL PATENTS

What is the licensing framework of standard essential patents (SEPs) for connectivity standards such as 5G and Wi-Fi? How will the framework change with the Internet of Things (IoT)? This book provides comprehensive answers to these questions.

For over two decades, connectivity standards have been the subject of litigation and controversy around the globe. Now, with the introduction of 5G and the emergence of the world of connected objects, or the IoT, the licensing framework for SEPs is becoming even more contentious. In order to bring clarity to the debate, this book analyses and explains key components of a fair, reasonable and non-discriminatory (FRAND) licence for SEPs; clarifies the economic, policy and market background of SEP disputes; examines the interrelated application of contract, patent and competition laws; and describes the approaches by courts and regulators in the EU, US and the UK. Importantly, the book also assesses how the experience from the smartphone and ICT industries can be applied in a new environment of the IoT, and considers what needs to be changed in the future SEP licensing landscape.

The book provides a holistic coverage of SEP licensing issues in an attempt to reduce uncertainty within this highly complex and technical area, and will be useful to practitioners, policy makers, SMEs and large technology companies in the IoT, as well as academics interested in the field.

Licensing Standard Essential Patents

FRAND and the Internet of Things

Igor Nikolic

•HART•
OXFORD • LONDON • NEW YORK • NEW DELHI • SYDNEY

HART PUBLISHING

Bloomsbury Publishing Plc

Kemp House, Chawley Park, Cumnor Hill, Oxford, OX2 9PH, UK

1385 Broadway, New York, NY 10018, USA

29 Earlsfort Terrace, Dublin 2, Ireland

HART PUBLISHING, the Hart/Stag logo, BLOOMSBURY and the Diana logo are trademarks of Bloomsbury Publishing Plc

First published in Great Britain 2021

A catalogue record for this book is available from the British Library.

Library of Congress Cataloging-in-Publication data

Names: Nikolic, Igor (Writer on patent law), author.

Title: Licensing standard essential patents : FRAND and the internet of things / Igor Nikolic.

Description: Oxford ; New York : Hart, 2021. | Based on author's thesis (doctoral - University College London, 2019). | Includes bibliographical references and index.

Identifiers: LCCN 2021041808 (print) | LCCN 2021041809 (ebook) | ISBN 9781509947553 (hardback) | ISBN 9781509947577 (pdf) | ISBN 9781509947560 (Epub)

Subjects: LCSH: Internet of things—Patents. | Patent licenses.

Classification: LCC K1519.C6 N55 2021 (print) | LCC K1519.C6 (ebook) | DDC 346.04/86—dc23

LC record available at https://lccn.loc.gov/2021041808

LC ebook record available at https://lccn.loc.gov/2021041809

ISBN: HB: 978-1-50994-755-3
ePDF: 978-1-50994-757-7
ePub: 978-1-50994-756-0

Typeset by Compuscript Ltd, Shannon

To find out more about our authors and books visit www.hartpublishing.co.uk. Here you will find extracts, author information, details of forthcoming events and the option to sign up for our newsletters.

FOREWORD

It gives me great pleasure to write this. For two main reasons. Firstly, I was the principal supervisor of Dr Igor Nikolic's PhD research project at UCL. His thesis is the foundation of this book. Those who read the book will not be surprised to learn that his examiners passed the thesis first time – there were no revisions or rewrites for Igor. It was a joy to supervise him, through the good and the dark times (nearly all PhD students go through at least one dark time). He was a ray of sunshine in the Faculty – when I said to the PhD admin staff that I would be getting another PhD student, one of them said 'Can we have another Igor?'

My second reason is that this is such a good book. The reality of the SEP system is that it works well. There are many standards for many technologies. For each standard there are many, many SEP-committed patents. There are thousands of complex negotiations and agreements between patentees and patentees, patentees and implementers, and thousands of licences and cross-licences which make the system work. The detail of this is largely hidden – but the result is not. That result is clearly the fastest sustained growth in technology the human race has ever seen. The SEP system is also the biggest and best example of worldwide cooperation between competitors. It is true that there have been, and will continue to be, conflicts by way of litigation in the courts or intervention by competition authorities. Because only the conflicts get publicity, they raise in some outsiders an impression that conflict is the norm and something ought to be done to stop conflict. They do not fully understand that disputes are the exception, not the norm, rather like a seafarer who has never seen an iceberg not realising that most of an iceberg cannot be seen. The visible tip of the FRAND iceberg has a whole host of various issues or arguments. Things and concepts such as holdup, holdout, what is non-discriminatory, top-down/bottom-up, royalty-stacking, patent thickets, over-declaration or antisuit and anti-antisuit injunctions, even the word FRAND itself, formed no part of the thinking or lexicon of competition lawyers, competition authorities, patent lawyers or judges only 20 years ago. Difficult to believe but true.

What this book does is set out each topic, clearly and fairly. It then describes the differing views on each topic. All this is done with full reference to cases, articles, competition authority actions. It does not promote Dr Nikolic's personal views on a point: that is for the reader who is given the evidence to do so. The book is a deceptively easy read because Dr Nikolic presents complex matter so well.

It will be a valuable resource for competition authorities and lawyers, patent lawyers, SEP holders and SEP implementers. Those who have it in mind to theorise about the FRAND system would do well to use it too – so as not to start off with theoretical opinions which they seek to justify. The book does it the other way round: start with the facts and form opinions later.

Sir Robin Jacob
Sir Hugh Laddie Chair of Intellectual Property Law
University College London
April 2021

ACKNOWLEDGEMENTS

This book originated from my PhD research at University College London and is the final product of the intellectual journey that took several years of research and writing. The book would not be possible without the help and support of many people along the way. Special thanks must particularly go to my supervisors and friends, Sir Robin Jacob and Dr Christopher Stothers, who shaped and guided my thinking in many ways. I am also very grateful to the European University Institute's School of Regulation – Communications & Media that allowed me to spend several months in Florence to finalise the book. I would like to thank the whole team at EUI – Pier Luigi Parcu, Chiara Carrozza, Niccolo Inocenti, Niccolo Galli and Marco Botta, also for conversations we had about many ideas from the book. Discussions with EUI's Lazar Radic is likewise kindly appreciated. I am also very grateful to the whole team at Hart for their support, professionalism and hard work.

Finally, the journey would not be possible without the patience and infinite support of my family – to Ivan, Jasmina, Aleksandar and to my beloved granny Mara, who is watching over and to whom this book is especially dedicated.

CONTENTS

PART II
THE MEANING AND CONTENT OF A FRAND LICENCE

PART III
STANDARD ESSENTIAL PATENT LICENSING IN THE INTERNET OF THINGS

ABBREVIATIONS

ABA	American Bar Association
ANSI	American National Standards Institute
ATIS	Alliance for Telecommunications Industry Solutions
BSI	British Standards Institution
CEN	European Committee for Standardization
CENELEC	European Committee for Electrotechnical Standardization
CJEU	Court of Justice of the European Union
EMVR	Entire market value rule
ETSI	European Telecommunications Standards Institute
FCC	(US) Federal Communications Commission
FRAND	Fair, reasonable and non-discriminatory
FTC	Federal Trade Commission
GDP	Gross domestic product
GSA	Global Mobile Suppliers Association
GSMA	Global System for Mobile Communications
HEVC	High Efficiency Video Coding
ICT	Information and Communications Technology
IEC	International Electrotechnical Commission
IEEE	Institute of Electrical and Electronics Engineers
IETF	Internet Engineering Task Force
IoT	Internet of Things
IP	Intellectual property
ISO	International Organization for Standardization
ITC	US International Trade Commission
IPR	Intellectual property right

ITU	International Telecommunication Union
ITU-R	ITU Radiocommunication Sector
ITU-T	ITU Telecommunication Standardization Sector
JEDEC	Joint Electron Device Engineering Council
MPEG	Moving Picture Expert Group
ND	Non-discrimination
NDA	Non-disclosure agreement
NPEs	Non-practising entities
R&D	Research and development
RAND	Reasonable and non-discriminatory
RF	Royalty-free
SDO	Standard-Development Organisation
SEP	Standard Essential Patent
SME	Small and medium-sized enterprise
SSPPU	Smallest saleable patent-practicing unit
TFEU	Treaty on the Functioning of the European Union
TIA	Telecommunications Industry Association
TSG	Technical Specification Group
UMTS	Universal Mobile Telecommunications System
WCDMA	Wideband Code Division Multiple Access
WG	Working Group
W3C	World Wide Web Consortium

LIST OF CASES AND LEGISLATION

European Union

Court of Justice of the European Union

European Commission

UK

Germany

United States

Courts

Agencies

Legislation and Agency Materials

European Union

Legislation

Agency Materials

United States

Legislation

Agency Materials

Introduction

I. Setting the Context

The 'Internet of Things' will change our everyday lives. It will bring internet connectivity to many different sectors of the economy. We are seeing cars, home appliances, buildings, utilities, healthcare devices all connected to the internet with the ability to communicate with each other and with users.[1] For example, smart cars would be able to notify passengers of traffic conditions and become self-driving. The smart home system will enable consumers to turn off burglar alarms, unlock doors and set up heating before they get home from work. Smart health devices will allow consumers to easily monitor and diagnose their health conditions. Factories will also benefit from the mass digitisation of production processes, allowing the monitoring and control of all aspects of production. We can only imagine future benefits that the 'Fourth Industrial Revolution' will bring.[2] Already around 20 billion devices are estimated to be connected to the internet with an expected rise to as many as 41 billion by 2025.[3] Studies have estimated the economic impact of the IoT at as much as $11.1 trillion per year in 2025,[4] and $12.3 trillion by 2035.[5]

[1] See: Commission, 'Staff Working Document, Advancing the Internet of Things in Europe' SWD(2016) 110 final; Federal Trade Commission, 'Internet of Things: Privacy & Security in a Connected World' (2015), available at: www.ftc.gov/system/files/documents/reports/federal-trade-commission-staff-report-november-2013-workshop-entitled-internet-things-privacy/150127iotrpt.pdf.

[2] See K Schwab, 'The Fourth Industrial Revolution: What it Means, How to Respond' (World Economic Forum, 14 January 2016), available at: www.weforum.org/agenda/2016/01/the-fourth-industrial-revolution-what-it-means-and-how-to-respond/.

[3] M Hung (ed), 'Leading the IoT: Gartner Insights on How to Lead in a Connected World' (2017), available at: www.gartner.com/imagesrv/books/iot/iotEbook_digital.pdf; IDC, 'The Growth in Connected IoT Devices is Expected to Generate 79.4ZB of Data in 2025, According to a New IDC Forecast' (18 June 2019), available at: www.businesswire.com/news/home/20190618005012/en/The-Growth-in-Connected-IoT-Devices-is-Expected-to-Generate-79.4ZB-of-Data-in-2025-According-to-a-New-IDC-Forecast#:~:text=A%20new%20IDC%20forecast%20estimates,ZB)%20of%20data%20in%202025.&text=IDC%20projects%20that%20the%20amount,the%202018%2D2025%20forecast%20period; Ericsson Mobility Report (June 2020) 23 (providing a more conservative but still significant estimate of 10 billion IoT devices in 2020 with expected growth to 24.6 by 2025).

[4] McKinsey Global Institute, 'The Internet of Things: Mapping the Value Beyond the Hype' (June 2015), available at: www.mckinsey.com/~/media/McKinsey/Industries/Technology%20Media%20and%20Telecommunications/High%20Tech/Our%20Insights/The%20Internet%20of%20Things%20The%20value%20of%20digitizing%20the%20physical%20world/The-Internet-of-things-Mapping-the-value-beyond-the-hype.pdf.

[5] IHS Economics & HIS Technology, 'The 5G Economy: How 5G Technology Will Contribute to the Global Economy' (January 2017), available at: cdn.ihs.com/www/pdf/IHS-Technology-5G-Economic-Impact-Study.pdf.

The internet connectivity is largely expected to be facilitated by the 5G cellular communication standard. The 5G is anticipated to be up to a hundred times faster than the existing 4G LTE.[6] The end-to-end latency will also go down to one millisecond allowing, for example, remote surgeries in healthcare that depend on uninterrupted transmission of data. The 5G thus creates the possibility of seamless connectivity between devices and interoperability enabled by standards are estimated to represent 40 per cent of the potential value of the IoT.[7]

A 5G standard, like many other technological standards, is covered by patented technology. Patents that are necessary for the implementation of a standard are called Standard Essential Patents. SEPs can be a valuable strategic asset. They enable their owners to shape future technological development, but also earn significant licensing revenues due to standards omnipresence in our everyday lives. Think about 4G, Wi-Fi, USB, or Bluetooth standards. Every smartphone, computer and consumer electronic device uses these standards, and every manufacturer of these devices would need to obtain a licence for SEPs. SEPs can thus earn significant revenues for their owners, and it is no wonder that companies have a financial incentive in owning as many SEPs as possible.

5G and other technical interoperability standards are typically developed within the framework of Standard-Development Organisations and often include a large number of SEPs. According to some estimates, there are over 45,000 and 39,000 patents declared essential to 4G LTE and 3G UMTS respectively,[8] and as many as 95,000 patent declarations for 5G.[9] In order to make SEPs widely available to users, patent owners working within SDOs are required to commit to license SEPs on fair, reasonable and non-discriminatory (FRAND) terms. While it could be argued that FRAND terms are intentionally left open to allow for flexibility in licensing negotiations and enable tailored solutions for each company, their vagueness has produced tensions and litigation.

Indeed, once first smartphones were introduced, major disputes arose concerning the interpretation of a FRAND licence. The smartphone patent wars of the past witnessed virtually every high-tech company such as Apple, Samsung, Microsoft, Google, Ericsson, Nokia, Qualcomm, Motorola, Huawei, ZTE and RIM (Blackberry) in bitter legal fights across the world – from the US and Europe to China and Japan – over the use of SEPs that read on smartphones and other consumer devices.[10] Patent wars were facilitated by new entrants in the smartphone

[6] 5GPPP, '5G Innovations for New Business Opportunities' (March 2017), available at: 5g-ppp.eu/wp-content/uploads/2017/01/5GPPP-brochure-MWC17.pdf.

[7] McKinsey Global Institute (n 4).

[8] J Baron and T Pohlmann, 'Mapping Standards to Patents Using Databases of Declared Standard-Essential Patents and Systems of Technological Classification' (2018) 27 *Journal of Economics & Management Strategy* 504, 521.

[9] T Pohlmann and K Blind, 'Fact Finding Study on Patents Declared to 5G Standards' (2020), available at: ipforbusiness.org/wp-content/uploads/2020/02/5G-patent-study_TU-Berlin_IPlytics-2020.pdf.

[10] See C Duhigg and S Lohr, 'Fighters in a Patent War' *New York Times* (7 October 2012), available at: archive.nytimes.com/www.nytimes.com/interactive/2012/10/08/business/Fighters-in-a-Patent-War.html (showing the list of companies and explaining the smartphone patent wars); S Segan, 'Infographic: Smartphone Patent Wars Explained' *PC Magazine* (19 January 2012) (showing the companies engaged

market enabled by 3G and 4G standards and the convergence between traditional telecommunication and consumer electronic industries. SEP wars raised many issues concerning the precise meaning of a FRAND licensing commitment such as: what are the principles and methodologies for calculating FRAND royalty? What royalty base should be used (a component or the end-product device)? What is the nature of a FRAND commitment (is it an enforceable contract or not)? What is the role of competition law in enforcing FRAND licensing? If and under what conditions are injunctions available for infringements of SEPs?

These and many other issues have been the subject of numerous cases and academic literature with polarising opinions and open issues remaining to date. For example, back in 2007 Qualcomm, a major SEP holder and a producer of baseband chips, was investigated in the EU and the US for charging excessive royalties for its patents essential for 2G and 3G telecommunication standards.[11] In 2009, Nokia sued Apple for infringing 10 SEPs relating to GSM and UMTS communication standards and sought injunctive relief in the US, Germany, the Netherlands and the UK.[12] In 2010, Motorola sued Microsoft for infringement of Wi-Fi SEPs and was successful in obtaining an injunction against Microsoft in Germany, prohibiting the sale of XBox and certain Windows software products.[13] Microsoft however, counter-sued in the US for breach of Motorola's commitment to license its SEPs on FRAND terms and asked the court to determine the level of FRAND royalty.[14] It was also able to obtain an anti-suit injunction against Motorola, prohibiting it from enforcing the German injunction.[15] Motorola also sued Apple in Germany for infringement of 2G SEPs and managed to obtain an injunction, temporarily blocking online sales of iPhones and iPads.[16] A SEP dispute between Huawei and ZTE was referred to the CJEU, which in 2015 gave a landmark ruling providing a framework for the use of injunctions for SEPs in the EU.[17]

The patent litigation between the two largest smartphone producers in the world – Apple and Samsung – marked the peak in smartphone patent wars and involved both SEPs and non-SEPs. In 2010, three years after Apple released its

in global smartphone patent wars), available at: www.pcmag.com/article2/0,2817,2399098,00.asp and www.pcmag.com/image_popup/0,1740,iid=325524,00.asp.

[11] See: Commission, 'Antitrust: Commission Initiates Formal Proceedings Against Qualcomm' MEMO/07/389 (2007); *Broadcom v Qualcomm* 2006 WL 2528545 (DC New Jersey 2006); *Broadcom v Qualcomm* 501 F.3d 297 (3rd Cir 2007). Cases ended with the European Commission terminating the investigation and Broadcom and Qualcomm settling in the US. See: Commission, 'Antitrust: Commission closes formal proceedings against Qualcomm' MEMO/09/516 (2009).

[12] See *Nokia v Apple*, 2011 WL 2160904 (D Del 2011). Nokia and Apple settled with Apple concluding a licensing agreement for the use of SEPs. See K O'Brien 'Nokia Settles 2-Year Fight With Apple on Patents' *New York Times* (14 June 2011), available at: www.nytimes.com/2011/06/15/technology/15nokia.html.

[13] *Microsoft v Motorola*, 795 F.3d 1024, 1032 (9th Cir 2015).

[14] *Microsoft v Motorola*, 2013 WL 2111217 (WD Wash 2013).

[15] *Microsoft v Motorola*, 696 F.3d 872 (9th Cir 2012).

[16] *Motorola – Enforcement of GPRS Standard Essential Patents* (Case AT.39985) Commission Decision C(2014) 2892 (29 April 2014).

[17] C-170/13, *Huawei v ZTE* ECLI:EU:C:2015:477.

iPhone, Samsung revealed its Galaxy S smartphone which looked similar to the iPhone, followed by an announcement in 2011 of a new tablet which also seemed to borrow from Apple's iPad. As a response, Apple sued Samsung for infringement of its non-SEPs, several design and utility patents, while Samsung counter-sued on its 3G SEP portfolio. At first, Apple managed to secure a $1billion verdict in 2012 for infringement of its non-SEPs,[18] which was subsequently lowered to $399 million.[19] The case went to the Supreme Court reversing the initial ruling and ordering new proceedings to calculate damages,[20] that ended in 2018 with a $539 million jury ruling in favour of Apple.[21] In the second case, Apple initially won $119.6 million in damages for infringement of non-SEPs relating to smartphone's interface, such as the slide-to-unlock feature, but this was reversed on appeal.[22] Samsung, on the other hand, appeared to be less successful with its SEPs but managed to attract attention from the competition authorities. It requested injunctions for infringement of 3G SEPs in Germany, the UK, France, the Netherlands and Italy,[23] and sought an exclusion order before the US International Trade Commission (ITC).[24] After finding an infringement of one SEP, the ITC granted an exclusion order directed at Apple's iPhone and iPad products. However, the exclusion order never came into effect because Apple managed to persuade the US Trade Representative to veto it.[25] The European Commission, on the other hand, opened an investigation against Samsung for alleged abuse of dominant position. In 2014 it accepted Samsung's binding five-year commitments not to seek injunctions on its SEPs against potential licensees that accept a specified licensing framework.[26] The US Department of Justice also opened an antitrust investigation of Samsung's pursuance of injunctions but closed the investigation after the ITC's exclusion order was vetoed by the US Trade Representative.[27]

Although the smartphone patent war litigation eventually dwindled down, there are still regular SEP disputes occurring around the world with many of the underlying issues regarding the precise content of a FRAND licence regularly emerging. For instance, the Federal Trade Commission in 2017 sued Qualcomm

[18] *Apple v Samsung*, 2012 WL 4078433 (ND Cal 2012).

[19] *Apple v Samsung*, 786 F.3d 983 (Fed Cir 2015).

[20] *Samsung v Apple*, 137 S.Ct. 429 (2016).

[21] *Apple v Samsung*, Case No 11-CV-01846-LHK (ND Cal 2018).

[22] *Apple v Samsung*, 67 F.Supp.3d 1100 (ND Cal 2014); 816 F.3d 788; *Apple v Samsung*, 816 F.3d 788 (Fed Cir 2016).

[23] AT.39939 *Samsung – Enforcement of UMTS standard essential patents*, Commission Decision C(2014) 2891 (29 April 2014).

[24] See: Certain Electronic Devices, Including Wireless Communications Devices, Portable Music and Date processing Devices, and Tablet Computers, Inv No 337-TA-794, Commission Opinion (4 June 2013).

[25] Letter from Michael BG Froman, Executive Office of the President, the US Trade Representative, to Hon Irving A Williamson, Chairman, US International Trade Commission, 3 August 2013 (US Trade Representative Letter), available at: ustr.gov/sites/default/files/08032013%20Letter_1.PDF.

[26] AT.39939 *Samsung – Enforcement of UMTS standard essential patents*, Commission Decision C(2014) 2891 (29 April 2014).

[27] Department of Justice, 'Statement of the Department of Justice Antitrust Division on Its Decision to Close Its Investigation of Samsung's Use of Its Standards-Essential Patents' (Press Release, 7 February 2014).

for alleged violation of US antitrust laws for its certain SEP licensing practices relating to refusing to license its SEPs to component chipmakers and reserving licensing only to end-device manufacturers. In 2019 the district court sided with the FTC by finding Qualcomm's licensing practice anti-competitive,[28] but reversed by the appeal court in 2020.[29]

The IoT will bring back SEP licensing issues again to the spotlight. Companies from many new industries – from automotive, utilities to healthcare wearables – now need to acquire a licence but are generally unfamiliar with the SEP licensing framework. Many of these companies will be SMEs that lack the resources to hire experienced staff dedicated solely to patent licensing. As with smartphones, the convergence between ICT and diverse IoT industries is expected to lead to a clash between the opposing business interests of different industries and will bring SEP licensing tensions back to the forefront.

Indeed, we may be witnessing the first signs of IoT patent wars in the automotive sector. New connected cars have been called 'smartphones on wheels' for integrating many different technologies and applications,[30] and one study estimates that by 2023 nearly 90 per cent of new vehicles in the US and 70 per cent worldwide will be shipped with embedded connectivity.[31] The licensing of connectivity standards to car manufacturers is leading to new SEP disputes. In November 2018, Daimler together with its component suppliers, filed a complaint with the European Commission against Nokia alleging that its refusal to license 3G/4G/5G SEPs to car component manufactures violates EU competition law. In 2019 Nokia retaliated by initiating a patent infringement suit against Daimler in Germany and in 2020 obtained a first instance injunction ruling.[32] Sharp and Conversant also followed suit and successfully sued for injunctions against Daimler in Germany,[33] while Sisvel and Conversant sued Tesla in the US for infringement of their 3G and 4G SEP portfolios.[34] In an effort to provide clarity, Düsseldorf Regional Court decided to make one more SEP licensing reference to the CJEU.[35] Ongoing cases and tensions evidence that SEP licensing disputes are far from over.

[28] *Federal Trade Commission v Qualcomm*, 411 F.Supp.3d 658 (ND Cal 2019).

[29] Federal Trade Commission v Qualcomm, 969 F.3d 974 (9th Cir 2020).

[30] C Heitzner, 'Mercedes Touts New A Class as 'Smartphone on Wheels' *Automotive News Europe* (2 February 2018), available at: europe.autonews.com/article/20180202/ANE/180209932/mercedes-touts-new-a-class-as-smartphone-on-wheels.

[31] B Heiden, J Padilla and R Peters, 'The Value of Standard Essential Patents and the Level of Licensing' (2020) 2, available at: papers.ssrn.com/sol3/papers.cfm?abstract_id=3717570.

[32] *Nokia v Daimler*, 2 0 34/19 Mannheim Regional Court (18 August 2020).

[33] M Klos, 'Setback for Daimler in Connected Cars Dispute Against Avanci Pool Members' *JUVE Patent* (11 September 2020), available at: www.juve-patent.com/news-and-stories/cases/setback-for-daimler-in-connected-cars-dispute-against-avanci-pool-members/; K Richter, 'Daimler Loses to Conversant Over Connected Cars SEP' *JUVE Patent* (28 October 2020), available at: www.juve-patent.com/news-and-stories/cases/daimler-loses-to-conversant-over-connected-cars-sep.

[34] B Brittain, 'Tesla, Dell Sued Over Wireless Tech by European Patent Licensor' *Bloomberg* (15 May 2020), available at: news.bloomberglaw.com/tech-and-telecom-law/tesla-dell-sued-over-wireless-tech-by-european-patent-licensor?context=search&index=4; R Lloyd, 'Tesla Targeted Again – this time by Conversant' *IAM* (27 April 2020), available at: www.iam-media.com/frandseps/tesla-targeted-again-in-new-infringement-suits-conversant.

[35] C-182/21 *Nokia Technologies* (23 March 2021).

Governments are also exploring ways in which to improve SEP licensing in the upcoming IoT. The European Commission is undertaking several initiatives aimed at improving the transparency and predictability of the SEP framework, facilitating licensing negotiations and quickly resolving disputes.[36] Some initiatives include the introduction of third-party essentiality checks and a form of industry coordination on the aggregate price of the standard.[37] Japan was the first country to introduce voluntary essentiality checks,[38] and the Japan Patent Office published a Guide on SEP Licensing Negotiations.[39] Industry members also attempted to bring some clarity but, after failing to reach a consensus, produced in 2019 two radically opposing guides to pertinent SEP licensing issues.[40]

Against this background, the book attempts to provide a comprehensive and systematic guide to the SEP licensing framework after almost two decades of evolving policy, case law and academic debates. The aim is to provide a clear overview and understanding of the standard development process, the market background of SEP disputes, and legal and policy issues surrounding the use of SEPs and the meaning of a FRAND licensing commitment. It will look at how courts shaped the content of a FRAND commitment over decades of litigation and will explain the interrelated application of patent, contract and competition laws that provide the legal framework for SEP disputes. The evolving policy debates about the use of SEPs and their impact on legal remedies and the licensing framework will be explained. Finally, the book will critically assess what lessons from SEP licensing in smartphone and ICT industries can be applied or need to be modified in the IoT and 5G environment. Given the changed environment, some proposals for licensing models in the IoT will be provided.

The book is intended to serve as a guide for lawyers, policymakers and academics to these complex legal and policy issues and hopes to be able to reduce litigation and uncertainty at the next stage of 5G patent battles.

[36] Commission, 'Setting Out the EU Approach to Standard Essential Patents' (Communication) COM(2017) 712 final; Commission, 'Making the Most of the EU's Innovative Potential: An Intellectual Property Action Plan to Support the EU's Recovery and Resilience' COM(2020) 760 final, 3.

[37] R Bekkers et al, 'Landscape Study of Potentially Essential Patents Disclosed to ETSI' (Publication Office of the European Union, 2020), available at: publications.jrc.ec.europa.eu/repository/handle/JRC121411; J Baron et al, 'Group of Experts on Licensing and Valuation of Standard Essential Patents – Contribution to the Debate on SEPs' (January 2021), available at: ec.europa.eu/docsroom/documents/45217.

[38] Japan Patent Office, 'Manual of 'Hantei' (Advisory Opinion) for Essentiality Check' (revised June 2019).

[39] Japan Patent Office, 'Guide To Licensing Negotiations Involving Standard Essential Patents' (June 2018), available at: www.jpo.go.jp/e/support/general/sep_portal/document/index/guide-seps-en.pdf.

[40] CEN-CENELEC, 'Principles and Guidance for Licensing Standard Essential Patents in 5G and the Internet of Things (IoT), Including the Industrial Internet' (June 2019), available at: www.cencenelec.eu/news/workshops/pages/ws-2019-013.aspx; CEN-CENELEC, 'Core Principles and Approaches for Licensing of Standard Essential Patents' (June 2019), available at: www.cencenelec.eu/news/workshops/Pages/WS-2019-014.aspx.

II. Structure

The book is divided into three parts. Part I provides a background on the standardisation process that is crucial for appropriately understanding SEP licensing issues. Chapter one provides an overview of different types of standards and explains the standard development process within SDOs. It also explains the notion of SEPs, the legal treatment of SEPs by SDO IPR policies, the concept of essentiality and how not all patents declared to be essential are truly essential (the over-declaration problem). Chapter two covers the discussion about patent holdup, royalty stacking and patent holdout theories that shaped and influenced the policy surrounding the use of SEPs. It will assess the merits of these notions, the evidence of their occurrence in practice and their impact on the available legal remedies.

Part II focuses on the meaning and content of the FRAND licensing framework. It will provide an analysis of all the elements of a FRAND licence, starting with a discussion on the legal nature of a FRAND commitment and the role of contract and competition law in regulating the enforceability of a FRAND commitment (chapter three); the principles and practical methodologies for calculating FRAND royalties (chapter four); the meaning of the non-discrimination part of a FRAND commitment (chapter five); the appropriate FRAND royalty base (chapter six); whether there is a legal requirement to license across the value chain (chapter seven); and remedies for infringements of SEPs (chapter eight).

Part III focuses then on the IoT. It looks at what measures can be implemented to improve the licensing framework in the changed environment of the IoT. The major shortcomings emerging from SEP litigation in ICT are the lack of knowledge of the number of truly essential patents and the aggregate royalty for a standard. Existing measures and proposals to improve the transparency and predictability of SEP licensing are discussed. However, the key problem in the IoT is the sheer size of potential new licensees from diverse industries making the current bilateral licensing model untenable. Thus, we should expect to see greater use of collective licensing via patent pools. Chapter nine explores the usability of patent pool licensing in the IoT. It addresses the obstacles in their formation and suggest ways to overcome them. Pool licensing could be a way for more efficient, balanced and transparent SEP licensing in the IoT.

The book was finalised on 1 July 2021 and includes cases, legislation, literature and data available up to that point.

PART I

The Standard-Development Environment

1

Standards, Standard-Development Organisations and Standard Essential Patents

This chapter will explain the standard-development environment, providing context to SEP licensing issues discussed in the rest of the book. It will first explain what standards are, their role in the economy and different types of standards. Next, the chapter will analyse the standard-development process within SDOs that are primarily responsible for developing technical interoperability standards such as 3G, 4G, 5G and Wi-Fi. It will examine how companies with different business models cooperate in the development of standards, the assessment and inclusion of technology in a standard, and the difference in technological contributions by SDO members. Finally, the chapter introduces the notion of standard essential patents. It will first explain the legal responsibilities of companies holding patents that may be essential to a standard, and will then clarify the meaning of essentiality and explain how not every patent declared as essential is not necessarily truly essential for a standard. The over-declaration of SEPs has a significant effect on licensing and impacts FRAND royalty determinations.

I. Standards

In simple terms, a standard can be defined as a set of technical specifications which provides a common design for a product or process.[1] Standards are all around us and come in various shapes and forms – from A4 paper size, the size of the railway tracks,

[1] M Lemley, 'Intellectual Property Rights and Standard-Setting Organisations' (2002) 90 *California Law Review* 1889, 1896; H Hovenkamp, 'Standards Ownership and Competition Policy' (2007) 48 *Boston College Law Review* 87; for a legal definition of standards see ISO/IEC Guide 2:2004, 'Standardization and Related Activities – General Vocabulary', 4th edn (2004) 12, available at: isotc.iso.org/livelink/livelink/fetch/2000/2122/4230450/8389141/ISO_IEC_Guide_2_2004_%28Multilingual%29_-_Standardization_and_related_activities_--_General_vocabulary.pdf?nodeid=8387841&vernum=-2 (defining standards as a 'document, established by consensus and approved by a recognized body, that provides, for common and repeated use, rules, guidelines or characteristics for activities or their results, aimed at the achievement of the optimum degree of order in a given context'); Regulation (EU) No 1025/2012 of 25 October 2012 on European Standardisation [2012] OJ L316/12 (EU Standardisation Regulation) Article 2 (defining standard as a 'technical specification, adopted by a recognised standardisation body, for repeated or continuous application, with which compliance is

the shape of electrical plugs to complex technical interoperability standards in the ICT sector. Examples are compact disc (CD) and Blue Ray data storage standards; Wi-Fi, Bluetooth, GSM (2G), UMTS (3G) and LTE (4G) communication standards; USB device connectivity standard and MPEG and PDF software standards.

Standards generate numerous benefits and play an important role in a modern economy.[2] They promote innovation, increase the quality and safety of products, enable jobs and growth and support to the global value chain.[3] Standards allow for the early market adoption of innovative products and services, make products less costly for companies to produce and more valuable to consumers.[4] If products contain the same technology, manufacturers may be able to achieve economies of scale more efficiently, reducing costs and price. Further, standards allow for interoperability or compatibility between products from different manufacturers to work together. For example, technical interoperability standards allow consumers to use their smartphones in different countries across the world, as well as to make and receive calls from smartphones from different manufacturers. Furthermore, interoperability leads to increased network effects where products are more valuable as the number of users increases.[5]

Studies have shown that standards produce positive benefits for the whole economy. In the EU, standards are estimated to have an impact on GDP growth between 0.3 per cent to 1 per cent.[6] In the UK standards are estimated to generate annual growth of around £8.2 billion or a third of annual GDP growth,[7] and in Germany standards contribute to annual growth of up to €17 billion or between 0.7 per cent and 0.8 per cent of GDP.[8]

not compulsory'); also Commission, 'Guidelines on the Applicability of Article 101 of the Treaty on the Functioning of the European Union to Horizontal Co-operation Agreements' (Communication) [2011] OJ C 11/01 (EC Horizontal Cooperation Guidelines 2011) 257 (defining standards as agreements that have 'as their primary objective the definition of technical or quality requirements with which current or future products, production processes, services or methods may comply').

[2] For an analysis of the benefits of standards, see generally: J Padilla, J Davies and A Boutin, 'Economic Impact of Technology Standards' (Compass Lexecon, 2017) 11–24, available at: www.compasslexecon.com/wp-content/uploads/2018/04/CL_Economic_Impact_of_Technology_Standards_Report_FINAL.pdf; Commission, 'European Standards for the 21st Century' (Communication) COM(2016) 358 final; US Department of Justice and Federal Trade Commission, 'Antitrust Enforcement and Intellectual Property Rights: Promoting Innovation and Competition' (2007).

[3] Commission, 'European Standards for the 21st Century' (n 2) 4–5.

[4] US Department of Justice and Federal Trade Commission, *Promoting Innovation and Competition* (n 2) 33.

[5] For network effects, see M Katz and C Shapiro, 'Systems Competition and Network Effects' (1994) 8 *Journal of Economics Perspectives* 93; C Shapiro and H Varian, *Information Rules: A Strategic Guide to the Network Economy* (Harvard Business School Press, 1999).

[6] Commission, 'A Strategic Vision for European Standards: Moving Forward to Enhance and Accelerate the Sustainable Growth of the European Economy by 2020' (Communication) COM(2011) 311 final, 1.

[7] Centre for Economics and Business Research, 'The Economic Contribution of Standards to the UK Economy' (British Standards Institution, 2015), available at: www.bsigroup.com/LocalFiles/en-GB/standards/BSI-standards-research-report-The-Economic-Contribution-of-Standards-to-the-UK-Economy-UK-EN.pdf.

[8] K Blind, A Jundgmittag and A Mangelsdorf, 'The Economic Benefits of Standardisation' (DIN German Institute for Standardisation, 2011), available at: www.din.de/blob/89552/68849fab0eeeaafb56c5a3ffee9959c5/economic-benefits-of-standardization-en-data.pdf.

However, standardisation may also have negative effects.[9] Because standardisation results in the adoption of one uniform solution it inevitably leads to the elimination of alternatives and the loss in variety. The costs associated with migration to a different or an improved version of a standard may slow down the implementation of better technologies. Countries may also use different national standards to erect barriers to trade and deter market access.[10] Nevertheless, positive effects are considered to outweigh any potential negative effects of standardisation.

A. Technical Interoperability Standards

Technical interoperability standards specify how different technologies interact with one another and work together successfully.[11] Technical interoperability standards are important in many industries but are especially relevant to the ICT sector and the IoT. They enable, for instance, the making and receiving of calls from smartphones from different manufacturers or for computer hardware components from various producers to be combined to create a functional computer. In the IoT they will enable connected devices such as cars, domestic appliances, wearables and industrial equipment to communicate seamlessly with each other, regardless of manufacturer, operating system, or other technical components.[12] Examples of technical interoperability standards are 3G, 4G, 5G cellular standards, WLAN, Wi-Fi and Bluetooth and USB connectivity standards.

There are many technical interoperability standards in the ICT and IoT industries. The Commission considers there are over 600 standards in the IoT sector,[13] while Baron and Spulber collected almost 800,000 standard documents and found that the majority relate to the ICT sector.[14] Other studies have looked at the

[9] For the analysis of the negative effects of standards, see International Telecommunications Union, 'Understanding Patents, Competition & Standardization in an Interconnected World' (ITU, 2014) 28–29, available at www.itu.int/en/ITU-T/Documents/Manual_Patents_Final_E.pdf; Commission, 'Patents and Standards: A Modern Framework for IPR Based Standardisation' (2014) 29, available at: pure.tue.nl/ws/files/3916785/391736021255721.pdf.

[10] International Telecommunications Union, 'Understanding Patents, Competition & Standardization in an Interconnected World' (n 9) 28 (showing how the growth of global TV market was slowed down by the fragmented national implementation of TV standards. The US and Japan supported NTSC; SECAM was adopted in France, Greece, Eastern Europe and Russia, while the rest of the world used PAL).

[11] On the benefits of interoperability see K Maskus and S Merrill (eds), 'Patent Challenges for Standard-Setting in the Global Economy: Lessons from Information and Communication Technology' (National Research Council, 2013) 16, available at: www.nap.edu/catalog/18510/patent-challenges-for-standard-setting-in-the-global-economy-lessons; B Biddle et al, 'The Expanding Role and Importance of Standards in Information and Communications Technology Industry' (2012) 53 *Jurimetrics* 177 (explaining the benefits of interoperability standards in the ICT industry).

[12] Commission, 'ICT Standardisation Priorities for the Digital Single Market' (Communication) COM(2016) 176 final, 2.

[13] ibid, 3.

[14] J Baron and D Spulber, 'Technology Standards and Standard Setting Organisations: Introduction to the Searle Center Database' (2018) 27 *Journal of Economics & Management Strategy* 462, 486–87.

prevalence of standards in particular products and found that the average laptop contains at least 251 interoperability standards,[15] while an average smartphone is estimated to contain a minimum of 30 interoperability standards.[16] Interoperability standards will reportedly generate 40 per cent of value in the IoT.[17] The licensing framework of these standards is the subject matter of the book.

B. Classification of Standards

Before going further into the specifics of patent licensing, it is important to recognise the distinction between different types of standards and their mutual relations. We can broadly observe two different classification:

i. Standards based on their source (de facto, collaborative and governmental standards).
ii. Standards based on the access to IP rights and openness in development process (open and closed standards).

i. Standards Based on their Source

a. De Facto Standards

De facto standards originate from one or several firms working together outside any institutional framework, whose products or solutions become widely adopted in the market.[18] Typically a company will develop a certain product or a solution that becomes so widely accepted by the market so as to become a standard. This may be possible in industries with strong network effects, where the value of the product increases as more users use it. Once a critical number of users are reached, the market 'tips' to one winner which becomes a standard in the market.[19] An example of a de facto standard is a QWERTY keyboard layout,[20] Microsoft's Windows operating system and Microsoft's word documents (.doc, .docx).

[15] B Biddle, A White and S Woods, 'How Many Patents in a Laptop (And Other Empirical Questions)?' (2010), available at: papers.ssrn.com/abstract=1619440.

[16] A Armstrong, J Mueller and T Syret, 'The Smartphone Royalty Stack: Surveying Royalty Demands for the Components Within Modern Smartphones' (2014), available at: papers.ssrn.com/sol3/papers.cfm?abstract_id=2443848.

[17] McKinsey Global Institute, 'The Internet of Things: Mapping the Value Beyond the Hype' (June 2015), available at: www.mckinsey.com/~/media/McKinsey/Industries/Technology%20Media%20and%20Telecommunications/High%20Tech/Our%20Insights/The%20Internet%20of%20Things%20The%20value%20of%20digitizing%20the%20physical%20world/The-Internet-of-things-Mapping-the-value-beyond-the-hype.pdf.

[18] See 'De Facto Standard Definition', BusinessDictionary.com, available at: www.businessdictionary.com/definition/de-facto-standard.html; see also D Teylas, *The Interface between Competition Law, Patents and Technical Standards* (Kluwer Law International, 2014) 34–35.

[19] On market 'tipping', see Katz and Shapiro (n 5) 105–06; Shapiro and Varian (n 5).

[20] Teylas (n 18) 34.

Sometimes, however, two or more opposing solutions may emerge that will compete to become a de facto standard in a 'standard war'.[21] An example is a battle for the video cassette recording standard in the 1980s between Sony's Betamax and JVC's VHS format. VHS prevailed in the end and become a de facto standard for video cassettes.[22] A more recent example is the battle in the 2000s between Toshiba's DVD HD and Sony's Blu-Ray for the establishment of the next high-definition optical disc format. Blu-Ray ended as the most widely accepted format, and Toshiba discontinued the support of DVD HD in 2008.[23]

Standard wars are generally inefficient.[24] They drain the resources of companies involved, while those that adopted the losing standard will end up with additional costs of switching to the winning format. Standard wars are also costly to consumers. Consumers may wait to purchase products until they see which solution will emerge as a standard. If they purchased a solution that was ultimately not successful, they would need to incur the additional costs of switching to the winning format. Standard wars also do not guarantee that the technologically superior solution will win. The success often goes to the solution that most rapidly reaches a critical mass of consumers and producers of complementary products, resulting in market tipping. For instance, some claim that Betamax offered superior picture and sound quality over the VHS, which prevailed because of an initially lower price and the possibility to record longer than Betamax.[25]

b. Collaborative Standards

Because of the inefficiencies of standard wars, companies may decide to work together on an industry-wide basis in order to jointly develop new standardised solutions. Collaborative standards can thus be defined as standards established by cooperation between two or more entities working within the framework of standard-development organisations.[26] The majority and the most important technical interoperability standards are collaborative standards developed within SDOs, including Wi-Fi, Bluetooth, 3G, 4G and 5G cellular standards.

From a terminological point, collaborative standards in the literature are often referred to as 'formal' or 'de jure' standards. A designation as 'formal' signifies that the process leading to the adoption of a standard is more or less formalised.[27] As such, the terms 'collaborative' or 'formal' standards may be used as synonyms. On the other hand, the term 'de jure' is misleading because it implies that there is a

[21] See Shapiro and Varian (n 5) 261–97 (describing standard wars).

[22] For an overview see Commission, 'Patents and Standards' (n 9) 71.

[23] ibid, 71–72; also Padilla, Davies and Boutin (n 2) 37–38.

[24] Padilla, Davies and Boutin (n 2) 37–38.

[25] ibid, 38.

[26] Teylas (n 18) 34–35; see also American Bar Association, Section of the Antitrust Laws, *Handbook on the Antitrust Aspects of Standard Setting* 2nd edn (ABA, 2011) 4; OECD, 'Standard Setting' (2011) DAF/COMP (2010)33, 23–24, available at: www.oecd.org/daf/competition/47381304.pdf.

[27] Teylas (n 18) 39–40.

legal requirement to adhere to SDO developed standards, which is often not the case. Standards developed within SDOs are voluntary and there is typically no legal requirement to comply with them.[28] The term 'de jure' standard should thus not be used to refer to collaborative standards but could be better used to describe governmental standards that are mandated by law.

c. Governmental Standards

Governmental standards are technical specifications that are adopted by the government and compliance is required by law.[29] Governmental standards can often be found relating to the issues of the public sphere, such as health, safety, or the environment, where it is necessary for the government to step in. The compliance with these standards is legally binding.[30] An example of governmental standards were the analogue TV standards in the US and Europe. The US Federal Communications Commission mandated the use of the NTSC standard, while Europe was divided between the French SECAM and the German–English PAL standards.[31] National governments also set 1G analogue telecommunication standards.[32] Because compliance with governmental standards is required by law, they may also correctly be referred to as 'de jure' standards.

The distinction in practice between de facto, collaborative, and governmental standards is not always clear-cut. For example, sometimes a de facto standard may be adopted by SDOs, becoming a formal standard. This was the case with Adobe's PDF format, which moved from de facto standard status to formal standard status when Adobe released specifications to the ISO.[33] Similarly, governments may also require compliance with a standard that has been widely adopted in the market. This was the case with the US NTSC television standard which in the 1950s was more successful than the government mandated standard for colour television. The FCC consequently adopted the NTSC standards as the US standard for colour television.[34]

[28] See: EU Standardisation Regulation (n 1) Article 2 ('standard means a technical specification, adopted by a recognized standardization body, for repeated or continuous application, *with which compliance is not compulsory*' (emphasis added)); also EC Horizontal Cooperation Guidelines (n 1) 280, 293 (holding that it may be an infringement of Article 101(1) TFEU if SSOs mandate the compliance with the standard).

[29] Teylas (n 18) 41. Governmental standards are numerous. See: ABA Section of the Antitrust Laws (n 26) 4 (noting that an estimated number of standards developed by US federal government agencies was approximately 44,000 in 2009); also Commission, 'European Standards for the 21st Century' (n 2) 5 (noting that as of 2016 there were approximately 4500 harmonised European standards).

[30] U Petrovcic, *Competition Law and Standard Essential Patents: A Transatlantic Perspective* (Kluwer Law International, 2014) 22; OECD, 'Standard Setting' (n 26) 24.

[31] Padilla, Davies and Boutin (n 2) 25–31.

[32] ibid, 2–3.

[33] See ISO, 'SO 32000-1:2008 Document Management – Portable Document Format', available at: www.iso.org/standard/51502.html and Adobe, PDF Reference and Adobe Extensions to the PDF Specification, available at: www.adobe.com/devnet/pdf/pdf_reference.html.

[34] Padilla, Davies and Boutin (n 2) 27.

Furthermore, governments may support the development of SDO standards and encourage their market adoption, while stopping short of mandating compliance by law. For instance, ETSI, a large formal European SDO, includes national standardisation bodies, national research institutions and state-owned network operators, as well as companies from the private sector.[35] This way national governments participate in the development of collaborative standards. European governments also actively supported and promoted the creation of 2G GSM standards developed by ETSI without legally requiring compliance.[36]

ii. *Open and Closed Standards*

A distinction could be made between open and closed standards based on the access to intellectual property rights and openness in the standard's creation. There is currently no commonly accepted definition of what constitutes an open standard.[37] The literature is broadly divided on whether the standard can be considered as open when the process of developing and approving the standard is open and transparent, or whether the standard must also be available royalty-free.[38] The ITU-T provides a process-oriented definition of open standards as those which are 'available to the general public and are developed (or approved) and maintained via a collaborative and consensus-driven process'.[39] Elements of open standards include a collaborative process, a reasonably balanced process not dominated by any interest group, due process in the development of standards, and that IP rights should be licensed either royalty-free or on FRAND terms.[40] On the other hand,

[35] See: ETSI, Membership, available at: www.etsi.org/membership.

[36] See: J Padilla, J Davies and A Boutin, 'Economic Impact of Technology Standards: Annexes to the Report' 3–4, available at: www.compasslexecon.com/wp-content/uploads/2018/04/CL_Economic_Impact_of_Technology_Standards_Annexes.pdf; OECD, 'Standard Setting' (n 26) 27.

[37] See: K Krechmer, 'Open Standards: A Call for Action' (2009) 47 *IEEE Communications Magazine* 88 (identifying 10 requirements of open standards); D Ernst, 'America's Voluntary Standards System – A "Best Practice Model" for Innovation Policy?' (2012) 128 East–West Center Working Paper 35 (noting that the concept of 'open standard' is elusive); R Shah and J Kesan, 'Lost in Translation: Interoperability Issues for Open Standards' (2012) 8 *I/S: A Journal of Law and Policy for the Information Society* 114 (defining open standards as 'a specification that is publicly available and freely implementable'); Baron and Spulber (n 14) 465 (considering standards established by SSOs and other industry groups to be open if they are not controlled by a single firm and the use of the standard is not restricted to a specified group of firms); B Lundel, J Gamalielsson and A Katz, 'On Implementation of Open Standards in Software: To What Extent can ISO Standards be Implemented in Open Source Software?' (2015) 13 *International Journal of Standardization Research* 47 (describing the debate about the definition of open standards and concluding that not all standards developed by SSOs can be regarded as 'open').

[38] See B Biddle, 'No Standards for Standards: Understanding the ICT Standards-Development Ecosystem' in J Contreras (ed), *The Cambridge Handbook of Technical Standardization Law: Competition, Antitrust, and Patents* (Cambridge University Press, 2018).

[39] ITU-T, 'Definition of Open Standards', available at: www.itu.int/en/ITU-T/ipr/Pages/open.aspx; see also the EU Standardisation Regulation (n 1) Annex II.

[40] For similar criteria of openness see ANSI, 'ANSI Essential Requirements: Due Process Requirements for American National Standards' (January 2021), available at: www.ansi.org/american-national-standards/ans-introduction/essential-requirements; Open Standards, 'Principles', available at: open-stand.org/about-us/principles/ (listing five fundamental principles of standards development: (i) due process, (ii) broad consensus, (iii) transparency, (iv) balance and (v) openness).

others consider standards to be open only if they are available royalty-free.[41] As a way of reconciling these two approaches, Dolmans proposes a compromise solution by arguing that the definition of an open standard has different meanings for different sectors.[42] Royalty-free licensing may be more appropriate for the software sector, while FRAND licensing is necessary for the telecommunications sector.[43]

Closed standards, on the contrary, are developed by one or more companies in a closed environment where access to the standard is not widely available. Companies owning a closed standard have full control of its development and implementation. They are free to choose whether they want to license the standard to others and under what terms. They may also decide to leave the production of standardised products or services exclusively to themselves. As such, closed standards are often referred to as 'proprietary'.[44]

The importance of the distinction between open and closed standards is due to the recognition that ICT standards should generally be open.[45] Regardless of the precise definition of openness, open standards ensure the widespread possible access to the technology and its downstream implementation. Policy measures should, therefore, aim to facilitate and support the creation of open standards. However, if policy actions result in too much restriction of intellectual property rights, IP owners may decide to abandon working on an open standard and opt for proprietary solutions instead. An appropriate policy framework should thus aim to ensure a balance between the interests of widespread access to standardised technology and the protection of IP rights.

II. Standard Development Organisations

SDOs are voluntary and non-profit organisations that coordinate the development of standards.[46] More precisely, they are in charge of 'developing, coordinating, promulgating, revising, amending reissuing, interpreting or otherwise maintaining standards'.[47] We have seen that collaborative standards are developed within a framework of SDOs.

[41] See: UK Policy Paper: 'Open Standards Principles' (April 2018) Open Source Initiative, 'Open Standards Requirements for Software', available at: opensource.org/osr; also Shah and Kesan (n 37).

[42] M Dolmans, 'A Tale of Two Tragedies – A Plea for Open Standards' (2010) 2 *International Free and Open Source Software Law Review* 115.

[43] ibid.

[44] See Padilla, Davies and Boutin (n 2); V Torti, *Intellectual Property Rights and Competition in Standard Setting: Objectives and Tensions* (Routledge, 2016) 53–56 (discussing the difference between open and proprietary standards).

[45] See Commission, 'ICT Standardisation Priorities for the Digital Single Market' (n 12).

[46] J Baron and T Pohlmann, 'Who Cooperates in Standards Consortia – Rivals or Complementors?' (2013) 9 *Journal of Competition Law & Economics* 905, 906.

[47] US Legal, 'Standard Setting Organizations Law & Legal Definitions', available at: definitions.uslegal.com/s/standard-setting-organization-sso/.

A terminological word of caution is warranted. SDOs are often referred to as Standard-Setting Organisations (SSOs) and the terms are widely used interchangeably. However, there is a crucial difference between 'setting standards' and 'developing standards'. The latter implies that there exist various equally efficient alternatives and the task is to merely chose one that will be 'set' as a standard. Examples are the selection of the shape of electrical outlets, the length of railway gauges or materials to be used in the production of conduits. On the other hand, the former implies simultaneous development of new technologies, often with great research and development (R&D) expenditure, and the adoption of the solution that offers superior performance.

Teece and Sherry emphasise that the standard-setting process should be associated with non-digital industries, while standard development better describes the process in digital industries.[48] The main difference is the extent to which R&D investment is needed for the development of new standardised solutions. In non-digital industries the selection of standardised solutions does not entail high research costs and there are often readily available existing alternatives. For example, quality and safety standards in non-digital industries relate to which safety component to use in heating boilers,[49] or whether electrical wires should be made of steel or plastic.[50] However, in the digital world there are often no ready off-the-shelf solutions and standardisation is not a simple matter of picking between equally good alternatives.[51] Rather, standardisation in digital markets consists of the parallel development of technological solutions during the standardisation process, the investment of millions (or even billions) of dollars in R&D, and the selection of technology that provides the best solution to a technical problem.[52] In other words, SDOs in digital industries do not actually *set* standards. Rather, they act as a venue for the development of technical specifications after which it is for the market to decide whether the standard will be widely adopted or not. There is no guarantee that a technical specification adopted by an SDO will turn into a widely accepted standard, which is why the term standard-setting organisation may be misleading.[53]

[48] D Teece, 'Profiting from Innovation in the Digital Economy' (2018) 47 *Research Policy* 1367, 1381; D Teece and E Sherry, 'Standard Setting, Standard Development and Division of Gains from Standardisation' (2016) *Competition Policy International* 1.

[49] *American Society of Mechanical Engineers, Inc v Hydrolevel Corporation*, 102 S.Ct.1935 (1982).

[50] *Allied Tube & Conduit Corp v Indian Head Inc*, 108 S.Ct. 1931 (1988).

[51] Teece (n 48) 1381.

[52] The standard-development process will be described in more detail in section II.C below.

[53] See Teylas (n 18) 37 (distinguishing SDOs as a sub-group of SSOs that have received official accreditation at the national, regional and international level); also Biddle et al (n 11) 183–84 (similarly holding that SSOs can be divided into two types: (i) SDOs, defined as SSOs that are formally recognised by a government authority, and (ii) consortia, which lack government recognition); also see Biddle, 'No Standards for Standards' (n 38).

Therefore, the distinction between SDO and SSO is not only linguistical but has important practical implications in understanding the standardisation process in the ICT and IoT context.

A. Types of SDOs

SDOs come in many different shapes and sizes. The European Commission distinguishes between: (i) 'formal' ('recognised' or 'accredited' SDOs) that are formally recognised by the government; (ii) 'quasi-formal' SDOs that are typically large, well organised and share many of the characteristics of formally recognised groups, but lack official governmental recognition; and (iii) 'consortia', which are small, privately run organisations (also referred to as 'special interest groups' or 'fora').[54]

Formal SDOs may operate on a global, regional, or national level. On a global level, the most important are the International Organisation for Standardization (ISO), the world's largest developer and publisher of international standards; the International Telecommunication Union (ITU) in charge of the standardisation in the telecommunications field, and the International Electrotechnical Commission (IEC) responsible for standardisation in the electrotechnical sector. Three formal SDOs operate on the EU level: the European Committee for Standardization (CEN), the European Committee for Electrotechnical Standardization (CENELEC) and the European Telecommunications Standardisation Institute (ETSI).[55] In the US, the American National Standards Institute (ANSI) is recognised by the US government as the private non-profit body that coordinates US national standards. ANSI does not develop standards itself, but it accredits other private SDOs which are responsible for developing American National Standards. On a national level, formal SDOs are typically national standardisation bodies such as the British Standards Institution (the UK), Detaches Institute for Normung (Germany) or Association Française de Normalisation (France).

Quasi-formal SDOs are large, well organised and influential SDOs but lacking official government recognition. However, standards developed by these organisations have broad impact and are widely accepted by the industry. Examples are the Institute of Electrical and Electronics Engineers (IEEE) responsible for the development of Wi-Fi standards; the Internet Engineering Task Force (IETF) developing internet protocol standards (TCP/IP) and the World Wide Web Consortium (W3C) known for internet standards HTML and xHTML.

On the other hand, consortia are smaller, privately run organisations, established with a specific purpose and limited membership.[56] They either work directly

[54] Commission, 'Patents and Standards' (n 9) 31–33; also J Baron et al, 'Making the Rules: The Governance of Standard Development Organizations and their Policies on Intellectual Property Rights' (EUR 29655 EN, Publication Office of the European Union, 2019), available at: ec.europa.eu/jrc/sites/jrcsh/files/sdo_governance_final_electronic_version.pdf.

[55] EU Standardisation Regulation (n 1) Annex I.

[56] Commission, 'Patents and Standards' (n 9) 33.

to develop their standards or, more often, facilitate and complement the workings of larger formal and quasi-formal SDOs. For example, different consortia have developed the USB, Bluetooth,[57] and Qi wireless charging standards.[58] Since they are smaller, standardisation in consortia can often proceed more expeditiously than in larger SDOs. Pohlmann estimates that over 60 per cent of standards are developed in standards consortia,[59] and Biddle and others found that in the average 2010 laptop there were at least 251 interoperability standards, the majority (44 per cent) developed by consortia, 36 per cent developed by formal SDOs and 20 per cent by single company de facto standards.[60]

Besides working on their own standards, consortia often develop technical specifications to be submitted as proposals for standardisation to formal or quasi-formal SSOs.[61] Companies often work ahead in informal consortia to settle their conflicts of interest and coordinate their complementary R&D programmes in advance of formal SDO meetings. Formal SDOs may even directly adopt the technical specification developed by consortia as their standards. The ISO and IEC have a unique transposition process which enables them to adopt a technical specification developed by consortia as formal ISO/IEC standards.[62]

Consortia may also work with formal and quasi-formal SDOs on the promotion, maintenance and enforcement of standards. For example, a consortia Wi-Fi Alliance played a crucial role in the initial promotion of the IEEE's 802.11 standard and is responsible for interoperability testing and rewarding compliant products with the right to use the 'Wi-Fi' name and logo.[63]

Overall, the standard-development ecosystem consists of a large number of SDOs, with the majority being small consortia. One database of SDOs lists 1,140 SDOs, most of them being consortia,[64] while another database includes a list of over 200 consortia.[65] Gandal and Régibeau found that the majority of SDOs come from the ICT sector.[66]

[57] Bluetooth SIG, 'About Us', available at: www.bluetooth.com/about-us/our-history; USB Implementers Forum, 'About USB IF', available at: www.usb.org/about; Biddle, White and Woods (n 15).

[58] Wireless Power Consortium, 'About the WPC', available at: www.wirelesspowerconsortium.com/about/about-wpc.

[59] T Pohlmann, 'The Evolution of ICT Standards Consortia' (2014) 95 *Communication & Strategies* 17, 19.

[60] Biddle, White and Woods (n 15).

[61] Baron and Pohlmann, 'Who Cooperates in Standards Consortia?' (n 46) 910; J Baron, Y Meniere and T Pohlmann, 'Standards, Consortia, and Innovation' (2014) 36 *International Journal of Industrial Organization* 22.

[62] Baron, Meniere and Pohlmann (n 61) 22; ISO/IEC, 'JTC 1 PAS Submitters', available at: jtc1info.org/page-3/page-4/jtc-1-pas-submitters/.

[63] Wi-Fi Alliance, 'Who We Are', available at: www.wi-fi.org/who-we-are; also Biddle, 'No Standards for Standards' (n 38).

[64] Consortium Info, 'Standard Setting Organizations and Standards List', available at: www.consortiuminfo.org/links/#.WOz-j_67rMA.

[65] Raising Standards, 'Comprehensive List of Consortia', 17th edn (August 2012), available at: www.raisingstandards.eu/new-page-1/.

[66] See N Gandal and P Régibeau, 'Standard-Setting Organisations: Current Policy Issues and Empirical Evidence' in P Delimatsis (ed), *The Law, Economics and Politics of Standardization* (Cambridge University Press, 2015).

B. Membership

SDOs have a diverse membership. According to one study a median SDO had 114 members, while five SDOs had over 1,000 members.[67] SDO membership can be broadly categorised as: (i) pure upstream companies; (ii) vertically integrated companies; (iii) pure manufacturing companies; and (iv) non-industry members.

SDOs members often pursue different business interests. Pure upstream companies, for instance, have an incentive to include their technologies in a standard and derive most of their revenues from SEP licensing.[68] On the other hand, pure manufacturing companies do not hold relevant IPRs, and their primary source of income comes through sales of downstream standard-compliant products.[69] Royalties represent a cost for them, and their incentive is to reduce or avoid payment of royalties altogether. Vertically integrated companies both produce standard-implementing products and invest in the R&D of standardised technologies. Their main incentive is securing a large enough SEP portfolio to use for cross-licensing with other vertically integrated companies and generate their income mostly from the sale of downstream products.[70] Often companies do not participate in just one but many different SDOs simultaneously in a given industry.[71] Finally, non-industry members include universities, research institutions, non-profit organisations, but also government bodies, national standardisation organisations and publicly owned companies. They pursue different objectives than industry members. They may be interested in having the best available technologies included in a standard, protecting the interest of consumers, or securing the public interest objectives in standardisation. Therefore, the diverse membership with competing business interests often creates conflicts within SDOs which are then frequently reflected in later licensing negotiations.

C. How SDOs Develop Standards

To properly appreciate the standardisation environment, it is necessary to understand the standard-development process itself. While the precise procedures vary between SDOs, there are nevertheless some commonly applicable principles. This section will describe the standard-development process at 3GPP, an umbrella SDO that consists of seven major formal SDOs.[72] The reason for choosing 3GPP

[67] Baron and Spulber (n 14) 483.

[68] EC Horizontal Cooperation Guidelines (n 1) 267; D Geradin and M Rato, 'Can Standard-Setting Lead to Exploitative Abuse? A Dissonant View on Patent Holdup, Royalty Stacking and the Meaning of FRAND' (2007) 3 *European Competition Journal* 101, 105–06.

[69] Geradin and Rato (n 68) 106.

[70] ibid.

[71] Baron and Spulber (n 14) 485 (finding that companies such as IBM, Intel, NEC, Hewlett-Packard, Motorola, Microsoft and Samsung participate in more than 40 SDOs simultaneously).

[72] The full list of members of 3GPP are: ARIB (Japan), CCSA (China), ETSI (Europe), ATIS (US), TTA (Korea), TTC (Japan), TSDSI (India). See 3GPP, 'Working Procedures' (20 October 2016), available at: www.3gpp.org/ftp/Information/Working_Procedures/3GPP_WP.pdf, Article 1.

is because it is responsible for the development of important communication standards – 3G UMTS and 3G W-CDMA, 4G LTE, and the 5G NR standard. Recent empirical studies of the 3GPP standard-development process have also shed some light on the behaviour of companies during the standardisation process.[73] Finally, the 3GPP procedures contain some universal principles similar to other SDOs.

The internal organisational structure of 3GPP, as well as other formal and quasi-formal SDOs, is divided between the decision-making body and lower bodies that are responsible for the actual technical development of a standard. The Project Co-Ordination Group (PCG) is the highest decision-making body in the 3GPP responsible for the overall management of 3GPP and includes representatives of seven member-SDOs.[74] Among others, the PCG is responsible for the final adoption of technical specifications as 3GPP standards, allocating resources for the internal working of 3GPP and ruling on appeals of the decisions of lower bodies.[75] The main technical work is done in Technical Specification Groups (TSGs) and smaller Working Groups (WGs).[76] In order to be more effective, a complex technological problem is broken into smaller and separate technological areas and assigned to a specific TSG where it can be examined by experts in the field. Each TSG is further separated into smaller WGs that work on more specific technological problems within TSG area.[77]

The standard-development process starts with the proposal for a new feature,[78] made by any member with the support of at least four individual member organisations.[79] The PCG decides whether to adopt a proposed new feature or not, and if it decides to move forward, the work on the feature will be broken down to smaller more manageable elements called 'building blocks' and assigned to a specific TSG.[80] Building blocks will then be further segregated into smaller 'work tasks' and allocated to one WG.[81]

The actual standard development proceeds in multiple WG and TSG meetings. 3GPP WGs typically meets six to eight times a year with hundreds of member representatives.[82] Each member may submit a technical contribution for addressing various technical issues and solutions.[83] The contributions are submitted and

[73] See: J Baron and K Gupta, 'Unpacking 3GPP Standards' (2018) 27 *Journal of Economics & Management Strategy* 433; K Gupta, 'How SSOs Work: Unpacking the Mobile Industry's 3GPP Standards' in J Contreras (ed), *The Cambridge Handbook of Technical Standardization Law: Competition, Antitrust, and Patents* (Cambridge University Press, 2018).

[74] See 3GPP, 'Working Procedures' (n 72) Article 15.

[75] ibid, Article 14.

[76] ibid, Article 20.

[77] ibid Articles 20, 22.

[78] 3GPP, 'Technical Specification Group Working Methods', TR 21.900, V14.0.0 (2017) 27, available at: www.etsi.org/deliver/etsi_tr/121900_121999/121900/14.00.00_60/tr_121900v140000p.pdf (defined as 'new, or substantially enhanced functionality which represents added value to the existing system').

[79] 3GPP, 'Working Procedures' (n 72) Article 39.

[80] 3GPP, 'Technical Specification Group Working Methods' (n 78) 27.

[81] ibid, 28.

[82] ibid, 37.

[83] See Gupta (n 73) 38 (describing the standardisation process).

made publicly available before each meeting. Interested members review contributions prior to the meeting and come prepared with comments and feedback. As reviewing and submitting technical contributions is quite complex, experienced engineers are mainly participating in WG and TSG meetings.

Voting in WGs and TSGs is based on a consensus, defined as the 'absence of sustained opposition to substantial issues'.[84] If consensus cannot be achieved, a technical contribution will be adopted if 71 per cent of votes are cast in favour.[85] After a series of such meetings, WGs and TSGs adopt 'technical specifications' which are the result of many technical contributions.[86] Often hundreds of technical contributions form one technical specification and many technical specifications form a standard. For example, according to one study, LTE Release 13 consisted of 1,261 technical specifications and around 300,000 technical contributions.[87]

Standardisation is an evolving process, and once a standard gets adopted it is not the end of the matter. Standards change and update over time. For example, there is not one single 3G UMTS and 4G LTE standard. Instead, there are different versions (called releases) of 3G UMTS and 4G LTE over time, each release adding new and improved features.[88] Development of a standard at one point becomes 'frozen' and is released to be implemented in standardised products. As soon as the work on one version of a standard is complete, the work continues for a new release. For instance, 5G NR release 15 was frozen in 2019, while in 2018 work had begun on the next release 16 which was then frozen in 2020 when the work on release 17 began.[89]

Although many companies participate in a standard's development, only a few submit their technologies and are responsible for the majority of a standard's contributions. Baron and Gupta found that out of almost 500 entities participating in 3GPP meetings, approximately one-third did not make a single contribution towards the development of 3G and 4G standards,[90] while only nine companies accounted for 60 per cent of all contributions.[91] Further studies confirmed this finding, with the top 10 companies together holding 82 per cent of all submitted 5G declarations,[92] and the top six companies out of total of 148 holding more than half of all disclosed SEP families at ETSI.[93] The reason for such a trend could

[84] 3GPP, 'Working Procedures' (n 72) Annex A.

[85] ibid, Article 25.

[86] Gupta (n 73) 39.

[87] ibid.

[88] See 3GPP, 'Releases', available at: www.3gpp.org/specifications/67-releases.

[89] ibid.

[90] Baron and Gupta (n 73) 447–48.

[91] ibid.

[92] T Pohlmann and K Blind, 'Fact Finding Study on Patents Declared to the 5G Standards' (January 2020) 10, available at: ipforbusiness.org/wp-content/uploads/2020/02/5G-patent-study_TU-Berlin_IPlytics-2020.pdf.

[93] R Bekkers et al, 'Pilot Study for Essentiality Assessment of Standard Essential Patents' (EUR 30111 EN, Publication office of the European Union, 2020) 65–68, available at: publications.jrc.ec.europa.eu/repository/handle/JRC119894 (finding also that out of 148 disclosing firms, 14 disclosed more than 500 patent families; 21 companies disclosed between 50 and 5,000 families; and 113 disclosed fewer than 50 families).

be explained by SDOs' diverse membership. Pure upstream companies and some vertically integrated companies have the incentive to actively participate in a standard's development and contribute their technologies to standards, while pure manufacturers and non-industry members might be more interested in being a part of a standardisation process only to gain information on the development of new technologies.

Figure 1 Standard Development Process at 3GPP[94]

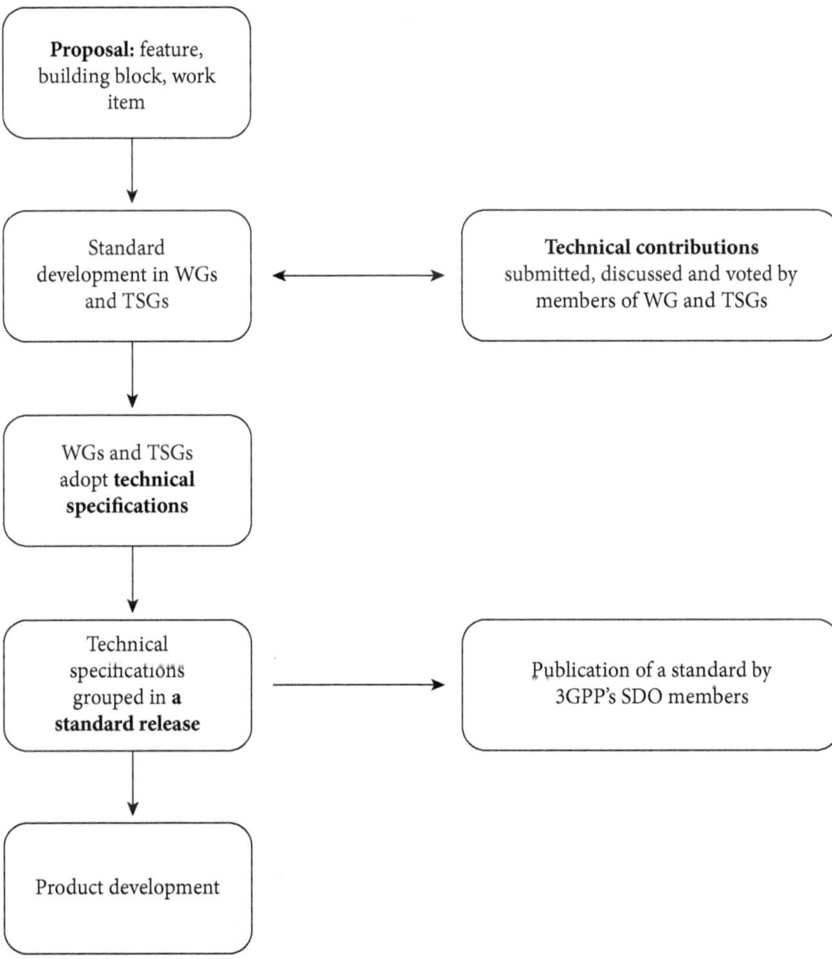

[94] See Baron and Gupta (n 73) 440; and Gupta (n 73) 34.

III. Standard Essential Patents

Collaborative standards often include patented technology from different SDO members. An SEP is defined as a patent that must be implemented to comply with a standard. In other words, there are no other ways to implement the standard without infringing the SEP. Well-known ICT standards often include hundreds or thousands of SEPs. According to some estimates, there are over 45,000 and 39,000 patents declared essential to 4G LTE and 3G UMTS respectively,[95] and as many as 95,000 patent declarations for 5G.[96] The video coding standards MPEG-2 and MPEG-4 are believed to have around 800 declared SEPs,[97] while the Wi-Fi standard was estimated to have around 3,000 declared SEPs.[98] The ETSI database alone contains 25,070 disclosed patent families.[99]

On a terminological note, it is common in the literature to use the term 'standard essential patent' while it is only specific *claims* of a patent that are essential to a standard.[100] Patents often include dozens of claims, some of which cover technology included in a standard and others which may not. Even within the claim, one part may be essential and the other not essential. The difference is important as disclosure and licensing obligations apply only to essential parts of patent claims, and do not extend to non-essential claims.[101] Therefore, the legally correct term would be 'standard essential claims of a patent' instead of 'standard essential patents'.

[95] See: J Baron and T Pohlmann, 'Mapping Standards to Patents Using Databases of Declared Standard-Essential Patents and Systems of Technological Classification' (2018) 27 *Journal of Economics & Management Strategy* 504, 521; see also *TCL v Ericsson*, 2017 WL 6611635 (CD Cal 2017) 27–28 (TCL's expert finding that there were over 153,000 patent and/or patent applications declared essential for 2G, 3G and 4G standards grouped into over 11,000 patent families).

[96] Pohlmann and Blind, 'Fact Finding Study' (n 92).

[97] Fraunhofer Institute, 'Study on the Interplay Between Standards and Intellectual Property Rights' (2011) 62, available at: ec.europa.eu/growth/content/study-interplay-between-standards-and-intellectual-property-rights-ipr-0_en.

[98] *In re Innovatio IP Ventures LLC Patent Litigation*, 2013 WL 5593609 (ND Illinois 2013) 43.

[99] Bekkers et al, 'Pilot Study for Essentiality Assessment of Standard Essential Patents' (n 93) 64.

[100] See American Bar Association, *Standards Development Patent Policy Manual* (ed J Contreras) (2007) (ABA, *Standards Development Patent Policy Manual*) 10–12; The Institute of Electrical and Electronics Engineers Standards Association (IEEE-SA), 'Standards Board Bylaws' (August 2020) Clause 6.1 (referring to essential patent claims), available at: standards.ieee.org/content/dam/ieee-standards/standards/web/documents/other/sb_bylaws.pdf; Bekkers et al, 'Pilot Study for Essentiality Assessment of Standard Essential Patents' (n 93) 113 ('it is the claims that determine the scope of exclusive rights conferred by the patents, and therefore determine essentiality').

[101] SDO IPR policies confirm this distinction. See ANSI, 'Essential Requirements: Due Process Requirements for American National Standards' (January 2021) 10 (speaking of 'essential patent claims'); ITU-ISO-IEC, 'Patent Statement and Licensing Declaration Form for ITU-T, ITU-R Recommendation, ISO or IEC Deliverable' (2 November 2018), available at: www.itu.int/dms_pub/itu-t/oth/04/04/T04040000020005PDFE.pdf (defining patents as 'claims contained in and identified by patents … solely to the extent that any such claims are essential'); courts also examine patent claims in disputes involving SEPs, see *In re Innovatio IP Ventures LLC Patent Litigation* 956 F.Supp.2d 925 (ND Ill 2013) (examining patent claims of 23 patents declared essential to Wi-Fi Standard); *Nokia Corp v InterDigital Technology Corp* [2007] EWHC 3077 (examining the essentiality of patent relating to 3G standard); *Unwired Planet v Huawei* [2015] EWHC 3366 (Pat) (examining all patent claims and finding them essential to 4G communication standard).

However, for the sake of simplicity, the term 'standard essential patents' will be used as it is common in the literature.

Studies have argued that SEPs are on average more valuable than non-SEPs. While measuring the quality of a patent is inherently subjective and imprecise, there are some external factors that could be used to compare patents. SEP holders are more likely to pay maintenance fees to keep SEPs in force in contrast to non-SEPs, thus viewing them as more valuable warranting expenditure maintenance fees.[102] A number of studies also found that SEPs receive a higher number of forward citations (ie, cited as a prior art by later patent applications) than non-SEPs.[103] Having more forward citations is generally considered as indication of a patent's quality.[104] SEPs are also likely to be patented in more countries than non-SEPs and have a larger family size.[105] Taken together, these factors suggest that SEPs have higher technical and economic significance and that SDOs are able to attract valuable technologies, although being part of a standard certainly contributes to the increase in value.

Some studies also claim that SEPs are more likely to be litigated than non-SEPs.[106] Accordingly, SEPs are estimated to be on average two to four times more litigated than non-SEPs.[107] This could be explained by the importance of SEPs and their widespread implementation in popular standards. Most litigated SEPs relate to communications standards, the IEEE's Wi-Fi and ETSIs 2G, 3G and 4G, while

[102] T Pohlmann and K Blind, 'Landscaping Study on Standard Essential Patents (SEPs)' (2016) 41; R Bekkers et al, 'Landscape Study of Potentially Essential Patents Disclosed to ETSI' (Publication Office of the European Union, 2020) 44–55.

[103] M Rysman and T Simcoe, 'Patents and the Performance of Voluntary Standard-Setting Organizations' (2008) 54 *Management Science* 1920, 1934 (finding that SEPs on average receive twice as many citations before disclosure and an additional rise in citations following disclosure); A Layne-Farrar, 'Innovative or Indefensible? An Empirical Assessment of Patenting within Standard Setting' (2011) 9 *International Journal of IT Standards and Standardization Research* 1 (finding that 3G UMTS SEPs received on average twice as many citations than non-SEPs); F Caviggioli et al, 'Patenting Strategies and Characteristics of Declared Inventions in the Long Term Evolution Standard' (2015) 46 *R&D Management* 664 (measuring forward citations for 4G LTE); Pohlmann and Blind, 'Landscaping Study on Standard Essential Patents (SEPs)' (n 102) 40; Baron and Pohlmann, 'Mapping Standards to Patents' (n 95) 521; Bekkers et al, 'Landscape Study of Potentially Essential Patents Disclosed to ETSI' (n 102) 44–55 (SEPs disclosed at ETSI receive on average twice as many forward citations than non-SEPs).

[104] However, a note of caution: SEPs may have more forward citations because they are more visible than non-SEPs and because of the requirement to ensure backward compatibility of new standard releases, newer SEPs would need to refer to older ones. See more in Bekkers et al, 'Landscape Study of Potentially Essential Patents Disclosed to ETSI' (n 102) 55.

[105] Pohlmann and Blind, 'Landscaping Study on Standard Essential Patents (SEPs)' (n 102) 40; Bekkers et al, 'Landscape Study of Potentially Essential Patents Disclosed to ETSI' (n 102) 44–55.

[106] But are also very likely to be settled. See M Lemley and T Simcoe, 'How Essential Are Standard Essential Patents?' (2019) 104 *Cornell Law Review* 607, 623 (finding that 75.9% of US SEP cases were settled and 16.1% were resolved on procedural grounds. Only 8% went to the merits).

[107] Commission, 'Patents and Standards' (n 9) 125 (6.7% of all essential patents in their dataset were the subject of litigation, while only 1.5% of non-SEPs were litigated); Pohlmann and Blind, 'Landscaping Study on Standard Essential Patents (SEPs)' (n 102) 41 (finding that almost 2% of all SEPs have been litigated at least once, while examined non-SEPs were litigated in only 0,45% of cases); also R Bekkers et al, 'Disclosure Rules and Declared Essential Patents' (2019) NBER Working Paper 23627.

other standards seem less contentious.[108] However, Gupta and Snyder claim that in smartphone patent wars non-SEPs were responsible for the majority of litigation and only one-third of asserted patents were SEPs.[109]

A. SEPs in IPR Policies of SDOs

SDO IPR policies typically impose two obligations on SEP owners: (i) the duty to disclose SEPs; and (ii) the duty to license SEPs.[110]

i. Disclosure Rules

The purpose of the disclosure rules is to inform SDO members if technical contributions are protected by patented technology in order to make a reasoned decision whether to include such technology into a standard or not. The precise nature of disclosure rules varies between SDOs, and it is possible to identify ex ante or ex post disclosures, and blanket or specific disclosures.

A disclosure of SEPs during the development of a standard is called ex ante disclosure, while the disclosure after the standard has been finalised is referred to as ex post disclosure.[111] The goal of ex ante disclosure is to provide early information to engineers working on the development of a standard about patented technology covered by technical contributions. Engineers may then make a reasoned decision whether to accept the inclusion of patented technologies into a standard or decide on a different (un)patented alternative. However, ex ante disclosures are inherently uncertain. The finally agreed version of a standard may not include technology disclosed early in the development process. Also, when a standard is under development, it may be difficult to assess with a sufficient degree

[108] See J Contreras, 'A Tale of Two Layers: Patents, Standardization and the Internet' (2016) 93 *Denver Law Review* 853 (finding that IETF's internet standards are rarely litigated compared with the IEEE and ETSI standards); J Contreras, 'Assertion of Standard Essential Patents by Non-Practicing Entities' in D Sokol (ed), *Patent Assertion Entities and Competition Law* (Cambridge University Press, 2017) (ETSI's 2G, 3G, 4G SEPs consisted of 53% of SEPs cases, while the IEEE's 802.11 SEPs were litigated in 35% of cases); Lemley and Simcoe (n 106) 619 (in the US SEP litigation in their sample ETSI and the IEEE's SEPs were responsible for 41% and 26% of cases, respectively).

[109] K Gupta and M Snyder, 'Smart Phone Litigation and Standard Essential Patents' (2014) Hoover IP2 Working Paper Series No 14006.

[110] On SDO IPR policy obligations, see generally: Lemley (n 1); ABA, *Standards Development Patent Policy Manual* (n 100); Commission, 'Patents and Standards' (n 9) 41–46; Torti (n 44) 60–82.

[111] R Bekkers and A Upgedrowe, 'A Study of IPR Policies and Practices of a Representative Group of Standards Setting Organizations Worldwide', Commissioned by the US National Academies of Science, Board of Science, Technology, and Economic Policy (17 September 2012) 59, available at: www.nap.edu/resource/18510/Bekkers-Updegrove%20Paper_092013.pdf (finding that all 12 examined SDOs IPR Policies provide for some form of early patent disclosure during the standard's development); P Régibeau, R De Coninck and H Zenger, 'Transparency, Predictability and Efficiency of SSO-based Standardisation and SEP Licensing: A Report for the European Commission' (2016) 46, available at: ec.europa.eu/growth/content/study-transparency-predictability-and-efficiency-sso-based-standardization-and-sep-licensing_en (discussing ex ante disclosures).

of accuracy whether a patent is essential and whether it would remain essential to a finally agreed version of a standard. A patent application at that time may still be pending and it is unclear whether the granted patent will ultimately read on a standard. As a result, early disclosure facilitates over-disclosure of patents that may not be essential for a standard.[112]

Another reason why ex ante disclosures are unreliable is because SEPs are often developed in parallel with the standardisation process and rarely exist before standardisation. Kang and Bekkers describe the phenomenon of 'just-in-time patenting' where companies apply for patents immediately before or right after SDO meetings and later negotiate their inclusion into a standard.[113] Pohlmann and Blind found that 71 per cent of all declared SEPs are granted after the final release of a standard.[114] These findings demonstrate that a standard development process rarely uses existing 'off-the-shelf' solutions; most technologies do not exist prior to standardisation but are made during a standard's development process. This will be important to bear in mind when analysing the merits of the ex ante incremental value approach for valuating SEPs and principles for calculating FRAND royalty.

Because of the difficulties associated with identifying SEPs early on in a standard's development, SDOs usually allow for ex-post disclosures after the standard is set. Ex-post disclosures are more accurate as companies now have the precise information on the finally agreed version of the standard and can more easily assess whether their patents cover the standard. Therefore, most of disclosures in practice occur ex post. Biddle shows that 44 per cent of disclosures for Wi-Fi standard occurred after the standard specifications were finalised.[115] The numbers are even higher for the 4G LTE standard where 100 per cent and 96 per cent of disclosures occurred after final versions of LTE release 8 and 11 were agreed, respectively.[116] However, the ex-post disclosures are contrary to the purpose of making engineers aware of patented technologies during the standard's development, and relying too much on ex-post disclosures may frustrate the goals of disclosures policies.

When making a disclosure, a patent owner may be required to precisely identify a patent or a patent application that may be essential for a standard (specific disclosure),[117] or it may only indicate that it may hold SEPs, while not revealing their full identity (blanket disclosures).[118] Specific disclosures increase transparency of

[112] See section III.C below.

[113] B Kang and R Bekkers, 'Just-in-Time Patents and the Development of Standards' (2015) 44 *Research Policy* 1948.

[114] Pohlmann and Blind, 'Landscaping Study on Standard Essential Patents (SEPs)' (n 102) 56.

[115] B Biddle, 'Five Reasons Why Patent Disclosure in Standard-Setting Organizations Doesn't Work (and what to do instead)' (2015) 5, available at: papers.ssrn.com/sol3/papers.cfm?abstract_id=2669893.

[116] ibid.

[117] See ETSI, IPR Information Statement and Licensing Declaration Form (3 September 2020), available at: www.etsi.org/images/files/IPR/etsi-ipr-policy.pdf (specific disclosure template); IEEE, Letters of Assurance (1 June 2019), available at: mentor.ieee.org/myproject/Public//mytools/mob/loa.pdf (providing options for both specific and blanket disclosure).

[118] See ETSI, IPR Licensing Declaration Form (3 September 2020)) (a blanket disclosure template form): www.etsi.org/images/files/IPR/etsi-ipr-policy.pdf IEEE-SA, 'Standards Board Bylaws' (August 2020) Clause 6.1 (defining blanket disclosures as an 'assurance that applies to all Essential Patent Claims for which a Submitter may currently or in the future … have the ability to license').

the SEP landscape and allow the assessment of the precise number of patents that are essential for a given standard. However, specific disclosures are more costly as patent owners may need to conduct extensive searches of their patent portfolios in order to identify specific patents that read on a standard. Blanket disclosures, on the other hand, decrease the transparency of the SEP landscape as the exact number of patents that may be covered by a standard are unknown but are easier for companies to implement and are usually tied in with a commitment to license any SEP that the company may have on FRAND or royalty-free terms. Therefore, while blanket disclosures do not convey the full picture of the SEP landscape, they at least ensure that all SEPs that a company holds will be available for licensing. SEP owners seem to prefer blanket disclosures due to lower costs and the wider assurance that, if there are any SEPs, they will be licensed on FRAND. Studies have shown that approximately 60 per cent of all disclosures are blanket ones.[119]

ii. Licensing Rules

Once a company declares it holds patents and patent applications that may be essential for a standard it is required to state its licensing position. SDO IPR policies typically require patent holders to license their SEPs either on fair, reasonable and non-discriminatory (FRAND) terms or royalty-free (RF) terms. Patent owners may also decide not to license their SEPs, in which case SDO members should decide whether to proceed with the inclusion of that technology into a standard or to adopt an alternative technology.[120]

Terminologically, some SDOs require licences to be available only on 'reasonable and non-discriminatory' (RAND) terms,[121] omitting the 'fair' requirement. It is commonly accepted in the literature that there are no substantive differences between FRAND and RAND terms and that the two should be treated as synonyms, unless and until SDOs or courts rule otherwise.[122]

The purpose of licensing rules is to secure widespread implementation of standards. They enable engineers to focus on adopting the best available technologies without worrying that the implementation of the standard may later be blocked by patent owners deciding not to license their technology. Licensing rules

[119] Commission, 'Patents and Standards' (n 9) 118–19; also Bekkers et al, 'Pilot Study for Essentiality Assessment of Standard Essential Patents' (n 93) 94 (as of January 2020, 68.7% of the IEEE's patent declarations for the 802.11 standard were blanket declarations).

[120] See ETSI, 'Intellectual Property Rights Policy' (3 September 2020), available at: www.etsi.org/images/files/IPR/etsi-ipr-policy.pdf, Clause 8 (describing the procedure if licences for SEPs are not available).

[121] See IEEE, 'Standards Board Bylaws' (August 2020) Clause 6 (including the term 'reasonable royalties'); ITU-T/ITU-R/ISO/IEC, 'Common Patent Policy', available at: www.itu.int/en/ITU-T/ipr/Pages/policy.aspx (speaking of 'reasonable terms and conditions').

[122] See: US Department of Justice and US Patent & Trademark Office, 'Policy Statement on Remedies for Standard Essential Patents Subject to Voluntary F/RAND Commitments' (8 January 2013) 1; Commission, 'Patents and Standards' (n 9) 40 (concluding that the term 'RAND' appears to be mostly used by US SDOs, while European SDOs prefer the term 'FRAND).

also ensure that licensing costs will be at a reasonable level, while also guaranteeing that SEP holders are fairly and adequately rewarded for the contribution of their best technologies.

However, the exact meaning and content of FRAND terms is not further defined. It is left for parties in good faith negotiations to arrive at terms that they see as fair and reasonable. The open-ended nature of FRAND terms naturally leads to some tensions, as what appears to be fair and reasonable to patent owners may not be for standard implementers. This may lead many authors and officials to argue for more precisely defined FRAND commitments.[123] As Lemley notes: 'It is all well and good to propose that SSOs require licensing on reasonable and non-discriminatory terms. But without some idea of what those terms are, reasonable and non-discriminatory licensing loses much of its meaning.'[124] However, others maintain that FRAND provides flexibility for parties to negotiate a licence tailored to their circumstances.[125] The very absence of a clear definition of FRAND terms makes it possible to specify licensing conditions for each licensee and to take into account the unique characteristics of certain sectors, contributing to the widest possible adoption of standards. According to Spulber, 'the incompleteness of FRAND commitments is a feature, not a flaw. It allows SEP holders and implementers to negotiate contingent patent licensing agreements that respond to changes in market conditions.'[126]

Despite the uncertainty, FRAND licensing appears to be the main licensing model for SEPs in the ICT industry. Pohlmann and Blind found that 68 per cent of all declared SEPs are licensed under FRAND terms,[127] while Baron and Spulber's study of the IPR policies of 37 SDOs found that 32 SDOs allowed for FRAND licensing, with the remaining five requiring royalty-free licensing.[128] The growth and the success of the ICT industry can also be evidence of the robustness of a FRAND commitment, and while there are some disputes the overall majority of

[123] D Swanson and W Baumol, 'Reasonable and Non-discriminatory (RAND) Royalties, Standards Selection, and Control of Market Power' (2005) 73 *Antitrust Law Journal* 1, 5; M Lemley and C Shapiro, 'A Simple Approach to Setting Reasonable Royalties for Standard-Essential Patents' (2013) 28 *Berkeley Technology Law Journal* 1135, 1137–38; R Hesse, Deputy Assistant Attorney General, US Department of Justice, 'Six Small Proposals for SSOs Before Lunch' (2012) Remarks as Prepared for the ITU-T Patent Roundtable, available at: www.justice.gov/atr/file/518951/download; K Uwe-Kuhn, F Scott-Morton and H Shelanski, 'Standard Setting Organisations Can Help Solve the Standard Essential Patent Licensing Problem' (March 2013) *CPI Antitrust Chronicle* 1.

[124] Lemley (n 1) 1964–65.

[125] Geradin and Rato (n 68) 112; P Larouche, J Padilla and R Taffet, 'Settling FRAND Disputes: Is Mandatory Arbitration a Reasonable and Non Discriminatory Alternative?' (2014) 10 *Journal of Competition Law & Economics* 581; G Sidak, 'The Meaning of FRAND Part II: Injunctions', (2015) 11 *Journal of Competition Law & Economics* 201; D Spulber, 'Licensing Standard Essential Patents with FRAND Commitments: Preparing for 5G Mobile Telecommunications' (2020) 18 *Colorado Technology Law Journal* 79.

[126] Spulber (n 125) 93.

[127] Pohlmann and Blind, 'Landscaping Study on Standard Essential Patents (SEPs)' (n 102) 36 (the remaining 32% declared SEPs do not specify the licensing conditions).

[128] Baron and Spulber (n 14) 479.

patent licensing agreements are concluded amicably. Thus, the flexibility of the FRAND notion seems to be an attractive option for market players.[129]

B. The Meaning of Essentiality

The precise meaning of essentiality varies from one SDO to another.[130] IPR policies generally make a distinction between *technical* and *commercial* essentiality. As such, the obligation to disclose and license SEPs depends on the exact notion of essentiality adopted by a particular SDO.

A patent is said to be technically essential if there is no other technical alternative to implement a standard without infringing the patent,[131] while a patent is commercially essential if it is not strictly technically required, but it is the only commercially feasible way a standard can be implemented.[132] The notion of commercial essentiality is thus broader and would require disclosure and licensing of more patents than under the pure technical essentiality definition. Moreover, the assessment of which patents are commercially essential is inherently unreliable and largely depends on the perspective of individual companies. For these reasons, it seems that most SDOs require disclosure and licensing only of technically essential patents. A study by Bekkers and Upgedrowe of 10 SDO policies found that eight required only technically essentiality.[133] ETSI, for instance, mandates disclosure only of technically essential patents,[134] while the IEEE requires the disclosure of commercially essential patents as well.[135]

Standards also contain different parts or features. A distinction can be made between *mandatory*, *optional* and *alternative* features of a standard. A mandatory feature includes criteria that must always be fulfilled in order to claim full conformity with a standard.[136] Optional features include criteria that may, but are not required, to be selected for the implementation of the standard.[137] It is common for a standard to include many optional features, some which may

[129] See Fraunhofer Institute, 'Study on the Interplay Between Standards and Intellectual Property Rights' (n 97) 115 (in this older study from 2011 there was a broad agreement among surveyed industry participants that the FRAND system works. It provides IPR owners with stronger incentives to invest in R&D, to patent and to contribute to standardisation).

[130] See Bekkers and Upgedrowe (n 111) 37.

[131] ibid, 39–40; ABA, *Standards Development Patent Policy Manual* (n 100) 18.

[132] ABA, *Standards Development Patent Policy Manual* (n 100) 18; Bekkers and Upgedrowe (n 111) 39–40; see also J Kesan and C Hayes, 'FRAND's Forever: Standards, Patent Transfers and Licensing Commitments' (2014) 89 *Indiana Law Journal* 231, 242; J Contreras, 'Essentiality and Standard-Essential Patents' in J Contreras (ed), *The Cambridge Handbook of Technical Standardization Law: Competition, Antitrust, and Patents* (Cambridge University Press, 2018).

[133] Bekkers and Upgedrowe (n 111) 37.

[134] ETSI, 'Intellectual Property Rights Policy' (3 September 2020) Clause 15, available at: www.etsi.org/images/files/IPR/etsi-ipr-policy.pdf.

[135] IEEE-SA, 'Standards Board Bylaws' (August 2020) Clause 6.1.

[136] ABA, *Standards Development Patent Policy Manual* (n 100) 16; Bekkers and Upgedrowe (n 111) 40; Contreras, 'Essentiality and Standard-Essential Patents' (n 132) 220–21.

[137] ABA, Standards Development Patent Policy Manual (n 100) 17.

never be implemented while some will become popular and used by almost every standard-implementer.[138] Additionally, there may be alternative features, where one or more alternative approaches must be selected in order to comply with the standard.[139] Proper drafting of the text of a standard is crucial in order to make this distinction. Often the use of terms such as 'shall', 'may', 'should', 'can' and 'is/has' in a standard's text have appropriate meaning and reflect the difference.[140]

A distinction between mandatory, optional and alternative features is relevant for many aspects of SEP licensing. For example, if the SEP holder has only patents essential for optional features of the standard the manufacturer may not need to take a licence in case it does not implement them. A patent would be standard essential but not infringed. Also, SEPs that read on core mandatory features are typically valued more than SEPs that read on optional or alternative features, which would have an impact on licensing negotiations and SEP valuations.[141]

C. The Problem of Over-Disclosure

Although a patent may be declared as essential, it may not be truly essential for a standard for a variety of reasons. Numerous studies and cases have confirmed that the number of truly essential patents is much lower than the number of declared essential patents. Back in 2004, Goodman and Mayers examined 7,796 patents and patent applications declared as essential for the 3G standard and found that only approximately 21 per cent of the declared patents were truly essential. In other words, 79 per cent of declared SEPs were non-essential.[142] Studies by Fairfield Research estimated that only 28 per cent, 29 per cent and 50 per cent of patent families declared essential to ETSI's 2G, 3G and 4G standards, respectively, were truly essential.[143]

[138] Bekkers and Upgedrowe (n 111) 41.

[139] Contreras, 'Essentiality and Standard-Essential Patents' (n 132) 221.

[140] Bekkers et al, 'Pilot Study for Essentiality Assessment of Standard Essential Patents' (n 93) 91.

[141] See *Microsoft v Motorola*, 2013 WL 2111217 (WD Wash 2013) 111 (confirming that mandatory portions are valued more than optional ones: 'a patent that is extremely important and central to the standard would reasonably command a higher royalty rate than a less important patent. Importantly, however, because an "essential" patent is one that is necessary to implement either an optional or mandatory provision of a standard, a specific SEP may contribute greatly to an optional portion of a given standard, but if the implementer does not use that portion, the specific SEP may have little value to the implementer') 325 ('patents that are essential to optional parts of the standard have a lower value than patents that are essential to the required portions').

[142] D Goodman and R Myers, '3G Cellular Standards and Patents' (2005) 13 *IEEE WirelessCom* 1. However, see also, D Martin and C de Meyer, 'Patent Counting, a Misleading Index of Patent Value: A Critique of Goodman & Myers and its Uses' (2006), available at: papers.ssrn.com/sol3/papers.cfm?abstract_id=949439 (criticising Goodman and Myers's paper for containing serious methodological flaws).

[143] Fairfield Resources International, 'Analysis of Patents Declared Essential to GSM as of 6 June 2007' (2008), available at: fair-standards.org/wp-content/uploads/2017/02/170213-FSA-Position-Paper Transparency-FRAND-1.pdf; Fairfield Resources International,' Review of Patents Declared Essential to WCDMA Through December 2008' (2009), available at: www.frlicense.com/wcdma1.pdf; Fairfield Resources International, 'Review of Patents Declared Essential to LTE and SAE (4G Wireless Standards) Through June 30, 2009' (2010), available at: frlicense.com/GSM_FINAL.pdf.

The Cyber Creative Institute also examined patents declared essential to the 4G LTE standard and found that 56 per cent of the sampled declared patents were truly essential, while 29 per cent were partially essential and 15 per cent were not essential at all.[144] 5G is likely to have similar essentiality rates.

Court cases also confirm this phenomenon. In *Unwired Planet v Huawei*, the court had to estimate, among other things, the total number of truly essential patents for ETSI's 2G, 3G and 4G standards. Out of thousands of declared SEPs, it was found that there are only 800 truly essential patents for 4G LTE standards, and 479 and 154 truly essential patents for 3G and 2G standards respectively.[145] The US court in *TCL v Ericsson* also examined the number of truly essential patents for ETSI's 2G, 3G and 4G standards and came to different result. It found that out of approximately 153,000 patents and patent applications in the ETSI database only 1,481 patents were found to be truly essential for 4G standards, and 953 and 365 truly essential patents for 3G and 2G respectively.[146] Other cases have also confirmed that not all asserted SEPs are in fact essential.[147]

The essentiality rate varies not only between standards but also between companies. For 4G, Unwired Planet's expert in *Unwired Planet v Huawei* estimated the essentiality rate of one large patent-holding company to be 15.9 per cent and 9.4 per cent for another.[148] For 5G, one study estimated essentiality rates between 15.8 per cent to as low as 5.4 per cent per company,[149] while another study was a bit more generous to SEP owners, with essentiality rates varying between 34 per cent and 19 per cent.[150]

What are the reasons for such a large number of declared essential patents turning out to be not truly essential? The main factor is over-disclosure. There are several reasons why SDO members may unintentionally or intentionally disclose patents that are non-essential.[151] First, the actual determination of the essentiality

[144] Cyber Creative Institute, Evaluation of LTE Essential Patents Declared at ETSI (2013), available at: www.cybersoken.com/file/lte03EN.pdf.

[145] *Unwired Planet v Huawei* [2017] EWHC 2988 (Pat) 377–78.

[146] *TCL v Ericsson*, 2017 WL 6611635 (CD Cal 2017) 27, 32.

[147] See: RPX Corporation, 'Standard Essential Patents: How do They Fare?' (2014), available at: www.rpxcorp.com/wp-content/uploads/2014/01/Standard-Essential-Patents-How-Do-They-Fare.pdf (finding that in the US, SEPs holders prevailed approximately 30–40% of the time); also *Nokia Corp v InterDigital Technology Corp* [2007] EWHC 3077 (finding only one patent to be essential to 3G standard out of four in the litigation); *IPCom v HTC* [2015] EWHC 1034 (Pat) (patent found to be valid but non-essential to 3G standard); however, see *In re Innovatio IP Ventures LLC Patent Litigation*, 956 F.Supp.2d 925 (ND Ill 2013) (finding all 23 patents in the litigation to be essential to the IEEE's 802.11 standard).

[148] *Unwired Planet v Huawei* [2017] EWHC 2988 (Pat) 333.

[149] M Noble, J Mutimear and R Vary, 'Determining Which Companies are Leading the 5G Race' (July/August 2019) *IAM Media* 35, 36, available at: www.twobirds.com/~/media/pdfs/news/articles/2019/determining-which-companies-are-leading-the-5g-race.pdf.

[150] Amplified, GreyB, 'Exploration of 5G Standards and Preliminary Findings on Essentiality' (2020), available at: static1.squarespace.com/static/59fa01a118b27d1bfef7f050/t/5ecc8c109259ee3d45ecda99/1590463526894/5G+SEP+Preliminary+Report.pdf.

[151] See generally: Commission, 'Patents and Standards' (n 9) 114–17; Biddle, 'Five Reasons' (n 115); G Sidak, 'The Meaning of FRAND, Part I: Royalties' (2013) 9 *Journal of Competition Law & Economics* 931, 956–60.

is left to the patent owner and SDOs do not double-check whether patents declared by their members are truly essential.[152] This leaves plenty of possibility for errors as determining essentiality is inherently subjective with a high potential for mistakes. Second, the duty to identify and disclose patents is typically limited to the personal knowledge of the individuals participating at SDO meetings. For example, the IEEE imposes a disclosure obligation for essential patents of which the 'individual participant is personally aware',[153] IETF requires disclosure of essential patents 'reasonably and personally known' to an individual participant,[154] while ETSI requires 'reasonable endeavours' to identify and disclose essential patents.[155] The extensive patent searches are not required because of the high costs and delays.[156] Errors may thus be possible as individual participants may not possess sufficient knowledge of the company's patent portfolio. Next, as explained the ex ante disclosures during the development of a standard are inherently inaccurate. Patents that are declared essential to a draft version of a standard may not end up in the final version that is ultimately approved. As seen, standard development is a continuous process, various technologies are debated and tested and only once the final version of the standard is approved would it be possible to make a definitive assessment of the technologies that are covered by the standard. Furthermore, standards evolve and change over time, and a patent essential to an earlier release of a standard may not be essential to a later one. Patents also expire or are invalidated in litigation. Most SDOs also require the disclosure of pending patent applications that may be essential to a standard and the scope of the finally issued patent may be narrowed or modified during the review by the national patent office and may no longer contain claims that are essential.[157] The patent application may also be rejected, successfully opposed, or abandoned. Thus, a declared patent application may not result in an issued patent. Finally, SDOs typically do not require updating patent disclosures.[158] This means that all those patents that are later found to be non-essential, expired, or invalidated are not reflected in the SDO's database.

[152] See: Common Patent Policy for ITU-T/ITU-R/ISO/IEC (2015) ('ITU, ISO or IEC are unable to verify the validity of any such information'); ETSI, 'Guide on Intellectual Property Rights' (19 September 2013) 59, available at: available at: www.etsi.org/images/files/ipr/etsi-guide-on-ipr.pdf ('Pursuant to ETSI IPR Policy, no investigation, including IPR searches, has been carried out by ETSI'); IEEE-SA, 'Standards Board Bylaws' (August 2020) Clause 6.2 ('The IEEE is not responsible for: 1. Identifying essential patent claims for which a license may be required; 2. Determining the validity, essentiality, or interpretation of patent claims'). A patent holder's determination of essentiality can only be challenged in court, see *Nokia Corp v InterDigital Technology Corp* [2005] EWCA Civ 614 (holding that issuing a determination of non-essentiality was within the court's power and discretion).

[153] IEEE-SA, 'Standards Board Bylaws' (August 2020) Clause 6.2.

[154] IETF, 'Intellectual Property Rights in IETF Technology' (May 2017) Article 5.1, available at: www.rfc-editor.org/rfc/pdfrfc/rfc8179.txt.pdf.

[155] ETSI, 'Intellectual Property Rights Policy' (3 September 2020) Clause 4.1.

[156] Bekkers and Upgedrowe (n 111) 58 (finding that all examined SDOs explicitly state that patent searches are not required).

[157] ibid, 44–45.

[158] ibid, 64–65. Also see ETSI, 'Guide on IPRs' (19 September 2013) Clause 2.1.4 ('Members are not obliged to inform ETSI of any updates to their essential IPR').

Patent holders may also have strong incentives to intentionally over-declare patents. A company that fails to disclose essential patents risks facing infringing competition law and allegations of deceptive conduct and fraud. The assertion of patents not disclosed to the SDO is referred to as 'patent ambush', with the legal consequence of unenforceability of patents.[159] On the other hand, there seem to be no material legal consequences for over-declaration. Patent owners thus have a strong incentive to err on the safe side and over-declare patents that have even a remote possibility of being essential to a standard, than to risk potential competition law liability and a patent's unenforceability. There is also a strong commercial incentive for companies to show they own a large SEP portfolio because licensing royalties are, to a large extent, based on the number of patents in a portfolio.[160] Vertically integrated companies may also want to show they have a large SEP portfolio for cross-licensing purposes. Having a sizable portfolio may also convey a message to the market that the company is innovative and a technological leader.[161]

Therefore, a number of factors contribute to companies unintentionally and intentionally over-declaring patents and the consequence is an unclear SEP landscape. Standard implementers do not know how many patents they need to license, and they understandably do not want to pay for non-essential patents. Over-declaration also affects FRAND royalty determinations as parties and courts try to establish the number of truly essential patents in a portfolio.[162] Thus, the unclear and non-transparent SEP market creates tensions in future licensing negotiations. Industry members are well aware of widespread over-declaration of SEPs, but there is no consensus on how to remedy this issue.[163] The merits of proposals for increasing the transparency of the SEP landscape and the reliability of a SEP declaration will be discussed in more detail in chapter nine.

[159] See *Rambus Inc v FTC*, 522 F.3d 456, 459 (DC Cir 2008) (non-disclosure of SEP, avoidance of giving a FRAND commitment and subsequent enforcement of SEP may be an antitrust offence); *Qualcomm v Broadcom*, 548 F.3d 1004 (Fed Cir 2008) (non-disclosure of SEPs in breach of SDOs IPR policy made SEPs unenforceable by doctrines of implied waver and equitable estoppel); *Hynix Semiconductor v Rambus*, 645 F.3d 1336 (Fed Cir 2011) (non-disclosed SEPs may be unenforceable by doctrines of implied waiver and equitable estoppel); *Core Wireless v Apple* 899, F.3d 1356 (Fed Cir 2020) (doctrine of implied waver may render non-disclosed SEP unenforceable); COMP/38.636 – *Rambus*, Commission Decision [2009] OJ C 30/17 (competition investigation concerning non-disclosure of SEPs). For detailed analysis of legal consequences of patent ambush see Petrovcic (n 30); B Lundqvist, *Standardisation Under EU Competition Rules and US Antitrust Law* (Edward Elgar, 2014); D Teylas, *The Interface Between Competition Law, Patents and Technical Standards* (Kluwer Law International, 2014).

[160] *Unwired Planet v Huawei* [2017] EWHC 711 (Pat) 182 (finding that the commercial practice for calculating royalties is to start with patent counting).

[161] C Tapia, *Industrial Property Rights, Technical Standards and Licensing Practices (FRAND) in the Telecommunications Industry* (Carly Heymanns Verlag, 2010) 13.

[162] See ch 4 for methodologies for calculating FRAND royalties.

[163] Fraunhofer Institute, 'Study on the Interplay Between Standards and Intellectual Property Rights' (n 97) 63–65; Commission, 'Patents and Standard' (n 9) 116; Régibeau, De Coninck and Zenger (n 111) 50.

IV. Conclusion

This chapter explained the standardisation environment and provided a background for better understanding of the SEP licensing issues in the rest of the book. It highlighted the importance of technical interoperability standards to ICT and IoT industries and explained the distinction and relations between different types of standards. The workings of SDOs and a typical standard-development process is discussed, which will help better understand the merits of some proposals for calculating FRAND royalties analysed in chapter four. The chapter also explained the duties to disclose and license SEPs and addressed the problems of essentiality and over-declaration that have a significant impact on future SEP licensing negotiations and valuations. The next chapter turns to the market and policy issues of SEP licensing in ICT and IoT industries.

2

The Dynamics of Standard Essential Patent Licensing: Patent Holdup, Holdout and Royalty Stacking

This chapter explains some of the problems relating to licensing SEPs in the ICT and the IoT industries. It will examine the market context under which SEP disputes emerged and will analyse the notions of patent holdup, holdout and royalty stacking that dominate SEP policy discussions, influencing policymakers and courts.

I. Industry Convergences and Changing Market Dynamics

The tensions relating to SEP licensing may be explained by placing them in the right market context. The convergence between the traditional telecommunications industry and the consumer electronics industry and the subsequent entry of new market players contributed to the emergence of mass SEP licensing disputes.

The ICT industry over the years has undergone a significant market change. The period of 1G, 2G and early 3G standards was characterised by a relatively few large vertically integrated players that both owned SEPs and manufactured downstream mobile handsets. All industry players at that time, Ericsson, Nokia, Siemens, Alcatel and Motorola, cross-licensed their SEPs and their primary source of revenue came from the sale of mobile handsets.[1] In the mid to late 2000s, in the period of late 3G and 4G standards, the traditional mobile phone that was used only for voice calls and text messaging was gradually being transformed into a multifunctional small computer. Smartphones combined features of traditional mobile phones, personal computers, media players and digital cameras. It also brought the convergence of two previously separate industries – telecommunications and consumers electronics – with different licensing traditions.

[1] See R Bekkers, B Verspagen and J Smits, 'Intellectual Property Rights and Standardization: The Case of GSM' (2002) 26 *Telecommunications Policy* 171; R Vary, 'Smartphone Patent Wars: A Phantom Menace' (November 2017), *CPI Antitrust Chronicle* 1.

Besides telecommunication standards, smartphones also incorporated many other standards from consumer electronics industries such as Wi-Fi for wireless connectivity, Bluetooth and USB for short-range connectivity, mp3, JPEG and MPEG for audio and video features and so on. These standards are typically licensed via patent pools,[2] and some even royalty-free.[3]

New entrants came to the smartphone market and changed the industry landscape. Companies such as Apple, Google, RIM, Microsoft, Samsung, Huawei, HTC, ZTE and many others were now producing smartphones and other consumer devices. Coming from a different industry they did not have relevant SEPs for cross-licensing, meaning they had to take a licence to all SEPs on a cash basis if they wanted to enter the market.[4] Recognising that they are generally net payees, they saw taking a licence to telecommunication SEPs as a cost of doing business and would prefer lowering the royalty burden as much as possible, or paying nothing at all. On the other hand, previous incumbents like Ericsson, Nokia, Alcatel and Motorola saw their market shares decline and gradually exited the smartphone handsets market altogether. However, they were left holding a considerable SEP portfolio and quickly realised that their main revenue stream now came from licensing of SEPs and other IP rights. As a result, declining incumbents and new entrants had radically opposed views on what exactly FRAND licensing terms mean and SEPs were quickly recognised as a strategic asset.[5]

The 5G NR standard is expected to bring even greater data connectivity and convergence with many different industries. The 5G standard will support data rates 100 times faster than the current 4G standard, and responsiveness 50 times better than 4G.[6] The first version of the 5G NR standard was released in 2018,[7] and the first commercial roll-outs started in 2020. These new network capacities will enable billions of other devices to be connected to the internet from a range of

[2] See MPEG LA patent pool audio video coding standards, available at: www.mpegla.com/main/default.aspx; VIA Licensing and Sisvel have managed two pools for Wi-Fi standard, see: www.via-corp.com/us/en/licensing/ieee-80211/overview.html; www.sisvel.com/licensing-programs/wireless-communications/wi-fi/introduction/.

[3] eg, for the use of the USB standard is SEP royalty-free, although companies are required to pay for the use of USB the trademark, as well as paying certification fees to show that their products comply with USB standard, see: www.usb.org/developers/logo_license/. Bluetooth also has a similar policy.

[4] Commission, 'Patents and Standards: A Modern Framework for IPR Based Standardisation' (2014) 64, available at: pure.tue.nl/ws/files/3916785/391736021255721.pdf (listing main net licensors and licensees for 3G and 4G standards).

[5] New entrants also sought to obtain SEPs through their own research and development and acquisition of SEP portfolios. See T Pohlmann and K Blind, 'Landscaping Study on Standard Essential Patents (SEPs)' (2016) 26–36, available at: ec.europa.eu (showing companies such as LG, Samsung, Huawei, Google and Blackberry are patenting new and/or acquiring existing SEPs).

[6] 5GPPP, '5G Innovations for New Business Opportunities' (March 2017), available at: 5g-ppp.eu/wp-content/uploads/2017/01/5GPPP-brochure-MWC17.pdf.

[7] 3GPP, Release 15 (3 March 2017), available at: www.3gpp.org/release-15; Dot Econ and Axon Partners Group, 'Study on the Implication of 5G Deployment on Future Business Models' (14 March 2018) 7, available at: berec.europa.eu/eng/document_register/subject_matter/berec/reports/8008-study-on-implications-of-5g-deployment-on-future-business models.

different industries such as automobiles, health, domestic appliances, construction and manufacturing. These industries have little experience of SEP licensing or may have a different licensing tradition from the ICT industry. They would also have to take SEP licenses on a cash basis, and one may expect that new potential IoT licensees would have much different views on what FRAND licensing terms mean than SEP-owning incumbents from the ICT industry.

These market dynamics, the convergence of different industries and the opposing business interests of market players explain the root cause of licensing tensions and lie behind academic and policy discussions about the notions of patent holdup, holdout and royalty stacking, discussed below.

II. Patent Holdup and Royalty Stacking

A. Patent Holdup

In their influential article in 2007, Carl Shapiro and Mark Lemley claimed that patent holdup is a serious problem in the ICT industry.[8] Patent holdup is defined as a situation where SEP owners wait until the patent is included in a standard and implementers are locked in producing standard-compliant products, and then charge excessive licensing fees and demand other more onerous licensing terms than they could have negotiated ex ante before the technology was made part of the standard.[9]

The patent holdup theory lies on the following premises: when a standard is under development by an SDO, many alternative technologies may compete for inclusion in the standard and, at this time (ex ante), the patent holder's market power is constrained by the available alternatives.[10] However, once the SDO agrees on the inclusion of one technology into the standard, other alternatives are eliminated and at this point (ex post) the market power of the SEP holder is increased. The additional market power of the SEP holder is said to originate from the collective action of SDO members and not necessarily from the technological superiority of the underlying technology. The requirement to ensure backward compatibility of later versions of the standard further augments the market power,

[8] M Lemley and C Shapiro, 'Patent Holdup and Royalty Stacking' (2007) 85 *Texas Law Review* 1991; and the follow-up version C Shapiro and M Lemley, 'The Role of Antitrust in Preventing Patent Holdup' (2020) 168 *University of Pennsylvania Law Review* 1.

[9] US Department of Justice and the Federal Trade Commission, 'Antitrust Enforcement of Intellectual Property Rights: Promoting Innovation and Competition' (2007) 35–36; ABA Section of the Antitrust Laws, *Handbook on the Antitrust Aspects of Standard Setting*, 2nd edn (ABA, 2011); Federal Trade Commission, 'The Evolving IP Marketplace: Aligning Patent Notice and Remedies with Competition' (2011) 191–92.

[10] US Department of Justice and Federal Trade Commission, *Antitrust Enforcement of Intellectual Property Rights* (n 9) 35–36; FTC, 'The Evolving IP Marketplace' (n 9) 191–92; J Farrell et al, 'Standard Setting, Patents and Hold-up' (2007) 74 *Antitrust Law Journal* 603.

as SEP cannot be so easily removed once the standard is set.[11] Since licensing negotiations typically begin after the standard is set, SEP holders may exploit the lock-in of standard implementers since it is too costly or even impossible to switch to alternative technologies. For instance, it is not possible nor commercially viable to make smartphones without 3G/4G technology or Wi-Fi connectivity. The availability of injunctions or even the threat of requesting an injunction before the courts are said to magnify patent holdup, as implementers may be required to stop selling downstream products if they infringe even one out of thousands of SEPs.[12] Therefore, the patent holdup notion is concerned with the potential *ex post* opportunism of SEP holders demanding excessive royalties once their technology becomes a part of the standard.

Patent holdup strategies by SEP holders are believed to lead to many negative effects.[13] The manufacturers of standard-compliant products may decide to pass on an increased royalty burden to final consumers by raising the price of downstream products. Follow-on innovation-building and improving on technologies claimed by SEPs by downstream manufacturers may be discouraged. Therefore, the patent holdup is said to act as a 'tax on innovation' and impedes the successful implementation of standards.[14] The dangers would be even more magnified in the IoT with numerous companies from diverse industry sectors needing to take SEP licences.

There are examples where courts found that the initial royalty demands by SEP holders were more than a FRAND rate, which are taken as instances of opportunistic holdup practices. In *Microsoft v Motorola*, Motorola initially demanded a royalty of 2.25 per cent of the end price of Microsoft's products for SEPs covering 802.11 (Wi-Fi) and H.264 audio-video encoding standards.[15] Applied to the average price of Microsoft's X-box of $500, the initially offered royalty would amount to $11.25 per X-box unit.[16] The court, assessing the importance of Motorola's patents to 802.11 and H.264 standard and the importance of these standards and SEPs to Microsoft's product, determined a FRAND royalty rate of 3.471 cents and 0.555 cents per unit for the 802.11 and H.264 SEP portfolios respectively.[17] Therefore, the adjudicated royalty rates were significantly lower than Motorola's initial offer.

[11] T Cotter, E Hovenkamp and N Siebrasse, 'Demystifying Patent Holdup' (2019) 76 *Washington & Lee Law Review* 1501 (discussing path dependency of later version of the standards).

[12] M Lemley, 'Ten Things to do About Patent Holdup of Standards (And One Not To)' (2007) 48 *Boston College Law Review* 149, 167 ('Denying such [injunctive] relief is the most powerful way to prevent patent holdup').

[13] Lemley and Shapiro, 'Patent Holdup and Royalty Stacking' (n 8); US Department of Justice and US Patent & Trademark Office, 'Policy Statement on Remedies for Standard Essential Patents Subject to Voluntary F/RAND Commitments' (2013); D Melamed and C Shapiro, 'How Antitrust Law Can Make FRAND Commitments More Effective' (2018) 128 *Yale Law Journal* 2110, 2116.

[14] See Melamed and Shapiro (n 13) 2116.

[15] *Microsoft v Motorola*, 2013 WL 2111217 (WD Wash 2013).

[16] ibid, 65 (Motorola subsequently modified its initial royalty demand and asked for between $3.00 and $4.50 for Wi-Fi SEPs and $0.50 to $0.63 for H.264 SEPs).

[17] ibid.

In another case, *In re Innovatio IP Ventures*,[18] Innovatio for its 23 SEPs for 802.11 Wi-Fi standard initially requested a royalty rate of 6 per cent of the end-product price. This resulted in per unit royalties of $3.39 per wireless access point, $4.72 per laptop, up to $16.17 per tablet, and up to $36.90 per bar code scanner.[19] However, the court ruled that the appropriate FRAND royalty rate for Innovatio's SEP portfolio was 9.56 cents per unit, many times lower than Innovatio's initial proposal. In other cases, such as *Unwired Planet v Huawei* and *TCL v Ericsson* courts also determined FRAND rates to be much lower than the SEP holder's initial proposals.[20]

Other conduct by SEP owners could also be used as a strategy to extract excessive royalties. In *Realtek v LSI* the court found that LSI breached its FRAND obligation by seeking an exclusion order before the International Trade Commission before offering Realtek a licence on FRAND terms.[21] One study found that in at least 75 per cent of SEP cases in the US, SEP owners used some sort of pressure towards infringers.[22]

B. Royalty Stacking

Royalty stacking concerns a situation when a standard is covered by a very large number of SEPs and if implementers had to pay royalties to all SEP owners royalties may stack on top of each other and become excessive in the aggregate.[23] Royalty stacking is said to be magnified in the presence of holdup when implementers have to pay individually excessive licensing rates.[24] However, royalty stacking can

[18] *In re Innovatio IP Ventures*, 2013 WL 5593609 (ND Illinois 2013).

[19] ibid, 12.

[20] See: *Unwired Planet v Huawei* [2017] EWHC 2988 (Pat) (Unwired Planet initially proposed a royalty for its 4G SEP portfolio of between 0.2% and 0.13%, in contrast to the court's determination of a 0.052% FRAND rate); *TCL v Ericsson*, 2017 WL 6611635 (CD Cal 2017) (Ericsson's initial proposed effective royalty rates of 1.988% and 1.074% for its 4G SEP portfolio, in contrast to the court's determination of a 0.450% FRAND rate).

[21] *Realtek Semiconductor Corp v LSI Corp*, 946 F.Supp.2d 998, 1005 (ND Cal 2013).

[22] B Love, Y Lefouili and C Helmers, 'Do Standard-Essential Patent Owners Behave Opportunistically? Evidence from US District Court Dockets' (2020), available at: papers.ssrn.com/sol3/papers.cfm?abstract_id=3727085. (These include: pursuing injunctions before courts and parallel exclusion orders before the International Trade Commission; engaging in worldwide litigation; failure to timely disclose SEPs before SDOs; over-declaration of SEPs; insisting on licensing on the end-device level; threatening to sue customers; offering discriminatory licensing rates or prior licences not being comparable. However, there is nothing opportunistic in these actions, and it could be said that SEP owners are forced to litigate because of opportunism on the side of implementers who avoid taking a licence and there is no other way to secure FRAND terms other than going to court. Challenging terms offered by implementers on all possible grounds could be another indicator of holdout. The results of this study should thus be considered with reservations.)

[23] See US Department of Justice and Federal Trade Commission, *Antitrust Enforcement of Intellectual Property Rights* (n 9) 61; ABA Section of the Antitrust Laws (n 9) 104–05; Lemley and Shapiro, 'Patent Holdup and Royalty Stacking' (n 8) 1993.

[24] Lemley and Shapiro, 'Patent Holdup and Royalty Stacking' (n 8) 2011.

occur even if there is no holdup, because the sheer number of licences needed to be concluded may make cumulative licensing costs excessively high. Therefore, while patent holdup concerns unilateral pricing by individual SEP owners, royalty stacking relates to cumulative licensing fees.

Indeed, often thousands of patents are declared essential for a single standard. As seen, there are approximately 45,000 and 39,000 patents declared essential to 4G LTE and 3G UMTS standards,[25] and as many as 95,000 patent declarations for 5G grouped in 21,571 patent families.[26] The video-coding standards MPEG-2 and MPEG-4 are believed to have around 800 declared SEPs,[27] while the Wi-Fi standard is estimated to have around 3,000 declared SEPs.[28] Furthermore, according to one estimate, there are 250,000 SEPs and non-SEPs that read on an average smartphone.[29] The sheer number of licences that need to be concluded raises concerns of potentially prohibitive royalty stack.

Economic theory also predicts that when complementary assets are priced independently, an aggregate price would be higher than if all complementary assets are priced together by a single monopolist. The theory of 'Cournot complements', based on the phenomenon observed by August Cournot back in 1838, explains that individual suppliers of complementary input typically do not consider the price charged by other suppliers, resulting in a collective the price that is higher than if the price were set by the single monopolist.[30] Since SEPs are perfect complements, the Cournot complements problem applies.

Several studies tried to estimate the actual amount of royalty stack. Stasik back in 2010 analysed the aggregate royalty burden on 4G LTE standard to which several major patent holders voluntarily announced royalty rates or ranges.[31] Based on those early announcements by nine major LTE SEP owners he found an aggregate royalty burden of 14.8 per cent of the end-product price. In 2014, Armstrong, Mueller and Syrett tried to calculate the total royalty stack on an average smartphone. They estimated that the aggregate patent royalty stack for a hypothetical

[25] See J Baron and T Pohlmann, 'Mapping Standards to Patents Using Databases of Declared Standard-Essential Patents and Systems of Technological Classification' (2018) 27 *Journal of Economics & Management Strategy* 504, 521.

[26] T Pohlmann and K Blind, 'Fact Finding Study on Patents Declared to the 5G Standard' (January 2020), available at: ipforbusiness.org/wp-content/uploads/2020/02/5G-patent-study_TU-Berlin_IPlytics-2020.pdf.

[27] Fraunhofer Institute, 'Study on the Interplay Between Standards and Intellectual Property Rights' (2011) 62, available at: ec.europa.eu/growth/content/study-interplay-between-standards-and-intellectual-property-rights-ipr-0_en.

[28] *In re Innovatio IP Ventures* (n 18) 41–42.

[29] J Kattan, 'FRAND Wars and Section 2' (2013) 27 *Antitrust* 30.

[30] See: A Cournout, *Researches Into the Mathematical Principles of the Theory of Wealth* (trans Nathaniel Bacon, MacMillan Company, 1897) (1838); also C Shapiro, 'Navigating the Patent Thicket: Cross Licensing, Patent Pools, and Standard Setting' (2000) 1 *Innovation Policy and the Economy* 119, 123; Lemley and Shapiro, 'Patent Holdup and Royalty Stacking' (n 8) 2013.

[31] E Stasik, 'Royalty Rates and Licensing Strategies for Essential Patents on LTE (4G) Telecommunications Standards' (September 2010) *les Nouvelles* 114.

$400 smartphone to be $120, or 30 per cent of the end-product price.[32] The 5G royalty stack could go as high as $25 for mobile handsets based on the publicly announced royalty rates of just four large SEP owners.[33]

C. The Influence of Patent Holdup and Royalty Stacking Theories

The notions of patent holdup and royalty stacking problems with SEPs have been very influential and are supported by parts of academia,[34] industry,[35] competition authorities[36] and courts,[37] in both the US and the EU.

[32] A Armstrong, J Mueller and T Syrett, 'The Smartphone Royalty Stack: Surveying Royalty Demands for the Components Within Modern Smartphones' (2014), available at: papers.ssrn.com/sol3/papers.cfm?abstract_id=2443848.

[33] E Stasik and D Cohen, 'Royalty Rates and Licensing Strategies for Essential Patents on 5G Telecommunication Standards: What to Expect' (September 2020) *les Nouvelles* 176 (analysing publicly announced royalty rates for 5G SEPs. Whether this number is too high or is a reasonable price for the innovation that 5G brings is another matter).

[34] For generally supportive academic literature see: Shapiro, 'Navigating the Patent Thicket' (n 30); Lemley and Shapiro, 'Patent Holdup and Royalty Stacking' (n 8); Lemley (n 12); Farrell et al (n 10); T Cotter, 'Patent Holdup, Patent Remedies and Antitrust Response' (2009) 34 *Journal of Corporation Law* 1151; D Lichtman, 'Understanding the RAND Commitment' (2010) 47 *Houston Law Review* 1023; C Shapiro, 'Injunctions, Hold-up, and Patent Royalties' (2010) 12 *American Law and Economics Review* 280; G Cary et al, 'The Case for Antitrust to Police the Patent Holdup Problem in Standard Setting' (2011) 77 *Antitrust Law Journal* 913; S Michel, 'Bargaining for RAND Royalties in the Shadow of Patent Remedies Law' (2011) 77 *Antitrust Law Journal* 889; D Carlton and A Shampine, 'An Economic Interpretation of FRAND' (2013) 9 *Journal of Competition Law & Economics* 531; M Lemley and C Shapiro, 'A Simple Approach to Setting Reasonable Royalties for Standard-Essential Patents' (2013) 28 *Berkeley Technology Law Journal* 1135; F Scott Morton and C Shapiro, 'Patent Assertion: Are We Any Closer to Aligning Reward to Contribution?' in J Lerner and S Stern (eds), *Innovation Policy and the Economy, vol 16* (National Bureau of Economic Research, 2016); W Lee and D Melamed, 'Breaking the Vicious Cycle of Patent Damages' (2016) 101 *Cornell Law Review* 385; Melamed and Shapiro (n 13); 77 US Professors Letter to Assistant Attorney General Delrahim, 'Speeches Patents and Holdups' (17 May 2018), available at: law.rutgers.edu/f/mc-05-18-2018.pdf; J Contreras, 'Much Ado About Holdup' (2019) 3 *University of Illinois Law Review* 875; Shapiro and Lemley, 'The Role of Antitrust in Preventing Patent Holdup' (n 8).

[35] See: Industry Letter to Department of Justice Regarding Standards, Innovation and Licensing (24 January 2018) available at: www.ccianet.org/wp-content/uploads/2018/01/Industry-Letter-to-DOJ-AAG.pdf (signed by industry bodies such as CCIA, the Fair Standards Alliance, the Software & Information Industry Association (SIAA) and ACT | The App Association, and major ICT companies such as Apple, Intel, Microsoft, Samsung, HP, Dell and Cisco); also letter signed by ACT, The App Association, Alliance of Automobile Manufacturers, Computer & Communications Industry Association (CCIA), High Tech Inventors Alliance (HTIA), National Retail Federation, Software & Information Industry Association (SIIA) and 'Standards, Licensing, and Innovation: A Response to DOJ AAG's Comments on Antitrust Law and Standard-Setting' (2018), available at www.ccianet.org/wp-content/uploads/2018/05/Multi-Assn-DOJ-White-Paper-053018.pdf.

[36] In the US see: (i) studies and reports by antitrust authorities: FTC, 'To Promote Innovation: The Proper Balance of Competition and Patent Law and Policy' (2003); US Department of Justice and Federal Trade Commission, *Antitrust Enforcement of Intellectual Property Rights* (n 9); FTC, 'The Evolving IP Marketplace' (n 9); US Department of Justice and US Patent & Trademark Office, 'Policy Statement on Remedies' (n 13); (ii) speeches by antitrust officials: R Hesse, Deputy Assistant Attorney General, Antitrust Division, US Department of Justice, Remarks as Prepared for the ITU-T

As a remedy for perceived dangers of patent holdup and royalty stacking, a number of proposals have been made regarding the legal framework for licensing SEPs. In general, they include: determining FRAND royalties as an ex ante incremental value of the patented technology before the standard is set and excluding any additional value created by standardisation; basing FRAND royalties on the smallest saleable patent-practising unit (ie, a component, as opposed to the value of the downstream end-products); concluding licences with component manufacturers; injunctions for infringement of SEPs not generally being available or, at least, being limited to exceptional circumstances; damages being the only remedy

Patent Roundtable, 'Six 'Small' Proposals for SSOs Before Lunch' (2012), available at www.justice.gov/atr/file/518951/download; R Hesse, Deputy Assistant Attorney General, Antitrust Division, US Department of Justice, 'Remarks Presented at the Global Competition Review: 2nd Annual Antitrust Law Leaders Forum, IP, Antitrust and Looking Back on the Last Four Years' (2013), available at: www.justice.gov/atr/file/518951/download; R Hesse, Deputy Assistant Attorney General, Antitrust Division, US Department of Justice, 'Remarks Presented at the Washington State Bar Association, 'The Art of Persuasion: Competition Advocacy at the Intersection of Antitrust and Intellectual Property' (2013), available at: www.justice.gov/atr/file/518356/download; R Hesse Deputy Assistant Attorney General, Antitrust Division, US Department of Justice, 'Remarks as Prepared for the Global Competition Review: GCR Live IP & Antitrust USA Conference, A Year in the Life of the Joint DOJ-PTO Policy Statement on Remedies for F/RAND Encumbered Standards-Essential Patents' (2014), available at: www.justice.gov/atr/file/517771/download; E Ramirez, Chairwoman, Federal Trade Commission, 'Address at the 8th Annual Global Antitrust Enforcement Symposium, Standard-Essential Patents and Licensing: An Antitrust Enforcement Perspective' (2014), available at: www.ftc.gov/system/files/documents/public_statements/582451/140915georgetownlaw.pdf; B Baer, Assistant Attorney General, Antitrust Division, US Department of Justice, 'Remarks as Prepared for Delivery at the 19th Annual International Bar Association Competition Conference, Reflections on the Role of Competition Agencies When Patents Become Essential' (2015), available at: www.justice.gov/opa/speech/assistant-attorney-general-bill-baer-delivers-remarks-19th-annual-international-bar; T McSweeney, 'Holding the Line on Patent Holdup: Why Antitrust Enforcement Matters' (2018), available at: www.ftc.gov/system/files/documents/public_statements/1350033/mcsweeny_-_the_reality_of_patent_hold-up_3-21-18.pdf. In the EU see: (i) Commission decisions: *Motorola – Enforcement of GPRS Standard Essential Patents* (Case AT.39985) Commission Decision C(2014) 2892 final, 418 (justifying intervention with the concern of patent holdup); *Samsung – Enforcement of UMTS Standard Essential Patents* (Case AT. 39939) Commission Decision C(2014) 2891 58 (justifying intervention with the concern of patent holdup); (ii) soft law: Commission, 'Guidelines on the Applicability of Article 101 of the Treaty on the Functioning of the European Union to Horizontal Co-operation Agreements' (Communication) [2011] OJ C 11/01, para 269 (listing patent holdup as a potential competitive concern); (iii) speeches: A Italianer, Director General for Competition, European Commission, 'Shaken not Stirred. Competition Law Enforcement and Standard Essential Patents' (2015), available at: ec.europa.eu/competition/speeches/text/sp2015_03_en.pdf; M Vestager, Commissioner for Competition, European Commission, 'Protecting Consumers from Exploitation' (2016), available at: wayback.archive-it.org/12090/20191129221154/https://ec.europa.eu/commission/commissioners/2014-2019/vestager/announcements/protecting-consumers-exploitation_en.

[37] See J Barnett, 'Has the Academy Led Patent Law Astray?' (2018) 32 *Berkeley Technology Law Journal* 1313 (finding that patent holdup or royalty stacking was mentioned by 37 federal court decisions, eight ITC proceedings and four FTC proceedings); also: *TCL v Ericsson* (n 20) 25–26 (justifying a 'top-down' approach to determining FRAND royalty because it reduces stacking and holdup risks); *Microsoft v Motorola*, 795 F.3d 1024 (9th Cir 2015) 1031 ('the tactic of withholding a license unless and until a manufacturer agrees to pay an unduly high royalty rate for an SEP is referred to as "hold-up"') 1052 ('the very purpose of the RAND agreement is to promote the adoption of a standard by decreasing the risk of hold-up'); *In re Innovatio IP Ventures* (n 18) 8 ('One of the primary purposes of the RAND commitment is to avoid patent hold-up, which occurs when the holder of a standard-essential patent demands excess royalties after standard implementers are already locked into using the standard').

for infringement of SEPs; and competition law being used more aggressively to police compliance with FRAND obligations. All these issues will be analysed in more detail in Part II.

III. Criticism of Patent Holdup and Royalty Stacking Theories

Despite wide recognition, there is also a large body of literature and public officials questioning the existence and the magnitude of patent holdup and royalty stacking phenomena in a standardisation context.[38]

[38] For academic literature see: D Geradin and M Rato, 'Can Standard-Setting Lead to Exploitative Abuse? A Dissonant View on Patent Holdup, Royalty Stacking and the Meaning of FRAND' (2007) 3 *European Competition Journal* 101; J Golden, 'Patent Trolls and Patent Remedies' (2007) 85 *Texas Law Review* 2111; G Sidak, 'Holdup, Royalty Stacking, and the Presumption of Injunctive Relief for Patent Infringement: A Reply to Lemley and Shapiro' (2008) 92 *Minnesota Law Review* 714; E Elhauge, 'Do Patent Holdup and Royalty Stacking Lead to Systematically Excessive Royalties?' (2008) 4 *Journal of Competition Law & Economics* 535; D Geradin, A Layne-Farrar and J Padilla, 'The Complements Problem Within Standard Setting: Assessing the Evidence on Royalty Stacking' (2008) 14 *Boston University Journal of Science and Technology Law* 144; V Denicolo et al, 'Revisiting Injunctive Relief: Interpreting eBay in High-Tech Industries With Non-Practicing Patent Holders' (2008) 4 *Journal of Competition Law & Economics* 571; B Kobayashi and J Wright, 'Federalism, Substantive Preemption, and Limits on Antitrust: An Application to Patent Holdup' (2009) 5 *Journal of Competition Law & Economics* 469; R Epstein, F Scott Kieff and D Spulber, 'The FTC, IP, and SSOs: Government Hold-Up Replacing Private Coordination' (2012) 8 *Journal of Competition Law & Economics* 1; L Froeb, B Ganglmair and G Werden, 'Patent Hold-Up and Antitrust: How a Well-Intentioned Rule Could Retard Innovation' (2012) 60 *Journal of Industrial Economics* 249; J Ratlif and D Rubinfeld, 'The Use and Threat of Injunctions in the RAND Context' (2012) 9 *Journal of Competition Law & Economics* 1; K Gupta, 'The Patent Policy Debate in the High-Tech World' (2013) 9 *Journal of Competition Law & Economics* 827; R Jacob, 'Competition Authorities Support Grasshoppers: Competition Law as a Threat to Innovation' (2013) 9 *Competition Policy International* 15; R Brooks, 'SSO Rules, Standardization, and SEP Licensing: Economic Questions from the Trenches' (2013) 9 *Journal of Competition Law & Economics* 859; G Langus, V Lipatov and D Neven, 'Standard-Essential Patents: Who Is Really Holding Up (and When)?' (2013) 9 *Journal of Competition Law & Economics* 253; D Geradin, 'Moving Away From High Level Theories: A Market Driven Analysis of FRAND' (2014) 59 *Antitrust Bulletin* 327; A Galetovic, S Haber and R Levine, 'An Empirical Examination of Patent Holdup' (2015) 11 *Journal of Competition Law & Economics* 549; G Sidak, 'Antitrust Division's Devaluation of Standard Essential Patents' (2015) 104 *Georgetown Law Journal Online* 48; D Teece, 'The "Tragedy of the Anticommons" Fallacy: A Law and Economics Analysis of Patent Thickets and FRAND Licensing' (2017) 32 *Berkeley Technology Law Journal* 1490; B Heiden and N Petit, 'Patent "Trespass" and the Royalty Gap: Exploring the Nature and Impact of Patent Holdout' (2018) 34 *Santa Clara High Technology Journal* 179; R Epstein and K Noroozi, 'Why Incentives for "Patent Holdout"' Threaten to Dismantle FRAND, and Why it Matters' (2018) 32 *Berkeley Technology Law Journal* 1381; A Galetovic, S Haber and L Zaretzki, 'Is there an Anti-Commons Tragedy in the Smartphone Industry?' (2018) 32 *Berkeley Technology Law Journal* 1527; US Professors' Letter to Assistant Attorney General Delrahim, 'Support of Evidence Based Antitrust Enforcement' (13 February 2018), available at: cpip.gmu.edu/wp-content/uploads/sites/31/2018/02/Letter-to-DOJ-Supporting-Evidence-Based-Approach-to-Antitrust-Enforcement-of-IP.pdf; G Sidak, 'Is Patent Holdup a Hoax?' (2018) 3 *Criterion Journal on Innovation* 401; G Werden and L Froeb, 'Why Patent Hold-up Does Not Violate Antitrust Law' (2019) 27 *Texas Intellectual Property Law Journal* 1; D Spulber, 'Licensing Standard Essential Patents with FRAND Commitments: Preparing for 5G Mobile Telecommunications' (2020) 18 *Colorado Technology Law Journal* 79.

As a preliminary matter, it is submitted that the definition of patent holdup is inadequate and risks equating holdup with normal patent infringement.[39] The notion of patent holdup, as it is being used in the literature, requires only that the implementer made an investment that is specific to the patented technology without first securing a licence, that a patent owner then approached an implementer with a request for a licence and, if negotiations failed, sought damages or an injunction.[40] However, this is an ordinary course of patent infringement which is the result of not having a licence in the first place. The danger is that the notion of patent holdup is being used any time a patent owner demands royalties which an implementer does not want to pay.[41] In other words, patent holdup is a one-sided notion used when an implementer believes SEP royalties are too high. Whether royalties are excessive or not is a subjective matter and can be ultimately resolved by courts.

Besides definitional matters, two main strands of criticism have been put forward against patent holdup and royalty stacking theories: the lack of real-world empirical evidence of their presence, and the mischaracterisation of the standardisation process and the legal licensing framework.

A. The Lack of Empirical Evidence of Systematic Negative Effects

Several studies tried to detect the presence of the negative effects of patent holdup and royalty stacking in the ICT industry. If they are indeed a problem and regularly occur in practice, the following negative effects would be possible to observe: (i) increasing prices of downstream products (excessive royalties are passed on to consumers); (ii) less availability of standardised products over time (manufacturers are exiting the market or reducing investment in the development of standardised products); (iii) downstream manufacturers experience reduced profit margins

For competition officials see: M Delrahim, Assistant Attorney General US Department of Justice, 'Take It to the Limit: Respecting Innovation Incentives in the Application of Antitrust Law' (10 November 2017), available at: www.justice.gov/opa/speech/file/1010746/download; M Delrahim, Assistant Attorney General US Department of Justice, 'The "New Madison" Approach to Antitrust and Intellectual Property Law' (16 March 2018), www.justice.gov/opa/speech/file/1044316/download; M Delrahim, Assistant Attorney General US Department of Justice, 'Antitrust Law and Patent Licensing in the New Wild West' (18 September 2018), available at: www.justice.gov/opa/speech/assistant-attorney-general-makan-delrahim-delivers-remarks-iam-s-patent-licensing; M Delrahim, Attorney General US Department of Justice, 'Broke … but Not No More: Opening Remarks – Innovation Policy and the Role of Standards, IP and Antitrust' (10 September 2020), available at: available at: www.justice.gov/opa/speech/assistant-attorney-general-makan-delrahim-delivers-remarks-leadership-virtual-series.

[39] See: Epstein, Scott Kieff and Spulber (n 38); A Galetovic and S Haber, 'The Fallacies of Patent Holdup Theory' (2017) 13 *Journal of Competition Law & Economics* 1, 25; Sidak, 'Is Patent Holdup a Hoax?' (n 38).

[40] Galetovic and Haber (n 39) 25.

[41] ibid, 26.

(the result of excessive royalties that cannot be passed on to consumers); and (iv) participants in standard development reduce investment in research and development. However, studies have shown the opposite results.

Regarding final consumer prices, Galetovic, Haber and Levine found that SEP-reliant products experienced faster price declines than any other goods between 1997 and 2013.[42] Looking only at smartphones, an industry where the most severe holdup and stacking effects were anticipated, studies found that the average selling price of a smartphone fell between 11.4 per cent and 24.8 per cent per year.[43] Putting this into perspective, the average price of a phone in 2013 was 79 per cent lower than in 1997.[44]

Studies also found that production output increased over time. Galetovic, Haber and Zaretzki showed that the number of smartphone devices sold each year is increasing by 20.1 per cent per year on average,[45] with 1.474 billion smartphone devices sold in 2016 alone.[46] In 2020, there were 10,406 different models of smartphone with 4G LTE connectivity on the market,[47] and a total of 16,807 different 4G LTE device models (including tablets, laptops, smart watches etc) from 779 different manufacturers.[48] These findings indicate a wide variety and choice available to consumers. Further, the consumer adoption of mobile communications is constantly rising. According to the GSMA, at the end of 2019, 5.2 billion people were subscribed to mobile services, accounting for 67 per cent of the population, with a projected growth to 5.8 billion or 70 per cent of world population by 2025.[49]

The ICT industry is very profitable and attracted the entry of numerous new market players. The Boston Consulting Group estimated that the mobile value chain generated almost $3.3 trillion in revenues globally in 2014,[50] with mobile handset revenues reaching $1.03 trillion in 2019.[51] The number of mobile device manufacturers rose from just two in 1994 to 103 in 2013.[52] Indeed, we can

[42] Galetovic, Haber and Levine (n 38).

[43] A Galetovic and K Gupta, 'The Case of the Missing Royalty Stacking in the World Mobile Wireless Industry' (2020) 29 *Industrial and Corporate Change* 827, 831; also K Mallinson, 'Don't Fix What Isn't Broken: The Extraordinary Record of Innovation and Success in the Cellular Industry Under Existing Licensing Practices' (2016) 23 *George Mason Law Review* 967, 992.

[44] Galetovic, Haber and Levine (n 38) 564–65.

[45] ibid.

[46] Galetovic, Haber and Zaretzki, 'Is there an Anti-Commons Tragedy in the Smartphone Industry?' (2018) (n 38) 1536.

[47] GSA, 'LTE Ecosystem Report: Status Update July 2020' (2020) 2, available at: gsacom.com/paper/lte-ecosystem-july-2020-global-status-report/.

[48] ibid, 3.

[49] GSMA, 'The Mobile Economy 2020' (2020) 3, available at: www.gsma.com/mobileeconomy/wp-content/uploads/2020/03/GSMA_MobileEconomy2020_Global.pdf.

[50] J Bezerra et al, 'The Mobile Revolution: How Mobile Technologies Drive a Trillion Dollar Impact' (Boston Consulting Group, 2015) 4, available at: www.bcg.com/publications/2015/telecommunications-technology-industries-the-mobile-revolution.

[51] GSMA (n 49) 16.

[52] Galetovic and Gupta (n 43).

observe from history how the mobile market changed over time, from having only Motorola in 1980, the dominance of Nokia, Ericsson, Alcatel and Motorola in the 1990s, their gradual decline in the 2000s and the entry of new players such as Samsung, Apple, Google, Huawei, HTC and others. Mallinson shows how the mobile industry concentration has declined over time from a highly concentrated to an unconcentrated market.[53]

Studies also report significant investment in research and development of new technologies. Companies in the mobile value chain invested $1.8 trillion in infrastructure and R&D from 2009 to 2013.[54] Moreover, operators are expected to invest $1.1. trillion for the roll out of 5G networks between 2020 and 2025.[55] Galetovic, Haber and Levine also show that the rate of innovation in the ICT industry is faster than the rest of the economy that is not reliant on SEPs. For instance, they found that the rate of innovation in phone equipment was 10 per cent per year faster than the economy-wide average,[56] while the rate of innovation in portable and laptop computers was even faster, 30 per cent per annum.[57]

Thus, the overall evidence suggests that the mobile telecommunications industry has significant positive effects on the whole economy. According to the GSMA, the mobile ecosystem generated 4.7 per cent of global GDP, a contribution that amounts to more than $4.1 trillion of added economic value.[58] In addition, the mobile ecosystem directly employs nearly 16 million people across the world, and indirectly supports another 14 million jobs in adjacent industries.[59]

As to individual cases where courts awarded significantly lower royalties than initially demanded by SEP owners, it is argued that a few individual cases are not representative to conclude that there is a widespread problem affecting the whole industry. In the words of Olhausen and Wright: 'the outcome of a handful of litigated cases says nothing about whether holdup is a widespread problem for competition and consumers',[60] while Layne-Farrar argues that litigation results from a few individual cases are 'highly fact-specific and should not be used as a benchmark for ecosystem reform'.[61] Authors also question the methodologies applied in these cases and point to several methodological deficiencies applied when evaluating SEPs.[62] Moreover, Gupta and Snyder studied the smartphone patent wars and found that

[53] Mallinson, 'Don't Fix What Isn't Broken' (n 43) 986.

[54] Bezerra et al (n 50) 4.

[55] GSMA (n 49) 17.

[56] Galetovic, Haber and Levine (n 38) 565.

[57] ibid.

[58] GSMA (n 49) 38.

[59] ibid, 39.

[60] M Ohlhausen and J Wright, 'Reply Submission on the Public Interest of Federal Trade Commissioners' In the Matter of Certain 3G Mobile Handsets and Components Thereof, ITC Case No 337-TA-613 (on remand) (2015) 7, available at: www.ftc.gov/public-statements/2015/07/reply-submission-public-interest-federal-trade-commissioners-maureen-k.

[61] A Layne-Farrar, 'Patent Holdup and Royalty Stacking Theory and Evidence: Where Do We Stand After 15 Years of History' (2014) DAF/COMP/WD(2014)84, 5.

[62] See G Sidak, 'The Meaning of FRAND, Part I: Royalties' (2013) 9 *Journal of Competition Law & Economics* 931 (criticising the methodologies used by the courts in *Microsoft v Motorola* and *Innovatio*).

SEPs were asserted in litigation only about one-third of the time and the majority of smartphone patent litigation actually came from non-SEPs.[63]

In the end, studies have tried to determine the actual cumulative royalty stack that device manufacturers are paying. Mallinson and Sidak looked at the revenues generated by major SEP owners and compared them with global mobile handsets revenues. This 'follow the money' approach focused on how much SEP holders earn from SEP licensing and estimates the licensing costs in the total mobile handsets revenues. They found that the maximum aggregate royalty yield for 2G, 3G and 4G SEPs was approximately 4 per cent to 5 per cent of global mobile handsets revenues.[64] A study by Galetovic, Haber and Zaretzki went further and tried to estimate the average cumulative SEP royalty yield on the average smartphone. They collected the data on the licensing revenues of 29 SEP licensors, the number of smartphones sold, their average selling price, and found that the cumulative SEP royalty yield was only 3.4 per cent of the smartphone's average selling price, or just $9.60.[65] Consequently, these studies found no excessive royalty stack.

Therefore, with no observable effects of patent holdup and royalty stacking, critics cast doubt on the existence of these phenomena in real life. In the words of Layne-Farrar:

> [C]ertainly the theories have been developed, but the empirical support is still lacking. Despite the 15 years proponents of the theories have had to amass evidence, the empirical studies conducted thus far have not shown that holdup or royalty stacking is a common problem in practice.[66]

As the US Federal Circuit observed: 'certainly something more than a general argument that these phenomena are possibilities is necessary'.[67]

In response, two counter-arguments have been put forward by authors claiming the dangers of patent holdup and royalty stacking. One is that empirical studies showing the growth of the ICT industry mean very little as there is no benchmark to compare whether the industry would grow even quicker without holdup. In other words, studies should establish a 'but-for world' in the absence of holdup and compare it with observable evidence.[68] The second

[63] K Gupta and M Snyder, 'Smartphone Litigation and Standard Essential Patents' (2014) Hoover IP2 Working Paper Series No 14006.

[64] K Mallinson, 'Cumulative Mobile SEP Royalties' (19 August 2015), available at: www.wiseharbor.com/pdfs/Mallinson%20on%20cumulative%20mobile%20SEP%20royalties%20for%20IP%20Finance%202015Aug19.pdf; G Sidak, 'What Aggregate Royalty Do Manufacturers of Mobile Phones Pay to License Standard-Essential Patents?' (2016) 1 *Criterion Journal on Innovation* 701.

[65] A Galetovic, S Haber and L Zaretzki, 'An Estimate of the Average Cumulative Royalty Yield in the World Mobile Phone Industry: Theory, Measurement and Results' (2018) 42 *Telecommunications Policy* 263; Galetovic, Haber and Zaretzki, 'Is there an Anti-Commons Tragedy in the Smartphone Industry?' (n 38); A Galetovic, S Haber and L Zaretzki, 'A New Dataset on Mobile Phone Patent License Royalties' (2017) Hoover IP2 Working Paper Series No 16011.

[66] Layne-Farrar (n 61) 1.

[67] *Ericsson v D-Link* 773, F.3d 1201, 1234 (Fed Cir 2014).

[68] Melamed and Shapiro (n 13) 2117; Shapiro and Lemley, 'The Role of Antitrust in Preventing Patent Holdup' (n 8) 24.

argument is that, while it is admittedly difficult to find direct empirical evidence of systematic holdup effects, we can deduct its existence from indirect evidence such as the presence of market institutions intended to mitigate its harmful effects. These are SDOs and FRAND commitments. According to Shapiro and Lemley: 'the near-universal recognition in the industry of the need for such a mechanism is strong evidence that companies view holdup as a problem they must build institutions to avoid'.[69]

However, these counter-arguments do not appear persuasive. No one has managed to construct this elusive but-for world without holdup, and even proponents admit that it would be impossible to do so.[70] We can only rely on observable evidence that shows success, growth and innovation in ICT industries. And while it is true that SDOs and FRAND commitments are intended to make the implementation of the standard widely available and prevent the negative effects of holdup and royalty stacking, the evidence indicates that the system has been a success. Thus, while it is true that widespread holdup and associated negative effects might have existed without FRAND commitments, they are in place precisely to prevent such an outcome.

B. The Misunderstanding of the Standardisation Process and Legal Licensing Framework

The second line of criticism of patent holdup and royalty stacking comes from their misunderstanding of the standardisation process and the legal licensing framework. As explained in chapter one, section II.C, standardisation is a lengthy and continuous process. Companies involved are repeat players and engaging in patent holdup strategy would single them out for a bad reputation. We would expect to see some retaliation from other players, such as denying inclusion of their technology into newer versions of a standard.[71] SEP owners actually have little interest in pricing excessively. They want the standard to succeed and be massively adopted because, if standards and products fail, they would also lose their revenues. SEP owners also need stable incomes to invest in the research and development of new technologies. Thus, repeated play, reputational effects and shared interests by SEP owners in the widespread and successful implementation of the standard mitigates the likelihood of patent holdup and royalty stacking.

Several other market factors diminish the possibility of systematic patent holdup and royalty stacking effects. Namely, they are unlikely between two vertically integrated companies because they will use each other's SEP portfolio for

[69] Shapiro and Lemley, 'The Role of Antitrust in Preventing Patent Holdup' (n 8) 26.
[70] ibid, 22.
[71] Geradin and Rato (n 38) 148; Epstein, Scott Kieff and Spulber (n 38) 20; P Larouche and F Schuett, 'Repeated Interaction in Standard Setting' (2018) *Journal of Economics & Management Strategy* 1.

cross-licensing, and neither would be able to impose excessive licensing terms on each other.[72] There are also some SEP holders that do not actively seek to enforce SEPs and keep them only for defensive purposes ('sleeping dogs'). Such companies focus instead on income generated by the sale of downstream products.[73] Therefore, only SEP owners that primarily rely on patent licensing income would have an incentive to monetise their SEP more aggressively, but their number is not that high, and they are constrained by repeat play and reputational effects. The patent holdup theory thus mischaracterises the SEP holders' economic incentives to seek exploitative licensing conditions.

Furthermore, the maximum licensing rates are often known in advance as the largest SEPs often publish their royalty rates. For example, for the 4G LTE standard, Ericsson, Nokia and Huawei publicly announced that their royalty rates would be about 1.5 per cent of handset price; Alcatel-Lucent announced a maximum royalty level of 2 per cent; Motorola's announced royalties were 2.25 per cent; and Qualcomm's royalties were 3.25 per cent.[74] Similarly, for the 5G NR standard, Ericsson announced that it would license its 5G SEP portfolio between $2.5 and 5$ per device;[75] Nokia up to €3 per device;[76] up to $1.2 by Interdigital;[77] and 3.25 per cent of the end-device price by Qualcomm.[78] There are also several patent pools operated by Sisvel, Via and MPEG LA that offer joint licences for many widely used standards. Although these publicly announced rates do not necessarily mean they are FRAND and do not prevent royalty stacking, they at least provide some market transparency and run contrary to the premises of the patent holdup theory that SEP owners wait until the standard is set and then surprise licensees with excessive rates.

The legal framework for the enforcement and licensing of SEPs also generally precludes the feasibility of opportunistic holdup practices by SEP owners. As will be seen, the availability of injunctions for infringement of SEPs is restricted both in the US and the EU.[79] It has become extremely difficult for the SEP holder to enjoin an infringer and requesting an injunction would hardly scare a potential licensee into paying excessive licensing fees. Moreover, if a FRAND commitment

[72] Geradin, 'Moving Away From High Level Theories' (n 38) 346–48.

[73] Commission, 'Patents and Standards' (n 4) 160.

[74] Stasik (n 31).

[75] Ericsson, 'Ericsson's FRAND Licensing Terms for 5G/NR in 3GPP Release 15' (3 March 2017), available at: www.ericsson.com/assets/local/tech-innovation/patents/doc/frand-licensing-terms-for-5g-nr-in-3gpp-release-15.pdf.

[76] Nokia, 'Nokia Licensing Rate Expectations for 5G NR Mobile Phones' (21 August 2018), available at: www.nokia.com/en_int/news/releases/2018/08/21/nokia-licensing-rate-expectations-for-5gnr-mobile-phones.

[77] Interdigital, 'Rate Disclosure', available at: www.interdigital.com/rate-disclosure.

[78] Qualcomm, '5G NR Royalty Terms Statement' (19 November 2017), available at: www.qualcomm.com/media/documents/files/qualcomm-5g-nr-royalty-terms-statement.pdf; Qualcomm, 'Examples of Royalties for Mobile Price Points' (1 April 2018), available at: www.qualcomm.com/media/documents/files/examples-of-royalties-for-smartphone-price-points.pdf.

[79] See ch 8 for the analysis of the use of injunctions for SEPs.

is interpreted as an enforceable contract, licensees would have the ability to request a judicial review of offered licensing terms and could ask the court to determine FRAND terms between the parties.[80] The possibility of judicial review effectively eliminates all likelihood of SEP owners unilaterally imposing excessive licensing terms on standard implementers. Competition law authorities around the world have also been scrutinising the conduct of SEP owners, with the consequence that SEP owners are now extremely careful when dealing with prospective licensees. In the words of the ITC judge, patent holdup is unlikely to be observed in practice because 'too many hostile eyes are watching'.[81] Consequently, the existing legal remedies in SEP cases mitigate the likelihood of opportunistic holdup strategies.

IV. Patent Holdout

While patent holdup and royalty stacking refer to the behaviour of SEP owners, others suggest that the real problem in the standardisation context is the opportunistic conduct of standard implementers – patent holdout.[82] Holdout is a situation where standard implementers avoid paying royalties as much as possible in order to pressure SEP holders to settle for sub-optimal rates or evade paying any royalties altogether. This strategy may be possible because the patent holder is unable to withhold the use of patented technology against manufacturers that do not accept licensing terms, but it must seek protection of its rights before courts, and only after a lengthy court procedure might it stop the unlicensed use of its technology. The negative effects of systematic holdout are that patent holders remain undercompensated for the use of their technologies, which diminishes incentives to innovate and invest in the development of new standardised technologies.

The legal remedies for the protection of IP rights play a large role in the feasibility of holdout strategy. If injunctions for infringement of SEPs are unavailable, and if damages for patent infringement are set at an inadequate level, implementers may rationally conclude that it would be more profitable to simply infringe patents, avoid taking a licence even at reasonable rates, and simply wait to be sued. Holdout may be also advantageous because the implementer might not be discovered and sued by the SEP holder, in which case the implementer

[80] See ch 3 for the contractual interpretation of a FRAND commitment.

[81] In the Matter of Certain 3G Mobile Handsets and Components Thereof, USITC Inv No 337-TA-613, 2015 WL 6561709, 31.

[82] For literature on holdout, see: Geradin and Rato (n 38) 119; D Geradin, 'Reverse Hold-ups: The (Often Ignored) Risks Faced by Innovators in Standardised Areas' (2010) paper prepared for the Swedish Competition Authority on the Pros and Cons of Standard-Setting, available at: papers.ssrn.com/sol3/papers.cfm?abstract_id=1711744; P Camasasca et al, 'Injunctions for Standard-Essential Patents: Justice is Not Blind' (2013) 9 *Journal of Competition Law & Economics* 285; Langus, Lipatov and Neven (n 38); C Chien, 'Holding Up and Holding Out' (2014) 21 *Michigan Telecommunications & Technology Law Review* 1; Heiden and Petit (n 38); Epstein and Noroozi (n 38).

would continue to use the technology for free. Even if the implementer were to be discovered and sued, it might be more profitable to litigate if the only consequence is the payment of a court determined FRAND rate, which it should have paid in the first place. In the meantime, the SEP owner may settle for below FRAND royalties if it does not have the financial resources to sustain protracted litigation, while the manufacturer could fund drawn-out litigation from profits made in downstream markets.[83] Therefore, we should be careful about undercompensating general purpose technologies (such as 2G, 3G, 4G and 5G standards) which generate much greater social returns than private returns due to the wide-ranging externalities they create.[84] The consequence would be underinvestment in R&D and lower innovation and growth.

On the other hand, Melamed, Shapiro and Lemley are sceptical that holdout is a concern and argue that it is just an elegant word for ordinary patent infringement. If the infringer is refusing to conclude a FRAND licence, the SEP owner has patent remedies available to address such behaviour, by suing for injunctions and/or requesting damages.[85] They see nothing exceptional in patent holdout warranting special rules. That is true, but it is precisely the weakening of patent remedies that creates incentives for holdout. While special rules may not be needed, the application of existing legal remedies should consider and aim to deter holdout practices by standard implementers.

Real examples of holdout can be found in the literature and case law. Bowman and Petit document different types of delaying tactics used by manufacturers to avoid taking a licence.[86] For example, manufacturers may offer negotiation terms that are not in line with industry practice, such as insisting on patent-by-patent and country-by-country licensing, endlessly postponing negotiation meetings or sending envoys with no authority to conclude licensing agreements.[87] They may also delay setting up arbitration panels, challenge the validity of individual patents in a portfolio, delay taking a licence for the whole portfolio until validity proceedings are completed, and complain about a patent owner's licensing practices to national competition authorities. While all these practices are perfectly legal, the overall effect is that is it becoming increasingly difficult to conclude SEP licences.

More colourful examples of holdout strategies may be found in the case law. In *Core Wireless v LG* in the US, Core Wireless sued LG for infringement of 3G and 4G SEPs.[88] After a long series of negotiations, LG stated that a lawsuit was 'preferable' to a licence and that LG would prefer to wait until another major cell

[83] R O'Donoghue and J Padilla, *The Law and Economics of Article 102 TFEU*, 2nd edn (Hart Publishing, 2013) 702–03.

[84] D Teece, 'Profiting from Innovation in the Digital Economy' (2018) 47 *Research Policy* 1367; Teece, 'The "Tragedy of the Anticommons" Fallacy' (n 38).

[85] Melamed and Shapiro (n 13) 2120; Shapiro and Lemley, 'The Role of Antitrust in Preventing Patent Holdup' (n 8) 30–33.

[86] Heiden and Petit (n 38) 220.

[87] ibid.

[88] *Core Wireless v LG*, 2:14-cv-912-JRG, Docket 47 (ED Tex 2016).

phone manufacturer licensed the portfolio.[89] Core Wireless ultimately prevailed in the litigation but was forced to spend nearly $8 million in legal and expert fees and incur many years of delay in order to obtain an award of $2.736 million.[90] In *TQ Delta v ZyXEL* parties were in negotiations for six years and once patents came close to expiring the implementer refused to take a licence on terms determined by the court.[91] TCL and Ericsson were also negotiating for more than six years before submitting to binding court adjudication of FRAND terms.[92] In *Sisvel v Haier*, it took the implementer seven months to reject a licensing offer and it waited almost a year to submit a counter-offer;[93] while in *NTT DoCoMo v HTC* the implementer submitted a counter-offer a year and a half after having received a licensing offer from the SEP owner and six months from the start of litigation.[94] In *Saint Lawrence Communications v Deutsche Telekom* it took an implementer five months to reply to a licensing offer.[95] The widespread holdout strategy may even bankrupt SEPs owners. In *Unwired Planet v Huawei*, the SEP owner was on the verge of insolvency because it could not conclude licences for its 3G and 4G SEP portfolio and had to engage in expensive and protracted worldwide litigation.[96] The SEP owner was ultimately acquired by another company that was able to fund the ongoing litigation.[97]

V. Conclusion

The commercial background behind the discussions on patent holdup, holdout and royalty stacking are industry convergence and the consequent tensions from having a certain number of companies holding SEPs and many other companies without SEP portfolios that would be net licensees. Both SEP owners and implementers can behave opportunistically in practice and the fact that there exists a large number of SEPs and SEP owners rightfully raises concerns about cumulatively prohibitive royalty stack. However, there is persuasive evidence that these notions have not produced systematic negative effects in real-world markets. The ICT industry is exhibiting rapid expansion and entry, falling consumer prices, increased output, and an extraordinary rate of innovation. It seems that FRAND commitments and existing legal remedies worked well and ensured overall

[89] ibid.
[90] ibid.
[91] *TQ Delta v ZyXEL* [2019] EWHC 745 (Pat) 12 ('on the evidence before me, I accept that this is a case of "hold-out" by ZyXEL').
[92] *TCL v Ericsson* (n 20) 6.
[93] *Sisvel v Haier*, 4a O 93/14 Regional Court Düsseldorf (3 November 2015).
[94] *NTT DoCoMo v HTC*, 7 O 66/15 Regional Court Mannheim (29 January 2016).
[95] *Saint Lawrence v Deutsche Telekom*, 2 O 106/14 Regional Court Mannheim (27 November 2015).
[96] *Unwired Planet v Huawei* (n 20).
[97] ibid, 404.

market success. Although individual SEP licensing disputes do occur, they have apparently not produced negative effects on the whole industry.

A key takeaway is that the SEP licensing framework and legal remedies need to take both holdup, holdout and potential royalty stacking into account in individual cases. Tilting the remedies and legal framework too much in favour of either side risks undermining innovation incentives and successful product implementation. Indeed, it will be seen that courts, competition authorities and policy officials are increasingly recognising that both concerns play a role in SEP cases and that a balanced approach must be adopted.

PART II

The Meaning and Content of a FRAND Licence

3

The Nature of a FRAND Commitment

Part II addresses the meaning and content of a FRAND licence as it has evolved over the years in court cases, academic literature and the policy documents of various governmental authorities. This chapter will first briefly explain the origins and principles of a FRAND commitment and will then turn to the legal nature of a FRAND commitment, its enforceability and the concurrent role of contract and competition laws in the SEP licensing context.

I. The Principles and the Text of a FRAND Commitment

Historically there is nothing new in licensing patents on FRAND terms; such commitments have been existing for decades. Professor Contreras traced the origins of FRAND patent licensing to US antitrust cases from the Second World War and up to and through the 1970s, where courts ordered patent holders to license their patents on FRAND terms as a remedy in antitrust cases involving perceived patent abuses.[1] The American Standards Association, as it then was, in 1959 adopted a policy permitting the inclusion of patents in standards, so long as the patent holder offered to license the relevant patents to others on 'reasonable terms'.[2] Therefore, since the requirement to license patents on FRAND terms has existed for over 50 years, it seem surprising that it still remains controversial.

A typical FRAND commitment consists of a patent holder submitting a written statement to the relevant SDO that it will license its essential patents on FRAND terms.[3] Depending on the SDO, such a statement may be called a 'licensing declaration',[4] or 'letters of assurance',[5] and may cover only individually disclosed

[1] J Contreras, 'A Brief History of FRAND: Analysing Current Debates in Standard Setting and Antitrust Through a Historical Lens' (2015) 80 *Antitrust Law Journal* 39.

[2] ibid, 43.

[3] However, see J Contreras, 'A Market Reliance Theory for FRAND Commitments and Other Patent Pledges' (2015) 2 *Utah Law Review* 479, 495–97 (distinguishing between seven different types of FRAND commitments).

[4] See: ITU/ISO/IEC, Patent Statement and Licensing Declaration Form for ITU-T, ITU-R Recommendation, ISO or IEC Deliverable' (2 November 2018), available at: www.itu.int/dms_pub/itu-t/oth/04/04/T04040000020005PDFE.pdf; ETSI, 'IPR Information Statement and Licensing Declaration' (3 September 2020), available at: www.etsi.org/images/files/IPR/etsi-ipr-policy.pdf.

[5] ANSI, 'ANSI Essential Requirements: Due Process Requirements for American National Standards' (January 2021) Clause 3.1.1, available at: www.ansi.org/american-national-standards/ans-introduction/essential-requirements; IEEE-SA, Letters of Assurance for Essential Patents (1 June 2019), available at: mentor.ieee.org/myproject/Public//mytools/mob/loa.pdf.

patents (a specific FRAND commitment), or any patent in a company's portfolio that may become essential (a blanket FRAND commitment).

One of the main principles of a FRAND commitment is securing access to standardised technologies and successful widespread implementation of the standard. Otherwise, standardisation efforts would be wasted if subsequent implementation of a standard were to be blocked because of unavailability of the patented technology.[6] Generally, patents give their holders the right to exclude others from using patented inventions. Normally patent holders are free to decide whether to license their patents (they may refrain from licensing), and if they do decide to make licences available, they are free to set the terms.[7] A FRAND commitment is a constraint on a patent holder's freedom to choose whether it wants to license or not, as well as on the terms of such a licence. Consequently, the FRAND commitment ensures that the patent holder will not deny licences for its SEPs and will also make them available under terms that are fair and reasonable.

The FRAND commitment, as opposed to royalty-free licensing, also protects the interests of patent holders who are assured that they will be adequately rewarded for the use of their technology.[8] They need adequate compensation for the investment in the research and development of new technologies, securing incentives to innovate in the future. Otherwise, there is a risk that patent holders will abandon open collaborative standardisation and opt instead for creating closed proprietary standards.[9]

The FRAND commitment therefore represents a balance between the interests of standard implementers and patent holders.[10] These interests are not opposed

[6] See K Maskus and S Merrill (eds), 'Patent Challenges for Standard-Setting in the Global Economy: Lessons from Information and Communication Technology' (National Research Council, 2013) 52–61, available at: www.nap.edu/catalog/18510/patent-challenges-for-standard-setting-in-the-global-economy-lessons (discussion of some objectives of FRAND licensing).

[7] See, eg: US Patent Act 35 USC 154 ('every patent shall contain a short title of the invention and a grant to the patentee, his heirs or assigns, of *the right to exclude others* from making, using, offering for sale, or selling the invention throughout the United States or importing the invention into the United States') (emphasis added); UK Patents Act 1977, ss 60–61; For an overview of patent rights see T Aplin and J Davies, *Intellectual Property Law: Text, Cases, and Materials*, 2nd edn (Oxford University Press, 2013) 562–63 ('patent law confers a property right, ie a right enforceable *in rem* rather than *in personam*. Thus, a patent owner can exercise her exclusive monopoly right against third parties'); L Bently and B Sherman, *Intellectual Property Law*, 4th edn (Oxford University Press, 2014) 610–12 ('the owner of a patent for product is given the right to make, dispose of, offer to dispose of, use, import, or keep the product, whatever for disposal or otherwise').

[8] See ETSI, 'Intellectual Property Rights Policy' (3 September 2020) Clause 3.2, available at: available at: www.etsi.org/images/files/IPR/etsi-ipr-policy.pdf ('IPR holders whether members of ETSI and their AFFILIATES or third parties, should be *adequately and fairly rewarded* for the use of their IPRs in the implementation of STANDARDS and TECHNICAL SPECIFICATIONS') (emphasis added).

[9] J Padilla, J Davies and A Boutin, 'Economic Impact of Technology Standards' (Compass Lexecon, 2017), available at: www.compasslexecon.com/wp-content/uploads/2018/04/CL_Economic_Impact_of_Technology_Standards_Report_FINAL.pdf (finding that open collaborative standards are more innovative and beneficial to the economy than closed propriety standards).

[10] ETSI, 'Intellectual Property Rights Policy' (n 8) Clause 3.1 ('the ETSI IPR POLICY seeks a balance between the needs of standardization for public use in the field of telecommunications and the rights of the owners of IPRs').

but are mutually reliant. Implementers want best available technologies to make successful innovative products, and standard developers are also interested in successful implementation of standardised technologies in order to earn adequate rewards for their R&D and invest in further innovation.

II. The Enforceability of a FRAND Commitment

Once given at the SDO, how is the FRAND commitment later enforced? The debate about the nature and enforceability of a FRAND commitment centres around whether it represents an enforceable contract that all third-party implementers may rely on or, in the alternative, whether it is enforced by competition law. Some other theories have also been developed in the literature with the aim of providing more consistent and efficient application of FRAND commitments.

A. Contract Law

Under a contract law approach, when the SEP holder submits a FRAND commitment it enters into a binding contract with the SDO that it will make licences available for its SEPs on FRAND terms to all third parties implementing the standard. Implementers of a standard may then rely on this FRAND contract between the SEP holder and the SDO as third-party intended beneficiaries. Accordingly, contract law lies at the heart of enforcing FRAND commitments.

The notion that a FRAND commitment is of a contractual nature has been widely, but not universally, recognised in the literature.[11] It is however important

[11] For literature supportive of contract law interpretation see: M Lemley, 'Intellectual Property Rights and Standard-Setting Organisations' (2002) 90 *California Law Review* 1889, 1909–17; D Crane, 'Patent Pools, RAND Commitments, and the Problematics of Price Discrimination' in R Dreyfuss, H First and D Zimmerman (eds), *Working Within the Boundaries of Intellectual Property* (Oxford University Press, 2010) 390 ('enforcement of the RAND obligation occurs as a matter of contract by any affected party'); R Brooks and D Geradin, 'Interpreting and Enforcing the Voluntary FRAND Commitment' (2011) 9 *International Journal of IT Standards and Standardization Research* 1, 2 ('a FRAND commitment is the result of a voluntary contract between essential patent holders and a standards-setting organization, with the important corollary that the meaning of that commitment must be determined through the legal methods of contractual interpretation'); H Hovenkamp, 'Competition in Information Technologies: Standard-Essential Patents, Non-Practicing Entities and FRAND Bidding' (2012) 12–32 University of Iowa Legal Studies Research Paper 13 ('Interpreting FRAND commitments requires courts to fill in the gaps in incomplete contracts'); T Cotter 'Comparative Law and Economics of Standard Essential Patents and FRAND Royalties' (2014) 22 *Texas Intellectual Property Law Journal* 311; R Jacob, *IP and Other Things: A Collection of Essays and Speeches* (Hart Publishing, 2015) 245 ('it is generally accepted that this commitment … is enforceable by third parties'); D Ginsburg, K Wong-Ervin and J Wright, 'The Troubling Use of Antitrust to Regulate FRAND Licensing' (2015) 10 *CPI Antitrust Chronicle* 2; G Sidak, 'The Meaning of FRAND, Part II: Injunctions' (2015) 11 *Journal of Competition Law & Economics* 201, 210 ('The SEP holder and the SSO are parties to the contract, whereas the implementer of the standard (the licensee) is a third-party beneficiary'); C Pentheroudakis and J Baron, 'Licensing Terms of Standard Essential Patents: A Comprehensive Analysis of Cases' (Joint Research Centre, Science for Policy Report, EUR 28302, 2017) 33–35, available at: publications.

to distinguish that a FRAND commitment does not automatically create a licensing agreement between the SEP holder and the standard implementer. Such a FRAND licensing agreement must be separately negotiated and concluded. Instead, the FRAND commitment creates a contract between the SEP holder and the SDO, where the SEP holder has the obligation to grant licences for its SEPs on FRAND terms to standard implementers. Because the terms of the future FRAND licence are not yet clear, a FRAND commitment represents a form of 'incomplete contract', with future terms to be decided by the parties or, in case of dispute, set by the court. Wright and Tsai view this contractual incompleteness not as a shortcoming, but as an intended and efficient feature because it allows for flexibility and taking into account various different circumstances between licensors and licensees.[12]

Courts in the US and UK have accepted that a FRAND commitment creates a binding contract between the SEP holder and the SDO, and that standard implementers may enforce it as third-party beneficiaries. In particular, courts analysed whether FRAND commitments given to IEEE, ETSI and ITU-T were enforceable contracts and found that they were.[13] For instance, in *Apple v Motorola*, Judge Crabb analysed Motorola's FRAND commitments given to the IEEE, from the perspective of Wisconsin law, and ETSI, from the perspective of French law. The court found that Motorola's membership in the IEEE and ETSI and the intellectual property declarations it made 'established a contractual relationship that required Motorola to license its essential patents to third parties on fair, reasonable and non-discriminatory terms'.[14] Judge Crabb then found that Apple could enforce these commitments as a 'third-party beneficiary of the agreements between Motorola and IEEE and Motorola and ETSI' because it was a user of the standards and a prospective licensee.[15] Similarly, Judge Robart in *Microsoft v Motorola* found that Motorola's commitment to the ITU created a binding contract which Microsoft could enforce as a third-party beneficiary, in particular because Microsoft was a member of ITU.[16]

In *Unwired Planet v Huawei* the UK court undertook extensive analysis of French contract law governing FRAND commitments given at ETSI. While holding

jrc.ec.europa.eu/repository/handle/JRC104068 (discussing the contract law interpretation of FRAND commitments); G Sidak, 'The FRAND Contract' (2018) 3 *Criterion Journal on Innovation* 1.

[12] See: J Tsai and J Wright, 'Standard Setting, Intellectual Property Rights, and the Role of Antitrust in Regulating Incomplete Contracts' (2015) 80 *Antitrust Law Journal* 157; also D Spulber, 'Licensing Standard Essential Patents with FRAND Commitments: Preparing for 5G Mobile Telecommunications' (2020) 18 *Colorado Technology Law Journal* 79, 93.

[13] *Apple v Motorola*, 886 F.Supp.2d 1061 (WD Wisc 2012); *Microsoft v Motorola*, 854 F.Supp.2d 993 (WD Wash 2012); *Innovatio IP Ventures, LLC Patent Litigation*, 921 F.Supp.2d 903 (ND Ill 2013); *Realtek Semiconductor v LSI*, 946 F.Supp.2d 998, 1005 (ND Cal 2013) ('There is no dispute in this case that defendants entered into a binding contract with the IEEE to license their declared standard-essential patents … on RAND terms, and that Realtek is a third party beneficiary to that contract'); also *TCL v Ericsson*, 2017 WL 6611635 (CD Cal 2017).

[14] *Apple v Motorola* (n 13) 1087).

[15] ibid.

[16] *Microsoft v Motorola* (n 13).

that a FRAND commitment represents an enforceable contract for the benefit of third parties, it also added a public interest argument in favour of making FRAND commitments contractually enforceable:

> Holders of essential IPR are not compelled to give a FRAND undertaking but it serves the public interest that they make it clear whether or not they are doing so, and it serves the public interest that if they do, the undertaking is public, irrevocable and enforceable. To avoid hold up, implementers need to know that they can hold SEP owners to a FRAND obligation.[17]

The UK Supreme Court subsequently confirmed that a FRAND commitment creates a contractual obligation which a third-party implementer can enforce against the SEP owner.[18]

Finally, we may soon see a French court giving an interpretation of a French law applicable to ETSI's FRAND commitment. In a dispute between TCL and Philips, the Paris court in an interim order indicated that it also sees ETSI's FRAND commitment as an enforceable contractual obligation for the benefit of third parties.[19] If the case is not settled before the court is able to decide on the merits, we might have an authoritative statement of a French court about the nature and enforceability of ETSI's FRAND commitment.

The benefits of conceptualising a FRAND commitment as an enforceable contract is that it gives all standard implementers the right to challenge the licensing terms offered by SEPs holders before a court. It is fundamentally a remedy against holdup. If the SEP holder offers excessive non-FRAND licensing terms, standard implementers have the right to sue the SEP holder for breach of contract and request the court to decide whether offered terms are FRAND and, if it finds that they are not, to determine the precise FRAND licensing terms. If the SEP holder is negotiating in bad faith, implementers may also bring a breach of contract action. Both parties are under a requirement to negotiate in good faith towards a FRAND licence, with corresponding sanctions if they do not. Indeed, courts in the US are asked to decide whether the SEP owner has breached its contractual obligations towards an SDO by negotiating in bad faith or offering non-FRAND terms.[20] By having the breach of contract action there can be no practical possibility for holdup, as implementers always have the option to go to court.

[17] *Unwired Planet v Huawei* [2017] EWHC 2988 (Pat) 146.

[18] *Unwired Planet v Huawei; Huawei and ZTE v Conversant* [2020] UKSC 37, 8.

[19] *TCL/Philips – ETSI*, Paris Court of First Instance, Interim Order, 6 February 2020, RG No 19/02085.

[20] See: *Realtek Semiconductor v LSI* (n 13) 1008 (seeking injunctions before offering licensing terms may be a breach of duty to negotiate in good faith: 'the court holds that defendants breached their contractual obligations to the IEEE and to Realtek as a third-party beneficiary of that contract by seeking injunctive relief against Realtek before offering Realtek a license'); *Microsoft v Motorola*, 2013 WL 2111217 (WD Wash 2013) (Microsoft initiated breach of contract action against Motorola for offering non-FRAND licensing terms); *HTC v Ericsson*, 6:18-vc-00243-JRG, Doc 538 (ED Tex 2019) (HTC alleging Ericsson breached its contractual obligation to ETSI by failing for offer SEP licence on FRAND terms).

However, the view that a FRAND commitment represents an enforceable contract is not universally shared and it is pointed out that there are some shortcomings.[21] Four lines of criticism can be identified: (i) it is unclear whether the non-members of an SDO can be considered as third-party beneficiaries of a FRAND commitment; (ii) the obligation to offer FRAND licensing terms is not sufficiently determinable to be enforceable; (iii) it is unclear if a contractual FRAND commitment follows the patent in case of a transfer of SEPs; and (iv) not all jurisdictions recognise third-party beneficiary rights. These arguments will be separately analysed.

i. Can SDO Non-Members Rely on a FRAND Contract?

A criticism of a contract law approach is that it is unclear whether all implementers of a standard could be regarded as third-party beneficiaries and whether they could all rely on a contractual FRAND commitment.[22] This is because third-party beneficiaries should be sufficiently identifiable to be able to enforce the contract. It is generally unproblematic for SDO members to rely on a FRAND commitment because it could be easily established that the SEP holder intended to make FRAND licenses available to other members of the SDO. However, the case is not straightforward for non-SDO members. Could the SEP holder have intended to confer third-party beneficiary rights to non-SDO members?

An answer to this question ultimately depends on the exact wording of the FRAND commitment. It seems that at least all the major SDOs included appropriate wording which does not make a distinction between members and non-members. Moreover, it is often specifically emphasised that the SEP holder should grant licences to *all* implementers of a standard, regardless of the membership of an SDO. For example, the ITU-T commitment reads that 'the Patent Holder is prepared to grant a license to an *unrestricted number of applicants*',[23] and the IEEE's FRAND commitment reads: 'The Submitter will make available a license for Essential Patent Claims under Reasonable Rates to an *unrestricted number of Applicants*'.[24] ETSI's FRAND commitment uses different wording, but has the same effect:

> [the SEP Holder] is prepared to grant irrevocable licences on fair, reasonable and non-discriminatory ('FRAND') terms and conditions under such IPR to at least the following extent: MANUFACTURE, including the right to make or have made customized components and sub-systems to the licensee's own design for use in MANUFACTURE; sell,

[21] For criticism see: Lemley (n 11) 1909–17 (discussing some shortcoming of the contract law enforceability of FRAND commitment); also Contreras, 'A Market Reliance Theory' (n 3).

[22] Contreras, 'A Market Reliance Theory' (n 3) 509–14 (expressing scepticism whether a non-SSO member could be intended third-party beneficiaries).

[23] ITU-ISO-IEC, 'Patent Statement and Licensing Declaration Form' (n 4) (emphasis added).

[24] IEEE, Letters of Assurance for Essential Patents (n 5) (emphasis added).

> lease, or otherwise dispose of EQUIPMENT so MANUFACTURED; repair, use, or operate EQUIPMENT; and use METHODS.[25]

Namely, the extensive enumeration effectively means that licences should be available to large numbers of entities, irrespective of whether they are ETSI members or not.[26]

Furthermore, Bekkers and Upgedrowe studied 12 SDO IPR policies and found that only one SDO (HDMI Forum) restricted the availability of FRAND licences only to its members, while for all other SDOs FRAND commitments are intended to benefit any implementer of the standard, irrespective of whether they are members or not.[27] At least one US court directly tackled the issue of whether non-members were intended third-party beneficiaries of a FRAND commitment given at the IEEE. Judge Holderman in *Innovatio* held that two manufacturers of equipment implementing the Wi-Fi standard who, although not members of the IEEE and thus not direct parties to the FRAND contract, were users of a standard and third-party beneficiaries of the contract.[28]

Therefore, it seems that at least all the major SDOs have clear wordings of their FRAND commitment that licences should be equally available to both SDO members and non-members and at least one US court has recognised that non-members of SDOs could also rely on a FRAND commitment as third-party beneficiaries. Indeed, the purpose of a FRAND commitment in enabling widespread and successful implementation of a standard would be defeated if a SEP owner could circumvent its FRAND obligation by asserting SEP against non-SDO members, such as final consumers or device manufacturers that were not involved in the standard-development process. It would be especially damaging to SMEs in the IoT context which would not be able to rely on a FRAND licence. Certainly, no one from the industry suggests that a FRAND commitment should not be applicable to non-members of SDOs.

ii. *Is a FRAND Commitment Sufficiently Clear to be an Enforceable Contract?*

Another issue with the contractual approach to a FRAND commitment is that it may be too vague and imprecise to be enforceable.[29] A contractual obligation should be sufficiently determinable otherwise it risks being unenforceable for indefiniteness. The ITC administrative law Judge Bullock held precisely that

[25] ETSI, 'Intellectual Property Rights Policy' (n 8) Clause 6.1.

[26] ETSI, 'Guide on Intellectual Property Rights' (19 September 2013) 56.

[27] R Bekkers and A Upgedrowe, 'A Study of IPR Policies and Practices of a Representative Group of Standards Setting Organizations Worldwide', Commissioned by the US National Academies of Science, Board of Science, Technology, and Economic Policy (17 September 2012) 77–78, available at: www.nap.edu/resource/18510/Bekkers-Updegrove%20Paper_092013.pdf.

[28] *Innovatio IP Ventures, LLC Patent Litigation* (n 13) 923–24.

[29] Contreras, 'A Market Reliance Theory' (n 3) 514–15.

in a dispute between Netlist and Hynix about the FRAND commitment given at JEDEC.[30] He analysed the FRAND commitment from the perspective of New York law and found that the 'the obligation to license on RAND terms, which appears to be a material term of the JEDEC Patent Policy, is anything but "reasonably certain"', and held that 'New York law appears to require that the agreement be considered unenforceable'.[31]

However, under the general principles of contract law, parties do not need to specify an exact price in order to create a binding agreement, as long as the price is determinable. In the absence of more precise terms, a court can determine a fair, reasonable and non-discriminatory royalty.[32] Indeed, all the cases so far have demonstrated that courts regularly decide whether terms offered by the parties are FRAND. If the implementer brings a breach of contract claim, a court would have to assess whether the terms offered by the SEP holder are FRAND in the light of the commercial practices and all circumstances of the case. In the words of Mr Justice Birss in *Unwired Planet v Huawei*:

> [I]t is possible for a court to adjudicate whether a licence is or is not FRAND. Whether terms are FRAND is an objective matter for a given set of circumstances and therefore whether a FRAND undertaking has been complied with can be determined as a matter of law. In that sense the undertaking is legally enforceable.[33]

Indeed, a standard of 'reasonableness' is nothing new in law, and courts are often called to adjudicate whether a party's conduct complies with the reasonableness requirement. Larouche, Padilla and Taffet show how the reasonableness standard is used in contract law, tort law, constitutional law, regulatory law, as well as in as in competition law and intellectual property law.[34] In all these cases, courts regularly give content to the notion of 'reasonableness'.

That said, the enforceability of a FRAND commitment should not be confused with the separate question of the enforceability of the *whole SDO IPR Policies*. For example, in *True Position v Ericsson*,[35] one of the issues was whether 3GPP's Working Procedures constituted a binding contract between True Position and 3GPP, and whether True Position breached that contract. The court, after analysing the provisions of the Working Procedures, held that the terms of the Working Procedures are too indefinite to be enforced, and 'the lack of specificity regarding a 3GPP members' obligations makes the Articles too indefinite to support the

[30] *In the Matter of Certain Memory Modules and Components Thereof, and Products Containing Same*, No 337-TA-1023, 195 (USITC, 14 November 2017) (Final Initial Determination).

[31] ibid.

[32] See Lemley (n 11) (discussing the enforceability of FRAND terms from the perspectives of the US contract law).

[33] *Unwired Planet v Huawei* [2017] EWHC 2988 (Pat) 138.

[34] P Larouche, J Padilla and R Taffet, 'Settling FRAND Disputes: Is Mandatory Arbitration a Reasonable and Non-discriminatory Alternative?' (2014) 10 *Journal of Competition Law & Economics* 581, 594.

[35] *True Position v Ericsson*, 977 F.Supp.2d 462 (ED Penn 2013).

formation of a contract'.[36] Similarly, the ITC administrative law Judge Essex, in a dispute between Interdigital against Nokia and ZTE, examined the ETSI Rules and Procedures and found that they do not constitute a binding contract between ETSI and the SEP holder. Instead, he held that ETSI's Rule and Procedures 'contain rules to guide the parties in their interactions with the organization, other members and third parties'.[37]

By way of analogy, some commentators argue that since IPR policies as a whole do not constitute a binding contract, the FRAND commitment equally lacks enforceability.[38] However, this view confuses two separate issues – the legal nature of IPR policies is distinct from the existence and enforceability of a FRAND commitment. IPR policies contain various provisions regarding the setting up and functioning of an SDO's internal committees, representations and voting rules, dispute resolution mechanisms, and other provision relating to the interaction between SDO members and the SDO. The FRAND commitment is a distinct obligation which arises separately only when the SEP holder signs and delivers to the SDO a specific declaration that it will license its SEPs on FRAND terms. Only then does the SEP holder create a binding contract with the SDO. Therefore, while the whole IPR policy may not constitute an enforceable contract, it is a separate and distinct issue from the enforceability of the FRAND commitment.

iii. Transferability of a FRAND Commitment

Like any other assets SEPs may be sold and transferred. The question is what happens to the FRAND commitment once the original holder transfers its SEPs to another entity? Does the FRAND commitment 'run with the patent'? If so, what legal mechanism provides for its transferability and what happens if the FRAND commitment is not transferred?

It is generally recognised that as a matter of policy, the FRAND commitment should run with the patent.[39] Otherwise, there is a serious risk that standardisation

[36] ibid, 470.

[37] *In the Matter of Certain Wireless Devices with 3G and/or 4G Capabilities & Components Thereof*, No 337-TA-868 (USITC, 13 June 2014) (Initial Determination) 77.

[38] Contreras, 'A Market Reliance Theory' (n 3) 506, 514–15.

[39] For the view of government authorities: Commission, 'Guidelines on the Applicability of Article 101 of the Treaty on the Functioning of the European Union to Horizontal Co-operation Agreements' (Communication) [2011] OJ C 11/01, 285 (EC Horizontal Cooperation Guidelines 2011); US Department of Justice and US Patent & Trademark Office, 'Policy Statement on Remedies for Standard-Essential Patents Subject to Voluntary F/RAND Commitments' (8 January 2013) 6. For the views of different authors, see: Geradin and Brooks (n 11) 14 (holding that transferability of FRAND is solvable by existing legal tools); R Hesse, Deputy Assistant Attorney General US Department of Justice, Remarks as Prepared for the ITU-T Patent Roundtable 'Six "Small" Proposals for SSOs Before Lunch' (10 October 2012), available at: www.justice.gov/atr/file/518951/download; K-W Uwe-Kuhn, F Scott Morton and H Shelanski, 'Standard Setting Organisations Can Help Solve the Standard Essential Patents Licensing Problem' *CPI Antitrust Chronicle* (March 2013); M Lemley and C Shapiro, 'A Simple Approach to Setting Reasonable Royalties for Standard-Essential Patents' (2013) 28 *Berkeley Technology Law Journal* 1135, 1158–60 (holding that FRAND obligation should travel with the patent); Maskus and Merrill (n 6) 81–95.

efforts would be undermined if by a mere transfer of SEPs to another entity a FRAND commitment could be circumvented.

Recognising this concern, SDOs have amended their IPR policies to provide that a FRAND commitment binds subsequent owners and that SEP holders should provide in patent transfer documents that the transferee accepts to be bound by a FRAND commitment. The IPR policies of ETSI, ANSI, IEEE, ITU-T and ISO now specifically provide that: (i) a FRAND commitment shall be interpreted as encumbrances that bind all successors in interest; (ii) the SEP holder must include provisions in any patent transfer agreement that the FRAND commitment is binding on the transferee; and (iii) the SEP holder must include provisions in any patent transfer agreement ensuring that the transferee shall, in a case of future transfers, include a similar provision to bind its subsequent transferees to respect the FRAND obligation and that transferees shall do the same in a case of any future transfer.[40] This is called a 'cascading' contractual approach, as it depends on each purchaser in the chain imposing the same contractual obligation on any future purchaser.[41]

A concern with the cascading approach is that is vulnerable to being broken as it depends on each purchaser in the chain imposing the required contractual obligation on the next purchaser.[42] If any purchaser breaks the chain, there is little the implementer can do to secure a FRAND licence. An implementer could challenge the party that broke the chain for not complying with the requirement to bind the successor in interest to the FRAND commitment. However, the party at fault may not be readily determined or found. If located, it could only compensate the implementer in damages, but cannot secure licences on FRAND terms as it no longer holds the SEP. Another option is to add the previous SEP holder that broke the cascading commitment chain as a party to the proceedings.[43] Courts could then find the breach of cascading FRAND contractual commitment and order specific performance, ie, transfer of a FRAND commitment, as well as any damages. These are admittedly very complicated, expensive and time-consuming solutions.

In the alternative, if the cascading chain is broken, courts may find that the purchaser had *actual or constructive notice* of a FRAND commitment at the time of

[40] See: ETSI, 'Intellectual Property Rights Policy' (n 8) Clause 6.1*bis*; ANSI, 'Essential Requirements: Due Process Requirements for American National Standards' (January 2021) Clause 3.1.1; IEEE-SA, 'Standards Board Bylaws' (August 2020) Clause 6.2. Policy, available at: standards.ieee.org/content/dam/ieee-standards/standards/web/documents/other/sb_bylaws.pdf; ITU-ISO-IEC, Patent Statement and Licensing Declaration Form (n 4); for an overview, see J Baron et al, 'Making the Rules: The Governance of Standard Development Organizations and their Policies on Intellectual Property Rights' (EUR 29655 EN, Publication Office of the European Union, 2019) 134–35, available at: ec.europa.eu/jrc/sites/jrcsh/files/sdo_governance_final_electronic_version.pdf.

[41] See Maskus and Merrill (n 6) 89–90 (describing cascading approach).

[42] ibid, 90–92; also Contreras, 'A Market Reliance Theory' (n 3) 547–48.

[43] eg, adding a party to the proceedings in the UK is possible pursuant to Practice Direction 19.2 which states: 'The court may order a person to be added as a new party if: (a) it is desirable to add the new party so that the court can resolve all the matters in dispute in the proceedings; or (b) there is an issue involving the new party and an existing party which is connected to the matters in dispute in the proceedings, and it is desirable to add the new party so that the court can resolve that issue'.

purchase and has *tacitly agreed* to license on FRAND terms. As FRAND declarations are made public by SDOs and purchasers are normally sophisticated industry players, it would be hard to imagine that the purchaser had no knowledge that it acquired SEPs and, further, that those SEPs were not encumbered by FRAND commitments. Indeed, because of these characteristics the courts may assume that the purchaser had actual or constructive knowledge of a FRAND commitment and tacitly accepted to be bound by it. This way the automatic transferability of a FRAND commitment could be ensured.

There is some support for this interpretation in US and UK case law. In *Rembrandt v Harris*,[44] AT&T owned SEPs subject to a FRAND licensing assurance which was transferred multiple times and ended up with Rembrandt, a patent assertion entity. Rembrandt asserted SEPs against Harris and disputed that it was bound by AT&T's FRAND commitment. The court, however, found that Rembrandt had either actual or constructive knowledge of AT&T's commitment to license its essential patents on FRAND terms at the time it acquired the respective SEPs, and Rembrandt later acknowledged that it was bound by that commitment. UK courts also recognise that in certain circumstances obligations of the assignor may bind the assignee which takes the patent with a notice of such obligations. The High Court held in *Dans Rekyltiffel Syndicat Aktieselkab v Snell* that 'the obligation to fulfil the terms of the agreement attached to the property which they acquired with *notice of the terms* upon which it was held by their assignor, disables them from holding the property without fulfilling the terms'.[45]

Admittedly, this interpretation does not provide a definite solution in cases where the purchaser had no knowledge that it has acquired SEPs and, once it does become aware that it does, and the cascading chain was indeed broken, refuses to accept compliance with the FRAND commitment. A simple and practical solution might be for courts to take the behaviour of the purchaser into account and decide not to grant an injunction if validity and infringement of SEPs have been established. Instead, courts could award damages based on the methodologies for determining FRAND royalties. This would be a sort of sanction imposed by courts for those purchasers that knowingly refused to be bound by the existing FRAND commitment.

An interesting interpretation of FRAND's transferability was provided by Düsseldorf Higher Regional Court in *Unwired Planet v Huawei*.[46] Although Unwired Planet did not dispute that it was bound by the FRAND commitment when acquiring the SEP from Ericsson, the Court said that a FRAND commitment irrevocably limits the exclusive right arising from a patent and is directly binding for the new patent holder without the need for any contractual provisions. In other words, this interpretation views FRAND commitments as pledges or servitudes on

[44] *Rembrandt Technologies v Harris Corporation*, 2009 WL 2490873 (Del Sup 2009).
[45] *Dans Rekyltiffel Syndicat Aktieselkab v Snell* [1908] 25 RPC 421.
[46] *Unwired Planet v Huawei*, I-2 U 31/16 Düsseldorf Higher Regional Court (22 March 2019).

property that follows the SEP to any future acquirer. It remains to be seen if such interpretation would be followed by other courts, but it provides a mechanism for securing automatic transferability of a FRAND commitment.

Therefore, the transferability of a FRAND commitment is secured by all the major SDOs that have in place provisions providing that a FRAND commitment should be interpreted as binding on all subsequent acquirers and SEP owners are required to ensure transferability of a FRAND commitment by all future transferees. In different ways, courts are also ensuring that a FRAND commitment survives SEP transfers and are not allowing acquirers to avoid complying with a FRAND commitment.

iv. Not All Jurisdictions Recognise Third-Party Beneficiary Rights

Finally, not all jurisdictions recognise third-party beneficiary rights, which may make a FRAND commitment contractually unenforceable in some countries. This argument is true and introduces an element of uncertainty and forum-shopping as depending on where SEPs are litigated the implementer may not have a contractual defence for the breach of a FRAND commitment. For example, German courts have held that a FRAND commitment represents a mere invitation for third parties to make offers,[47] and are yet to recognise that a FRAND commitment creates third party-beneficiary rights. Instead, they analyse FRAND issues via a competition law defence to injunction suits brought by SEP owners in the framework of the CJEU's *Huawei v ZTE* case. The *Huawei v ZTE* framework is analysed in detail in chapter eight but suffice to say at this stage that it is a way in which competition law in the EU indirectly ensures the compliance with FRAND commitments even in jurisdictions that do not recognise the contractual nature of FRAND commitments. Thus, it is a form of backstop to prevent rendering a FRAND commitment meaningless and unenforceable.

The situation may be overcome by SDOs selecting the applicable law for a FRAND commitment which recognises third-party beneficiary rights. ETSI's IPR Rules, for instance, specify that the FRAND commitment is governed by French law which recognises third-party beneficiary rights.[48] Courts hearing a FRAND case would then have to interpret the FRAND commitment in accordance with the applicable law, which could enable the enforceability of a FRAND commitment even in jurisdictions that do not recognise third-party beneficiary rights.

[47] Cotter (n 11) 318 (referring to two German cases); however for the contrary argument, see C Tapia, *Industrial Property Rights, Technical Standards and Licensing Practices (FRAND) in the Telecommunications Industry* (Carly Heymanns Verlag, 2010) 18–36, 39–40 (arguing how under German law it may be possible that a FRAND commitment constitutes a binding pre-contract for the benefit of third parties).

[48] ETSI, 'Intellectual Property Rights Policy' (n 8) Clause 12; also *Unwired Planet v Huawei* [2017] EWHC 2988 (Pat) 133 (referring to the French Civil Code's provisions on the agreement for the benefit of third parties).

v. SDOs Could Clarify the Contractual Nature of a FRAND Commitment

As seen, the enforceability of a FRAND commitment as a third-party beneficiary contract ultimately depends on the precise wording of the FRAND commitment and the law applicable to it. The clearer the wording, the fewer disputes about the nature of a FRAND commitment. While the majority of SDOs specify that licences should be offered to all implementers, they are not so precise as to directly state that the FRAND commitment forms a contract between the SEP holder and the SDO, nor that all implementers regardless of whether they are SDO members or not could be third-party beneficiaries. Unambiguous wording would increase certainty and prevent different interpretations. SDOs should also ensure that the appropriate law applicable to a FRAND commitment is one which recognises third-party beneficiary rights.

An amendment to the text of the FRAND commitment would not be too difficult to achieve, as it is fairly uncontroversial that a FRAND commitment should have a binding effect and be enforceable by implementers. It should be expected that there will be unanimity or at least broad support among SDO members.[49] The following wording may be used in order to ensure better clarity and enforceability of a FRAND commitment: 'MEMBER and the SDO acknowledge that by delivering this LICENSING ASSURANCE it creates a binding contract between the MEMBER and the SDOs to which all IMPLEMENTERS of a STANDARD may rely on as third-party beneficiaries. This LICENSING ASURANCE shall be governed by the laws of [....]'.

B. Competition Law

As an alternative to contract law, it has been suggested that competition law could be used as the principal enforcement mechanism of FRAND commitments. According to this view, the SEP holder's breach of a FRAND commitment would be an infringement of competition law.[50]

A support for this interpretation comes from competition law's prohibition of excessive and discriminatory pricing, as well as from prohibiting any conduct

[49] The IPR Policies of SDOs regularly evolve over time, especially in response to legal and practical developments. See A Layne-Farrar, 'Proactive or Reactive? An Empirical Assessment of IPR Policy Revisions in the Wake of Antitrust Actions' (2014) 59 *Antitrust Bulletin* 373; Tsai and Wright (n 12). Also, uncontroversial proposals supported by government or competition authorities are often widely adopted, see Baron et al, 'Making the Rules' (n 40) 129–31.

[50] See: M Dolmans, 'Standards for Standards' (2002) 26 *Fordham International Law Journal* 163; P Chappatte, 'FRAND Commitments: The Case for Antitrust Intervention' (2009) 5 *European Competition Journal* 319; Arguing for the application of US antitrust law: G Cary et al, 'The Case for Antitrust Law to Police the Patent Holdup Problem in Standard Setting' (2011) 77 *Antitrust Law Journal* 913; D Melamed and C Shapiro, 'How Antitrust Law Can Make FRAND Commitments More Effective' (2018) 128 *Yale Law Journal* 2110.

by dominant companies that harms competition which is not based on competition on the merits.[51] Accordingly, competition law could provide another route to preventing the imposition of non-FRAND licensing terms. The relationship between competition law and FRAND commitments and the role of competition law in ensuring compliance with FRAND licensing terms will be analysed in this section.

i. EU Competition Law and Breach of FRAND Commitments

EU competition law prohibits dominant companies from imposing excessive and discriminatory prices. Excessive prices for the purposes of EU competition law have been defined as those that 'have no reasonable relation to the economic value'.[52] The legal test for proving excessive prices requires, first, determining whether the difference between the costs actually incurred and the price actually charged is excessive.[53] If the answer is affirmative, then it must be established whether the price is unfair in itself or when compared with competing products.[54] The legal test for excessive prices applies equally to excessive royalties for intellectual property rights.[55] On the other hand, the legal test for proving anti-competitive price discrimination requires establishing: (i) that a dominant company entered into equivalent transactions with other trading parties; (ii) that it applied dissimilar conditions to equivalent transactions; (iii) that the discrimination placed the other trading party at a competitive disadvantage; and (iv) that there are no objective justifications.[56]

Applying competition law doctrines of excessive and discriminatory prices to FRAND royalties may not be an easy or appropriate task.[57] As a preliminary

[51] See Treaty on the Functioning of the European Union [2011] OJ C 326, Article 102(a) and (c) ('Any abuse by one or more undertakings of a dominant position within the internal market or in a substantial part of it shall be prohibited as incompatible with the internal market in so far as it may affect trade between Member States. Such abuse may, in particular, consist in:

> directly or indirectly imposing *unfair purchase or selling prices or other unfair trading conditions*
>
> ...
>
> (c) applying dissimilar conditions to equivalent transactions with other trading parties, thereby placing them at a competitive disadvantage') (emphasis added).

[52] Case 27/76 *United Brands v Commission* [1978] ECR 207, 250.

[53] R Whish and D Bailey, *Competition Law*, 9th edn (Oxford University Press, 2018) (overview of excessive pricing regulation under EU competition law) 762–66; A Jones and B Sufrin, *EU Competition Law: Text, Cases, and Materials*, 6th edn (Oxford University Press, 2016) 566–71 (discussing excessive pricing under EU competition law).

[54] *United Brands v Commission* (n 52) 252.

[55] See C-177/16 *Biedrība 'Autortiesību un komunicēšanās konsultāciju aģentūra – Latvijas Autoru apvienība' Konkurences padome (AKKA/LAA)* ECLI:EU:C:2017:689 (a copyright collective management organisation accused of charging excessive copyright royalties).

[56] For an overview of price discrimination under EU competition law, see: Whish and Bailey (n 53) 779–82; Jones and Sufrin (n 53) 559–66.

[57] For an excellent overview, see: M Botta, 'The Challenge of Sanctioning Unfair Royalty Rates by the SEP Holder: "When", "How" and "What"' (2021) 44 *World Competition* 3; M Botta, 'Non-Discrimination in Standard Essential Patents: ND Prong v Art 102(c) TFEU' (2021) *Journal of Competition Law & Economics* (forthcoming).

step it would have to be established whether the SEP owner holds a dominant position in the market. However, the SEP does not automatically confer a dominant position and dominance would need to be proven in each case. A dominant position may be true for SEPs reading on 4G and 3G cellular standards that are indispensable for all modern smartphones, but it may not necessarily be the case for other, less popular standards.[58] Not every collaborative standard developed by SDOs succeeds on the market. Some collaborative standards are ultimately not widely accepted and are not implemented by a substantive number of manufacturers. In this case, holding a SEP for such a standard would hardly confer a dominant position. An example would be the first SDRAM standard adopted by JEDEC, which was not implemented as quickly or widely as anticipated, leading JEDEC to work on a next generation standard.[59] A standard may also face competition from other standards or from non-standardised products. This was the case with Toshiba's DVD HD and Sony's Blu-Ray standard wars, for the establishment of the next high-definition optical disc format. When there are two competing alternative standards, dominance would be hard to establish. Therefore, competition law would be inapplicable to SEP holders' conduct in the case of standards which do not have a dominant position in the market, rendering the FRAND commitment meaningless.

Even if dominance is established, further difficulties exist in proving the legal tests for excessive and discriminatory royalties under EU competition law.[60] The first step in finding excessive royalties requires comparing whether the difference between the costs actually incurred and the price charged is excessive. However, applying a costs-based principle may not be suitable in an IPR context because the costs of developing technology are substantial, but the marginal costs of licensing are close or equal to zero.[61] Considering that the costs of developing the technology are also imprecise, as they often fail to take into account the costs of failed

[58] D Geradin and M Rato, 'FRAND Commitments and EC Competition Law: A Reply to Phillippe Chappatte' (2010) 6 *European Competition Journal* 129, 167; U Petrovcic, *Competition Law and Standard Essential Patents: A Transatlantic Perspective* (Kluwer Law International, 2014) 71–73 (discussing the establishment of dominance in cases of SEPs).

[59] Petrovcic, *Competition Law and Standard Essential Patents* (n 58) 71–72.

[60] See M Mariniello, 'Fair, Reasonable and Non-Discriminatory (FRAND) Terms: A Challenge to Competition Authorities' (2011) 7 *Journal of Competition Law & Economics* 523 (describing difficulties in applying competition law to regulating FRAND royalties); Botta, 'The Challenge of Sanctioning Unfair Royalty Rates by the SEP Holder' (n 57).

[61] The European Commission also acknowledged the inadequacy of applying cost-based methods in the context of IPRs. See: EC Horizontal Cooperation Guidelines 2011 (n 39) 289. ('In principle, cost-based methods are not well adapted to this context because of the difficulty in assessing the costs attributable to the development of a particular patent or groups of patents'); see also the Opinion of AG Jacobs in Case C-395/87 *Ministere public v Jean-Louis Tournier* (1989) ECLI:EU:C:1989:215, 53 ('it is pointed out that it is inappropriate in the present context to proceed on the basis of comparison between the costs of production and the selling price because it is impossible to determine the cost of the creation of a work of the imagination such as a musical work'); Opinion of AG Wahl in Case-C-177/16 *AKKA/LAA* ECLI:EU:C:2017:286, 37 ('a cost-price comparison makes little sense with regard to the supply of certain intangible goods such as – in the case in the main proceedings – copyright musical work').

projects, or different strands of R&D which all indirectly contributed to the development of the technology.[62] Another issue is determining whether the difference between the costs and the royalty is excessive. Setting royalties well above R&D costs may represent fair compensation for innovative technologies and provide incentives for further risky innovation. Conversely, erroneous decisions may harm innovation and consumer welfare. Recognising this, the CJEU in *AKKA-LA* held that there is no single adequate method with which to assess whether prices are unfair and that competition authorities have a margin for manoeuvre.[63] Typically in IP cases a benchmarking method is used to compare the price charged by a dominant company with the price charged by competitors, the prices of licensors in different geographical markets and to different customers, and the change of price over time.[64] However, the benchmarking method is far from simple and straightforward to apply. Besides requiring data that may not be readily available, it ultimately comes down to a subjective estimate of what is 'unfair' in relation to IP rights. As seen, any valuation of the price of technology must take into account the total costs of the development of technology, including the costs of failed projects, and incentives for future innovation. This is not an easy task for any authority and involves a high risk of false positives.

The difficulty in applying Article 102 TFEU to excessive non-FRAND royalties by SEP holders was apparent in two cases investigated by that the European Commission. In *Rambus*, the European Commission challenged the imposition of royalties for the use of SEPs that were considered as excessive.[65] However, *Rambus* is a peculiar case where no FRAND commitment was given. Instead, Rambus' conduct consisted of a 'patent ambush', an intentional deception of the SDO by concealing the existence of patents and patent applications during the development of a standard and later, once its technology had been adopted into the standard, claiming unreasonably high royalties.[66] Thus, because of a patent ambush, Rambus managed to avoid giving a FRAND commitment and charged unconstrained royalties for the use of its SEPs.

The European Commission also investigated whether Qualcomm was charging non-FRAND royalties for the use of its SEPs contrary to Article 102 TFEU.[67] Qualcomm participated in the standardisation process and committed to license its SEPs for the WCDMA standard on FRAND terms. Later, complainants

[62] Dolmans (n 50) ('More important, a cost-based analysis ignores the value of the sparks of imagination that may represent the essence of the innovation. Cost-based pricing also ignores risk, which is especially high in sectors relying on expensive R&D'.).

[63] *AKKA/LAA* (n 55) 49.

[64] Botta, 'The Challenge of Sanctioning Unfair Royalty Rates by the SEP Holder' (n 57).

[65] Commission, 'Antitrust: Commission Confirms Sending a Statement of Objections to Rambus' MEMO/07/330 (2007).

[66] ibid.

[67] Commission, 'Antitrust: Commission Initiates Formal Proceedings Against Qualcomm' MEMO/07/389 (2007).

alleged that Qualcomm failed to comply with its FRAND licensing commitment. In opening the investigation, the European Commission stated that it would evaluate whether Qualcomm's breach of a FRAND commitment consisted of an abuse of dominant position. In the words of the European Commission: 'a finding of exploitative practices by Qualcomm in the WCDMA licensing market contrary to Article [102] of the EC Treaty may depend on whether the licensing terms imposed by Qualcomm are in breach of its FRAND commitment'.[68]

However, neither investigation resulted in a definite finding of the abuse of dominant position. The *Rambus* case was closed with a commitments decision, where Rambus undertook to lower its royalties, but did not determine whether the challenged conduct represented an abuse of dominant position.[69] The investigation of Qualcomm was terminated after complainants withdrew their claims.[70] The results of the European Commission's investigations demonstrate the difficulties of applying competition law to SEP royalties.

A principal problem with the application of competition law's prohibition of excessive prices is that it confuses and conflate two separate notions – a contractual obligation to license SEPs on FRAND terms and a competition law prohibition of excessive prices. The contractual obligation to license on FRAND terms is stricter than competition law. Namely, the SEP holder may offer terms that are slightly above a contractual FRAND obligation, representing a breach of its contractual duties to an SDO, but may not yet reach the threshold of being excessive in a competition law sense. Thus, while both competition law and FRAND commitments use similar language ('excessive', 'unreasonable') and apply to the level of royalties, making it tempting to confuse them, they are nevertheless two separate legal instruments.

The distinction was properly recognised by Mr Justice Birss in *Unwired Planet v Huawei*. Having found that the SEP holder's offers were not FRAND, he was asked to assess whether they were also excessive within the meaning of Article 102 TFEU. He disagreed in principle that a rate that is higher than FRAND would automatically be abusive from a competition law perspective. In his words:

> I hold as a matter of law that the boundary of what is and is not a FRAND rate is different from the boundary of what is and is not an unfair price contrary to Art 102(a). If the rate imposed is FRAND then it cannot be abusive. But a rate can be higher than the FRAND rate without being abusive too.[71]

[68] ibid.

[69] Commission, 'Antitrust: Commission accepts commitments from Rambus lowering memory chip royalty rates' IP/09/189 (2009) (Rambus agreed to charge zero royalties for the SDR and DDR chip standards that were adopted when Rambus was a JEDEC member, and a maximum royalty rate of 1.5% for the later generations of JEDEC DRAM standards, instead of the 3.5% that Rambus was previously charging).

[70] Commission, 'Antitrust: Commission closes formal proceedings against Qualcomm' MEMO/09/516 (2009).

[71] *Unwired Planet v Huawei* [2017] EWHC 2988 (Pat) 757.

Mr Justice Birrs held that a non-FRAND rate could be abusive only if it is 'so far above FRAND as to act to disrupt or prejudice the negotiations themselves'.[72] On the facts of the case, he found that the SEP holder's initial offers of one and a half to six times more than the determined FRAND rates were not so high as to disrupt the negotiations and were accordingly not found to be abusive within the meaning of EU competition law.[73]

The same difficulties are present in applying competition law's prohibition of discriminatory pricing. To date, no court or competition agency in the EU has found that the SEP holder abused its dominant position by using discriminatory licensing terms. As seen, EU competition law requires, in addition to finding of 'dissimilar conditions' to 'equivalent transactions', proof of 'competitive disadvantage'. Applying different royalties to similarly situated licensees would not be anti-competitive unless it is capable of distorting competition between the parties.[74] This issue was extensively analysed in *Unwired Planet v Huawei*.[75] There, Unwired Planet concluded a licensing agreement with Samsung on much more favourable terms than the ones offered to Huawei. Having established that Samsung and Huawei were similarly situated licensees and that terms between them were indeed dissimilar, the court had to decide whether the difference was such as to distort competition between them.[76] After careful examination it was established that, although the difference in the royalty rates between Samsung and Huawei were large, the difference was not large enough to distort competition.[77] Consequently, no infringement of competition law was found. However, if we adopt a contractual interpretation of a FRAND commitment, there would be no requirement to prove 'competitive disadvantage', making it easier to enforce and impose stricter obligations than competition law.[78]

In conclusion, the competition law legal tests for establishing excessive and discriminatory royalties are not an adequate general enforcement mechanism for FRAND commitments.[79] To date there has been no case in the EU that conclusively established the abuse of dominant position by the SEP holder for charging excessive or discriminatory royaltics. Consequently, conceptualising a FRAND commitment as an enforceable contract provides better enforceability and reliability.

[72] ibid, 765.

[73] ibid, 772–77.

[74] C-525/16 *Meo-Serviços de Comunicações e Multimédia*, ECLI:EU:C:2018:942, 28, 31.

[75] *Unwired Planet v Huawei* [2017] EWHC 2988 (Pat).

[76] ibid, para 503.

[77] ibid, para 518. Confirmed on appeal, see *Unwired Planet v Huawei* [2018] EWCA Civ 2344.

[78] See ch 5 for the non-discrimination requirement of a FRAND commitment.

[79] For more arguments against the application of EU competition and inadequacies of competition law for regulating FRAND commitments, see Geradin and Rato (n 58); D Geradin, 'Pricing Abuses by Essential Patent Holders in a Standard-Setting Context: A View From Europe' (2009) 76 *Antitrust Law Journal* 329; D Geradin, 'The European Commission's Policy Towards The Licensing of Standard-Essential Patents: Where do We Stand?' (2013) 9 *Journal of Competition Law & Economics* 1125; for a comparative analysis of competition law approaches to non-FRAND royalties, see Petrovcic, *Competition Law and Standard Essential Patents* (n 58).

Indeed, competition law debate in the EU has moved from focusing on pricing to looking at the conduct of SEP owners. Chapter eight will show how the European Commission intervened in *Motorola* and *Samsung* cases concerning the use of injunctions for infringement of SEPs and holding that under certain conditions they represent an abuse of dominant position.[80] The CJEU in *Huawei v ZTE* confirmed that seeking injunctions for SEPs may lead to an abuse of dominant position and provided a negotiation framework for both parties to adhere to.[81] The *Huawei v ZTE* competition framework now governs the use of injunctions in the EU and ensures that injunctions are not be granted unless the SEP owner offers or court establishes FRAND licensing terms.

ii. US Antitrust Law and Breach of FRAND Commitments

US antitrust law is even more difficult to apply because, unlike the EU, it does not prohibit excessive prices charged by dominant companies. The Supreme Court held that:

> [C]harging of monopoly prices, is not only not unlawful, but it is important element of the free market system. The opportunity to charge monopoly prices, at least for a short period of time, is what attracts business acumen in the first place; it induces risk taking that produce innovation and economic growth.[82]

Therefore, charging excessive non-FRAND royalties as such is not actionable antitrust conduct. On the other hand, the Robinson–Patman Act prohibits discriminatory pricing that has anti-competitive effects,[83] but establishing competitive harm by a SEP holder's discriminatory pricing may not be an easy task. To date it appears that no US court has successfully applied the prohibition of anti-competitive price discrimination in SEP cases.

Instead, the US antitrust law is concerned with the illegitimate obtainment or maintenance of monopoly power, and not how a legitimate monopolist should use its monopoly power. Section 2 of the Sherman Act makes it unlawful to 'monopolize, or attempt to monopolize … any part of the trade or commerce among the several States'.[84] To prevail on a claim for monopolisation or attempted monopolisation, the plaintiff must prove that the defendant had power in the relevant market and wilfully sought, acquired, or maintained that power in an unlawful manner.[85]

[80] *Motorola – Enforcement of GPRS standard essential patents* (Case AT.39985) Commission Decision C(2014) 2892 (29 April 2014); *Samsung – Enforcement of UMTS standard essential patents* (Case AT.39939), Commission Decision C(2014) 2891 (29 April 2014).

[81] C-170/13 *Huawei Technologies v ZTE*, ECLI:EU:C:2015:477.

[82] *Verizon Communications v Law Offices of Curtis v Trinko*, 540 US 398, 407 (2004).

[83] 15 US Code § 13.

[84] 15 US Code § 2.

[85] *United States v Grinnell Corp*, 384 US 563, 570–71 (1966); also E Elhauge and D Geradin, *Global Competition Law and Economics*, 2nd edn (Hart Publishing, 2011) 265–70 (explaining the application of s 2 of the Sherman Act).

Accordingly, antitrust claims in SEP cases have been centred around the accusation that the SEP holder *deceived* an SDO in order to unlawfully acquire monopoly power. In *Broadcom v Qualcomm*,[86] Broadcom alleged that Qualcomm deceived the SDO to include its SEPs into the standard by falsely promising to license its patents on FRAND terms, and then breached such promise by licensing its technology on non-FRAND terms. The Third Circuit held that for the violation of section 2 of the Sherman Act it must be proven that: (i) the SEP holder intentionally falsely promised to license its SEPs on FRAND terms; (ii) the SDO relied on that promise when including the technology in a standard; and (iii) the patent holder subsequently breached that promise.[87] Only then would the conduct represent unlawful acquisition of monopoly power. The legal test represents a significant hurdle, making US antitrust laws impractical as a general framework for the enforcement of FRAND commitments.[88]

What's more, in *Rambus v FTC* the US Court of Appeals for the DC Circuit held that a plaintiff must prove that the SDO would have adopted alternative technology but for deception.[89] In other words, it should be established that alternative technologies would have been adopted in the standards if there was no deceptive conduct from the SEP owner. Deception should directly contribute to the exclusion of alternative technologies. The *Rambus* case concerned patent ambush, where Rambus was alleged to have intentionally concealed the existence of its patents and patent applications during the development of a standard and once its patents were included in a standard it started asserting them against implementers However, by concealing the existence of its SEPs during standardisation, Rambus avoided giving a FRAND commitment, thus enabling it to insist on allegedly non-FRAND terms. The FTC considered such conduct anti-competitive and a violation of section 2 of the Sherman Act because Rambus's deception enabled it either to acquire a monopoly though standardisation of its patented technology and the exclusion of possible alternatives, or to avoid the limitation on its patent licensing terms by giving a FRAND commitment. The DC Circuit, however, disagreed and held that mere avoidance of a FRAND commitment in itself does not represent anti-competitive conduct: 'an otherwise lawful monopolist's use of deception

[86] *Broadcom v Qualcomm*, 2006 WL 2528545 (DC NJ 2006); *Broadcom v Qualcomm*, 501 F.3d 297 (3rd Cir 2007).

[87] *Broadcom v Qualcomm*, 501 F.3d 297, 314 (3rd Cir 2007); also *Microsoft v Interdigital*, 2016 WL 1464545 (D Del 2016).

[88] Several authors are critical of the use of competition laws as a general mechanism of enforcement of FRAND commitments: B Kobayashi and J Wright, 'The Limits of Antitrust and Patent Holdup: A Reply to Cary et al' (2012) 78 *Antitrust Law Journal* 701; U Petrovcic, 'Patent Hold-up and the Limits of Competition Law: A Transatlantic Perspective' (2013) 50 *Common Market Law Review* 1363; Cotter (n 11) 327–42; Ginsburg, Wong-Ervin and Wright (n 11); Contreras, 'A Market Reliance Theory' (n 3) 523–34; M Ohlhausen, 'The Elusive Role of Competition in the Standard-Setting Antitrust Debate' (2017) 20 *Stanford Technology Law Review* 93.

[89] *Rambus Inc v Federal Trade Commission*, 522 F.3d 456 (DC Cir 2008).

simply to obtain higher prices normally has no particular tendency to exclude rivals and thus to diminish competition'.[90] Only a proof that the SDO would have standardised alternative technology without the SEP owner's deception represents an actionable antitrust conduct as it leads to exclusion of competition. If the SDO had standardised the SEP owner's technology regardless of the deception, because there were no alternatives or the technology was more superior than alternatives, and would have been standardised even without requesting a FRAND commitment, then the SEP owner's deception would not produce anti-competitive effects.

US cases struggled with proving deception to the requisite standards, and we have no final court judgment to date that has definitively established the violation of section 2 of the Sherman Act for deceptive breach of a FRAND commitment. Some courts, like Northern District Court of Texas in *Continental v Avanci* went so far as to wholly reject that the deception of an SDO constitutes anti-competitive conduct reiterating that charging higher prices alone does not exclude rivals and diminish competition.[91] Others allowed claims to proceed but required pointing to alternative technologies that might have been excluded due to deceptive conduct.[92] However, no case ultimately led to a final judgment affirming antitrust liability. The difficulty in proving that deception led to elimination of alternatives is that, as explained in chapter one, there are typically no ready 'off-the-shelf' alternatives that compete for inclusion in a standard, but rather technologies are developed collaboratively with the intention to respond to a standard's technical requirements. In addition, proving that the SEP owner at the time of making a FRAND commitment intentionally knew that it would later renegade on it represents a significant additional burden.

In some cases, the FTC challenged the conduct of SEP holders via section 5 of the FTC Act that prohibits unfair methods and acts of competition in cases relating to patent ambush,[93] the transfer of a FRAND commitment,[94] the use of

[90] ibid, 464.

[91] *Continental Automotive Systems v Avanci*, 2020 WL 5627224 (ND Tex 2020) 12.

[92] *Research in Motion v Motorola*, 644 F.Supp.2d 788, 798 (ND Tex 2008) ('RIM pleads that IEEE and ETSI did not incorporate Motorola's technology into their standards because of Motorola's business acumen or because its technology was superior. Instead, RIM asserts, the IEEE and ETSI relied on Motorola's false promises that it would license its patents on FRAND terms'); *Apple v Samsung*, 2012 WL 1672493 (ND Cal 2012) 8 ('Apple presents alternatives that the working group could have adopted to perform the same functionality as that performed by each Declared-Essential Patent asserted. Additionally, Apple alleges that, since the working group knew of alternatives to Samsung's technologies, had it known that Samsung did not intend to license on FRAND terms the adopted patents, ETSI would not have adopted the standard because of the negative lock-in effect'); *Microsoft v Interdigital*, 2016 WL 1464545 (D Del 2016) 1 ('Microsoft alleges that IDC, in order to induce ETSI to incorporate IDC's patented technology into the 3G and 4G standards, falsely promised to license its SEPs on FRAND terms. But for IDC's deception, Microsoft alleges, ETSI would have included in the standards alternate technologies or not specified any technology at all'); *Wi-Lan v LG Electronics*, 382 F.Supp.3d 1012 (SD Cal 2019).

[93] *Dell Computer Corporation*, Docket No C-3658, 121 (FTC 1996); *Union Oil Company of California*, Docket No 9305 (FTC 2005).

[94] *In the Matter of Negotiated Data Solutions*, File No 051-0094 (FTC 2008).

injunctions for SEPs.[95] These cases did not concern the level of royalties and section 5 of the FTC Act is of limited use as only the FTC can bring actions, private litigation is not permitted,[96] and the boundaries of unfair competition liability are still relatively unclear.[97]

Therefore, the mere breach of a FRAND commitment in itself is not actionable antitrust behaviour in the US.[98] Various US courts have explicitly confirmed this. In *TCL v Ericsson*, the court held that:

> [T]he crux of TCL's argument seems to be that because TCL has evidence that Ericsson has breached FRAND, TCL has evidence that Ericsson has necessarily done so in an anticompetitive way … The Court has not been provided with any authority for this kind of bootstrapping of a breach of contract case, without more, into a violation of the policy or spirit of antitrust laws. Instead … it is clear that there needs to be some other conduct by Ericsson than mere breach of its FRAND obligations.[99]

In *Continental v Avanci*, Judge Lynn held that 'it is not anticompetitive for an SEP holder to violate its FRAND obligations. A lawful monopolist's charging of monopoly prices is not only not unlawful; it is an important element of the free-market system'.[100] And the Ninth Circuit in *FTC v Qualcomm* concluded that if the SEP owner breached its FRAND commitments, 'the remedy for such a breach lies in contract and patent law', not antitrust laws.[101]

iii. The Role of Competition Law in the SEP Context

Besides positive arguments that demonstrate the difficulty in applying competition law doctrines to breaches of contractual FRAND commitments, there are additional policy reasons against competition law intervention in pure SEP pricing cases. First, the larger involvement of national competition authorities would effectively represent government regulation of technology prices.[102] The European

[95] *In the Matter of Robert Bosch GmbH*, Docket No C-4377 (FTC 2013); *In the Matter of Motorola Mobility LLC and Google Inc*, File No 121-0120 (FTC 2013).

[96] 15 US Code § 45.

[97] No court to date has yet confirmed the application of section 5 of the FTC Act to the conduct of SEP holders. Also, several of the FTC's Commissioners dissented from the use of stand-alone s 5 liability for the conduct of SEP holders. See: Dissenting Statement of Commissioner Kovacic, *In the Matter of Negotiated Data Solutions*, File No 051-0094 (FTC 2008); Dissenting Statement of Commissioner Maureen K Ohlhausen, *In the Matter of Robert Bosch GmbH*, Docket No C-4377 (FTC 2013); Dissenting Statement of Commissioner Maureen K Ohlhausen, *In the Matter of Motorola Mobility LLC and Google Inc*, File No 121-0120 (FTC 2013).

[98] See Ohlhausen (n 88) 121–22; also M Delrahim, Assistant Attorney General US Department of Justice, 'Antitrust Law and Patent Licensing in the New Wild West' (18 September 2018), available at available at: www.justice.gov/opa/speech/assistant-attorney-general-makan-delrahim-delivers-remarks-iam-s-patent-licensing.

[99] *TCL v Ericsson*, SACV 14-0341 JVS (CD Cal 2016) 9–10.

[100] *Continental Automotive Systems v Avanci* (n 91) 11.

[101] *Federal Trade Commission v Qualcomm*, 969 F.3d 974, 1005 (9th Cir 2020).

[102] See Geradin and Rato (n 58) 168.

Commission, as well as other national competition authorities, have been rightly reluctant to intervene in ordinary business transactions and act as price regulators outside situations of natural and legal monopolies.[103] Moreover, a government technology-price regulation is not justified in the light of other available remedies, like arbitration and court adjudication, which are more adequately placed to settle private disputes. Second, competition law remedies may not provide an adequate redress to standard implementers. National competition authorities in the EU may issue fines, and in the US successful plaintiffs can obtain treble damages, but this does not provide adequate satisfaction to the standard implementers who need access to standardised technology and whose genuine remedy is getting a licence on FRAND terms. Certainly, national competition authorities may also either directly regulate the price or leave it for the dominant company to devise new FRAND pricing terms and monitor its compliance. However, this would draw government authorities even further into price regulation and micromanagement of technology prices.

Finally, and more fundamentally, equating competition law prohibition of excessive and discriminatory prices with a contractual breach of a FRAND commitment practically renders a FRAND commitment meaningless. If a FRAND commitment does not impose any additional pricing obligations over and above those required by competition law, then there would be no point in giving a FRAND commitment in the first place. Instead, a contractual commitment to license on FRAND terms imposes stricter pricing requirements over and above those of competition law.[104]

A proper interpretation of the FRAND commitment should distinguish between a contractual requirement to license on FRAND terms and a competition law prohibition of excessive and discriminatory pricing. These two notions are not the same and should not be equated, but they coexist and operate at two separate levels, each constraining the pricing of SEP owners.[105] The evidence needed to prove the infringement of competition law and the breach of contract are different, as well as their remedies. Competition law requires a difficult burden of proof and many above-FRAND offers would hardly reach the threshold of competition law, but they would be caught by a stricter contractual interpretation of a FRAND commitment.

What is then the role of competition law in a SEP context? It remains applicable as a positive boundary on a firm's behaviour when relevant conditions

[103] Jones and Sufrin (n 53) 567 ('outside the regulatory context, exploitative high prices which do not have exclusionary potential are better dealt with by contract or consumer protection law rather than competition law').

[104] This interpretation was confirmed in *Unwired Planet v Huawei* [2017] EWHC 2988 (Pat). Also, *Unwired Planet v Huawei* [2018] EWCA Civ 2344, 200 (finding that if there is a competitive harm from the SEP holder's discriminatory pricing, it is better addressed via competition law).

[105] See J Atik, 'The FRAND Ceremony and the Engagement of Article 102 TFEU in the Licensing of Standard Essential Patents' (2019) 42 *Fordham International Law Journal* 949.

relating to market power and anti-competitive conduct are satisfied.[106] There are cases where the conduct of SEP holders was considered anti-competitive under traditional competition law doctrines. For example, the European Commission in 2018 fined Qualcomm for the abuse of dominant position for supposedly entering into an exclusivity agreement with Apple for the purchase of LTE baseband chips.[107] The FTC similarly considered that Qualcomm's refusal to license its SEPs to chip competitors and exclusionary terms with Apple were anti-competitive, but the Ninth Circuit disagreed.[108] The European Commission in 2019 again fined Qualcomm for alleged predatory pricing of its 3G baseband chips.[109] Under certain conditions conditional refusal to license SEPs, tying of SEPs, grant-back and cross-licences could also violate competition laws.[110] Thus, competition law acts as a constraint on a SEP owner's conduct when conditions relating to market power and abuse are established in an individual case.

C. Alternative Theories on the Enforceability of FRAND Commitments

Several authors have suggested different theories for conceptualising FRAND commitments in order to make them more effective and address potential shortcomings in contractual approach. Professor Kesan and Professor Hayes proposed viewing FRAND commitments as encumbrances (servitudes) on real property (the equitable servitudes theory).[111] Under this approach, a FRAND commitment would be interpreted as a servitude on patents, making it tied to the patent and automatically running with the patent in a case of transfer irrespective of whether it is specifically included in the transfer documents.[112] It would also make the

[106] See H Hovenkamp, 'FRAND and Antitrust' (2020) 105 *Cornell Law Review* 101, 102 ('the question of an antitrust violation does not depend on whether the conduct breached a particular agreement but rather on whether it restrained trade under § 1 of the Sherman Act, was unreasonably exclusionary under § 2 of the Sherman Act); J Contreras, 'Much Ado About Holdup' (2019) 3 *University of Illinois Law Review* 875, 903 ('In order for a violation of law to occur, a defendant must be shown to have engaged in legally prohibited conduct using established standards of conduct, not the ill-defined economic concept of hold-up.').

[107] Commission, 'Antitrust: Commission fines Qualcomm €997 million for abuse of dominant market position' (Press Release) IP/18/421 (2018).

[108] *Federal Trade Commission v Qualcomm* (n 101).

[109] Commission, 'Antitrust: Commission fines US Chipmaker Qualcomm €242 Million for Engaging in Predatory Pricing' (Press Release) IP/19/4350 (2019).

[110] See Hovenkamp, 'FRAND and Antitrust' (n 106); C Shapiro and M Lemley, 'The Role of Antitrust in Preventing Patent Holdup' (2020) 168 *University of Pennsylvania Law Review* 1; J Padilla, D Ginsburg and K Wong-Ervin, 'Antitrust Analysis Involving Intellectual Property and Standards: Implications from Economics' (2019) 33 *Harvard Journal of Law & Technology* 1 (discussing proving market power in an IP context and antitrust analysis of refusal to license, tying and bundling, grant-backs and cross-licences and requests for injunctive relief).

[111] J Kesan and C Hayes, 'FRAND's Forever: Standards, Patent Transfers, and Licensing Commitments' (2014) 89 *Indiana Law Journal* 231, 286–87.

[112] ibid, 287.

FRAND commitment easier to enforce as there is no need to prove the existence of an enforceable contract, nor to invoke the third-party beneficiary theory. The FRAND commitment would be tied to the SEPs as a servitude enforceable by any standard implementer.

Professor Contreras, on the other hand, proposes a market reliance theory that conceptualises FRAND commitments as forming a promissory estoppel and adding a rebuttable presumption of reliance.[113] A promissory estoppel is a contractual doctrine in some jurisdictions that makes unilateral promises enforceable if it causes detrimental reliance of the other party.[114] The problem in applying promissory estoppel to a FRAND commitment is that a manufacturer would need to prove that it actually and justifiably relied on a FRAND commitment to its detriment, which may be difficult.[115] Also, the identity of the person to which a promise is made must be specified; promissory estoppel doctrine does not recognise third-party beneficiary rights.[116] Professor Contreras, therefore, proposes making a rebuttable presumption of reliance by all standard implementers. This is justified because the SEP holder has publicly given FRAND commitments, technology markets are dependent on FRAND licensing and the obligation to license on FRAND terms is well known to market participants.[117] The benefit of the market reliance theory is that it greatly simplifies the enforcement of a FRAND commitments by all standard implementers. The only thing that needs to be established is that the original patent owner made a FRAND commitment, and that the implementer manufactures or sells a product that uses a standard.[118] The manufacturer can then simply rely on a FRAND commitment and demand FRAND licensing terms. The market-reliance theory also ensures that the FRAND commitment is tied to the SEP and does not depend on the number of times SEPs are transferred, nor on the ultimate patent owner. If a manufacturer is sued for patent infringement, it needs only to determine that the technology is part of a market characterised by a FRAND commitment and that asserted patents were once owned by a party that gave a FRAND commitment.[119]

Although both proposals are interesting and resolve the issues of enforceability and transferability of a FRAND commitment, the practical implementation would require judicial recognition or legislative action, which remains uncertain.[120] However, we have seen how Düsseldorf Higher Regional Court in *Unwired Planet v Huawei* appears to have echoed the equitable servitudes theory by holding that the FRAND commitment irrevocably limits the exclusive patent rights and is

[113] Contreras, 'A Market Reliance Theory' (n 3).
[114] ibid, 517–18.
[115] ibid, 519.
[116] ibid.
[117] ibid, 542.
[118] ibid.
[119] ibid, 547–48.
[120] ibid, 556–57.

directly and indispensably binding for the new patent holder without the need for any contractual provisions.[121] It remains to be seen if other courts or the German Federal Supreme Court will endorse it.

III. Conclusion

The chapter demonstrated that a FRAND licensing commitment is of a contractual nature and that competition and contract laws coexist and operate at two separate and distinct levels, each constraining the conduct of SEP holders and standard implementers in its own way. A contractual FRAND commitment imposes stricter pricing obligations over and above competition law pricing restraints, protects implementers against excessive non-FRAND royalty demands, and requires good faith negotiations from both parties. However, a mere breach of a contractual FRAND commitment does not necessarily imply infringement of competition law. Competition law is generally ill-suited for pure royalty disputes, but it does play a role in regulating the behaviour of SEP holders when the conditions of market power and anti-competitive conduct are satisfied.

[121] *Unwired Planet v Huawei*, I-2 U 31/16 Düsseldorf Higher Regional Court (n 46).

4

FRAND Royalty

Having discussed the nature and enforceability of the FRAND commitment, this chapter will analyse what a FRAND royalty is and how it can be determined. The principles of FRAND royalty will first be discussed, followed by practical calculation methods used before courts.

At the outset, however, it is important to emphasise that SDO IPR policies typically do not define how FRAND royalties should be determined. Instead, they leave the determination to market-based bilateral negotiations between parties. There is thus no requirement on SEP owners to commit to a certain price level. For example, CEN-CENELEC stress that 'FRAND has no precise pricing content, but instead is a "comity device" designed to promote good faith negotiation between patent owners and prospective licensees'.[1] The only exception seems to be the IEEE which in a 2015 revision of its IPR policy provided a specific definition of what value FRAND royalty should include and how it should be calculated.[2] The discussion about the principles and definitions of FRAND royalties mainly comes from economic literature and policymaking circles. To the extent that these interpretations find their way into court judgments means they may become binding upon parties and influence future market royalty negotiations. The views and advocacy on FRAND royalties from various government authorities, such as the European Commission, the US Department of Justice, or the Federal Trade Commission may influence bilateral bargaining of SEP owners and implementers, but they are not legally binding.

Next, since the obligation to license SEP on FRAND terms is a contractual obligation of the SEP owner, a FRAND royalty should be interpreted by contractual principles and we should not confuse it with national patent damages rules. The determination of FRAND royalties in practice often comes in patent litigation after SEPs have been found to be valid and infringed and the court is then asked to determine damages for past use and future royalties. This led US courts to use the principles of patent damages laws providing that 'the court shall award the claimant damages adequate to compensate for the infringement

[1] CEN and CENELEC, 'Standard Essential Patents and Fair, Reasonable and Non-Discriminatory (FRAND) Commitments' (2016) 2, available at: www.cencenelec.eu/News/Policy_Opinions/PolicyOpinions/EssentialPatents.pdf.

[2] IEEE-SA, 'Standards Board Bylaws' (August 2020) Clause 6.1. Definitions, available at: standards.ieee.org/content/dam/ieee-standards/standards/web/documents/other/sb_bylaws.pdf.

but in no event less than a reasonable royalty' for calculating FRAND royalties.[3] However, while both notions contain the word *reasonable*, the contractual FRAND obligation and the rules of national patent damages laws should not be conflated.[4] The court should be interpretating the contractual obligation to license on FRAND terms, which is independent from national patent damages rules. Otherwise, the amount of FRAND royalty would depend on the patent damages laws of the country where the SEP litigation is initiated. This is not what is intended by a FRAND commitment. National patent damages laws remain relevant for non-FRAND patents, but not for FRAND-committed ones. Having this distinction is mind is important when analysing suggested interpretations of a FRAND royalty and methods for calculation.

I. The Principles of FRAND Royalty

Economists and policymakers have tried to distil some FRAND royalty principles. Three distinctive values may be observed in the literature: (i) the 'sunk cost value', meaning the costs of standard implementers related to the development of standard-implementing products, including implementer's costs of switching to alternative technologies; (ii) the 'value of standardisation', meaning any value added by the standardisation of the technology (ie, any additional value that increases the importance of technology upon standardisation due to the presence of network effects); and (iii) 'the value of the technology itself', meaning the value of the technology before it was included in a standard.

The consensus is the patent holder should not be able to capture sunk and switching costs of standard implementers, ie, 'sunk cost value' (point i). Indeed, obtaining this value would represent a classic example of patent holdup. On the other hand, the critical disagreement is whether SEP holders should be able to capture some value of standardisation (point ii), or whether the SEP royalties should be confined only to the value of the technology itself before it was included in a standard (point iii). Those that see patent holdup and royalty stacking as prevailing problems in the ICT industry advocate that FRAND royalties should be capped at the value of the technology itself before it was included in a standard. Others question whether this approach secures appropriate returns to SEP holders and incentives to innovate. The following section will compare and contrast competing notions of the SEP value and suggest some guiding principles for the interpretation of FRAND royalties.

[3] US Patent Act 35 USC 284; see *Microsoft v Motorola*, 2013 WL 2111217 (WD Wash 2013); *In re Innovatio IP Ventures*, 2013 WL 5593609 (ND Ill 2013).

[4] J Contreras et al, 'The Effect of FRAND Commitments on Patent Remedies' in B Biddle et al (eds), *Patent Remedies and Complex Products* (Cambridge University Press, 2019) 167.

A. The Value of the Technology Itself (the Ex Ante Incremental Value Approach)

As a remedy to perceived patent holdup and royalty stacking, it is suggested that SEP royalties should be based on the value of the technology itself, without any additional value created by the standardisation. The method for arriving at such value is the use of the ex ante incremental value of the patent as compared with the next best alternative at the time the standard is set.[5]

The premises of the ex ante incremental value approach lie in the following scenario: during standard's development, different patented and unpatented technologies compete for the inclusion in a standard.[6] At that stage, the patent holder would only be able to charge an incremental value of its technology over the next best alternative. However, once a patented technology is chosen to be a part of the standard, other alternative technologies are eliminated. At that stage, the patent holder would allegedly be able to capture not only the incremental value of its technology over the next best alternative but also the full value of the standard, even though its technology makes only a modest contribution, as well as implementers' switching costs. Accordingly, it is alleged that the patent holder should not be able to capture this additional 'holdup' value.[7] Instead, the patent owners should be compensated only for the value of their technology before it was included in a standard.

[5] For supporters of this approach, see generally: D Swanson and W Baumol, 'Reasonable and Non-discriminatory (RAND) Royalties, Standards Selection, and Control of Market Power' (2005) 73 *Antitrust Law Journal* 1; M Lemley and C Shapiro, 'Patent Holdup and Royalty Stacking' (2007) 85 *Texas Law Review* 1991, 2040–43; J Farrell et al, 'Standard Setting, Patents and Hold-up' (2007) 74 *Antitrust Law Journal* 603, 637; D Lichtman, 'Understanding the RAND Commitment' (2010) 47 *Houston Law Review* 1023; C Cary et al, 'The Case for Antitrust to Police the Patent Holdup Problem in Standard Setting' (2011) 77 *Antitrust Law Journal* 913; S Michel, 'Bargaining for RAND Royalties in the Shadow of Patent Remedies Law' (2011) 77 *Antitrust Law Journal* 889; Federal Trade Commission (FTC), 'The Evolving IP Marketplace: Aligning Patent Notice and Remedies with Competition' (2011) 22–23; D Carlton and A Shampine, 'An Economic Interpretation of FRAND' (2013) 9 *Journal of Competition Law & Economics* 531, 545; M Lemley and C Shapiro, 'A Simple Approach to Setting Reasonable Royalties for Standard Essential Patents' (2013) 28 *Berkeley Technology Law Journal* 1135, 1147–48; J Ordover and A Shampine, 'Implementing the FRAND Commitment' (2014) 10 *Antitrust Source* 1; F Scot Morton and C Shapiro, 'Strategic Patent Acquisitions' (2014) 79 *Antitrust Law Journal* 463; G Leonard and M Lopez, 'Determining RAND Royalty Rates for Standard-Essential Patents' (2014) 29 *Antitrust* 86; J Contreras and R Gilbert, 'A Unified Framework for RAND and Other Reasonable Royalties' (2015) 30 *Berkeley Technology Law Review* 1451; W Lee and D Melamed, 'Breaking the Vicious Cycle of Patent Damages' (2016) 101 *Cornell Law Review* 385; R Grasso, 'Standard Essential Patents: Royalty Determination in the Supply Chain' (2017) 8 *Journal of European Competition Law & Practice* 283; T Cotter et al, 'Reasonable Royalties' in B Biddle et al (eds), *Patent Remedies and Complex Products* (Cambridge University Press, 2019).

[6] FTC (n 5) 192; Carlton and Shampine (n 5) 536–38.

[7] FTC (n 5) 192. But see T Cotter, E Hovenkamp and N Siebrasse, 'Demystifying Patent Holdup' (2019) 76 *Washington & Lee Law Review* 1501 (arguing that holdup royalty consists of sunk costs plus the opportunity cost of not having chosen the non-infringing alternative ex ante).

A typical example is a scenario where two alternative technologies compete for the inclusion in a standard, technology A with the value of $50 and technology B with the value of $40.[8] The incremental value between technology A over B is $10, which is then assumed to be the maximum amount the user would be willing to pay for technology A. If the holder of technology A demands royalty that is too high, the SDO would presumably adopt the alternative technology B for a lower price.

Further support for the application of the ex ante incremental value is found in the US patent damages laws. The US Patent Act provides that upon finding of patent infringement the court shall 'award damages adequate to compensate for the infringement but in no event less than a reasonable royalty'.[9] Reasonable royalties, on the other hand, are determined in accordance with 15 non-exhaustive factors set out in the *Georgia-Pacific Corp v US Plywood Corp* case.[10] In particular, Factor 9 requires comparing the 'utility and advantages of the

[8] Farrell et al (n 5) 612.

[9] US Patent Act 35 USC 284.

[10] *Georgia-Pacific Corp v US Plywood Corp*, 318 F. Supp. 1116, 1120 (SDNY 1970), modified and af'd 446 F.2d 295 (2nd Cir 1971) The *Georgia-Pacific* factors are the following:

'1. The royalties received by the patentee for the licensing of the patent in suit, proving or tending to prove an established royalty.
2. The rates paid by the licensee for the use of other patents comparable to the patent in suit.
3. The nature and scope of the license, as exclusive or non-exclusive; or as restricted or non-restricted in terms of territory or with respect to whom the manufactured product may be sold.
4. The licensor's established policy and marketing program to maintain his patent monopoly by not licensing others to use the invention or by granting licenses under special conditions designed to preserve that monopoly.
5. The commercial relationship between the licensor and licensee, such as, whether they are competitors in the same territory in the same line of business; or whether they are inventor and promotor.
6. The effect of selling the patented specialty in promoting sales of other products of the licensee; the existing value of the invention to the licensor as a generator of sales of his non-patented items; and the extent of such derivative or convoyed sales.
7. The duration of the patent and the term of the license.
8. The established profitability of the product made under the patent; its commercial success; and its current popularity.
9. The utility and advantages of the patent property over the old modes or devices, if any, that had been used for working out similar results.
10. The nature of the patented invention; the character of the commercial embodiment of it as owned and produced by the licensor; and the benefits to those who have used the invention.
11. The extent to which the infringer has made use of the invention; and any evidence probative of the value of that use.
12. The portion of the profit or of the selling price that may be customary in the particular business or in comparable businesses to allow for the use of the invention or analogous inventions.
13. The portion of the realizable profit that should be credited to the invention as distinguished from non-patented elements, the manufacturing process, business risks, or significant features or improvements added by the infringer.
14. The opinion testimony of qualified experts.

patent property over the old modes or devices, if any, that had been used for working out similar results' while Factor 15 provides that the reasonable royalty should take into account 'the amount that a licensor and a licensee would have agreed upon at the time the infringement began if both had been reasonably and voluntarily trying to reach an agreement'. These two factors have been interpreted as supporting the ex ante incremental value approach. Namely, what a willing licensor and willing licensee would normally agree at the time before the infringement is said to be capped at the incremental value of the patented technology over the next best alternative,[11] the maximum that a willing licensee would accept.[12] Consequently, the *Georgia-Pacific* factors from the US patent damages law provided a legal basis for the introduction of the ex ante incremental value approach in FRAND royalty determinations, at least in the US.

The main principle behind the ex ante incremental value approach is to confer all the value of the standardisation to standard implementers. The only reward for SEP holders would be the increase in the volume of royalty-bearing sales of standard implementing products.[13] These new licensing opportunities are said to be sufficient reward for the SEP holder for developing the technology chosen for inclusion in the standard.[14] Any other value apart from the ex ante value is labelled as a 'holdup value', and the FRAND commitment is interpreted as preventing the SEP holders from capturing this value.[15] In the words of Professor Carlton and Professor Shampine:

> A 'reasonable' royalty paid by a firm in the context of FRAND and an SSO is a royalty that does not include any hold-up value: the royalty that would have been negotiated ex ante, before the patented technology at issue had been adopted into the standard and prior to the licensee incurring sunk costs. The maximum royalty ex ante is based on the incremental value that the technology brings to the licensee compared with the next-best alternative available.[16]

> 15. The amount that a licensor (such as the patentee) and a licensee (such as the infringer) would have agreed upon (at the time the infringement began) if both had been reasonably and voluntarily trying to reach an agreement; that is, the amount which a prudent licensee who desired, as a business proposition, to obtain a license to manufacture and sell a particular article embodying the patented invention would have been willing to pay as a royalty and yet be able to make a reasonable profit and which amount would have been acceptable by a prudent patentee who was willing to grant a license'.

[11] FTC (n 5) 185–87.

[12] ibid.

[13] D Melamed and C Shapiro, 'How Antitrust Law Can Make FRAND Commitments More Effective' (2018) 127 *Yale Law Journal* 2110, 2118.

[14] ibid.

[15] FTC (n 5) 192 ('Were patentees able to obtain the hold-up value, this overcompensation could raise prices for consumers while undermining efficient choices made among technologies competing for inclusion in a standard'); Melamed and Shapiro (n 13) 2118 ('Ex ante value reflects what the SEP holder would have been paid by implementers of the standard in an ex ante bargain, and is the proper measure of the market value of the SEPs.').

[16] Carlton and Shampine (n 5) 545.

i. Reception in Practice

The ex ante incremental value approach to evaluating SEPs has been very influential. It has been accepted by US courts and principally endorsed by the US and EU competition authorities. For instance, in a dispute between Apple and Motorola, Judge Posner held that as a matter of principle 'the purpose of the FRAND requirements … is to confine the patentee's royalty demand to the value conferred by the patent itself as distinct from the additional value – the hold-up value – conferred by the patent's being designated as standard-essential'.[17] In *Microsoft v Motorola*, Judge Robart held that 'from an economic perspective, a RAND commitment should be interpreted to limit a patent holder to a reasonable royalty on the economic value of its patented technology itself, apart from the value associated with incorporation of the patented technology into the standard',[18] and that 'the parties to a hypothetical negotiation under a RAND commitment would consider alternatives that could have been written into the standard instead of the patented technology. The focus is on the period before the standard was adopted and implemented (ie, *ex ante*)'.[19] Judge Robart also held that 'rewarding the SEP owner with any of the value of the standard itself would constitute hold-up value and be contrary to the purpose behind the RAND commitment'.[20] In the same vein, Judge Holderman in *Innovatio* noted that 'the court's RAND rate, therefore, must, to the extent possible, reflect only the value of the underlying technology and not the hold-up value of standardization'.[21] The US Federal Circuit in *Ericsson v D-Link*,[22] and *CSIRO v Cisco*[23] also appears to have endorsed the principle that a FRAND royalty rate must be based 'on the value of the invention, not any value added by the standardization of that invention'.[24] In other words, according to the Federal Circuit, 'any royalty award must be based on the incremental value of the invention, not the value of the standard as a whole or any increased value the patented feature gains from its inclusion in the standard'.[25] Therefore, as a matter of law, it seems that in the US FRAND royalties must be based on the ex ante incremental value.

[17] *Apple v Motorola*, 869 F.Supp.2d 901, 913 (ND Ill 2012).

[18] *Microsoft v Motorola* (n 3) 74.

[19] ibid, 106.

[20] ibid, 109.

[21] *In re Innovatio IP Ventures* (n 3) 9.

[22] *Ericsson v D-Link* 773 F.3d 1201 (Fed Cir 2014).

[23] *CSIRO v Cisco*, 2015 WL 7783669 (Fed Cir 2015).

[24] *Ericsson v D-Link* (n 22) 1235; *CSIRO v Cisco* (Fed Cir 2015) (n 23) 8.

[25] *Ericsson v D-Link* (n 22) 1235; also *CSIRO v Cisco* (Fed Cir 2015) (n 23) 8 ('reasonable royalties for SEPs … must not include any value flowing to the patent from the standard's adoption'). ibid ('the royalty for SEPs should reflect the approximate value of that technological contribution, not the value of its widespread adoption due to standardization. In other words, a royalty award for a SEP must be apportioned to the value of the patented invention (or at least to the approximate value thereof), not the value of the standard as a whole. Therefore, damages awards for SEPs must be premised on methodologies that attempt to capture the asserted patent's value resulting not from the value added by the standard's widespread adoption, but only from the technology's superiority').

The US and EU competition authorities also endorsed the view that FRAND royalties should be based on the value of the technology itself, excluding any value arising out of standardisation. The FTC in the 2011 Evolving IP Marketplace Study held that 'a definition of RAND based on the ex-ante value of the patented technology at the time the standard is set necessary for consumers to benefit from competition among technologies to be incorporated into the standard – competition that the standard-setting process itself otherwise displaces',[26] and recommended to courts to 'cap the royalty at the incremental value of the patented technology over alternatives available at the time the standard was defined'.[27] More recently, the European Commission in its 2017 Communication on Standard Essential Patents recommended that a FRAND royalty for SEPs should primarily 'focus on the technology itself and in principle should not include any element resulting from the decision to include the technology in the standard'.[28] A FRAND royalty should also be 'irrespective of the market success of the product which is unrelated to the patented technology'.[29]

Finally, SDOs themselves may provide a definition of FRAND royalties in their IPR policies. To date, this was only done by one SDO – the IEEE – which in its IPR policy provides that FRAND royalty must exclude the value resulting from the inclusion of the patented technology into the IEEE standard.[30] In other words, FRAND royalties for the IEEE's standards should also be based on the 'value of the technology itself'. Any value arising out of standardisation should presumably go to implementers of the IEEE's standards.

ii. Criticism of the Ex Ante Incremental Value Approach

Despite the wide influence, the ex ante incremental value approach to FRAND royalties is not universally accepted and can be criticised on four major grounds for: (i) misunderstanding the standardisation process and the way standardised technologies are developed; (ii) depreciating the value of SEPs; (iii) not being

[26] FTC (n 5) 194.

[27] ibid.

[28] Commission, 'Setting out the EU Approach to Standard Essential Patents' (Communication) COM(2017) 712 final, 6. However, the EC acknowledged that there might be cases where the technology is developed in order to be a part of the standard and has little market value outside the standard. In such a situation, an alternative evaluation should be considered such as the relative importance of the technology in the standard compared with other contributions. The EC also mentions that FRAND valuation should ensure continued incentives for SEP holders to contribute their best available technology to standards. Thus, the EC appears to have adopted a more nuanced approach.

[29] ibid, 6–7. But the Commission also added an alternative criterion when the technology is developed mainly for the standards and has little market value outside the standards, discussed in section II below.

[30] IEEE-SA, 'Standards Board Bylaws' (n 2) Clause 6.1. Definitions ('Reasonable Rate' shall mean appropriate compensation to the patent holder for the practice of an Essential Patent Claim excluding the value, if any, resulting from the inclusion of that Essential Patent Claim's technology in the IEEE Standard')

used in real-world commercial transactions; and (iv) the impossibility of applying directly in practice.[31] These arguments will be discussed in detail below.

a. Misunderstanding the Standard-Development Process

One of the principal problems with the ex ante incremental value approach is that it adopts a simplified idea of the standardisation process, which does not correspond with the reality of the standard-development process within SDOs. Namely, it is based on the premise that on SDO working group meetings deciding which technology to include in a standard there are ideally two (or more) already fully developed alternative technologies. The SDO's working group then only needs to decide which technology to choose based on the ex ante price. Returning to the example at the beginning of the chapter, if the value of technology A is $50, and the value of the technology B is $40, the incremental value between them is $10 which would represent the maximum amount the user would be willing to pay. The working group would then evaluate different alternative technologies based on their quality and ex ante price.

However, this idealised solution does not resemble the practical realities of the standardisation process within SDOs. As seen in chapter one, section II and section II.C, standard development is a continuous and cooperative process that lasts for years and proceeds in many working group meetings. Technologies are not selected for a standard in a single step, nor in one single meeting. Instead, standard development is a process whereby different technologies at different meetings are discussed, added, changed and later removed as standardisation evolves. Therefore, it may not always be possible to point to an exact working group meeting where it was deliberated which alternative technology to include in a standard. The operationalisation of the ex ante incremental value approach would require going through the minutes of the working group meetings to decipher when exactly deliberations took place and what arguments the working

[31] For literature criticising the ex ante incremental value approach see: R Teffet and H Wellford, 'Questioning the FTC's Incremental Value Test and Claims of Widespread Hold-up in Technology Standards' (2012) 57 *Antitrust Bulletin* 161; R Epstein, F Scott Kieff and D Spulber, 'The FTC, IP, and SSOs: Government Hold-up Replacing Private Coordination' (2012) 8 *Journal of Competition Law & Economics* 1; G Sidak, 'The Meaning of FRAND, Part I: Royalties' (2013) 9 *Journal of Competition Law & Economics* 931; F Scott Kieff and A Layne-Farrar, 'Incentive Effects from Different Approaches to Holdup Mitigation Surrounding Patent Remedies and Standard-Setting Organisations' (2013) 9 *Journal of Competition Law & Economics* 1091; D Geradin, 'The Meaning of "Fair and Reasonable" in the Context of Third-Party Determination of FRAND Terms' (2014) 21 *George Mason Law Review* 919; A Layne-Farrar and G Llobet, 'Moving Beyond Simple Examples: Assessing the Incremental Value Rule Within Standards' (2014) 36 *International Journal of Industrial Organization* 57; D Teece et al, 'Maintaining Ecosystem Innovation by Rewarding Technology Developers: FRAND, Ex Ante Rates and Inherent Value' (2017) Tusher Center for the Management of Intellectual Capital Working Paper Series No 2; A Galetovic and S Haber, 'SEP Royalties: What Theory of Value and Distribution Should Courts Apply?' (2019) Hoover IP2 Working Paper Series 19001.

group members used to adopt one technology over another. The sheer volume of the task weighs negatively on the practicality of applying the ex ante incremental value approach.

The ex ante incremental value approach also wrongly assumes that there are already readily available ('off-the-shelf') technologies and the only task of the working group is to choose between similar alternatives. However, this is often not what happens with standard development in the digital world. As seen, SEPs are developed with the aim of being part of the standard, and technology may not exist independently of the standard-development context.[32] Technology developers invest significant resources into R&D precisely to be part of the standard, and technological solutions are developed and refined in parallel with standard development. Thus, there are often no alternative technologies. Such a situation occurred in *Innovatio*, where Judge Holderman found that there were no feasible alternatives that would provide all the functionalities of Innovatio's patents.[33] Therefore, the ex ante incremental value model accurately describes the standard-setting process in a non-digital context but does not relate to standard development in digital technologies.

Further complications arise if there exist two alternative technologies, but both are patented. Some economics suggest that, if two patented and equally effective alternatives cost the same, patent owners would negotiate the price down to effectively zero because of the desire to have their technology incorporated into the standard.[34] However, no patent holder would realistically accept having its technology used for free or close to nothing. Instead of driving the price down to zero, patent holders have an option to simply decline to include their technology into a standard or seek to establish their own competing proprietary standards.[35]

The ex ante incremental value approach also presumes that there already exists some ex ante price allowing for price comparison. Again, this is usually not the case because SEP licensing occurs ex post, once the standard is adopted and standard-compliant products appear on the market.[36] Because SEP royalties are rarely negotiated ex ante, there are no ex ante rates to compare. Using the ex ante incremental approach would require guesswork and estimating what the ex ante price would be without having any real-world market evidence to rely on. This makes the application of the ex ante incremental value approach unreliable.

[32] Sidak, 'The Meaning of FRAND, Part I: Royalties' (n 31) 932.

[33] *In re Innovatio IP Ventures* (n 3).

[34] See Swanson and Baumol (n 5) 18–19; A Layne-Farrar, J Padilla and R Schmalensee, 'Pricing Patents for Licensing in Standard-Setting Organizations: Making Sense of FRAND Commitments' (2007) 74 *Antitrust Law Journal* 671; Carlton and Shampine (n 5) 539.

[35] See A Layne-Farrar, G Llobet and J Padilla, 'Payments and Participation: The Incentives to Joint Cooperative Standard Setting Efforts' (2014) 23 *Journal of Economics & Management Strategy* 24; Scott Kieff and Layne-Farrar (n 31) ('the incremental value rule would likely cause unintended harmful effects, such as reduced SSO participation and sub optimal investment in innovation').

[36] Teece et al (n 31) 21.

b. Depreciating the Value of SEPs

The ex ante incremental value approach may seriously depreciate the value of SEPs and reduce innovation incentives. Some technologies may make a significant contribution to the standard, but their incremental value may be small. For instance, Teece, Grindley, Sherry and Mallinson provide examples of two very useful and costly to develop technologies, the incremental value between them may be small, but the contribution of either to the total value of the product may be significant.[37] Under the ex ante incremental value approach, the royalty rate should be determined by this small increment. However, the contribution of the technology to the standard and to products implementing the standard is large. Thus, the ex ante incremental value approach would fail to properly recognise the contribution of the technology to the full value of the standard and its importance to downstream products.[38]

Other factors could also undervalue SEPs. It is difficult to presume that there exists one unique number that is the incremental value of the patent.[39] Different parties value patented technology differently, some prefer technology A, some technology B, while others prefer technology C. Searching for the subjective ex ante price might either over-appreciate or depreciate SEPs depending on the use of individual licensees. It was also suggested that SEPs have a 'combinatorial value',[40] or can be characterised as 'innovative complements',[41] meaning they have value only when used in combination with all other patents essential for a standard.

[37] ibid, 13.

[38] Teece provides further good examples on how the application of ex ante incremental value in practice would not properly reflect the value of patented technology, see D Teece, 'Patent Counting and the "Top-Down" Approach to Patent Valuations: An Economic and Public Policy Appraisal of Reasonable Royalties' (2020) 5 *Criterion Journal on Innovation* 157, 176. ('Suppose that there is a freely available public domain technology (call it *PD*) that enables firms to make some good at a cost of $100 per unit. Suppose that there is a patented alternative technology (call it *P*) that enables firms to make the same good at a cost of $80 per unit. Then the incremental value of the patented technology relative to the public domain technology is $20 per unit. Now suppose that there is a second patented alternative technology (call it Q) that enables firms to make the same good at a cost of $78 per unit. In this example, the incremental value of Q relative to the public domain technology PD is $22 per unit. But the incremental value of Q relative to P is only $2 per unit. Unless one believes that the royalty for P will be $0, there is no reason to believe that the royalty for two will be driven down to $2 per unit … Now consider a different example in which both P and Q lower the cost of making the given good to $78 per unit. Now the incremental value of each relative to the public domain technology is $22 per unit, but the incremental value of each patented technology relative to the other patented technology is $0. Suggesting that the royalty rates for both P and Q "should" be $0 because the incremental value of each patented technology relative to the other is $0 allows no return to the innovation, despite the fact that both innovations yield considerable value (of $22 per unit) relative to the public domain technology.')

[39] Epstein, Scott Kieff and Spulber (n 31) 37.

[40] Sidak, 'The Meaning of FRAND, Part I: Royalties' (n 31) 932.

[41] D Spulber, 'Finding Reasonable Royalty Damages: A Contract Approach to Patent Infringement' (2019) 2 *University of Illinois Law Review* 616, 688.

If a patent is truly essential from making downstream products, then 'it logically follows that patent does not have a substitute or a non-infringing substitute',[42] and all SEPs must be used in the fixed proportion in order to implement a standard.[43] Thus the ex ante incremental value approach may only be applicable to non-SEPs,[44] but would not be appropriate for valuating SEP.

Finally, basing the value of SEPs at the moment of technology's inclusion in a standard may create a disbalance between parties.[45] The implementer at that point has not yet sunk any costs in developing standard-implementing products, but the patent holder has already sunk significant R&D costs in developing patented technology. In order to truly restore the balance between the parties, it was suggested that the moment of the hypothetical negotiation between the parties should be pushed further back in time, to the moment when the patent holder decides whether to monetise its invention through a standard developed by the SDO, rather than a proprietary standard outside the SDO or some other business strategy.[46] At that earlier moment, neither party is subject to lock-in or holdup.

c. Not Used in Real-World Commercial Transactions

Perhaps the most significant deficiency of the ex ante incremental value approach is that it is not used in real-world licensing negotiations.[47] Actual licences are the result of bilateral negotiations between SEP holders and implementers, normally ex post after the standard has been adopted and standard implementing products appeared on the market. When negotiating for a licence, parties take into account a number of market factors: they consider the scope of patents; their claims; whether the declared SEPs are actually essential; the validity and infringement of SEPs; the success of the standard in the market; the importance of standard to the products in question; the actual volumes and prices of infringing products; the value of mutual cross-licences, etc. Assessing whether the SEP had alternatives at the time it was included in a standard, and if so, comparing the value between the alternatives is not what parties in commercial transactions do.

Consequently, if prices in competitive markets are not formed on the basis of the ex ante incremental value over next best alternatives, it is questionable whether such approach should be artificially imposed on the market by courts or competition authorities.

42 Sidak, 'The Meaning of FRAND, Part I: Royalties' (n 31) 932.
43 ibid.
44 ibid, 933.
45 ibid, 983.
46 ibid; Epstein, Scott Kieff and Spulber (n 31) 10.
47 Teece et al (n 31) 13.

d. Inapplicability in Practice

Finally, from a practical perspective, the ex ante incremental value approach may be excessively difficult if not impossible to apply. It puts courts in the impossible position of double-checking the decisions of engineers working on standard development; evaluating different technological proposals; finding the one which may represent the best alternative; estimating the ex ante price of technologies and making comparisons in order to arrive at an incremental value between alternatives. This is a tremendous task and does not seem to be a practical or realistic option for courts.

Indeed, although US courts have endorsed the principle that FRAND royalties should be based on the value of the technology itself before inclusion in a standard, no court has directly managed to apply the ex ante incremental value approach.[48] In *Microsoft v Motorola*, Judge Robart noted that FRAND royalties should be based on the value of patented technology itself, excluding the value associated with inclusion of the patented technology into the standard,[49] but he rejected the application of the ex ante incremental value method because it 'lacks real-world applicability'.[50] In his words:

> [I]n practice, approaches linking the value of a patent to its incremental contribution to a standard are hard to implement. Calculating the incremental value for multi-patent standards gets very complicated because when you take one patent out of a standard and put another one in you may make other changes, the performance of the standard is multidimensional, different people value different aspects.[51]

Instead, Judge Robart based his FRAND royalty determination primarily on comparable licences and patent pool royalties, and the assessment of the importance of SEPs to the standard and to standard-implementing products.[52]

In *Innovatio*, Judge Holderman similarly held that the FRAND rate must reflect only 'the value of the underlying technology and not the hold-up value of standardization'.[53] He also considered applying the ex ante incremental value method and was faced with two preliminary issues. The first was whether patent holders would negotiate the price down to effectively zero if there existed equally effective patented alternatives.[54] Judge Holderman disagreed and correctly

[48] Galetovic and S Haber (n 31) 36 ('it is an irony that while the logic underpinning the [ex ante incremental value] approach has been widely embraced by competition authorities, the technique itself has never actually been applied').

[49] *Microsoft v Motorola* (n 3) 74.

[50] ibid, 77.

[51] ibid, 79.

[52] ibid, 113.

[53] *In re Innovatio IP Ventures* (n 3) 9.

[54] ibid, 20.

held that it is 'implausible that in the real world, patent holders would accept effectively nothing to license their technology'.[55] He recognised that

> even assuming that patent holders agreed to essentially give away their technology so that it will be adopted into the standard, such a low return for the patent holders would discourage future innovators from investing in new technology and from contributing their technology to future standards.[56]

The next issue was what alternatives to take into account – whether to focus only on alternatives that were presented at an SDO's working group meetings or whether all possible publicly known alternative technologies should also be considered.[57] Judge Holderman decided to focus only on technologies that were presented and deliberated by the SDO. In his words:

> [R]ather than second guessing the technical expertise of the many engineers and technicians who participated in the development of the 802.11 standard, the court will assume that technology that did not even merit a mention by the IEEE in its deliberations about the standard was not likely to have been a serious contender for adoption into the standard.[58]

Such an approach is correct, as expanding the enquiry to all possible alternatives that were not even considered by the SDO would unduly complicate already difficult assessment. In the end, Judge Holderman found that there were no alternatives at the time of standardisation that would have provided all the functionalities of Innovatio's patents. Therefore, the ex ante incremental value method was not used for determining FRAND royalties.

In *TCL v Ericsson*, Judge Selna was also sceptical about the applicability of the ex ante incremental value approach.[59] Comparing alternatives would require assessing whether they are mutually consistent with each other, what would be their performance on the standard, and whether they would be able to create a viable, functioning standard.[60] Indeed, all these decisions are better left to engineers. Courts are inadequate places for second-guessing decisions made by qualified technical experts. While the judge endorsed the principle that a FRAND royalty should be 'based on the incremental value that the patented invention adds to the product, not any value added by the standardisation of that technology',[61] he did not apply the ex ante incremental value approach but relied on comparable licences and the top-down methods discussed below.

[55] ibid.
[56] ibid.
[57] ibid.
[58] ibid.
[59] *TCL v Ericsson*, 2017 WL 6611635 (CD Cal 2017).
[60] ibid, 42.
[61] ibid, 108.

The US Federal Circuit, in *Ericsson v D-Link*[62] and *CSIRO v Cisco*[63] also held that the FRAND royalty rate must be based 'on the value of the invention, not any value added by the standardization of that invention',[64] and that 'any royalty award must be based on the incremental value of the invention, not the value of the standard as a whole or any increased value the patented feature gains from its inclusion in the standard'.[65] However, the Federal Circuit did not explain the precise method to be used to arrive at such value, nor what should happen if it were not possible to apply the ex ante incremental value approach.

Finally, from a legal perspective, it is unclear whether the *Georgia-Pacific* criteria in the US requires the use of the ex ante incremental value. Factor 9 requires comparison of 'the utility and advantages of the patent property over the old modes or devices, if any, that had been used for working out similar results', but the technologies here are not old versus new models. Instead, they are existing at the same time and competing to be a part of the standard, which is different than Factor 9 suggests. Moreover, Factor 15 providing that the reasonable royalty should take into account 'the amount that a licensor and a licensee would have agreed upon at the time the infringement began if both had been reasonably and voluntarily trying to reach an agreement' also does not lend unquestionable support to the ex ante incremental value approach. As seen, the real-world willing licensor and willing licensee do not use the ex ante incremental value approach in their royalty negotiations. Interpreting Factor 15 of the *Georgia-Pacific* criteria as mandating the use of the ex ante incremental value method in hypothetical negotiations between a willing licensor and a willing licensee, does not have a basis in commercial reality. Consequently, a careful reading of the *Georgia-Pacific* criteria does not appear to require an automatic application of the ex ante incremental value approach in calculating reasonable royalty patent damages.

In any event, the *Georgia-Pacific* criteria for determining reasonable royalties in patent damages should not be relied on for determining FRAND royalties. As explained in the introduction of this chapter, they are conceptually two different notions. *Georgia-Pacific* criteria originate from patent damages law, while FRAND royalties are contractual commitments of the SEP owner given to the SDO, and no SDO points to the use of *Georgia-Pacific* criteria or any other national patent damages laws for determining FRAND royalties. Patent damages law comes to play only after the patent has been litigated to be valid and infringed, while when determining FRAND royalties courts are asked to interpret incomplete contractual terms. The only similarity is that they both use the term 'reasonable', which appears to have led US courts to invoke their patent damages case law on reasonable royalties and *Georgia-Pacific* factors.[66] Outside the US, courts have not relied

[62] *Ericsson v D-Link* (n 22).
[63] *CSIRO v Cisco* (Fed Cir 2015) (n 23).
[64] *Ericsson v D-Link* (n 22) 1235; *CSIRO v Cisco* (Fed Cir 2015) (n 23) 8.
[65] *Ericsson v D-Link* (n 22) 1235.
[66] See Contreras et al (n 4) 167.

on national patent damages laws and have considered more practical ways of calculating FRAND royalties.[67]

Therefore, although considered by US courts the ex ante incremental value approach was ultimately not applied due to insurmountable practical difficulties. If parties in real-world commercial licensing negotiations never use the ex ante incremental value calculations and courts were never able to apply it in practice, a question could rightly be raised as to why we keep on insisting on it. A conclusion could correctly be borrowed from Epstein, Kieff and Spulber: 'although the whole concept of "incremental value" is a useful intellectual construct when describing purchaser conduct in simplified academic models, the complexity of the real world makes it essentially useless as a tool for prescribing pricing'.[68]

B. Sharing the Value of Standardisation

A different approach to conceptualising FRAND royalties is to share the value of standardisation between SEP owners and users, but exclude the sunk cost value of implementers.[69] The value of standardisation, explained by Sidak, consists of two elements: (i) transaction costs savings for implementers of the standard and for SEP holders; and (ii) the network effects generated by interoperability between standard-compliant products.[70] SEP holders help create the value of standardisation by contributing their best available technologies into a standard. It is difficult to justify the denial to SEP holders of any portion of the value of the standard they helped create and to accrue all the benefits of standardisation to standard

[67] ibid; also discussion in section II below.

[68] Epstein, Scott Kieff and Spulber (n 31) 37.

[69] There is a relatively small but growing literature which argues that SEP holders should enjoy some value created by standardisation. See G Sidak, 'The Value of Standard vs the Value of Standardisation' (2016) 68 *Baylor Law Review* 59; N Siebrasse and T Cotter, 'The Value of The Standard' (2017) 101 *Minnesota Law Review* 1159 (distinguishing between, 'sunk costs holdup', 'network value appropriation' and 'apportionment', and arguing that SEP holders should capture some part of the network value appropriation that arises out of network effects created by the standard, but should not capture the implementer's sunk costs nor the value of other SEPs in a standard); Teece et al (n 31) (arguing that SEP holders should capture some value created by standardisation); CEN-CENELEC, Principles and Guidance for Licensing Standard Essential Patents in 5G and the Internet of Things (IoT), Including the Industrial Internet' (June 2019 7, available at: www.cencenelec.eu/news/workshops/pages/ws-2019-013.aspx ('Fair and reasonable' compensation should be based upon the value of the patented standardised technology to its users'); P Picht, 'FRAND Determination in *TCL v Ericsson* and *Unwired Planet v Huawei*: Same but Different? (2018) Max Planck Institute for Innovation and Competition Research Paper No 18-07, 37 ('distributing the added value seems, prima facie, fair and we cannot tell, by way of a generally applicable formula, how the distribution should be made. But there is no reason a SEP holder, of all parties involved, should receive nothing of the *added* value'); B Neurohr, 'Dynamically Efficient Royalties for Standard-Essential Patents' (2020) 16 *Journal of Competition Law & Economics* 298; but see: R Stern, 'Who Should Own the Benefits of Standardization and the Value it Creates?' (2018) 19 *Minnesota Journal of Law, Science & Technology* 108 (arguing that the benefits of standardisation should flow to consumers).

[70] Sidak, 'The Value of Standard vs the Value of Standardisation' (n 69).

implementers. Otherwise, there would be little incentive to continue contributing best technologies to collaborative standardisation.[71]

A FRAND royalty could then be conceptualised along the following lines:

1. It should exclude any 'sunk cost value' of standard implementers, by setting the level of royalties before implementers have started manufacturing standardised products (preventing patent holdup and promoting widespread access to the standard).
2. it should fairly share the 'value of standardisation' between SEP holders and standard implementers (securing incentives to innovate).
3. It should be proportionate in relation to the contribution of the patented technology to the standard and be proportionate to the overall royalty for the standard (preventing royalty stacking and apportionment to the value of the SEP in question).

The benefits of this approach are securing the incentives to innovate by technology developers and, at the same time, ensuring that standard implementers are protected from negative holdup and royalty stacking effects.

However, this approach is not without criticism. Melamed and Shapiro argue that technology developers make 'speculative investments' and bear the risk that their technology will not be successfully adopted in the market or be sufficiently compensated.[72] They claim that the situation facing a technology developer seeking to license its intellectual property is no different from anyone else making a speculative investment, 'whether in technology, real estate, corporate securities, or any other industry'.[73] They conclude that 'requiring that buyers guarantee an adequate return to those who make speculative investments would be antithetical to the operation of the market system and would badly distort investment incentives'.[74] However, they appear to misunderstand the nature of collaborative standardisation. Rather than making speculative investments, technology developers are collaborating with manufacturers within SDOs to create successful and widely implemented standards. The success of the standard does not depend only on implementers; both SEP owners and implementers cooperate in the standard-development process to create and adopt technologies that would solve technical problems and create opportunities for successful downstream innovation. While their argument may hold true for non-SEPs, it does not adequately describe the standard-development process in digital markets.

Another argument is that SEP holders would be appropriately compensated by the increase in royalty-bearing sales of standardised products, even if royalties are based on the value of the technology itself (ex ante incremental value).[75] However, if

[71] G Sidak 'Apportionment, FRAND Royalties and Comparable Licenses after *Ericsson v D-Link*' (2016) 4 *University of Illinois Law Review* 1811, 1864–67; Layne-Farrar, Llobet and Padilla (n 35).

[72] Melamed and Shapiro (n 13) 2119.

[73] ibid.

[74] ibid.

[75] ibid, 2134.

rates are too low no amount of higher volumes of royalty-bearing sales can adequately compensate SEP holders to the level which incentivises further R&D. Both rates and volumes should be taken into account. This view also conflates the notions of sunk cost value with the value of standardisation. The value of standardisation can properly be shared only through an appropriate royalty rate; relying only on increased volumes with low rates would accrue all the benefits of standardisation to implementers.

It appears that at least one court recognised the distinction between the 'sunk costs value' and the 'value of standardisation'. In *Unwired Planet v Huawei* in the UK, Mr Justice Birss correctly interpreted the FRAND commitment as inconsistent with capturing an implementer's sunk costs. The question was then whether, as a matter of principle, the SEP holder should enjoy some value created by the inclusion of its technology into the standard. Mr Justice Birss answered in the affirmative. In his words:

> When talking about FRAND economists refer to the idea that the FRAND rate represents the rate which would be agreed 'ex ante', in other words before the patented invention is adopted into the standard. This is another way of saying that the rate seeks to eliminate hold up and to that extent is uncontroversial. In the concurrent evidence session Prof Neven explained that he did not regard FRAND as a scheme which meant the patentee could not appropriate some of the value that is associated with the inclusion of his technology into the standard and the value of the products that are using those standards … Neither side disputed this and to the extent it is a matter for the economists, I accept their evidence. The economists' opinions show that it is not necessary to deprive the patentee of its fair share of those two sources of value in order to eliminate hold up and fulfil the purpose of FRAND. To that extent I may be differing from certain parts of the decisions in *Innovatio IP Ventures* and *Ericsson v D-Link* in the US but it is not necessary to look into that any further since neither side before me took the point.[76]

The European Commission also cautiously accepted that basing royalties on the value of the technology itself may not be possible in all SEP cases. A 2017 Communication on Standard Essential Patents provided that certain licensing principles should be taken into account when valuating SEPs. The first principle is that the value of SEPs should be based on the technology itself and should not include value arising from the decision to include the technology in the standard.[77] However, it then added an alternative criterion in cases where the technology is developed for the standard and has little market value outside the standard that

[76] *Unwired Planet v Huawei* [2017] EWHC 2988 (Pat) para 97.

[77] Commission, 'Setting Out the EU Approach to Standard Essential Patents' (n 28) 6–7 (the full text is as follows: 'licensing terms have to bear a clear relationship to the economic value of the patented technology. That value primarily needs to focus on the technology itself and in principle should not include any element resulting from the decision to include the technology in the standard. In cases where the technology is developed mainly for the standard and has little market value outside the standard, alternative evaluation, such as the relative importance of the technology in the standard compared to other contributions in the standard, should be considered').

other valuation methods could be used, such as the relative importance of the technology in the standard compared with other contributions in the standard. The second principle is that FRAND value should take into account the present added value of the patented technology which, as will be explained in section II.C below, requires looking at market-based evidence of income generated by such technology. Thus, the European Commission seems to cautiously acknowledge that the benefits of standardisation should be shared between technology developers and standard-implementers and that FRAND royalty determinations should be based on market evidence.

Nevertheless, the main shortcoming of the sharing the value of standardisation approach, like the ex ante incremental value method, is that it would be difficult to directly implement in practice and, importantly, it is also not used in real-world licensing negotiations. As most idealised theoretical models its practical application is challenging, if not impossible. Nevertheless, the approach is still useful because it appropriately takes into account the nature of a standard's development, protects the interests of both technology developers and standard implementers, and may thus serve as a useful benchmark to more practical royalty calculation models. With this in mind, we may focus less on idealised theoretical concepts and place more attention on practical models that help parties and courts reach an understanding on FRAND royalties. The next section therefore explains the methods courts use in determining FRAND royalties.

II. Calculating FRAND Royalties in Practice

As a preliminary matter, patent royalties in licensing agreements can be structured in several ways: (i) by agreeing on a lump-sum payment; (ii) by identifying a unit and calculating royalties as a dollar (or any other currency figure) per unit (unit-based royalties); or (iii) by identifying a base product and calculating royalties as a percentage of the revenue obtained from the sale of such product or percentage of the sales price of such product (running royalties). There is no precise rule which royalty structure is FRAND or not and in practice all three methods are used, either individually or in combination.

There are two broad approaches to calculating FRAND royalties in practice: (i) a 'bottom-up' approach, which determines the value of SEPs based on comparable licences or other market-based comparators, but without taking into account overall royalty for a standard; and (ii) a 'top-down' approach, which first seeks to establish the overall royalty for a standard and then calculates a share to an individual SEP.[78] These approaches are not necessarily mutually exclusive. As will be

[78] For an overview of these approaches, see Japan Patent Office, 'Guide to Licensing Negotiations Involving Standard Essential Patents' (5 June 2018), available at: www.jpo.go.jp/e/support/general/sep_portal/document/index/guide-seps-en.pdf.

seen, courts in the UK and the US have applied a combination of both approaches to arrive at a FRAND royalty rate.[79] This chapter will compare and contrast these approaches, highlight their merits and deficiencies, and suggest avenues for improvements.

A. Comparable Licences

A way for determining FRAND royalties is to look at the actual royalty rates agreed in the marketplace between parties in bilateral negotiations. This is done by analysing comparable prior licences for the SEPs in question. The use of comparable licences is often taken as the best evidence of the value of SEPs,[80] and a royalty that is voluntarily agreed by the parties is naturally said to be fair and reasonable.[81] Indeed, comparable licences provide real-world evidence on how commercial companies evaluate standardised technology. Recognising this fact, US courts have held that 'an established royalty is usually the best measure of a "reasonable" royalty for a given use of an invention'.[82]

However, the reliance on comparable licences has been criticised both on theoretical grounds, whether they accurately reflect the value of the technology, and on their practical usability. According to some authors, prior licences should be disregarded from the royalty analysis because they tend to overcompensate patent holders.[83] Lee and Melamed claim that because licences are generally concluded ex post, after implementers have started practising the standard, they may reflect implementers' switching costs and the costs of avoiding litigation, not

[79] *Unwired Planet v Huawei* (n 76) (applying comparable licences, but then using a top-down approach as a cross-check); and *TCL v Ericsson* (CD Cal 2017) (n 59) (applying a top-down approach, but then analysing comparable licences as a cross-check).

[80] See D Geradin and M Rato, 'Can Standard-Setting Lead to Exploitative Abuse? A Dissonant View on Patent Holdup, Royalty Stacking and the Meaning of FRAND' (2007) 3 *European Competition Journal* 101, 156 ('The existence of licensing agreements entered into following arm's-length negotiations between IPR holder and licensee is arguably the best indicator of a reasonable royalty rate'); R Brooks and D Geradin, 'Interpreting and Enforcing the Voluntary FRAND Commitment' (2011) 9 *International Journal of IT Standards and Standardization Research* 1, 12 ('royalties received under prior and existing licences for the very patents being litigated often represent the most influential factor in determining "reasonableness" under the *Georgia-Pacific* framework, and should arguably have the same role in the context of FRAND litigation'); Sidak, 'The Meaning of FRAND, Part I: Royalties' (n 31) 1000; A Layne-Farrar and K Wong-Ervin, 'Methodologies for Calculating FRAND Damages: An Economic and Comparative Analysis of the Case Law from China, the European Union, India, and the United States' (2017) 8 *Jindal Global Law Review* 127, 150; Spulber (n 41).

[81] Sidak, 'The Meaning of FRAND, Part I: Royalties' (n 31).

[82] *Monsanto Co v McFarling*, 488 F.3d 973, 978 (Fed Cir 2007).

[83] Lemley and Shapiro, 'Patent Holdup and Royalty Stacking' (n 5) 2022; Lee and Melamed (n 5); J Masur, 'The Use and Misuse of Patent Licenses' (2015) 110 *Northwestern University Law Review* 115; C Pentheroudakis and J Baron, 'Licensing Terms of Standard Essential Patents: A Comprehensive Analysis of Cases' (2017) (Joint Research Centre, Science for Policy Report, EUR 28302) 149–50, available at: publications.jrc.ec.europa.eu/repository/handle/JRC104068.

necessarily only the value of the technology. Patent licensing rates, at least in the US, are supposedly inflated due to a 'vicious cycle', where courts tend to award higher royalties based, in part, on ex post licensing agreements.[84] Higher litigation damages then result in higher licensing royalties, since patent licences are negotiated under a shadow of litigation and the more a patent holder can obtain from litigation the more an infringer has to pay the patent holder to avoid litigation. Licences concluded under a threat of injunction also skew royalties too high. As a result, they suggest that all ex post licences are 'tainted' and should be disregarded from royalty analysis.[85]

On the other hand, others suggest that relying too much on prior licences may in fact undercompensate patent holders.[86] This is the case because licences are typically discounted due to the probability that some patents in a portfolio may not be valid or be infringed. After litigation, however, courts have established the validly and infringement of patents and relying on existing licences for the assessment of damages will lead to double discounting and undervalue the patents in suit.[87] Patent holders in some cases may also conclude licences on unfavourable terms that do not accurately reflect the value of the technology. Such is the case when the patent holder has only limited resources to enforce its patent rights and may thus be forced to license under unfavourable terms, or even leave many users unlicensed. A patent holder may also choose to promote early widespread adoption of the technology by offering favourable lower licensing rates.[88] Therefore, using prior licences may not properly reflect the value of the standardised technology, as rates may be under-valued.

On a more practical side, a concrete problem is finding licences that are sufficiently comparable. It is usually difficult to find licences with identical sets of terms. They may differ, for example, in the number of patents (licences may include more or fewer patents for the same standard; may bundle together patents for different standards in one licence or bundle SEPs with non-SEPs); include different

[84] Lee and Melamed (n 5) 388–89; Pentheroudakis and Baron (n 83) 150.

[85] Lee and Melamed (n 5) 419–20; Also: IEEE-SA, 'Standards Board Bylaws' (n 2) Clause 6.1. Definitions: 'Reasonable Rate' (recommendation that reasonable rates should exclude licensing agreements concluded under a threat of injunctions); However, see E Hovenkamp and J Masur, 'How Patent Damages Skew Licensing Markets' (2018) 36 *Review of Litigation* 379 (finding that basing patent damages royalties on prior licences creates inefficient outcomes. It discourages patent holders from licensing at anything less than a high royalty rate, due to the fear that anything less would weaken the patent by limiting its future recovery in litigation. It also disincentivises patent holders to price discriminate. They also show how patent licences may take into account different circumstances, making reliable comparison difficult).

[86] E Elhauge, 'Do Patent Holdup and Royalty Stacking Lead to Systematically Excessive Royalties? (2008) 4 *Journal of Competition Law & Economics* 535 (arguing that reasonable royalty patent damages in the US patent may actually undercompensate patent holders); M Akemann, J Blair and D Teece, 'Patent Enforcement in an Uncertain World: Widespread Infringement and the Paradox of Value for Patented Technologies' (2016) 1 *Criterion Journal on Innovation* 861.

[87] Hovenkamp and Masur (n 85); Cotter et al (n 5) 36–37.

[88] Akemann, Blair and Teece (n 86).

royalty structures (running royalty, per-unit royalty or lump-sum royalty); include different licensing terms (cross-licensing provision between parties, grant-backs, exchange of other considerations such as joint R&D, strategic partnerships or have different rates based on the downstream use of the technology); or be concluded as a part of the settlement of litigation or arbitration (the agreed royalties may include some part of the costs of litigation and the uncertainty about the litigation outcome, as opposed to be purely based on the value of SEPs). Therefore, it may happen that there are simply no licences that are sufficiently comparable. On the other hand, in a case of new technologies that have just been developed, there may be no licences at all as they are yet to be concluded. Another difficulty is the confidentiality of licensing agreements meaning that, apart from the SEP holder's own licences, it may not be possible to obtain licences from other SEP owners to use as a comparator. Therefore, the use of comparable licences in FRAND determination may not always be possible.

Despite these shortcomings, comparable prior licences provide real-world evidence of how parties in commercial transactions value SEPs.[89] Arguments that licences over or undercompensate SEP holders should be taken into account at the stage of assessing their comparability, and not as an argument for outright rejection of their use.[90] For example, if the implementer claims that prior licences contain unreasonably high royalties because they are concluded under the threat of injunction, it should prove how the feasibility of injunction influenced the acceptance of higher royalty rates and why such rates are not FRAND. Conversely, if the patent holder claims that prior licences contained a discount for the early adoption of the technology, it should adduce evidence to that account and then provide the information on the actual royalty level without an early-adoption discount. As to practical differences between licences, these can be overcome by the process of 'unpacking' ie, by using different economic methods of translating all the elements of a licence to arrive at an effective one-way royalty rate paid by the licensee.[91] In case there are no prior or comparable licences, we might try to estimate the market price of the portfolio by looking at its purchase price (if patents have been

[89] Layne-Farrar and Wong-Ervin (n 80) 150; Sidak, 'The Meaning of FRAND, Part I: Royalties' (n 31) 1000 (arguing that ex post licences are the best reliable evidence on FRAND royalties as they represent a voluntary agreement between the parties on what is FRAND. Further, injunctive relief is not a credible threat in the case of SEPs and, even assuming it is, there is no reason to assume that licences negotiated under such threat are not FRAND); C Chien and E Schulman, 'Patent Semi-Comparables' (2018) 25 *Texas Intellectual Property Journal* 215 (arguing that many licences may be useful for comparison although the facts and terms are not identical).

[90] See *Ericsson v D-Link* (n 22) 1227 (holding that while prior licences 'are almost never perfectly analogous' this shortcoming 'generally goes to the weight of the evidence, not admissibility').

[91] *Unwired Planet v Huawei* (n 76) 186–97 (explaining the method of unpacking licences); *TCL v Ericsson* (CD Cal 2017) (n 59) 54, 62–64 (explaining unpacking). See also G Sidak, 'Converting Royalty Payment Structures for Patent Licenses' (2016) 1 *Criterion Journal on Innovation* 901 (explaining different economic methods in translating running royalties, per unit and lump-sum royalties into effective royalty).

previously acquired), the purchase price of other comparable patents, or the value of intangible assets to the company.[92]

Finally, a way for more efficient use of comparable licences might be for SEP holders to make public their effective royalty rates.[93] All things being equal, these rates would apply to every similarly situated licensee. Some SEP owners already publish their rates. For instance, in relation to 5G, Ericsson announced that it would license its 5G SEP portfolio at between $2.5 and 5$ per device,[94] Nokia up to EUR 3 per device,[95] Qualcomm at 3.25 per cent of the end-device price,[96] and Huawei up to $2,5 per handset.[97] Patent pools have also had their rates published. Sisvel licenses its 2G, 3G and 4G SEP portfolio for a fixed-unit fee of between €0.14 and €0.06 depending on the quantity of licensed products,[98] while Via Licensing patent pool charges for its 4G LTE portfolio at between $1 and $2.1.[99] Knowing the starting effective royalty rates may make the comparison between licences significantly easier.[100] During negotiations parties might agree on a different amount, but the difference could then be more easily explained by factors such as the value of cross-licences, the value of other SEPs or non-SEPs, or the value of settling ongoing litigation. The failure of the SEP owner to justify the divergence from the announced rate and the concluded rate would weigh heavily in favour of finding the offer as non-FRAND.

i. Application in Practice

Comparable licences play a large role in FRAND royalty determinations and are the most widely used method by courts, although there are struggles to find

[92] See Spulber (n 41) 656–67.

[93] See R Gilbert, 'Deal or No Deal? Licensing Negotiations in Standard Setting Organizations' (2011) 77 *Antitrust Law Journal* 855, 875 (proposing that SEP owners make publicly available different royalty schedules); see also ch 5 in relation to a non-discrimination obligation.

[94] Ericsson, 'Ericsson's FRAND Licensing Terms for 5G/NR in 3GPP Release 15' (3 March 2017), availableat:www.ericsson.com/assets/local/tech-innovation/patents/doc/frand-licensing-terms-for-5g-nr-in-3gpp-release-15.pdf.

[95] Nokia, 'Nokia Licensing Rate Expectations for 5G NR Mobile Phones' (21 August 2018), available at: www.nokia.com/en_int/news/releases/2018/08/21/nokia-licensing-rate-expectations-for-5gnr-mobile-phones.

[96] Qualcomm, '5G NR Royalty Terms Statement' (19 November 2017), available at: www.qualcomm.com/media/documents/files/qualcomm-5g-nr-royalty-terms-statement.pdf; Qualcomm, 'Examples of Royalties for Mobile Price Points' (1 April 2018), available at: www.qualcomm.com/media/documents/files/examples-of-royalties-for-smartphone-price-points.pdf.

[97] Huawei, 'Huawei Releases White Paper on Innovation and Intellectual Property 2020' (16 March 2021), available at: www.huawei.com/en/news/2021/3/huawei-releases-whitepaper-innovation-intellectual-property-2020.

[98] Sisvel, Wireless Program License Terms, available at: www.sisvel.com/licensing-programs/wireless-communications/wireless/license-terms.

[99] Via Licensing, LTE License Fees, available at: www.via-corp.com/us/en/licensing/lte/licensefees.html.

[100] See Gilbert, 'Deal or No Deal?' (n 93) 875 (proposing that SEP owners make publicly available different royalty schedules).

licences that are sufficiently comparable and difficulties with the application of precise unpacking formulas.

Microsoft v Motorola was the first case where the court was tasked with setting a FRAND royalty between parties.[101] It involved Motorola's portfolio of SEPs for the IEEE's Wi-Fi 802.11 and ITU's H.264 standard. The court first considered and then rejected the application of the ex ante incremental value approach as lacking real-world applicability. Judge Robart then proceeded to determine FRAND royalty by considering comparable licences and the importance of the patent portfolio to the standard and to infringing products.[102] The problem, however, was finding licences that were sufficiently comparable. Judge Robart dismissed Motorola's previous licences as not comparable because they were concluded as a part of the settlement of litigation,[103] had broad cross-licensing provisions,[104] or bundled relevant SEPs together with other standards, and SEPs with non-SEPs.[105] Instead, as a comparable, the court used patent pool royalties holding that 'under certain circumstances, patent pools can serve as indicators of a royalty rate that falls within the range of royalties consistent with the [F]RAND commitment'.[106] As a general matter, Judge Robart agreed that 'patent pools tend to produce lower royalty rates than those that could be achieved through bilateral negotiations'.[107] Another problem is that patent pools implement royalty structure based on patent counting and value all patents equally, which may disincentive patent holders with valuable SEPs to participate in the patent pool. However, in this specific case the court held that patent pool rates serve as good indicators of FRAND royalty rate because Motorola's SEPs were found to have a relatively low value.

Innovatio concerned a portfolio of 19 SEPs for the IEEE's Wi-Fi 802.11 standard.[108] The court there also started first with the ex ante incremental value approach but dismissed it after finding that Innovatio's patents had no viable alternatives. Judge Holderman then turned to prior licences and faced similar problems in finding licences that were sufficiently comparable. Innovatio's SEP acquisition agreement was dismissed because it was not possible to isolate the value of SEPs from the rest of the transaction.[109] Licensing agreements that were concluded as a part of the settlement of litigation were also rejected, holding that they do not represent an accurate market rate because they mainly reflect the desire to settle litigation and are not focused only on the value of SEPs.[110] Finally, one licensing

[101] *Microsoft v Motorola* (n 3).

[102] ibid, paras 110–13.

[103] ibid, 415 and 431 (holding that licensing agreements concluded as a settlement of litigation do not provide evidence that the other party would voluntarily agree to royalties for SEPs apart from the broader agreement to settle existing litigation).

[104] ibid, 426–29.

[105] ibid.

[106] ibid, 508.

[107] ibid, 499.

[108] *In re Innovatio IP Ventures* (n 3).

[109] ibid, 30.

[110] ibid, 32–34.

agreement was dismissed because it included a large number of SEPs and covered a newer version of the standard than the one under litigation.[111] Having found no sufficiently comparable licences, Judge Holderman then considered patent pool royalty rates. However, in contrast to *Microsoft v Motorola*, he found that patent pool rates were not appropriate because Innovatio's patents were considered to be of moderate to moderate-high importance, while patent pool rates could be applicable only to relatively low-value SEPs.[112] Therefore, in *Innovatio* neither prior licences nor patent pool royalties were found to be sufficiently comparable, and the court eventually used the top-down approach discussed below.

In *CSIRO v Cisco*,[113] Judge Davis was tasked with determining damages for one SEP for the IEEE's Wi-Fi standard and was similarly faced with the difficulty of finding sufficiently comparable agreements. In this case, there was only one prior licence concluded with the company that had a specific relationship with the SEP holder. Namely, the licensee was founded by three ex-employees of the SEP owner, and it had a number of obligations towards the SEP holder, such as the disclosure of its business plans, the minimum performance obligation, the grant of a royalty-free grant-back licence for any improvements and the assignment of all rights in those improvements upon termination of the agreement.[114] Because of these characteristic, Judge Davis held that the prior licensing agreement was not sufficiently comparable and, instead, based his royalty determination on the parties' licensing offers made in negotiations.[115] On appeal, the Federal Circuit vacated the judgment and instructed the district court to re-evaluate the relevance of this licence as comparable licence valuations 'may be the most effective method of estimating the asserted patent's value'.[116]

In *HTC v Ericsson* the court was asked to rule whether Ericsson's offer to HTC for the 4G SEP portfolio was FRAND.[117] The court did not have to determine the rate as in previous cases, but only had to verify the compliance of Ericsson's offer with FRAND terms. In doing so it relied on Ericsson's prior licences and held that 'comparable licenses provide the best market-based evidence of the value of Ericsson's SEPs and that Ericsson's reliance on comparable licenses is a reliable method of establishing fair and reasonable royalty rates that is consistent with a FRAND commitment'.[118] Finding that Ericsson's offer to HTC was consistent with rates in comparable licences the court ruled that Ericsson fulfilled its FRAND obligation.

[111] ibid, 35.
[112] ibid, 35–36.
[113] *CSIRO v Cisco* 2014 WL 3805817 (ED Tex 2014).
[114] ibid, 10.
[115] ibid, 12.
[116] *CSIRO v Cisco* (Fed Cir 2015) (n 23).
[117] *HTC v Ericsson* 6:18-vc-00243-JRG, Doc 538 (ED Tex 2019).
[118] ibid, 11.

As mentioned, the hurdle of finding and using licences that are sufficiently comparable can be overcome by unpacking different elements of a licence to arrive at an effective royalty rate that a licensee pays. The unpacking method was applied extensively in *TCL v Ericsson*.[119] The case concerned the determination of a FRAND royalty rate of Ericsson's 2G, 3G and 4G SEP portfolio. Judge Selna applied both comparable licences and a top-down approach. The court unpacked Ericsson's licences that included different provisions: a combination of lump-sum payments together with per-unit or percentage royalties; cross-licensing provisions; some agreements that were concluded as a settlement of litigation, or contained additional provisions relating to sale of equipment, SEPs or business cooperation.[120] By using different economic models, the court was able to translate all the various elements into one effective rate which every licensee pays to Ericsson. Effective rates enabled comparison of rates between different licensees. As an illustration, unpacking comparable licences led to a range of rates of between 0.321 per cent and 0.662 per cent for Ericsson's 4G SEPs and between 0.321 per cent and 0.679 per cent for 3G SEPs.[121]

In the UK, Mr Justice Birss in *Unwired Planet v Huawei* also determined FRAND royalty by unpacking comparable licences.[122] There, Unwired Planet acquired a part of Ericsson's SEP portfolio for 2G, 3G and 4G standards and asserted them against a number of manufacturers, among them Huawei. In determining the FRAND royalty rate, Mr Justice Birss first considered two of Unwired Planet's prior licensing agreements, but discarded them as not sufficiently comparable.[123] One agreement was found to mix SEPs with non-SEPs, and running royalties with lump-sum payments, while the other was concluded as a part of the wider arrangement with a company that bought Unwired Planet, which at that time was suffering serious financial difficulties and was close to insolvency.[124] Instead, Mr Justice Birss relied on Ericsson's prior licences and determined that they are sufficiently comparable.[125] After unpacking he arrived at an effective royalty rate of 0.8 per cent for 4G SEPs and 0.67 per cent for 2G/3G SEPs,[126] and as a next step scaled down the royalties to the value of Unwired Planet's smaller portfolio.[127]

It is interesting to observe how Mr Justice Birss in *Unwired Planet v Huawei* and Judge Selna in *TCL v Ericsson* both unpacked Ericsson's licences but arrived at a different result. The royalty rate of 0.8 per cent in *Unwired Planet v Huawei*

[119] *TCL v Ericsson* (CD Cal 2017) (n 59).
[120] ibid, 62–89.
[121] ibid, 93.
[122] *Unwired Planet v Huawei* (n 76).
[123] ibid, 383–409.
[124] ibid.
[125] ibid, 462.
[126] ibid, 466.
[127] ibid, 475–77.

is almost twice the size of the 0.45 per cent royalty awarded by Judge Selna for Ericsson's 4G SEPs. The disparity in rates can be explained by the difference in licences that judges accepted as comparable. Judge Selna excluded licences with ZTE and Coolpad, but included Apple, while Mr Justice Birss did the opposite, included ZTE and Coolpad but excluded Apple. The unpacking formula also varied. This shows that unpacking is not an exact science; the result can vary depending on what licences are taken into account and the factors considered in the unpacking formula. Nevertheless, if properly used, unpacking can give a sense of the effective rate paid by licensees and may enable easier comparison of licences.

German courts also rely heavily on comparable licences when reviewing whether the offers of parties are FRAND. In *Saint Lawrence v Vodafone*, Düsseldorf District Court said that the higher the number of concluded licensing agreements on similar conditions, the stronger the presumption that such terms are FRAND.[128] After looking at six licence agreements the SEP owner concluded with other licensees for royalty rates of between \$0.20 and \$0.40 per device, the Court held that it was sufficient to prove that the offer was in accordance with industry practice and FRAND terms. Similarly, in *Fraunhofer-Gesellschaft (MPEG-LA) v ZTE* and *Tagivan (MPEG-LA) v Huawei*, Düsseldorf District Court held that comparable agreements are an important indicator of the FRANDness of offers and that the SEP owner will need to provide information on its comparable licensing agreements.[129] Accordingly, approximately 2,000 standard licensing agreements concluded by MPEG LA patent pool provided a strong presumption that underlying licensing terms are FRAND, which defendants failed to refute.

Comparable licences are also used to assess whether the offer of the SEP owner is discriminatory. The non-discrimination obligation is analysed in chapter five.

B. Top-Down Approach

According to the top-down approach, the SEP owner should receive a proportional share of the total aggregate royalty of a standard. It requires first establishing a cumulative royalty for a standard and then calculating the share in the total royalty of an individual SEP owner. The advantage of the top-down royalty calculation is that it addresses royalty stacking and patent holdup concerns.[130] Namely, it ensures that individual patent holders would only receive a royalty that is proportional to their share of SEPs, while individual royalties in the aggregate would not exceed the overall price of the standard. Additionally, the top-down approach increases

[128] *Saint Lawrence v Vodafone*, 4a O 73/14 Düsseldorf District Court (31 March 2016).

[129] *Fraunhofer-Gesellschaft (MPEG-LA) v ZTE*, 4a O 15/15 Düsseldorf District Court (9 November 2018); *Tagivan (MPEG-LA) v Huawei*, 4a O 17/15 Düsseldorf District Court (15 November 2018).

[130] For arguments in support of this approach, see P Chappatte, 'FRAND Commitments: The Case for Antitrust Intervention' (2009) 5 *European Competition Journal* 319, 339–43.

transparency in the market as manufacturers are aware of the ultimate price of the standard.

However, the top-down approach poses significant challenges and its wider application and usability by courts is questionable.[131] It must be emphasised that no SDO requires the use of the top-down approach in FRAND royalty determination; it emerged from court cases as a way to ensure that the overall royalty stack would not be excessive in the aggregate. Its application requires resolving important questions of how to determine the aggregate royalty cap and how to divide the aggregate royalty to an individual SEP owner.

Regarding the aggregate royalty for a standard, no such cap currently exists in the industry and estimating the aggregate royalty that licensees are currently paying would require publicly disclosing the rates of all licensing agreements and calculating the total royalty being paid. However, such is not practically feasible as courts could only order the disclosure of confidential licensing agreements from the parties to the litigation, not from third parties. Nor would this approach be appropriate as some implementers are not licensed or are not comprehensively licensed with all SEP owners, so there is no aggregate royalty that is being paid by all implementers.

In theory, the best place for setting the aggregate royalty for the standard would be within SDOs. Régibeau, De Coninck and Zengler suggest that aggregate royalties should be set by SEP holders that hold a significant number of SEPs,[132] while Contreras proposes that SEP holders and standard implementers should engage in joint negotiations to set mutually agreed aggregate royalty caps.[133] Common to both approaches is some form of industry-wide agreement on a standard's price. The main problem, however, is that such an agreement involves direct price fixing between competitors, which is strongly prohibited by competition laws.[134]

[131] For criticism, see: Geradin and Rato, 'Can Standard-Setting Lead to Exploitative Abuse? (n 80) 138–40; Layne-Farrar Padilla and Schmalensee (n 34) 682–85; D Geradin and M Rato, 'FRAND Commitments and EC Competition Law: A Reply to Phillipe Chappatte' (2010) 6 *European Competition Journal* 129, 157–63.

[132] P Régibeau, R De Coninck and H Zenger, 'Transparency, Predictability and Efficiency of SSO-based Standardisation and SEP Licensing: A Report for the European Commission' (2016) 44–45, available at: ec.europa.eu/growth/content/study-transparency-predictability-and-efficiency-sso-based-standardization-and-sep-licensing_en.

[133] J Contreras, 'Aggregated Royalties for Top-Down Royalty Determination: Revisiting "Joint Negotiations"' (2017) 62 *Antitrust Bulletin* 690.

[134] Commission, 'Guidelines on the Applicability of Article 101 of the Treaty on the Functioning of the European Union to Horizontal Co-operation Agreements' (Communication) [2011] OJ C 11/01, 247 ('Any agreements to reduce competition … as a cover to jointly fix prices either of downstream products or of substitute IPR or technology will constitute restrictions of competition by object'); US Department of Justice and the Federal Trade Commission, *Antitrust Enforcement of Intellectual Property Rights: Promoting Innovation and Competition* (2007) 51 ('summary condemnation would be justified if IP holders were to reach naked agreements on the licensing terms they will propose to an SSO'). Indirect price-fixing agreements are also caught by competition law, see N Zingales and O Kanevskaia, 'The IEEE-SA Patent Policy Update Under the Lens of EU Competition Law' (2016) 12 *European Competition Journal* 195 (arguing that the IEEE Patent Policy update which introduced certain criteria for calculating FRAND royalties could be prohibited by EU competition law as a restriction of

In order to implement aggregate royalty proposals, competition authorities would need to create a special exception for price fixing in the area of standardisation.[135] As a result, no SDO to date has implemented aggregate royalty caps in its IPR policy. Knowing the aggregate royalty rate for a standard might, however, be a good policy option which will be discussed more in chapter nine, but without industry agreement, it is doubtful whether courts should take on themselves the task of regulating technology prices

A separate issue is to how to distribute royalties to individual SEP owners. There are generally two approaches: (i) a numerical proportionality method, where a share in total royalties is allocated in proportion to the number of SEPs a company owns; and (ii) a patent quality-based method, where a share in total royalties is allocated based on the contribution of SEPs to the overall value of the standard. Both methods have their positive and negative sides.

A numerical proportionality method is relatively simple and straightforward to apply. All that is needed is to count the number of SEPs each company holds and distribute the standard's aggregate royalty in proportion to the number of SEPs. However, the downside of this approach is that it does not take into account the fact that not all SEPs are of equal value; some SEPs contribute more to the value of the standard than others. As seen in chapter one, section III.B, SEPs that read on core (mandatory) functions of a standard contribute more to the value than SEPs that read on optional or peripheral features. Economists have found that the economic value of patents is highly skewed, with only a relatively small number of patents providing the most value.[136] The result of the numerical proportionality method would be that patent owners with valuable SEPs would be under-rewarded, while those with low-quality SEPs would be over-rewarded. This creates perverse incentives for companies to declare patents of questionable value and disincentives contributing patents of significant value to the standard.[137]

A further problem with the numerical proportionality method is that it does not take into account the fact that not all declared patents are in fact essential.

competition by effects); M Lo Bue, 'Are these Cartels? Price Guidelines Adopted by Standard Setting Organisations (US, Institute of Electrical and Electronics Engineers)' (2016) 7 *Journal of European Competition Law & Practice* 537 (finding that the updated IEEE Patent Policy represents a focal point influencing decision on prices); N Petit, 'The IEEE-SA Revised Patent Policy and its Definition of "Reasonable" Rates: A Transatlantic Antitrust Divide?' (2017) 27 *Fordham Intellectual Property, Media & Entertainment Law Journal* 211 (arguing that the IEEE Patent Policy update represents price fixing, a restriction of competition by object, prohibited by EU competition law).

[135] Even authors who support the introduction of aggregate royalties admit that this would require a more flexible interpretation of competition laws. See Régibeau, De Coninck and Zenger (n 132) 45; Contreras, 'Aggregated Royalties' (n 133).

[136] M Schankerman, 'How Valuable is Patent Protection? Estimates by Technology Field' (1998) 29 *RAND Journal of Economics*, 77, 94; J Allison et al, 'Valuable Patents' (2004) 92 *Georgetown Law Journal* 435; B Hall, A Jaffe and M Trajtenberg, 'Market Value and Patent Citations' (2005) 36 *RAND Journal of Economics* 16.

[137] See Geradin and Rato, 'FRAND Commitments and EC Competition Law: A Reply to Phillipe Chappatte' (n 131) 158–59.

As shown in chapter one, section III.C, over-declaration is a significant problem, and the numerical proportionality method would incentivise companies to over-declare patents as much as possible in order to have as high a stack as possible so that they could receive a larger share of the total royalty for a standard.[138] It would effectively award royalties even for patents that are not in fact essential. As a result, the implementation of the numerical proportionality method would need to include some form of essentiality checks to identify the number of patents that are truly essential for a standard as well as the proportion of truly essential patents that a company holds, which may not be a simple task.

A final problem with the numerical proportionality method is that it needs to take into account the fact that the number of patents in a standard varies over time.[139] Some patents expire or are no longer essential, while new patents for latest versions of a standard are added. As the number of patents for a standard varies over time, so does the share of patents that a company owns in a standard. A numerical proportionality method would thus need to consider the fluctuating share of SEPs that a company holds.

On the other hand, a patent quality-based method is fairer and provides a more accurate picture as it recognises that not all SEPs hold the same value and assigns a larger share of royalties to more valuable SEPs. However, the implementation of this approach is much more complex and requires a difficult assessment of the value of each SEP and its comparison with others. At minimum, it requires knowing which patents are truly essential and which not, and distinguishing which SEPs read on mandatory or optimal features, as mandatory features are by definition more valuable. Other factors could then be added for a more precise estimation, for example it might be possible to look at the number of forward citations of a patent (economists have found that the number of citations that a patent receives is one of the indicators of the value and technological impact of underlying technology),[140] the geographic coverage of patents (more valuable patents are excepted to have larger international coverage) or the number and quality of contributions that a certain company made to SDO working groups during the development of a standard.[141] While neither the forward citations or standard's contributions in themselves are the most accurate method for establishing a

[138] Layne-Farrar, Padilla and Schmalensee (n 34) 683.

[139] Geradin and Rato, 'FRAND Commitments and EC Competition Law: A Reply to Phillipe Chappatte' (n 131) 161–62.

[140] G Sidak and J Skog, 'Citation Weighting, Patent Ranking, and Apportionment of Value for Standard-Essential Patents' (2018) 3 *Criterion Journal on Innovation* 201; Hall, Jaffe and Trajtenberg (n 136); D Harhoff et al, 'Citations Frequency and the Value of Patented Inventions' (1999) 81 *Review of Economics and Statistics* 511.

[141] Signals Research Group, 'The Essentials of Intellectual property, From 3G Through LTE Release 12. Quantifying Technology Leadership in the Development of the 3G and LTE Standards from their Inception Through December 2014' (May 2015), available at: signalsresearch.com/issue/the-essentials-of-intellectual-property-from-3g-to-lte-release-12-5/.

patent's value and could be criticised on a number of grounds,[142] the combination of all these methods could provide a useful indication of the strength of a company's portfolio and the value of individual SEPs. The downside is that elaborate estimations and comparisons of patent value are costly and time-consuming to apply.

i. Application in Practice

The top-down approach has been used in only a few cases to date. It was first applied by Judge Holderman in *Innovatio* for determining FRAND rate for Innovatio's portfolio of Wi-Fi SEPs.[143] The top-down approach was applied as a necessity because all other methods failed. As seen, there were no licences that were sufficiently comparable; patent pool rates did not represent an adequate proxy as Innovatio's patents were of moderate to high importance, and the ex ante incremental value approach was not applicable because there were no alternatives to Innovatio's patents. Only then was the top-down approach adopted as suggested by an expert witnesses.

As a first step, Judge Holderman had to decide on the aggregate royalty for a standard. He took the average profit of chip manufacturers as the maximum royalty cap, holding that this would be the maximum that the chipmaker would be willing to pay as otherwise he would exit the chipmaking business.[144] The profit of chip manufacturers, instead of device manufacturers, was justified by the argument that the SEP owner cannot discriminate on the basis of a licensee's position in the market. The profit margin of chip manufacturers was also held to alleviate concerns of royalty stacking, as the total royalty stack would not exceed an amount that would force chipmakers out of business. The judgment includes information on the average chip price from 2000 to 2013 showing how chip prices were falling every year. The average chip price from 2000 to 2013 was only $3.99 and the average profit margin 12.1 per cent. Including the data of chip prices from 1997, when the infringement began, the average price was held to be $14.85. Applying the average profit margin, the court arrived at an average profit of $1.80 per chip,[145] which was taken to represent the aggregate royalty for Wi-Fi standard.

In the next step, Judge Holderman had to establish the total number of SEPs for the Wi-Fi standard. He recognised that many of the declared essential patents

[142] J Baron, 'Counting Standard Contributions to Measure the Value of Patent Portfolios: A Tale of Apples and Oranges' (2020) 44 *Telecommunications Policy* 1 (criticising the use of contributions to SDOs as an indicator of the value of a SEP portfolio as unreliable due to the heterogeneity of contributions in type, outcome and impact, and susceptible to manipulation); D Abrams, U Akcigit and J Grennan, 'Patent Value and Citations: Creative Destruction or Strategic Disruption?' (2018) NBER Working Paper 19647 (finding that the relationship between citations and value forms an inverted-U with fewer citations at the high end of value than in the middle).

[143] *In re Innovatio IP Ventures* (n 3) 37–40.

[144] ibid, 38.

[145] ibid, 43.

may not be actually essential but did not undertake a detailed essentiality analysis. The court relied on a study showing there are approximately 3,000 potentially essential patents for Wi-Fi standard.[146]

As a final step, Judge Holderman decided to apply an estimate of patent quality, thus rejecting the pure numerical proportionality approach. The court relied on an article by Professor Mark Schankerman that the top 10 per cent of all electronics patents account for 84 per cent of the value. Given that Innovatio's patents were found to be of moderate to high importance to the standard, they were placed among the top 10 per cent of all SEPs for Wi-F standard providing most of the value.[147] After performing the relevant calculations, the court arrived at a royalty rate of 9.56 cents per chip for Innovatio's portfolio of 19 SEPs.

The approach in *Innovatio* can be criticised. Using the average profit margin of unlicensed chip prices as the total royalty for a standard is an inappropriate proxy for a standard's value. The value of IP is generally independent from the value of its physical components, otherwise we would be valuing paintings based on cost of the ink and canvass spent in production, or the value of books solely by the number of pages. The low-profit margins of chip manufacturers may not provide adequate return to SEP owners, would significantly depreciate the value of SEPs and harm incentives to innovate. Indeed, it is hard to imagine that the value of the whole Wi-Fi connectivity is worth less than $1.80 and, paradoxically, the value of the Wi-Fi technology is worth almost ten times less than its physical implementation. As a response to the price of intellectual property exceeding their current profit margin, chip manufacturers may simply raise prices. Judge Holderman recognised this possibility but nevertheless decided to stick with profit margins of unlicensed chips.[148] On the other hand, the court in *Innovatio* correctly recognised that not all patents have the same value and refused to apply a simple numerical proportionality approach, although a more elaborate analysis of patent quality could have been performed. It is quite likely that given further inputs the valuation could have changed. In *Ericsson v TCL*, for example, one economic expert testified that the top 10 per cent of SEPs provide 65 per cent of the value; applying that study would have produced an even lower royalty rate.[149]

The second case where the top-down method was applied is the UK's *Unwired Planet v Huawei*. There Mr Justice Birss used the top-down method as a cross-check of the reasonableness of determined rates from unpacked comparable licences. It was not used as the primary method for the establishment of royalty rates.

Regarding the aggregate royalty rate, Mr Justice Birss decided to leave it open and did not proceed to fixing it in advance. This was mainly because of the lack of sufficient proof of the aggregate royalty that the industry is paying. He first examined various statements from individual companies given from 2008 to 2010 about

[146] ibid.
[147] ibid.
[148] ibid, 38.
[149] *TCL v Ericsson* (CD Cal 2017) (n 59) 38.

the expected aggregate royalty stack for the 4G LTE standard.[150] This included statements from Ericsson, Alcatel-Lucent, NEC Corporation, NextWave Wireless, Nokia, Nokia Siemens Networks and Sony Ericsson that the maximum aggregate royalty for 4G SEPs should be in the single-digit percentage of the sales price; Ericsson's statement that it believes a reasonable aggregate royalty to be between 6 per cent and 8 per cent of a handset's price; and Huawei's statement that it supports a low single-digit percentage of sales price end-user devices as a reasonable maximum aggregate royalty.[151] Based on these, Huawei submitted that the aggregate royalty stack should be capped at 8 per cent. Mr Justice Birss rejected these statements as self-serving,[152] since they are being given by companies claiming the overall royalty is low, but that they are entitled to a larger share. Putting weight on these statements also does not take into account what SEP owners and implementers actually agreed in preceding years in concrete licensing agreements.[153] He decided to leave this question open and assess the aggregate royalty rate indirectly when checking the reasonableness of determined rates from comparable agreements.

The second step required finding the total number of SEPs for 4G/3G/2G standards and Unwired Planet's share in the total number of SEPs. Mr Justice Birss correctly recognised that not all declared SEPs are truly essential and proceeded to determine the number of truly essential patents. Parties proposed two different essentiality checks to filter out truly essentiality patents out of thousands of SEP declarations. After applying various essentiality filters, he held that there are 800 truly essential patents for 4G LTE standards, and 479 and 154 truly essential patents for 3G and 2G standards respectively.[154]

The final step required estimating a SEP owner's share in the overall royalty and the court decided on the numerical proportionality method. Mr Justice Birss correctly recognised that not all patents carry the same weight, as some may be more important to the standard than others.[155] However, having found that both parties in the proceedings used patent counting in their negotiations and given the vast number of SEPs,[156] he held that it would be a 'disproportionate task of evaluating every single patent thoroughly in order to compare each one with all the others',[157] and that 'some sort of patent counting is the only practical approach at least for a portfolio of any size'.[158] In other words, the court decided to use the numerical proportionality method because the parties themselves suggested such an approach.

[150] *Unwired Planet v Huawei* (n 76) 264.
[151] ibid.
[152] ibid, 269.
[153] ibid, 270.
[154] ibid, 377–78.
[155] ibid 184.
[156] ibid, 182.
[157] ibid, 183.
[158] ibid, 184.

The top-down approach was applied as a cross-check for the reasonableness of the rates arrived from unpacked comparable licences. Unpacking comparable licences produced Ericsson's effective royalty rate for a multimode 2G/3G/4G handset of 0.8 per cent, which scaled down to Unwired Planet's share of SEPs lead to 0.062 per cent royalty. Applying this rate on the total share of SEPs produces a total royalty burden for 4G LTE of 8.8 per cent.[159] This was considered as reasonable and lower than the aggregate royalty implied by rates suggested by the parties: Huawei's proposal would lead to the aggregate royalty of 13 per cent and Unwired Planet's 10.4 per cent.

The use of the top-down method in *Unwired Planet v Huawei* can be commended. It was effectively applied as a 'sanity check' to rates derived from comparable licences which, as seen, are concrete market-based evidence of the value of SEPs. The court avoided imposing binding aggregate royalty caps and did not get drawn into regulating technology prices. The use of statements by some SEP owners is indeed self-serving and diverges from the actual rates from concluded licensing agreements. Additionally, their application for setting the aggregate royalty rate would be difficult to justify in relation to those companies that have not given or refused to give such statements.

The last case applying the top-down method is *TCL v Ericsson* in the US.[160] Judge Selna used both the top-down method and comparable licences to determine FRAND rates for Ericsson's SEP portfolio.

Regarding the aggregate rate, Judge Selna decided to rely on public statements made by Ericsson and other industry participants on 2G, 3G and 4G rates, the same as Mr Justice Birss in *Unwired Planet v Huawei* disregarded. Statements contained an indication of the overall royalty rate and endorsement of the numerical proportionality principle in patent valuations. For instance in a 2002 press release concerning 2G and 3G standards, Ericsson together with Nokia, Siemens and NTT DoCoMo, publicly endorsed the numerical proportionality valuation of SEPs by stating that it will license its essential patents 'at rates that are proportional to the number of essential patents owned by each company'.[161] In the same press release, companies suggested total royalties of a 'modest single-digit level'.[162] Nokia specifically endorsed a 5 per cent royalty, and NTT DoCoMo suggested 'keeping cumulative royalty rate below 5%'.[163] For the 4G standard, Ericsson issued two public statements where it said to expect a 'reasonable maximum aggregate royalty level of 6–8%', and together with Alcatel-Lucent, NEC, Next Wave Wireless and Nokia announced that it 'supports the reasonable aggregate royalty level for LTE' in a 'single-digit percentage of the sales price'.[164] Based on the foregoing,

[159] ibid, 475–76.
[160] *TCL v Ericsson* (CD Cal 2017) (n 59).
[161] ibid, 20.
[162] ibid.
[163] ibid.
[164] ibid, 22.

Judge Selna applied the 5 per cent figure to 2G/3G, and both the 6 per cent and 10 per cent figure to the 4G standard.[165]

Regarding the total number of SEPs for 2G/3G/4G standards and Ericsson's share, like Mr Justice Birss in *Unwired Planet v Huawei*, Judge Selna recognised that not all declared SEPs are truly essential and that it is necessary to determine the number of truly essential patents. The court started by finding that as of September 2015, there were approximately 153,000 patents and patent applications in the ETSI database declared essential for 2G, 3G and 4G standards.[166] It then applied various essentiality filters, removing duplicated and expired patents, and patents not published in English. This produced 11,469 patent families with at least one active patent published in English.[167] After excluding patent families that did not have any patents with claims to user equipment, there were 7,106 patent families remaining. The court then accepted TCL's sample essentiality study to arrive at an estimate of how many declared patents were truly essential. The court held that there are 1,481 truly essential patents for 4G standard, and 365 and 953 truly essential patents for 2G and 3G standards respectively.[168] Ericsson's share was similarly calculated, although the parties naturally disagreed on the numbers.

In the final step, Judge Selna decided on a numerical proportionality method for evaluating SEPs. TCL proposed the application of a patent quality-based method to adjust Ericsson's share in total royalty by the relative strength of its portfolio. A proposed method was based on evaluating alternatives that were available to Ericsson's SEPs at the time the standard was set.[169] It assigned a different value to SEPs based on whether there were no alternatives (the highest value), whether SEPs provided moderate to marginal improvement over alternatives, or no improvement at all.[170] It then assigned value based on the assumption that the top 10 per cent of SEPs provide 65 per cent of the value of the standard. As a cross-check, TLC's expert used a forward citation analysis, attempting to determine the strength of patents by examining how often they are cited in future patent applications.[171] These methods produced an estimate of Ericsson's SEP share based on the number of its truly essential SEPs adjusted for quality estimate.[172] However, Judge Selna rejected this method because it failed to consider the relative value of all SEPs in the standard, so there was nothing to compare Ericsson's SEPs with.

[165] ibid, 26.
[166] ibid, 27.
[167] ibid, 28.
[168] ibid, 32.
[169] ibid, 38–40.
[170] ibid, 38.
[171] ibid, 40.
[172] ibid ('Using the 10%/65% ratio, this led to Ericsson owning 3.1% of the US 4G patent value share, 4.0% of the US 3G patent value share, and 6.7% of the US 2G value share … The results of the forward citation analysis demonstrate that Ericsson owns a 4.0% value share of US 4G patents, a 5.7% value share of US 3G patents, and an 8.1% value share of 2G patents').

It also did not consider whether alternative technologies would be inconsistent with each other, would perform worse, or would maintain a viable functioning standard, rendering the comparison with alternative technologies only speculative. TCL's analysis also did not examine who owns alternatives. Finally, the court was not persuaded by the analysis that the top 10 per cent of SEPs provide 65 per cent of the value of the standard and it questioned why a different skew was used in *Innovatio*, where it was held that the top 10 per cent of SEPs provided 84 per cent of the value.[173]

As a result, due to the failure of proof, the court adopted a numerical proportionality method, treating all patents as having the same value.[174] The rates obtained by using the top-down approach were then compared with the rates obtained from unpacked comparable licences and the court decided that the US rate for Ericsson's 4G SEP portfolio should be 0.45 per cent, and for 0.3 per cent and 0.164 per cent for the 3G and 2G SEP portfolios respectively.

However, Judge Selna's FRAND royalty determination was in the end annulled on appeal by the Federal Circuit on procedural grounds, finding that Ericsson was entitled to a jury trial.[175] Consequently, the top-down method was not analysed by the Federal Circuit and it remains to be seen what its further application in practice will be.

TCL v Ericsson demonstrates the practical difficulties in applying the top-down method. Every step of the way is fraught with uncertainty, from how to determine the aggregate royalty level, how to conduct the essentiality analysis of the total number of SEPs and patentees' share, and how to evaluate SEPs. Tweaking any factor in the analysis can lead to significantly different results. Determining the aggregate royalty level based on past statements from certain SEP owners is problematic. It is unclear how much public statements could be legal binding, and even if they were to bind the declarant, they could not apply to those SEP owners that did not make such statements. Indeed, it seems Ericsson has learned the lesson and neither it nor any other SEP owner announced the aggregate royalty expectation for 5G. Essentiality calculations are also not an easy task. When analysing the essentiality of 4G LTE SEPs, *Unwired Planet v Huawei* and *TCL v Ericsson* arrived at different results. *TCL v Ericsson's* 1,481 truly essential patents are almost double the size of the 800 patents held to be essential in *Unwired Planet v Huawei*. Both cases in the end resorted to a numerical proportionality valuation of SEPs, despite acknowledging that not all patents confer the same value. The difficulty in evaluating a SEP portfolio was especially noticeable in *TCL v Ericsson*.

In conclusion, the principal problem with using the top-down approach is that it involves courts setting and controlling the aggregate rates that has no basis in

[173] ibid, 41–42.

[174] ibid, 16 ('court adopts a simple patent counting system which treats every patent as possessing identical value').

[175] *TCL v Ericsson*, 943 F.3d 1360 (Fed Cir 2019).

the industry. Until the market arrives at an aggregate price of the standard, it is questionable if courts should assume the role of regulatory price agencies. As seen, courts have struggled in finding a way to determine the aggregate price in the absence of industry-wide agreement. The top-down approach is also not used in licensing negotiations, casting doubt on the merits of its wider use. While it is true that a top-down approach resolves concerns about royalty stacking, it seems as a rather blunt instrument. It could be better used as a sanity check to rates derived from comparable licences as applied by Mr Justice Birss in *Unwired Planet v Huawei*, rather than a direct rate-setting method.

C. Other Approaches

Other methods that do not rely on comparable licences but use other observable market factors have been suggested for determining FRAND royalties. The European Commission in its SEP Communication recommended the use of the present value-added method: 'determining a FRAND value should require taking into account the present value added of the patented technology. That value should be irrespective of the market success of the product which is unrelated to the patented technology'.[176] However, the application of this method is not further elaborated by the Commission.

The present value-added method is a traditional income approach to evaluating IP rights.[177] The income approach estimates the future cash flows expected from the patent, which are then discounted back at an appropriate discount rate.[178] The goal is to determine the increase in the value of the product attributable to the standard and SEP portfolio.[179] Several direct or indirect methods can be used to estimate future cash flows. A direct way is to use the incremental income analysis by looking at the value of the product and asking what it would be worth with or without patented technology. If there are products that use patented technology and those that do not, it might be possible to determine the value added of the patented technology. Often, however, it will not be possible to find two products with and without SEPs, so indirect methods for estimation would need to be used. They can be customer surveys that look at how customers value different patented features and calculate the increase in consumers' willingness to pay for standardised technology, or the residual value approach that deducts the value of all other

[176] Commission, 'Setting out the EU Approach to Standard Essential Patents' (n 28) 7.

[177] See R Ghafele and J Schmitz, 'Economic Perspectives on FRAND' (2020) 11 *Journal of European Competition Law & Practice* 90, 91; H Goddar and U Moser, 'Traditional Valuation Methods: Cost, Market and Income Approach' in F Munari and R Oriani (eds), *The Economic Valuation of Patents: Methods and Applications* (Edward Elgar, 2011).

[178] Ghafele and Schmitz (n 177) 92.

[179] J Baron et al, 'Group of Experts on Licensing and Valuation of Standard Essential Patents: Contribution to the Debate on SEPs' (January 2021) 110–11, available at: ec.europa.eu/docsroom/documents/45217.

assets and technologies in a product order to arrive at the 'residue' that represent the value of standardised technology.[180]

The benefit of the present value-added method lies in its understanding of how patents create market value and its efforts to measure this added value. As it does not rely on prior comparable licences it can be used in situations when there are no licences, such as with new and unlicensed technologies like 5G, or with SEP owners that lack prior licensees. The drawback, however, is finding reliable data on the increased value of products directly attributable to SEPs. Additionally, comparable licensing agreements should not be completely disregarded when they exist, as they represent reliable market evidence of how commercial companies evaluate SEPs. The present value-added method might then be used only in situations when there are no comparable licences or as an additional factor supplementing the comparable licences analysis.

Another approach to evaluating SEPs is to use hedonic pricing.[181] Hedonic price analysis looks at observed prices and features in the market of each of the components of a multicomponent product in order to isolate the value attributable to each component. By regressing a product's total price on the product's characteristics, hedonic price analysis enables determining how much consumers are willing to pay for individual components of a multicomponent product. Thus, hedonic price analysis could quantify consumers' willingness to pay for features such as screen size, battery life or 3G/4G/5G cellular connectivity. The method has been suggested by Sidak and is a variant of the present value-added method as it seeks to determine the future royalty streams of standardised technology based on consumers' willingness to pay. Hedonic price analysis can be used to find an aggregate royalty for a standard, which then needs to be apportioned to the individual SEP owner based on the quality of its SEPs.

Like the present value-added method, hedonic price analysis could be useful when there are no comparable licences in a case of new standards or for a SEP holder without any licensees. When there are comparable licences, hedonic price analysis could be used as a cross-check in assessing the aggregate rate for the standard.

III. Conclusion

The chapter examined the principles of a FRAND royalty and practical methods for its calculation. As seen, SDOs typically do not define what FRAND terms are and leave royalty determinations to bilateral negotiations between the parties.

[180] Goddar and Moser (n 177) 129–30.

[181] G Sidak and J Skog, 'Hedonic Prices and Patent Royalties' (2017) 2 *Criterion Journal on Innovation* 601; G Sidak and J Skog, 'Hedonic Prices for Multicomponent Products' (2019) 4 *Criterion Journal on Innovation* 301.

Normative proposals of what value FRAND royalties should include largely come from economists and policymaking circles.

The most widely used normative interpretation of FRAND royalties provides that they should be based on the value of the technology itself, ie, the ex ante incremental value compared with the next best alternative prior to standardisation. It is based on the premise that SEP owners should be precluded from capturing any value arising from standardisation and accruing all the benefits to standard implementers. It was demonstrated how the ex ante incremental value approach suffers from serious practical deficiencies, making it unsuitable as a guiding normative principle for FRAND royalty interpretation. It confuses a simple standard-setting process in a non-digital context with complex and innovative standard-development in digital industries. It depreciates the value of SEPs and expropriates all the benefits that SEP technologies create for standard implementers. Importantly, the ex ante incremental value method is impossible to apply in practice, as demonstrated by the fact that no court has managed to directly use it to date and, moreover, it is not used by parties in real-world commercial transactions and SEP valuations. Thus, the discussion about the ex ante incremental value approach to FRAND royalties should be gently put to rest.

If some overreaching FRAND royalty principles are to be devised, the following could be used:

1. Exclude any 'sunk cost value' of standard implementers, by setting the level of royalties before implementers have started manufacturing standardised products.
2. Fairly share the 'value of standardisation' between SEP holders and standard implementers.
3. Proportionality in relation to the contribution of the patented technology to the standard, and proportionality to the overall royalty for the standard.

Such a normative interpretation aims to strike the balance between the interests of SEP owners, standard implementers and consumers. However, like any idealised theoretical models it also suffers from practical difficulties in application. This may be a further argument that we should be focusing less on elusive normative models and turn more attention to practical approaches to calculating FRAND royalties.

When it comes practical methods for determining FRAND royalties, comparable licences provide the best market evidence of the value of SEPs and should be used as a starting point in any royalty determinations. However, finding licences that are sufficiently comparable and unpacking them to arrive at an effective one-way royalty rate remains challenging. A top-down approach alleviates royalty stacking concerns, but its wider application is questionable due to the fundamental problem of setting a standard's aggregate royalty rate without industry-wide agreement. It could be more adequately used only as a cross-check to royalties derived from unpacked comparable licences. Finally, the present value-added method proposed by the European Commission or hedonic price analysis are interesting proposals that may find more application in the future. They could be used if there are no comparable licences, when there is a new unlicensed standard or SEP owner without prior licensees, or also as a cross-check to rates derived from comparable licences.

To conclude, Judge Selna correctly observed that: 'the search for precision and absolute certainty [in determining FRAND royalties] is a doomed undertaking'.[182] Indeed, any third-party determination of bilateral licensing terms is inherently imprecise. Chapter nine will discuss some ways of how SEP licensing may become more transparent and efficient in the IoT context.

[182] *TCL v Ericsson* (CD Cal 2017) (n 59) 14.

5

The Non-Discrimination Requirement of a FRAND Commitment

This chapter analyses the non-discrimination part of a FRAND commitment. In addition to royalties being fair and reasonable, a FRAND commitment requires them to be non-discriminatory as well. The general economic and welfare effects of price discrimination and its implication for SEP licensing will first be explained, followed by an analysis of the legal obligation of SEP holders in the text of FRAND commitments and the IPR policies of different SDOs. Next, the chapter will proceed by examining different interpretations of the scope of the ND obligation in the literature and case law. It concludes with a framework for the interpretation and application of the ND requirement and the use of non-disclosure agreements and confidentiality obligations necessary for the verification of its compliance.

At the outset, it is important to reiterate the distinction between discrimination that violates contractual provision of a FRAND commitment and discrimination that infringes competition law. The two notions are not the same and should not be confused.[1] By giving a FRAND commitment the SEP owner undertakes a contractual obligation that can be further specified by SDOs. On the other hand, competition law already applies to the pricing conduct of SEP owners by virtue of competition legislation. The non-discrimination obligation of a FRAND commitment would be effectively meaningless if it adds nothing more than the requirement to respect competition laws. Thus, the contractual ND commitment imposes obligations over and above those of competition law.

The distinction between contractual and anti-competitive discrimination is important because the burdens of proof are different. Proving contractual discrimination is much simpler and only requires establishing: (i) the existence

[1] See ch 3, section II.B. Also, M Botta, 'Non-Discrimination in Standard Essential Patents: ND Prong v Art 102(c) TFEU' (2021) *Journal of Competition Law & Economics* (forthcoming); J Contreras and R Gilbert, 'Non-Discrimination – FRAND's Last Stand? (21 December 2020) *CPI Antitrust Chronicle* 2; G Sidak, 'Fair and Unfair Discrimination in Royalties for Standard-Essential Patents Encumbered by a FRAND or RAND Commitment' (2017) 2 *Criterion Journal on Innovation* 301.

of a contractual of obligation (ie, a FRAND commitment); (ii) discriminatory conduct (applying dissimilar conditions to equivalent transactions); and (iii) no objective justification for discrimination. On the other hand, proving anti-competitive discrimination is much more complex and generally requires establishing: (i) the market power on the side of the SEP owner; (ii) discriminatory conduct; (iii) anti-competitive effects; and (iv) the absence of objective justifications. The evidence that discrimination led to anti-competitive effects is difficult to adduce and is fact intensive. Under a contractual approach, however, there is no need for a complex enquiry into market power and the anti-competitive effect of price discrimination.

A final argument against equating the ND obligation of a FRAND commitment with competition law lies in the fact that different jurisdictions have different criteria of what constitutes anti-competitive price discrimination. Thus the scope and applicability of the ND obligation would vary depending on the jurisdiction hearing the dispute. For example, the threshold for establishing market power and anti-competitive effects differs between the US and the EU, and potentially even more compared with Asian jurisdictions like China, Japan, India, or South Korea. This is clearly not what is intended by the FRAND commitment.

Therefore, although they are two separate notions, the contractual ND requirement of a FRAND commitment and anti-competitive price discrimination coexist and apply independently to the pricing conduct of SEP owners. In a concrete case, price discrimination by the SEP owner could breach contractual ND obligations but may not rise to the level of competition law prohibition and vice versa. Price discrimination may be in accordance with FRAND obligation, but if it causes competitive disadvantage between licensees it can be prohibited by competition laws. The chapter focuses on a contractual interpretation of the non-discrimination requirement of a FRAND commitment.

I. Positive and Negative Aspects of Price Discrimination in Standard Essential Patent Licensing

Price discrimination in the economic sense means selling the same product to different customers for different prices not directly corresponding to the difference in costs of production or supply.[2] Price discrimination is not necessarily harmful and can have both positive and negative effects.

[2] R Whish and D Bailey, *Competition Law*, 9th edn (Oxford University Press, 2018) 777.

On the one hand, price discrimination may be beneficial to consumer welfare.[3] This is because the seller can offer its products at a lower price to those consumers that are price-constrained and sell at a higher price to consumers that are not. Without price discrimination, price-constrained consumers might not be able to purchase the product. For example, a producer may charge $10 per product in prosperous areas and $5 per product in a poorer area. If price discrimination were prevented, the producer may sell the product at a uniform price of $7 in both areas with the result that fewer people in poorer areas would buy the product. Moreover, many companies offer discounts to students and elderly people who generally have a lower willingness to pay in order to make products more affordable and accessible to all. In this sense, price discrimination is beneficial as it leads to more consumers purchasing the product and greater output.

On the other hand, price discrimination may also have negative effects.[4] It may distort competition between customers if they compete with each other in the downstream market. For example, if vertically integrated companies charge different prices for inputs from their competitors, this may distort competition in the downstream market by raising competitors' costs and favouring a vertically integrated company's own products.

Economists distinguish between three degrees of price discrimination.[5] A first-degree price discrimination involves a firm setting a price for each product equal to each consumer's willingness to pay. Examples are personalised pricing tailored for each consumer based on its individual characteristics. A second-degree price discrimination involves a firm setting a menu of prices for its product, such as volume discounts or offering versions of the product with different quality levels and prices. A third-degree price discrimination involves setting prices for different groups of customers, like student discounts or discounts for the elderly. Economist generally agree that first, second- and third-degree price discriminations are pro-competitive as they increase output, ensure that more consumers have affordable prices, can increase competition between products and create dynamic incentives for innovation.[6] Only the first-degree price discrimination raises some concerns as it may allow the seller to capture the total surplus by matching the maximum reservation price of each consumer. However, the concrete anti-competitive effects, if any, of the first-degree price discrimination need to be established on a case-by-case basis.

[3] See S Bishop and M Walker, *The Economics of EC Competition Law: Concepts, Application and Measurement*, 3rd edn (Sweet & Maxwell, 2010) 256; G Niels, H Jenkins and J Kavanagh, *Economics for Competition Lawyers*, 2nd edn (Oxford University Press, 2016) 182–84; Whish and Bailey (n 2) 777. For the early discussion on the welfare effects of price discrimination see F Ramsey, 'A Contribution to the Theory of Taxation' (1927) 37 *Economic Journal* 47.

[4] Bishop and Walker (n 3); Niels, Jenkins and Kavanagh (n 3) 184–85.

[5] See OECD, 'Price Discrimination' (2016) DAF/COMP(2016)15, 7.

[6] ibid, 9–10.

General economic insights on price discrimination apply equally in the SEP context,[7] and we may observe all three degrees of price discrimination. For example, the SEP holder may offer more favourable licensing terms to a manufacturer of smart meters than to a smartphone manufacturer, or to licensees in different geographic markets (a third-degree price discrimination). Discrimination in licensing terms for different uses of the technology would be justified because licensees do not use the standard to the same extent and functionality. A smartphone uses full functionality of cellular standards, and a willingness to pay the smartphone manufacturer would be higher than that of a smart meter manufacturer who uses only limited functionality of a cellular standard. If price discrimination were to be prohibited, and the SEP holder had to use one uniform price, then access to the standard might be unaffordable to smart meter manufacturers if the SEP holder used the price charged to smartphone manufacturers as a uniform price. Conversely, it would be unprofitable for the SEP holder to charge the smartphone manufacturers a lower price than it offers to smart meter manufacturers. SEP owners are also often offering quantity discounts where royalty rates are falling based on the increase of the quantity of royalty-bearing products, and early-bird discounts for companies that sign up to licences within a certain time frame (a second-degree price discrimination). SEP owners may also engage in cross-licensing and attach further mutual obligations like business cooperation and strategic partnership, in which case we may talk about first-degree price discrimination. All these practices ensure price affordability to as many licensees as possible and provides widespread access to the standard, while at the same time securing incentives to innovate to SEP owners.

However, price discrimination in SEP licensing may also produce negative welfare effects. SEP owners may distort competition in the downstream market by unfairly imposing substantially larger royalties on some licensees.[8] Vertically integrated SEP owners may in particular have strong incentives to discriminate against their downstream competitors.[9] They may demand significantly higher licensing royalties from competitors in order to increase their costs and make their downstream products less appealing to consumers.

[7] A Layne-Farrar, 'Nondiscriminatory Pricing: Is Standard Setting Different?' (2010) 6 *Journal of Competition Law & Economics* 811 (discussing price discrimination in the SEP context); J Contreras and A Layne-Farrar, 'Non-Discrimination and FRAND Commitments' in J Contreras (ed), *The Cambridge Handbook of Technical Standardization Law: Competition, Antitrust, and Patents* (Cambridge University Press, 2018).

[8] See K Maskus and S Merrill (eds), 'Patent Challenges for Standard-Setting in the Global Economy: Lessons from Information and Communication Technology' (National Research Council, 2013) 53–54, available at: www.nap.edu/catalog/18510/patent-challenges-for-standard-setting-in-the-global-economy-lessons.

[9] D Swanson and W Baumol, 'Reasonable and Non-discriminatory (RAND) Royalties, Standards Selection, and Control of Market Power' (2005) 73 *Antitrust Law Journal* 1, 25–30; D Crane, 'Patent Pools, RAND Commitments, and the Problematics of Price Discrimination' in R Dreyfuss, H First and D Zimmerman (eds), *Working Within the Boundaries of Intellectual Property* (Oxford University Press, 2010) 373; Layne-Farrar (n 7) 824–27.

Therefore, the proper interpretation of the non-discrimination part of a FRAND commitment should aim at preventing the negative effects of price discrimination while allowing for beneficial differential pricing that promotes widespread adoption of the standard. The question is then not whether any differentiation in pricing is prohibited, but rather what degree of discrimination is allowed.

II. The Non-Discrimination Requirement in the Text of a FRAND Commitment

The starting point in the interpretation of the ND requirement is to consult the precise text of a FRAND commitment and the IPR policy of the relevant SDO. We may observe that the wording of the ND obligation varies slightly between SDOs and that SDOs typically do not define further its precise content. Instead, the concrete implementation of the non-discriminatory licensing condition is to be specified in market based bilateral negotiations between the parties.

A common version of the ND commitment requires licensing on 'fair, reasonable and non-discriminatory' terms. For example, ETSI's FRAND commitment states that the SEP holder should be 'prepared to grant irrevocable licences on fair, reasonable and non-discriminatory ("FRAND") terms'.[10] In a similar manner, the FRAND commitment in ITU-T, ISO and IEC reads: 'the Patent Holder is prepared to grant a license to an unrestricted number of applicants on a worldwide, non-discriminatory basis and on reasonable terms and conditions',[11] while TIA simply states that licences will be available 'under terms and conditions that are reasonable and non-discriminatory'.[12] In these cases, the non-discrimination commitment is said to be unqualified as it does not further elaborate on the conditions of discrimination.

A slightly different version of the non-discrimination commitment calls for licensing that is 'demonstrably free of unfair discrimination'. For example, ANSI's Essential Requirements asks that licences be available 'under reasonable terms and conditions that are demonstrably free of any unfair discrimination'.[13] The IEEE's Patent policy has similar wording and requires SEP owners to make licences

[10] ETSI, 'Intellectual Property Rights Policy' (3 September 2020) Clause 6.1, available at: www.etsi.org/images/files/IPR/etsi-ipr-policy.pdf.

[11] ITU-ISO-IEC, 'Patent Statement and Licensing Declaration Form for ITU-T, ITU-R Recommendation, ISO or IEC Deliverable' (2 November 2018), available at: www.itu.int/dms_pub/itu-t/oth/04/04/T04040000020005PDFE.pdf.

[12] TIA, 'Intellectual Property Rights Policy' (21 October 2016) 8, available at: www.tiaonline.org/wp-content/uploads/2018/05/TIA_Intellectual_Property_Rights_Policy.pdf.

[13] ANSI, 'Essential Requirements: Due Process Requirements for American National Standards' (January 2021) 11, available at: www.ansi.org/american-national-standards/ans-introduction/essential-requirements.

available 'under Reasonable Rates, with other reasonable terms and conditions that are demonstrably free of any unfair discrimination'.[14] A non-discrimination commitment in these cases is said to be qualified, as it prohibits only unfair discrimination while presumably allowing for discrimination that is fair.

Whether there exists a practical difference between qualified and unqualified discrimination is currently an open question.[15] One interpretation may be that the full text of a FRAND commitment requires all terms and conditions to be fair and reasonable, which applies to non-discrimination as well. Even the text of unqualified discrimination would then require all terms and conditions of a licence to be fair and reasonable, meaning that discrimination should also be fair. Consequently, what is prohibited is unfair discrimination between licensees.

Further definition of the content of the ND requirement of a FRAND commitment is typically not elaborated by SDOs, leaving the precise determination of FRAND licensing terms to bilateral market-based negotiations between the parties. For instance, ITU-T provides that 'negotiations are left to the parties concerned and are performed outside the ITU-T/ITU-R',[16] and similarly ETSI specifies that 'specific licensing terms and negotiations are commercial issues between the companies and shall not be addressed within ETSI'.[17] The IEEE warns that it is 'not responsible for determining whether any licensing terms or conditions provided in connection with submission of a Letter of Assurance, if any, or in any licensing agreements are reasonable or non-discriminatory'.[18] TIA also elaborates that 'the precise terms and conditions are left to the parties, or if the parties fail to agree and dispute the reasonable and nondiscriminatory character of what the licensor offers, the matter is left to the courts'.[19] CEN-CENELEC go further by holding that 'FRAND has no precise pricing content, but instead is a "comity device" designed to promote good faith negotiations between patent owners and prospective licensees'.[20] In a similar vein TIA provides that 'the term of "non-discrimination" implies a standard of even-handedness'.[21]

[14] IEEE-SA, 'Standards Board Bylaws' (August 2020) Clause 6.2. Policy, available at: standards.ieee.org/content/dam/ieee-standards/standards/web/documents/other/sb_bylaws.pdf.

[15] See J Contreras, 'Global Markets, Competition and FRAND Royalties: The Many Implications of *Unwired Planet v Huawei*' (2017) 8 *Antitrust Source* 1, 5–6; Sidak, 'Fair and Unfair Discrimination' (n 1) 308–15; Contreras and Layne-Farrar (n 7) 189–90.

[16] ITU-ISO-IEC, 'Patent Statement and Licensing Declaration Form' (n 11).

[17] ETSI, 'Guide on Intellectual Property Rights' (19 September 2013) Clause 4.1.

[18] IEEE-SA, 'Standards Boards Bylaws' (August 2020) 18.

[19] TIA, 'Guidelines to the Telecommunications Industry Association Intellectual Property Rights Policy' (1 May 2014) 4, available at: available at: www.tiaonline.org/wp-content/uploads/2018/05/Guidelines_to_the_Intellectual_Rights_Policy_of_the_Telecommunications_Industry_Association.pdf.

[20] CEN-CENELEC, 'Standard Essential Patents and Fair, Reasonable and Non-Discriminatory (FRAND) Commitments' (2016) 2, available at: www.cencenelec.eu/News/Policy_Opinions/PolicyOpinions/EssentialPatents.pdf.

[21] TIA, 'Guidelines to the Telecommunications Industry Association' (n 19) 4.

Therefore, since the content of the ND obligation of the FRAND commitment is not further elaborated by SDOs, courts hearing SEPs disputes struggled to define its precise application. The next section reviews various interpretations by courts and the literature on the meaning of the ND obligation.

III. No Requirement to Apply Uniform Terms to All Licensees

It appears that the only consensus is that the ND requirement does not mean that the SEP holder must grant licences on identical terms to all implementers.[22] In other words, the ND requirement does not require the use of a uniform price for all licensees. The support for such interpretation comes from the text of the FRAND commitment itself, as well as from the general economics of price discrimination. Namely, if the goal of the FRAND commitment is to impose identical prices to all licences, then it could have been drafted in that way. Instead, as seen, the IPR policies typically state that the negotiations of licences are left to the parties concerned and are conducted outside SDOs, which confirms that licensing terms can differ between licensees as they are subject to negotiations. If the licensing terms have to be uniform, then there would be nothing left to negotiate. TIA explicitly confirms this, by stating that

> the term 'non-discriminatory' does not mean or imply that licensing terms must be the same for all applicants. Discrimination and difference are not the same. It is understood that the process of license negotiations and the components of consideration between parties can vary substantially yet be fair.[23]

From the economic perspective, charging the same price to differently situated licensees is discriminatory just as charging different prices to similarly situated licensees would be. It may have negative welfare effects as implementers who cannot not afford a uniform price would not be licensed and could not enter the market, reducing overall output and consumer welfare.

The interpretation that the ND requirement does not mean an obligation to charge uniform price to all licensees has been recognised by courts in the US and EU. In *TCL v Ericsson*, Judge Selna interpreted ETSI's FRAND commitment as 'not requiring a single rate that is necessarily FRAND, and different rates offered

[22] See Swanson and Baumol (n 9) 25; R Gilbert, 'Deal or No Deal? Licensing Negotiations in Standard Setting Organizations' (2011) 77 *Antitrust Law Journal* 855, 827 ('it is artificial and counterproductive to impose a definition that requires identical licensing terms for every licensee'); D Carlton and A Shampine, 'An Economic Interpretation of FRAND' (2013) 9 *Journal of Competition Law & Economics* 531; G Sidak, 'The Meaning of FRAND, Part I: Royalties' (2013) 9 *Journal of Competition Law & Economics* 931, 997; M Lemley and C Shapiro, 'A Simple Approach to Setting Reasonable Royalties for Standard-Essential Patents' (2013) 28 *Berkeley Technology Law Journal* 1135, 1141–42.

[23] TIA, 'Guidelines to the Telecommunications Industry Association' (n 19) 4.

to different licensees may well be FRAND given the economics of the specific licensee'.[24] Based on the drafting history of ETSI's IPR policy he concluded that the drafters 'did not intend "non-discriminatory" to ensure the exact same treatment or identical license terms for all licensees to the same portfolio of essential patents'.[25] The same conclusion was reached by Mr Justice Birss in *Unwired Planet v Huawei* where he held that if a royalty should be the same for all licences then a FRAND commitment could have been written in that way, and there is accordingly no reason to interpret ETSI's FRAND commitment in such a strict way.[26] The German Federal Supreme Court in *Sisvel v Haier* also held that the FRAND obligation does not mean that the SEP owner has to apply a 'uniform tariff' granting the same conditions to all licensees.[27]

However, apart from the understanding that licensing terms do not need to be uniform, there is no agreement as to what extent licensing terms can differ and still be non-discriminatory.

IV. Interpretations of the Non-Discrimination Requirement of a FRAND Commitment

Various interpretations are trying to give substance to the non-discrimination requirement of a FRAND commitment. There is currently no universally accepted approach, and a few court cases to date do not provide a definitive answer. This section presents evolving interpretations of the ND requirement in the literature and case law to date.

A. Prohibition of Discrimination between Different Levels of the Production Chain

One interpretation is that the ND requirement of a FRAND commitment requires SEP owners to offer licences to *all* standard implementers that request one, regardless of their position in the production chain.[28] This argument is related to

[24] *TCL v Ericsson*, 2017 WL 6611635 (CD Cal 2017) 109.

[25] ibid.

[26] *Unwired Planet v Huawei* [2017] EWHC 2988 (Pat) 497.

[27] *Sisvel v Haier*, KZR 36/17 Federal Court of Justice (5 May 2020) 81.

[28] M Mariniello, 'Fair, Reasonable and Non-Discriminatory (FRAND) Terms: A Challenge to Competition Authorities' (2011) 7 *Journal of Competition Law & Economics* 523, 525 ('the FRAND commitment waives the patent holder's right to refuse to license its IP rights to anybody seeking such a license'); Carlton and Shampine (n 22) 546 ('"Non-discriminatory", in the context of a SSO setting standards for competing firms, can be interpreted to mean that all implementers of the standard should be offered licenses to the technology'); S Barazza, 'Licensing Standard Essential Patents Part One: The Definition of FRAND Commitments, the Determination of Royalty Rates' (2014) 9 *Journal*

whether the SEP holder can choose the level of the production chain to license, for example by licensing only to final downstream manufacturers, or whether the SEP holder must also license to component manufacturers if they request it.

Issues relating to value-chain licensing will be analysed in more detail in chapter seven. Suffice to say at this point that it would be too broad to read into the non-discrimination requirement of a FRAND commitment as imposing an obligation to license at every level of the production chain. If the SEP holder decides to license only at the end-device level but not at the component level, there is arguably no discrimination between component and end-device manufacturers because they are not similarly situated and there is no mutual competition between them. A duty to license at every level of the supply chain may exist only if expressly specified by other elements of a FRAND commitment, as will be explained in chapter seven.

B. Prohibiting Price Discrimination of Vertically Integrated SEP Holders against Downstream Competitors

One interpretation of the non-discrimination requirement of a FRAND commitment is that the vertically integrated SEP holder cannot discriminate on the basis of whether or not it competes downstream with the licensee.[29] Swanson and Baumol argue that the non-discrimination requirement principally applies only to vertically integrated SEP holders because they may use discriminatory prices to create or enhance their market power in downstream markets for standard-compliant products or services.[30] The vertically integrated SEP holder may charge their downstream competitors significantly higher licensing rates in order to raise their production costs and make competing downstream products more expensive for consumers. Swanson and Baumol propose the use of the 'efficient component

of Intellectual Property Law & Practice 465, 471 ('"non-discriminatory" principle requires the SEP holder to offer a licence to all prospective licensees'); R Grasso, 'Standard Essential Patents: Royalty Determination in the Supply Chain' (2017) 8 *Journal of Competition Law & Practice* 283, 292 ('The SEP-holder's refusal to license component-level implementers simply based on the implementers position in the supply chain is contrary to its commitment not to discriminate').

[29] See Swanson and Baumol (n 9) 27 ('we interpret the "nondiscrimination" component of the RAND obligation as applying to and regulating the licensing conduct of vertically integrated but not pure-licensors for the purpose of preventing anticompetitive acts in the market for downstream products and services'); J Farrell et al, 'Standard Setting, Patents and Hold-up' (2007) 74 *Antitrust Law Journal* 603, 640; Crane (n 9) 382 ('at a minimum, the commitment should be understood as an assurance that [the SEP holder] will not use discriminatory licensing patentees' power downstream from the patents to the standardized product'); Layne-Farrar (n 7); A Layne-Farrar and K Wong-Ervin, 'Methodologies for Calculating FRAND Damages: An Economic and Comparative Analysis of the Case Law from China, the European Union, India, and the United States' (2017) 8 *Jindal Global Law Review* 127, 143 ('the "ND" portion of RAND prevents SEP holders from discriminating on the basis of whether or not it competes directly with the licensee').

[30] Swanson and Baumol (n 9) 26.

pricing rule' (ECPR), which is a price that the SEP holder charges itself for the use of its own SEPs in order to identify whether a price is discriminatory.[31] Any royalty that substantially deviates from the ECPR could be deemed to violate the non-discriminatory requirement of a FRAND commitment.

Prohibiting discrimination by vertically integrated SEP holders against competitors is certainly a part of the ND obligation, but is not sufficient to provide a comprehensive answer. Such interpretation is too narrow. NPEs can also distort downstream competition by offering favourable licensing terms to some standard implementers and more restrictive terms to others. There are no reasons why the anti-competitive effects of price discrimination should be restricted only to vertically integrated SEP holders, and not to NPEs. The text of the FRAND commitment also does not make a distinction between the business models of submitters. Any company that makes a FRAND commitment undertakes to comply with the non-discrimination requirement, regardless of whether it is vertically integrated or not.

Furthermore, the proposed use of ECPR would be difficult, if not impossible to apply in practice.[32] Arriving at a price that the SEP holder charges itself for the use of SEPs would require calculating the incremental costs of producing downstream components minus the downstream product price. However, precisely determining the incremental costs of producing a product is not an easy task, especially in high-tech industries.[33] The ECPR test also does not appreciate the fact that the SEP holder itself may need a licence for other SEPs, and it does offer a solution to how to disaggregate the value that the SEP holder is paying to all other licensors from the value that it is paying for the use of its own SEPs. As Layne-Farrar observes: 'for all its intuitive appeal, then, the ECPR likely would be unworkable in most real-world standard-setting context'.[34]

C. Prohibiting Discrimination against Similarly Situated Licensees

The commonly accepted interpretation of the ND requirement of a FRAND commitment is that similarly situated licensees should be treated similarly.[35]

[31] ibid, 30.

[32] Crane (n 9) 385; Layne-Farrar (n 7) 829–31.

[33] Crane (n 9) 385.

[34] Layne-Farrar (n 7) 831.

[35] See Gilbert (n 22); Lemley and Shapiro (n 22) 1141–42 ('A patent owner making a FRAND commitment is obliged to offer similar terms to similarly situated parties. However, this does not mean that everyone must always pay the same price'); D Geradin, 'The Meaning of "Fair and Reasonable" in the Context of Third-Party Determination of FRAND Terms' (2014) *George Mason Law Review* 919, 928 ('non-discrimination does not mean that licensing terms should be identical for all licensees, as such an interpretation would ignore economic realities, but that "similarly situated" licensees should have

The support comes both from the case law and literature. However, the application is not as simple as it may seem and it opens up additional issues where courts and commentators radically diverge, such as: (i) how to determine if licensees are similarly situated; (ii) how to determine dissimilarity in treatment, ie, is it sufficient to show a mere divergence of terms or do we require more, like the proof of competitive harm?; and (iii) what is the remedy in case of discrimination? Each point is important and will be analysed in turn.

i. Which Licensees are Similarly Situated?

For various reasons licensees differ and it may not be so straightforward to identify which licensees are similarly situated. For example, licensees vary in terms of quantities of produced standard-implementing products (big corporations versus SMEs); industries where they are present (smartphone manufacturers versus smart car manufacturers); geographical presence (global versus local players); whether a licensee has a corresponding portfolio to cross-license or not; and other circumstances that may apply to a particular licensee (for example, concluding a business cooperation agreement together with a licence, accepting to promptly conclude a licence and secure an early-bird discount as opposed to companies choosing to hold out and negotiate and litigate for years, or licences concluded under financial duress). Each criterion may differentiate a licensee, and the question is which conditions are relevant and which are not for classifying licensees as similarly situated.

Carlton and Shampine propose that firms are 'similarly situated if *ex ante* they expect to obtain the same incremental value from the patented technology compared with the next best available alternative available to be incorporated into the standard'.[36] This would distinguish firms based on industries where they operate. Smartphone makers and car manufacturers that use cellular connectivity are different, as they obtain different value from standardised technology and do not compete against one another, meaning they can pay different rates. However, what about other criteria that may differentiate licensees from the same industry?

In *Unwired Planet v Huawei* the question was whether Samsung and Huawei were similarly situated. Samsung concluded a favourable licence with Unwired Planet using Unwired Planet's very difficult financial situation. Namely, Unwired Planet was close to insolvency and running short of cash, as it was able to conclude only one licence for its portfolio and was engaged in protracted and expensive multijurisdictional patent litigation against Huawei and other implementers.[37]

access to the same licensing terms'); Sidak, 'Fair and Unfair Discrimination' (n 1); CEN-CENELEC, 'Principles and Guidance for Licensing Standard Essential Patents in 5G and the Internet of Things (IoT), Including the Industrial Internet' (June 2019) 7, available at: www.cencenelec.eu/news/workshops/pages/ws-2019-013.aspx.

[36] Carlton and Shampine (n 22) 546.

[37] *Unwired Planet v Huawei* [2018] EWCA Civ 2344, 138.

After Unwired Planet was bought by another company, a deal was struck with Samsung whereby Samsung paid an undisclosed lump sum in cash and assigned a portfolio of patents in return for a worldwide licence under Unwired Planet's SEP and non-SEP portfolio.[38] Although Mr Justice Birss held that the licence did not represent useful evidence of the market value of Unwired Planet's patent portfolio, the question was whether it could still be used in the non-discrimination analysis. Huawei contended that it was being discriminated against by Unwired Planet as it was offered much higher licensing terms than Samsung.

The High Court and the Court of Appeal held that Huawei and Samsung were similarly situated as they are both very large multinational telecommunications manufacturers active in the same handsets and infrastructure markets.[39] This was enough to characterise them as similarly situated. Courts recognised the difference in circumstances under which Samsung's licence was entered – financial condition of the licensor and wider strategic cooperation between Unwired Planet and Samsung – but different market conditions do not render a transaction not equivalent. Such market conditions could, however, be assessed under the objective justification part of the ND analysis.[40]

In *TLC v Ericsson* the court accepted the general principle that companies using the technology in the same market and at similar level of the value chain should be treated as similar in the ND analysis.[41] This narrowed down the focus only to the mobile phone market. The question was whether we can further distinguish licensees from the mobile phone market based on their characteristics, and what those characteristics may be. The court said that the factors that matter are of a geographic scope, licences required by the firm and sales volume.[42] Factors that do not matter are a company's overall financial success or risk, brand recognition, the operating system, or the existence of retail stores. The geographic scope was the most important factor in determining which firms are similarly situated, and the court distinguished between global firms and local firms that are active in only one country (local kings).[43] Global firms and local kings are held not to be similarly situated because they serve different markets and customers, and because local firms receive different kinds of licences limited only to SEPs in one jurisdiction, and a rate that reflects the portfolio strength in that jurisdiction. On the other hand, global firms receive a global portfolio licence at a global blended rate which averages out higher rates in some countries with lower rates in others with weaker or non-existent patent protection.[44] The court in the end concluded that TCL is similarly situated to global firms such as Apple and Samsung, but not with strong local players like Karbon from India and Coolpad from China.

[38] ibid, 144.
[39] *Unwired Planet v Huawei* [2017] EWHC 2988 (Pat) 488.
[40] *Unwired Planet v Huawei* [2018] EWCA Civ 2344, 169.
[41] *TCL v Ericsson* (n 24) 57.
[42] ibid, 58.
[43] ibid, 59.
[44] ibid.

Therefore, the case law and literature correctly make a distinction between companies using the technology in different downstream markets. As mentioned, the 5G standard has a different use and provides a different value to a smartphone, connected car or a smart utility meter. Whether and how to distinguish between licensees in the same market is a point of contention. Often, the main factors will be the geographical coverage and the size of licensees, while other factors such as market background under which a licence was entered could be examined in the objective justification part of the ND analysis.

ii. When is Dissimilar Treatment Discriminatory?

The second question is how to determine the threshold of dissimilarity of terms that triggers the ND obligation. In the case law and literature, we can broadly identify two tendencies: (i) a 'quick-look' approach based on the observation that rates or conduct of the SEP owner appear dissimilar; or (ii) that a dissimilarity of terms should lead to competitive harm between licensees. Neither approach is universally accepted, and each has its own distinct features.

The 'quick-look' approach was applied by some US and German courts where they only summarily examined the divergence of terms or looked at some external factors to find discriminatory treatment. For example, in *TCL v Ericsson* in the US, the court compared the offers that Ericsson made to TCL with licences concluded with other similarly situated licensees and found that offers were 'radically divergent'.[45] This was sufficient to find that the ND obligation was breached, but the court did not elaborate on its decision further. In *Philips v Wiko*, Karlsruhe Higher Reginal Court found that Philip's offer was discriminatory because it did not adequately explain why it agreed a lump-sum payment with one party and not a running royalty as offered to Wiko.[46] This is also an example of the indirect way of the assessment of the compliance with the ND obligation, although the question could have been resolved by the unpacking of licences and a comparison of effective rates.

In *Unwired Planet v Huawei*,[47] Düsseldorf Higher Regional Court focused on the conduct of the SEP owner and held that prior to granting the very first FRAND licence the SEP owner should select a specific licensing concept which is then binding upon the future licensing conduct of the SEP owner and any potential successors.[48] Any deviation from the terms in the very first FRAND licence would automatically trigger a breach of ND obligation. A change in licensing

[45] *TCL v Ericsson* (n 24) 94.
[46] *Philips v Wiko*, 6 U 183/16 Karlsruhe Higher Regional Court (30 October 2019).
[47] *Unwired Planet v Huawei*, I-2 U 31/16 Düsseldorf Higher Regional Court (22 March 2019).
[48] ibid, 413.

terms would be possible only if it is agreed that all licences expire at the same time; only at that time could the SEP owner choose a new licensing concept applicable to all licensees.[49] Such an interpretation, however, treats the ND requirement like the most favoured licensee clause that has negative welfare effects in a SEP licensing context and goes against the legislative history of ETSI's FRAND commitment, discussed further below. Additionally, it represents significant regulatory interference by courts in patent licensing markets and appears too rigid and inflexible to apply in evolving and fast-changing market circumstances. It would be advisable for such interpretation to be avoided and it remains to be seen how it will stand in appeal.[50]

The selective enforcement of SEPs against only some, but not all potential licensees was also deemed by Düsseldorf Regional Court as discriminatory.[51] The Court recognised that depending on the circumstances it would not have been possible for the SEP owner to enforce its SEPs against all other infringers, and initially targeting only infringers with market strength could be justified.[52] However, on the facts of the case, the Court held that suing only three companies without asserting SEPs against the remaining competitors was discriminatory and the SEP owner should at least have contacted and requested a licence from other companies as well.[53] However, tying the non-discrimination obligation with the mass enforcement of SEPs might not be the most optimal outcome. It could incentivise mass litigation, even with little merit, only to fulfil court-imposed interpretation of the ND requirement. While it is true that selectively licensing only to some competitors in the downstream market could cause competitive harm and an uneven playing field, as operating costs would be raised only to companies that take a licence while others would remain unlicensed, this could be better addressed by other market mechanisms, like patent pool licensing,[54] rather than the interpretation of the contractual ND obligation of a FRAND commitment.

Therefore, the 'quick-look' approach to determining discriminatory treatment does not appear to be optional. Applying rigid formulas, like prohibiting divergence from the first granted FRAND licence or selectively enforcing SEPs, risks disincentivising SEP licensing and upsetting patent licensing markets, which need to be flexible to accommodate many different business models and market circumstances. While a quick-look approach offers stability and faster resolution of cases, it comes at a high cost of harming flexibility and efficiency of complex licensing

[49] ibid, 414, 420.

[50] At the time of writing, the judgment of Düsseldorf Higher Regional Court in *Unwired Planet v Huawei* is under appeal to the Federal Supreme Court.

[51] *Intellectual Ventures v Vodafone*, 4C O 81/17 Düsseldorf Regional Court (11 July 2018).

[52] ibid, 274.

[53] ibid, 276–77.

[54] See discussion in ch 9.

markets and prevents the beneficial welfare effects of adjusting licensing agreements to the specific circumstances of parties and industries.

The second interpretation provides that the dissimilarity of terms should lead to competitive harm in order to be discriminatory. The German Federal Supreme Court in *Sisvel v Haier* held that the standard for assessment of the ND requirement of a FRAND commitment is the same as the competition law prohibition of discriminatory pricing from Article 102 TFEU.[55] On the facts of the case, Sisvel was found to have offered a licence to Haier on a much higher rate than to Haier's competitor. Sisvel argued that this other licensee was a state owned Chinese mobile phone maker and was granted a below-FRAND rate due to pressure from the Chinese government. Düsseldorf Higher Regional Court did not accept the argument as a valid objective justification for dissimilar treatment and found that the difference in rates was discriminatory within the meaning of Article 102 TFEU.[56] The Federal Supreme Court agreed that the standard of assessment for ND obligation is the competition law prohibition of discriminatory pricing, but accepted the fact that the SEP owner was forced to accept a below-FRAND rate in view of the lack of a realistic possibility for judicial enforcement of patents and pressure from the government as an objective justification.[57] Thus, the dissimilar treatment was not found to have breached an ND obligation.

On the other hand, the UK's *Unwired Planet v Huawei* is against equating competition law analysis with the assessment of the compliance with the ND obligation of a FRAND commitment. As a matter of principle, Mr Justice Birss held that a non-discrimination obligation should mean that a benchmark FRAND rate should be arrived at which is applicable to all licensees seeking the same kind of licence (a 'general' non-discrimination).[58] However, if the ND obligation means that a licensee has the right to demand the very same rate that has been granted to another licensee which is lower than the benchmark rate (which he coined as 'hard-edged' non-discrimination) then the obligation only applies if the difference would distort competition between the two licensees.[59] Analysing the hard-edged interpretation of the ND requirement, the court found that although the difference in the royalty rates between Samsung and Huawei was large, it was not large enough to distort competition between them.[60] Consequently, a breach of hard-edged ND requirement was not found.

Other cases also held that competition law should not be placed in the ND assessment. *TCL v Ericsson* held that the US Sherman Act and its long history provide no guidance to understanding ETSI's non-discrimination under FRAND.[61]

[55] *Sisvel v Haier*, KZR 36/17 (n 27) 81.
[56] *Sisvel v Haier*, 15 U 65/15 Düsseldorf Higher Regional Court (13 January 2016) 260–87.
[57] *Sisvel v Haier* (n 27) 102.
[58] *Unwired Planet v Huawei* [2017] EWHC 2988 (Pat) 177, 503.
[59] ibid, 503.
[60] ibid, 518.
[61] *TCL v Ericsson* (n 24) 91.

The court distinguished between harm to competition which is actionable under US antitrust laws, and harm to a competitor which is not, but is caught under FRAND analysis.[62] The UK Court of Appeal and the Supreme Court in *Unwired Planet v Huawei* rejected the 'hard-edge' interpretation of the ND obligation and confirmed there is no need to prove competitive harm in the ND analysis of a FRAND commitment. They correctly recognised that discrimination that causes competitive harm could well be addressed through the application of competition law, and therefore there was no need to apply it in the FRAND analysis as well.[63]

In conclusion, we can see that courts are struggling to find a uniform interpretation of the degree of dissimilarity of terms needed to trigger the breach of ND obligation. Neither the quick-look approach nor using competition law analysis provide a satisfactory framework. Recognising this deficiency, the European Commission's SEP Expert Group proposed an interesting model for the assessment of the ND obligation.[64] It suggested developing a benchmarking model where the terms of a licence would be compared with all other licensing agreements concluded with similarly situated licensees and the degree of dissimilarity of terms mapped against other licences.[65] This would supposedly enable easier comparison of licensing terms. The applicability of this method could be further explored.

iii. *What are the Remedies for Discrimination?*

A final issue to be addressed is the remedy for the SEP owner's breach of its ND obligation. Two interpretations from the literature and case law can be identified: (i) a discriminated licensee should receive the same rate as the other similarly situated licensee; or (ii) a discriminated licensee should receive a general FRAND rate applicable to all other similarly situated licensees.

Under the first approach, if the ND requirement is breached a remedy should be the payment of the same rate that another similarly situated licensee pays.[66] If for any reason the SEP holder concludes a more favourable licence with any licensee, the SEP holder must offer the same terms to all other similarly situated licensees.[67] For example, if the SEP holder concludes more favourable licensing

[62] ibid.

[63] *Unwired Planet v Huawei* [2018] EWCA Civ 2344, 200; *Unwired Planet v Huawei; Huawei and ZTE v Conversant* [2020] UKSC 37.

[64] J Baron et al, 'Group of Experts on Licensing and Valuation of Standard Essential Patents – Contribution to the Debate on SEPs' (January 2021) 121, available at: ec.europa.eu/docsroom/documents/45217.

[65] ibid.

[66] Carlton and Shampine (n 22) 546 ('"Non-discriminatory" … can be interpreted to mean that … all "similarly situated" firms should pay the same royalty rate').

[67] A Shampine, 'Applying the Non-Discrimination Requirement of FRAND when Rates Change' (2016) 8 *Antitrust Source* 1.

terms with any handset manufacturer, it must offer the same terms to all other handset manufacturers. This is effectively the 'hard-edge' version of the ND requirement supported by Huawei in *Unwired Planet v Huawei*. It would arguably lead to the same level playing field between licensees.

However, such interpretation of the ND requirement of a FRAND commitment would transform it into a Most Favoured Licensee (MFL) clause. Neither general economic studies into the welfare effects of MFL clauses nor the text or legislative history of FRAND commitments provide support for such interpretation. MLF clauses in patent licensing agreements are likely to discourage licensing, as SEP owners would be dissuaded from offering lower royalties in the fear that it would become binding to all other licensees.[68] Licensing would become inflexible and economists caution that MFL clauses often result in higher overall prices in the market, as companies are reluctant to offer discounts even in most efficiency-justified cases.[69] Salop and Scott-Morton show that MFL clauses can also have exclusionary effects by raising the costs of rivals or entrants that try to compete by attempting to unsuccessfully negotiate lower prices from vertically integrated SEP holders.[70] The MFL clause interpretation thus has the potential to harm the technological development of standards if it has the effect of compelling the SEP owner to accept a level of royalty which does not reflect the value of the licensed technology.[71]

The text and legislative history of FRAND commitments also does not support the interpretation of the non-discrimination requirement as imposing an MFL obligation. Geradin and Brooks examined negotiations leading to ETSI's first IPR policy and found nothing to support that ETSI intended the FRAND commitment to be the same as the MFL clause.[72] ETSI's first interim patent policy in 1993 expressly included an MFL requirement, but this provision was quickly withdrawn in the face of substantial opposition, evidencing that ETSI members did not want the MFL clause to be a part of the FRAND commitment.[73]

The courts in *TCL v Ericsson* and *Unwired Planet v Huawei* examined and rejected the interpretation that the ND requirement of ETSI's FRAND

[68] Gilbert (n 22) 880.

[69] S Salop and F Scott Morton, 'Developing and Administrable MFN Enforcement Policy' (2013) 27 *Antitrust* 15.

[70] ibid.

[71] *Unwired Planet v Huawei* [2018] EWCA Civ 2344, 198.

[72] R Brooks and D Geradin, 'Interpreting and Enforcing the Voluntary FRAND Commitment' (2011) 9 *International Journal of IT Standards and Standardization Research* 1, 15.

[73] ibid ('Given this history, we conclude that any attempt to equate the "non-discriminatory" component of an ETSI FRAND commitment with thoroughgoing "Most Favoured Licensee" obligations would be mistaken as a matter of intent-based contract interpretation'). The relevant clause reads: 'include a clause requiring the licensor to promptly notify a licensee of any licence granted by it to a third party for the same IPRs under comparable circumstances giving rise to terms and conditions that are clearly more favourable, in their entirety, than those granted to the licensee and allowing the licensee to require replacement of the terms and conditions of its licence, in their entirety, either with those of the third party licence, or with such other terms and conditions as the parties may agree'.

commitment entails an MFL obligation.[74] The UK Supreme Court recognised that there are commercial circumstances where the SEP owner may choose to license its portfolio at a below-FRAND rate not reflecting its true value, such as offering royalties to the first implementer to take a licence in order to encourage others to seek licences as well, or a 'fire sale' licensing in order to secure financial survival when the SEP owner is in commercial difficulties.[75]

The second interpretation is that the discriminated licensee should be offered a benchmark FRAND rate applicable to all other similarly situated licensees. In other words, this is the 'general' non-discrimination obligation introduced by Mr Justice Birss in *Unwired Planet v Huawei* and endorsed by the UK Court of Appeal and the Supreme Court.[76] It requires establishing a benchmark rate that reflects the value of the SEP portfolio without taking into account the characteristics of the individual licensee.[77] Such a benchmark FRAND rate is then offered to all similarly situated licensees. Simply put, 'there is to be a single royalty price list available to all'.[78] A benchmark FRAND rate can be adjusted downwards depending on the characteristics of individual licensees (such as, for example, volume and early-bird discounts) or any special circumstances of the licensor (ie, financial duress), but it cannot be set higher than the benchmark level and a particular licensee cannot demand a lower rate granted to another licensee.

The benchmark royalty approach has merits; it is based on the value of the portfolio and not on the individual characteristics of the parties. It prevents driving down royalties to sub-optimal levels and associated negative welfare effects under the MFL interpretation, but at the same time prevents holdup as every similarly situated licensee should be offered the same benchmark FRAND rate. Thus, the amount of royalties does not depend solely on the bargaining strength of the

[74] *TCL v Ericsson* (n 24) 13, 14, 91; *Unwired Planet v Huawei* [2018] EWCA Civ 2344, 199 ('It is difficult to identify any underlying purpose which would support the hard-edged discrimination rule contended for by Huawei. Its effect is akin to the insertion of the rejected "most favoured licensee" clause in the FRAND undertaking. It is of course possible that those behind formulating the undertaking thought that the same effect as a most favoured licensee term could be achieved by the "ND" limb of FRAND, but we consider that it is far more likely that the industry would have regarded such a term as inconsistent with the overall objective of the undertaking'); also *Unwired Planet v Huawei; Huawei and ZTE v Conversant* (n 64).

[75] *Unwired Planet v Huawei; Huawei and ZTE v Conversant* (n 64) 125.

[76] The UK Supreme Court also added that the ND obligation has no separate meaning, a FRAND commitment imposes a single unitary obligation and should be read as a composite whole: 'There are not two distinct obligations, that the licence terms should be fair and reasonable and also, separately, that they should be non-discriminatory. Still less are there three distinct obligations, that the licence terms should be fair and, separately, reasonable and, separately, non-discriminatory'; *Unwired Planet v Huawei; Huawei and ZTE v Conversant* (n 64) 113–14. However, such an interpretation is difficult to accept. While it is true that concepts of fair, reasonable and non-discriminatory are closely linked, they provide answers to different questions. A FRAND royalty is concerned with the valuation of SEPs, while the ND asks whether similarly situated licensees are treated similarly by being offered the same FRAND rate.

[77] *Unwired Planet v Huawei* [2018] EWCA Civ 2344, 195–98.

[78] *Unwired Planet v Huawei; Huawei and ZTE v Conversant* (n 64) 114.

licensee as the upper amount is constrained by the benchmark FRAND rate. The next section examines how the general framework of the ND requirement could be applied.

V. The Application of the Non-Discrimination Requirement of a FRAND Commitment

As seen, courts have struggled to arrive at a coherent framework for analysing the ND requirement of a FRAND commitment. The conflicting judgments concern what factors make licensees similar/dissimilar; the degree of dissimilarity triggering the breach of ND obligation; and the remedies against discriminatory treatment. This section summarises and provides a framework for the interpretation of the ND requirement of a FRAND commitment.

In accordance with the majority of case law and literature, the ND part of the FRAND commitment should be interpreted as prohibiting the SEP holder from offering dissimilar licensing terms to similarly situated licensees without objective justification. This approach is grounded in contractual interpretation of the ND requirement and does not require proof of the anti-competitive effects of dissimilar treatment.

The efficient operationalisation of the ND obligation would require, as a first step from SEP owners that decide to monetise their SEP, the publication of detailed royalty programmes and terms and conditions applicable to all similarly situated licensees.[79] Such royalty programmes would act as a benchmark FRAND royalty rate. For example, for 3G/4G/5G portfolios a separate royalty programme could be set for different downstream markets and uses of the technology. Rates could differ for the smartphone market, motor vehicles or consumer devices. SEP owners should define in advance where they will license in the production chain (end-device or component) and whether they will use a running royalty, per-unit royalty, a lump-sum payment or a combination of them all. Further refinements could be made within each royalty programme, for instance the amount of volume discounts depending on the quantity of royalty-bearing units, early-bird discounts for signing up to a licence within a certain time frame or specifying royalty caps and floors in a case of running royalties.[80] Selective enforcement of patents should not be held to be discriminatory as it cannot be expected that the SEP owner should simultaneously target the whole industry. Only if there is clear evidence

[79] Publication of royalty programmes by SEP owners was already discussed and proposed in the literature by Gilbert (n 22) 875 (proposing that all licensees should be able to choose from the same schedule of royalties, which may be a fixed fee, a fixed per-unit running royalty, royalty that declines with the output. As such each licensee could choose which royalty schedule best fits with its business model); Contreras and Gilbert (n 1); recently Baron et al (n 65) 120.

[80] Baron et al (n 65) 119.

that selective enforcement is intentionally made to distort competition should it be further scrutinised.[81]

This proposal is not radical as patent pools and some SEP owners are already implementing it. Major patent pools such as Avanci, Sisvel and Via-Licensing publish their royalty programmes. For cellular 3G/4G/5G portfolios they differentiate between different industries (different programmes for mobile phone and motor vehicle markets), provide per-unit royalty rates, volume and early-bird discounts. For example, Via-Licensing for its portfolio of 3G and 4G SEPs has a separate licensing programme for mobile devices and connected vehicles. For mobile devices, the licensing rate varies between $1.50 and $2.25 per unit depending on the quantity and a 50 per cent discount is provided if the licence is executed within six months,[82] while the rate for connected motor vehicles varies between $3.00 and $.2.25 per unit.[83] Avanci, the largest patent pool, currently offers portfolio licences for 2G/3G and 4G SEPs for connected vehicles at $15 per vehicle and promises that it will provide different royalty programmes for a wide range of IoT industries.[84] As mentioned before, some of the largest cellular SEP owners – Qualcomm, Nokia, Ericsson, Interdigital – have published their maximum royalty rates for 3G/4G and 5G. However, their announcements lack the specificity of those from patent pools and they could in the future provide more information, especially since the IoT will bring countless numbers of companies from different industries that would need to take a licence.

Publicly announced royalty programmes and terms and conditions applicable to all similarly situated licensees provides a more transparent and predictable licensing framework. It enables easier compliance with the ND requirement and ensure licensees know in advance the maximum amount of royalty costs. Every similarly situated licensee would be offered the same rate, thus ensuring the level playing field between implementers. Individually negotiated royalties may be lower than the published rates, but this will be based on transparent and objective criteria, not solely on the bargaining strength of the individual licensee. Of course, an offered royalty must be fair and reasonable and able to be immediately accepted by the implementer without further negotiations to ensure that it would not be discriminatory to other licensees. Transparently set licensing programmes in accordance with FRAND royalty principles would prevent most royalty disputes.

[81] ibid.

[82] Via Licensing, Mobile Devices & General Products Sub-Program, License Fees, available at: www.via-corp.com/licensing/mg-multi-generational-wireless/mobile-devices-general-products/mg-mobile-patent-license-fees/.

[83] Via Licensing, Connected Motor Vehicles & Component, License Fees, available at: www.via-corp.com/licensing/mg-multi-generational-wireless/connected-motor-vehicles/mg-connected-motor-vehicles-license-fees/.

[84] Avanci, Marketplace, Pricing, available at: www.avanci.com/marketplace/#li-pricing.

Once publicly announced royalty programmes are set, it would be easier to apply the ND obligation. As discussed, the contractual approach to the interpretation of the ND obligation consists of the following three-part legal test: (i) are licensees similarly situated? (ii) Has the SEP holder offered dissimilar terms? (iii) Are there any objective justifications?

The first step should establish whether licensees are similarly situated. The comparison now will be easier as the licensor has already made different royalty programmes available for different licensees depending on the industry and the use of SEPs, the position in the production chain, geographical scope of the licence (worldwide or regional) and volumes of licensed products.

The second step is to establish if the licensee is treated dissimilarly. The object of the enquiry should be on whether the licensee was offered the same royalty programme as other similarly situated licensees. The focus is then not on finally concluded licences, as they will naturally vary even between similarly situated licensees.[85] The difference between a licence offer and the royalty that the licensee will ultimately pay under the negotiated licence agreement depends on many factors, such as whether payments are negotiated as a lump sum, per unit or running royalty; the difference between projected and actual sales; whether early-bird discount was applied or a licence was concluded after prolonged negotiations and litigation; the length of the agreement; whether cross-licensing is involved; and whether the licence is tied with some other business cooperation between licensor and licensee. Thus, the ultimate paid royalty will naturally vary. What is important is that the licensee is being *offered* the same terms as all other similarly situated licensees. This approach is more simple and easier to apply as there is no need to measure the differences between ultimately paid rates. All that is needed is to check if each similarly situated licensee is offered the same royalty programme; the licensee can then decide how best to proceed and negotiate the most optimal terms.

If it is established that the SEP owner offered dissimilar terms to similarly situated licensees, then the burden should be on the SEP owner to provide any objective justifications for such treatment. An example of objective justification is financial duress on the side of the SEP owner, when it may accept below-FRAND royalties in order to ensure financial liquidity, which is what happened in *Unwired Planet v Huawei*. Another example could be favourable offers to secure valuable cross-licence or associated business cooperation with the other party.

The remedy for the breach of ND obligation should be to offer to the licensee the same royalty programme as was applied to all similarly situated licensees. The ND obligation interpreted in this way does not have the negative effects of an MFL clause that would force down royalties to below-FRAND levels and discourage the beneficial welfare effects of price discrimination, but it ensures that all

[85] See similarly Sidak, 'Fair and Unfair Discrimination' (n 1) 364–65.

similarly situated licensees would be treated equally in a transparent and predictable manner. Once the same royalty programme is offered to all, a licensee can negotiate the precise terms and conditions with the licensor that consider its unique situation.

VI. Confidentiality Agreements and Disclosure of Licences

Under the current system, where many licensing programmes are not fully transparent, the SEP owner needs to disclose to the court and the prospective licensee its prior licences in order to prove that its offer is on FRAND terms. As seen, comparable prior licences are a key method in determining FRAND royalty rates and are also crucial in verifying the compliance with the ND obligation. A licence, however, includes many information that is strictly confidential and unrestricted disclosure would put licensees at a competitive disadvantage and commercial risk. For example, licences may include information about past and future sales of a licensee, sales forecasts, plans for expansion and geographical coverage, the terms of the business cooperation between licensor and licensee, the price of the cross-licensed portfolio etc. Given that similarly situated licensees are often mutual competitors, the unrestricted disclosure of prior licences would allow licensees to obtain sensitive commercial information about their competitors. On the other hand, some information from prior licences must be available to the court and the prospective licensee in order to verify whether the SEP owner made a FRAND offer. Such information includes the list of patents to be licensed, details on the agreed royalty rates, rebates, caps and other financial information regarding royalty terms.

As a result, non-disclosure agreements (NDAs) are typically concluded to reconcile the tension between the need for disclosure of prior licences in the FRAND context and the need to protect confidential business secrets. The tensions about the precise structure of NDAs have begun to emerge in SEP litigation.[86] On the one hand, NDAs can be structured under the 'external eyes only' principle where licences would be disclosed only to external lawyers and experts who keep the information confidential from their clients and use the information to verify whether the offered terms are FRAND. While such an approach ensures the maximum possible protection of confidential business

[86] See Fair Standards Alliance, 'Transparently FRAND: The Use (and Misuse) of Confidentiality Obligations in FRAND Licensing Negotiations' (13 February 2017), available at: fair-standards.org/wp-content/uploads/2017/02/170213-FSA-Position-PaperTransparency-FRAND-1.pdf; S Makris and C Tapia, 'Confidentiality in FRAND Licensing After *Huawei v ZTE*: National Courts in Europe Searching for Balance' (April 2019) *les Nouvelles* 210.

information, it prevents the prospective licensee from finding out itself if the offered terms are in line with other prior licences. If the case goes to court, such a disclosure regime would prevent the prospective licensee from relying on key documents in the case, calling into question the right to a fair trial. On the other hand, NDAs can be structured as a 'confidentiality club' where access to licences is provided only to a limited number of company representatives of the implementer and its external experts, who enter into confidentiality obligations not to further disclose such information to the implementer. This approach attempts to limit the exposure of confidential information to a limited number of implementer's representatives. The downside, however, is that once confidential information is acquired by the implementer's representatives it cannot be unlearned and the implementer's representatives would not realistically be able to avoid its use in the future.

The practice of courts regarding the scope of NDAs is slowly emerging. In Germany, courts have recommended that parties enter into confidentiality club arrangements and have not accepted the external eyes only principle.[87] In the UK, in *TQ Delta v Zyxel*, the request by the SEP owner to disclose prior licences solely under the external eyes only principle was also rejected, arguing that it would exclude access to key documents in the trial for one of the parties.[88] However, the judge indicated that it might be possible for *some* documents to be reserved for external eyes only when there are exceptional circumstances that justify it, but that a confidential club arrangement is sufficient to guarantee the protection of confidential information. *Mitsubishi and Sisvel v Oppo and Xiaomi* combined both principles – external eyes only for some exceptionally sensitive documents, and a confidentiality club for the remaining documents.[89] A member of the confidentiality club, however, must not include persons who are involved in licensing negotiations or FRAND litigation with the SEP owner and parties to disclosed licensing agreements.[90] This is intended to ensure that representatives of the implementer in the confidentiality club would not be able to use the confidential information obtained in future negotiations with the SEP owner or its competitors.

Parties could then structure their NDAs in a tiered way. Most licences could be disclosed to the confidential club comprised of representatives of the implementer and external experts who would need to keep the information obtained confidential from the implementer. Company representatives should not be involved in future SEP licensing negotiations with other SEP owners, although they can be members of internal IP, legal or economic teams. Sensitive information about competitors that is irrelevant for the establishment of FRAND terms could

[87] ibid.
[88] *TQ Delta v Zyxel* [2018] EWHC 1515(Ch) 21–24.
[89] *Mitsubishi and Sisvel v Oppo and Xiaomi* [2020] EWHC 2641 (Pat).
[90] ibid, 55.

be redacted. This could apply, for instance, to the names of counterparties, terms of business cooperation, cross-licensing terms, projected future sale plans, etc. If, however, such information needs to be disclosed for the unpacking of licences, a separate external-eyes only tier could be set up which would be able to read this unredacted information. External eyes-only tiers could also be tasked to review some particularly sensitive licences not disclosed to a confidentiality club, for example licences of direct competitors of the implementer. Structuring NDAs in this way would ensure the protection of confidential business information and also enable the implementer to verify whether it was offered FRAND terms as other similarly situated licensees.

Admittedly, the process of entering into a proper NDA arrangement, and then disclosing, assessing and comparing information from prior licences can be slow and demanding. The process is also liable to potential abuse by implementers who intentionally delay the conclusion of licensing agreements, and the risk of leakage of confidential information cannot be averted. The European Commission's SEP Expert Group thus proposed establishing a confidential repository of licensing agreements with a special market transparency body, where access to the repository would be allowed only to courts, competition authorities, arbitrators and other agreed upon trusted persons.[91] The repository would facilitate comparison of terms, enabling easier assessment of the compliance with ND obligations and determining whether SEP royalties are fair and reasonable. This proposal could be explored further as it indeed has the potential to simplify licensing negotiations and protect business secrets at the same time. Additionally, if SEP owners were to make public their licensing programmes and terms, as suggested, the same terms would be offered to all similarly situated licensees which would obviate many of the concerns with discriminatory licensing.

VII. Conclusion

The ND requirement of a FRAND commitment is a contractual obligation separate from the competition law prohibition of anti-competitive discriminatory pricing, which imposes stricter pricing restrictions than under competition law. The ND obligation is commonly interpreted as preventing dissimilar treatment of similarly situated licensees, but the precise implementation has varied between courts which struggled with its application. However, it appears to be well established that the ND requirement should not represent an MFL clause that would compel the SEP owner to conclude licensing agreements at the same rate with all similarly situated implementers. This chapter has suggested that SEP owners should make

[91] Baron et al (n 65) 143–44.

public different royalty programmes applicable to all similarly situated licensees, and publish precise royalty terms and conditions, which would go a long way to addressing any ND concerns and lead to a more transparent and predictable licensing framework. A confidential repository of licensing agreements could also be considered as an additional mechanism to facilitate licensing and faster resolution of disputes.

6

FRAND Royalty Base

I. Introduction: The End-Product or Component?

This chapter addresses the royalty base that can be used for FRAND royalties. It will first provide a policy analysis of which royalty base best reflects the value of SEPs and will then proceed to discussing whether there is a legal requirement to use a particular royalty base. In conclusion it will look at how courts in SEP litigation resolved this question.

A disagreement between practice and the literature is whether SEPs should be based on final end-products or components. Some argue that SEPs are fully implemented in components and applying royalties on end-products is unjustified as it systematically overcompensates patent holders enabling them to capture the value of other unrelated patented and unpatented features and components.[1] Basing royalties on end-products would thus represent a 'tax' on successful implementers who have made a significant investment in the development of downstream products and other valuable follow-on non-standardised technologies.[2] Accordingly, a proper approach would be to use components that fully use a standard's functionality. In the case of cellular 3G, 4G, 5G, and wireless communication Wi-Fi standards would often be a baseband chip. It is also frequently pointed out that US patent damages law requires the use of the 'smallest saleable patent-practicing unit' (SSPPU) in damages calculations in cases of multi-component products.[3] The US antitrust agencies at one point endorsed the approach that FRAND royalties should be based on the SSPPU.[4]

[1] For the literature supportive of using components as a royalty base in SEP licensing, see: M Lemley and C Shapiro, 'Patent Holdup and Royalty Stacking' (2007) 85 *Texas Law Review* 1991, 2024; J Ordover and A Shampine, 'Implementing the FRAND Commitment' (2014) 10 *Antitrust Source* 1, 10 ('our concern about using the price of the downstream device is that its market price can reflect a great deal of value to consumers derived from other sources … with respect to the value of the technology, the standard is implemented in the component'); J Kattan, 'The Next FRAND Battle: Why the Royalty Base Matters' (31 March 2015) *CPI Antitrust Chronicle* 1; J Kattan, J Ordover and A Shampine, 'FRAND and the Smallest Saleable Unit' (2016) 9 *Competition Policy International* 1; W Lee and D Melamed, 'Breaking the Vicious Cycle of Patent Damages' (2016) 101 *Cornell Law Review* 385, 428; R Grasso, 'Standard Essential Patents: Royalty Determination in the Supply Chain' (2017) 8 *Journal of Competition Law & Practice* 283; CEN-CENELEC, 'Core Principles and Approaches for Licensing of Standard Essential Patents' (June 2019) 35, available at: www.cencenelec.eu/news/workshops/Pages/WS-2019-014.aspx.

[2] Grasso (n 1) 287.

[3] Lee and Melamed (n 1) 428; Grasso (n 1) 290.

[4] The Federal Trade Commission (FTC), 'The Evolving IP Marketplace: Aligning Patent Notice and Remedies with Competition' (2011) 212 ('the practical difficulty of identifying a royalty rate that

On the other hand, others point out that final end-devices should be used as a royalty base for SEP licensing because the full value and functionality of the standard is realised only in end-devices.[5] A long-standing industry practice is to use end-products as a royalty base recognising the fact that end-products are often the most adequate proxy of a standard's value. Basing royalties on components would, consequently, systematically devalue SEPs and undercompensate SEP owners, diminishing incentives to innovate and participate in the development of future standards. It is also pointed out that US patent damages law does not require the use of the SSPPU in all cases and is not a substantive rule of law.[6] Recently, the US Department of Justice reversed its position, recognising that parties should be free to set the royalty base that encourages efficient licensing and innovation, including the use of end-devices, and warning that mandatory imposition of the use of the SSPPU as a royalty base in SDO IPR policies may warrant antitrust scrutiny.[7]

accurately reflects the invention's contribution to a much larger, complex product often counsels toward choosing the smallest priceable component that incorporates the inventive feature'); Department of Justice, Letter from Renata Hesse, Assistant Attorney General to Michael Lindsey (2 February 2015) 12 ('the Smallest Saleable Compliant Implementation may be appropriate in calculating a royalty that is correctly tied to the patented invention, particularly when the product is complex and incorporates many patented technologies').

[5] For the literature supportive of using final end-devices as a royalty base in SEP licensing, see: D Geradin and A Layne-Farrar, 'Patent Value Apportionment Rule for Complex, Multi-Component Products' (2011) 27 *Santa Clara High Technology Law Journal* 763; G Sidak, 'The Proper Royalty Base for Patent Damages' (2014) 10 *Journal of Competition Law & Economics* 989, 991 ('Using the price of the smallest salable patent-practicing component as the royalty base risks undercompensating the patent holder, because it ignores (1) the effects that the patented technology has on the value of the downstream product and (2) the value that synergies between complementary technologies create'); C Caffarra and P Régibeau, 'Patent Explosion and Patent Wars: Holdup, Royalties and Misunderstandings over 'Market Value' (2014), available at: ecp.crai.com/wp-content/uploads/2017/11/Caffarra_et_al_SEP_and_market_value_revised_clean.pdf ('we conclude that claims that "the market value of a device is not the appropriate base on which to calculate a FRAND royalty" are misplaced, as are corresponding concerns about the choice of royalty base in agreements between SEP holders and licensees'); L Froeb and M Shor, 'Innovators, Implementers and Two-Sided Holdup' (2015) 8 *Antitrust Source* 1; M Blecker, T Sanchez and E Stasik, 'An Experience-Based Look at the Licensing Practices that Drive the Cellular Communications Industry: Whole Portfolio/Whole Device Licensing' (December 2016) *les Nouvelles* 221, 223 ('the whole-device licensing model has functioned well, simplified the process for both the licensee and licensor, and enabled the cellular communications industry to become a historic success story'); B Heiden and J Andreasson, 'Reevaluating Patent Damages in the Knowledge Economy: The Intellectual Value Chain in the Royalty Base for Standard-Essential Patents' (2016) 1 *Criterion Journal on Innovation* 229; D Teece and E Sherry, 'On the "Smallest Salable Patent-Practicing Unit" Doctrine: An Economic and Public Policy Analysis' (2016) Tushner Center for the Management of Intellectual Capital Working Paper No 11 ('the [SSPPU] doctrine makes no economic sense and is completely at odds with the long standing view that in determining reasonable royalties one should mimic licensing practices in the real world'); A Gautier and N Petit, 'Smallest Salable Patent Practicing Unit and Component Licensing: Why 1$ is not $1' (2019) 15 *Journal of Competition Law & Economics* 690.

[6] D Cawley and L Leavitt, 'The Federal Circuit Disavows Mandatory Smallest Salable Patent Practicing Unit "Rule"' (2017) 36 *Review of Litigation* 52; D Kappos and P Michel, 'The Smallest Salable Patent-Practicing Unit: Observations of its Origin, Development and Future' (2018) 32 *Berkeley Technology Law Journal* 1433.

[7] See M Delrahim, Assistant Attorney General US Department of Justice, 'Take it to the Limit: Respecting Innovation Incentives in the Application of Antitrust Law' (10 November 2017), available at: www.justice.gov/opa/speech/file/1010746/download ('While the so-called "smallest salable component" rule may be a useful tool among many in determining patent infringement damages for

The question of a royalty base is closely connected with the issue of where to license in the supply chain discussed in chapter seven. They are, however, two distinct notions – a royalty base is a factor in determining the amount of royalty, while a licensing level is concerned with whom the licence should be concluded. Often the two will overlap; if components are used as a royalty base licences will also be concluded with component makers and vice versa, but this is not necessary. Licences could also be concluded with end-device manufacturers using the price of components as a royalty base, or licences with components manufacturers could be structured to be based on the value of the end-devices where their components will be used.

Ultimately, the debate about a proper royalty base comes down to price. A royalty applied to higher valued end-devices would lead to a larger amount than when applied to a lower price of components. This applies both to running and per-unit royalties. For example, using the same percentage royalty (1 per cent) on the price of an end-device ($500) or a component ($10) leads to substantially different amounts (in this case, $5 and $0.5 respectively). Similarly, a per-unit royalty of $5 would be easier to justify and collect on a $500 end-device, than on a $20 or $10 component. Given that profit margins of components are set at a low level in order to stay competitive, a SEP royalty may exceed the current profit margin of component manufacturers who would be unable to pay SEP royalties or, if they do, will need to increase the price of components, which may put them at a competitive disadvantage against other component manufacturers that have not yet taken a licence. Therefore, it becomes critical to know where the value of the standard comes from and whether a component or end-device best reflects that value.

II. The Appropriate FRAND Royalty Base

A proper FRAND royalty base should adequately reflect the value of SEPs. To find out whether the end-product or a component is an appropriate base, we should look at where the standard realises its full functionality and value. The analysis here will focus on connectivity standards, but the overall principle can be applied to other standards and industries.

The argument of using components as a royalty base is that a standard's functionality is fully implemented in a component and basing royalties on the end-device would allow SEP holders to capture the value of other components and the implementer's own follow-on innovations. Because the SEP holder's invention

multi-component products, its use as a requirement by a concerted agreement of implementers as the exclusive determinant of patent royalties may very well warrant antitrust scrutiny'); Department of Justice, Letter from Makan Delrahim, Assistant Attorney General to Sophia Muirhead (10 September 2020) (IEEE III Business Review Letter) 8 ('Ultimately, there is no single correct way to calculate a reasonable royalty in FRAND context. The Department believes parties should be given flexibility to fashion licenses that reward and encourage innovation').

has nothing to do with the presence of other features or components, it should not be able to capture this additional value. An example is a gold-plated smartphone that sells for $10,000, or a smartphone with 64 GB memory that retails for $700 and 265 GB memory that retails for $800. The price difference in these examples is attributable to other features unrelated to standardised technology. Using running royalties based on the selling price of the smartphone would allow SEPs holders to charge higher royalties to smartphones with better features and components than smartphones with fewer features. Instead, the price of a chip which generally costs around $15 should be used as a royalty base because it provides the same 3G/4G connectivity to every smartphone regardless of its final retail price.[8]

On the other hand, the argument of using end-devices as a royalty base is that SEPs realise their functionality and bring value to the whole product and not just on a component representing only its physical implementation.[9] Cellular connectivity in a smartphone brings significant value to consumers; in addition to making and receiving calls it enables access to the internet, sending and receiving pictures, the use of applications, emails, chat and messenger applications, online games. Moreover, the combination of different patented or unpatented features and components creates synergies and increases the value of the downstream product.[10] For example, having more memory enables the smartphone to handle larger files and that enhances the value of data connectivity because users value more data connectivity that can transfer larger files faster, and having better data connectivity likewise enhances the value of having additional memory.[11]

Indeed, a standard's value varies and depends on its downstream use. The value of 4G technology to a smartphone that uses its full functionality is different from a smart meter that uses only limited cellular connectivity. Similarly, in the IoT a smart car uses cellular connectivity frequently and to a fuller capacity than a smart refrigerator that would use connectivity only occasionally and with limited functionality. Basing royalties on final downstream devices appreciates this distinction.

Therefore, using chips as a royalty base would not capture the full value and benefits that standards bring to end-devices and consumers. Examples below illustrate this point. Given that the prevailing industry practice is to use end-devices as a royalty base, current component prices do not reflect the value of IP and basing royalties on the price of unlicensed chips may produce sub-optimal results. In *Innovatio* the court calculated FRAND royalties for Innovatio's 19 patents

[8] Grasso (n 1) 10 ('with respect to the value of the technology, the standard is implemented in the component').

[9] Blecker, Sanchez and Stasik (n 5) 231–32.

[10] See Teece and Sherry (n 5) 17 ('the combination of the patented feature and the presence (or absence) of other unpatented features can result in synergies in the value that users associate with the product as sold'); Sidak (n 5) 989 (explaining how SEPs have complementarity and network effects resulting from interaction with other patented and non-patented components of downstream products); Caffarra and Régibeau (n 5) ('the economic contribution of the technology would also have to include additional value obtained from features that are independent of the technology to the extent that total sales of the device are increased by the presence of the technology').

[11] Teece and Sherry (n 5) 17.

essential for Wi-Fi standard by looking at the average price of a Wi-Fi chip and using the average profit margin as the maximum royalty cap that a chip manufacturer would pay.[12] The court found that the average Wi-Fi chip price between 1997 and 2003 was $14.85 yielding an average profit of $1.80 on each chip, which is taken to be the maximum price for Wi-Fi standard. It is hard to imagine that the value of the whole Wi-Fi connectivity to end-users is worth less than $1.80 and, moreover, it would be paradoxical that the value of the Wi-Fi technology is almost ten times less than its physical implementation. An even more extreme example would be if the court in *Innovatio* used the average chip price between 2000 and 2013 as suggested by the implementers' damages expert. Since the average price of Wi-Fi chips is falling each year, this would lead to an average price of $3.99 per chip.[13] Applied to the average profit margin of 12.1 per cent this would produce an average profit of only $0.4 per chip and thus the maximum price for Wi-Fi technology.[14] The incentives to invent and participate in further standardisation would be seriously undermined if the interpretation that Wi-Fi connectivity is worth less than 0.4 cents is adopted.

It is also interesting to observe the difference in price of a product with and without cellular connectivity. iPad with Wi-Fi currently retails at only $329, while iPad with added cellular connectivity retails at $459. The difference of $130 exemplifies the added value that cellular connectivity brings to the end-product and how the average chip price does not adequately reflect the standard's value.

In relation to the IoT, recent studies have tried to estimate the value of connectivity standards to smart vehicles. One study looked at how much consumers are paying for connected car applications showing that on average consumers are paying approximately $3,900 per vehicle over an average car's lifetime, or between $330 and $22,645 depending on the brand and connectivity package.[15] Another study looked at the revenue derived by vehicle manufacturers from a connected vehicle ecosystem to be $670 in the US and $593 worldwide per connected vehicle.[16] The total revenue from connectivity-enabled products and services in the automotive sector was calculated to grow from $223 billion to $483 billion from 2018 to 2023, with forecasts predicting as much as $2 trillion by 2030.[17] This does not suggest that SEP owners should capture the whole value that connectivity brings to cars and consumers, but it does indicate that low profit margins of unlicensed components is not an adequate representative of the value created by SEPs.

[12] *In re Innovatio IP Ventures, LLC Patent Litigation*, 2013 WL 5593609 (ND Ill 2013).

[13] ibid, 40.

[14] ibid, 41.

[15] S Arya, 'The Value of Standardized Technology to Connected Cars' (2020) 69 *GRUR International* 365.

[16] B Heiden, 'The Value of Connectivity in the Automotive Sector – A First Look' (2019) 42, available at: papers.ssrn.com/sol3/papers.cfm?abstract_id=3521488.

[17] ibid.

Petit provides a good example of the value that a standard brings to end-devices with the Wireless Avionics Intra-Communications (WAIC) standard providing wireless communication between two or more points in an aeroplane.[18] WAIC is used primarily for safety-related applications: the release of oxygen masks, trigger of oxygen flow, emergency lighting and cabin pressure. By using WAIC aircraft manufacturers can cut significant costs by eliminating around 30 per cent of electrical wires in an aircraft. The reduction in weight coming from the elimination of wires is translated to jet fuel costs savings and reduced CO2 emissions. Taking just the fuel cost savings for the typical Airbus A-380, Petit estimates savings of $3.02 million per plane. Therefore, the WAIC standard's functionality and added benefits are realised by the whole plane and not just by a chip. He estimates the value of the radio frequency equipment that implements the WAIC standard to be $1000. Even if the key patent holder sought only half of the costs savings realised by the aircraft manufacturers as compensation for the benefits that patented technology realises, the royalty rate would be in excess of 1,510 per cent of the component price, which every component manufacturer would surely complain is unreasonable.[19]

Judge Davis in *CSIRO v Cisco* also recognised that the price of a physical component may not be an adequate proxy for a standard's value by providing a colourful example:

> The benefit of the patent lies in the idea, not in the small amount of silicon that happens to be where that idea is physically implemented. Basing a royalty solely on chip price is like valuing a copyrighted book based only on the costs of the binding, paper, and ink needed to actually produce the physical product. While such a calculation captures the cost of the physical product, it provides no indication of its actual value.[20]

He also added that the price of unlicensed components is artificially low and does not adequately reflect a standard's value:

> [C]ompounding this problem is the depression of chip prices in the damages period resulting from rampant infringement which occurred in the wireless industry, no company in the industry sought a license from CSIRO to the [patent] and CSIRO received no royalties whatsoever for that technology. It is simply illogical to attempt to value the contributions of the [patent] based on wireless chip prices that were artificially deflated because of pervasive infringement.[21]

The additional practical problem of basing royalties on components is that their prices may not always be available, while prices of the downstream products are readily observable. For example, a component may not be sold independently on the market but is made only for use in downstream products or only for use by a

[18] N Petit, 'The Smallest Salable Patent-Practicing Unit Experiment, General Purpose Technologies and Coase Theorem' 4IP Council (2016), available at: www.4ipcouncil.com/application/files/8914/5554/8353/SSPPU_rule_GPTs_and_the_Coase_Theorem_-_N_Petit_15_02_16.pdf.

[19] The example is taken from A Layne-Farrar, 'The Patent Damages Gap: An Economist's Review of US Statutory Patent Damages Apportionment Rules' (2018) 26 *Texas Intellectual Property Law Journal* 31.

[20] *CSIRO v Cisco*, 2014 WL 3805817, 11 (ED Tex 2014).

[21] ibid; also Heiden and Andreasson (n 5) 273 (using the term 'royalty lacking' to describe downward pressure on component prices due to the fact that components remain unlicensed because licensing happens downstream at end-device level).

particular manufacturer. In this case, the price of the component might be heavily discounted, or the component price may vary between different downstream manufacturers based on internal factors such as payment terms, warranty, quantities and taxes.[22] The use of estimates would be required to calculate the 'real' price of the component. On the other hand, the use of easily observable prices of downstream products would be more efficient than using estimated and unprecise prices of components.[23] Moreover, even if components are sold independently on the market, the prices of unlicensed components would not be a reliable proxy because, as we have seen, they do not take into account the value of IP rights.

Additionally, claims of SEPs for cellular connectivity standards are often not confined only to a chip but relate to complete downstream products or a combination of components. The reason is because cellular standards are intended to ensure interoperability between user equipment and a network, and thus require a device to function in a network environment. Putnam and Williams analysed Ericsson's patents declared essential for 2G/3G and 4G standards and found that they read on: (i) various components alone; (ii) various components in combination; (iii) complete handsets alone; and (iv) complete handsets in networks.[24] They further found that none of Ericsson's SEPs claimed only the baseband chip.[25] Instead, around 71 per cent of SEPs claimed some aspect of user equipment (downstream products), either alone or in combination with claims to the network.[26] Similar findings were reached in litigation. In *Unwired Planet v Huawei*, two SEPs that were held valid and infringed claimed combination of components and whole networks,[27] and in Germany several litigated SEPs involved claims relating to a combination of components,[28] and even over whole networks.[29] Consequently, there is often no single component that would claim the whole portfolio of SEPs.

[22] See Blecker, Sanchez and Stasik (n 5).

[23] This problem may be observed in a few cases that used the SSPPU discussed in more detail below. See *Cornell University v Hewlett-Packard Co*, 609 F.Supp.2d 279, 290 (ND NY 2009) (selling price of the SSPPU had to be estimated using a 'combination of economic and statistical techniques'); *LaserDynamics, Inc v Quanta Computer, Inc*, 694 F.3d 51, 69–70 (Fed Cir 2012) (rejected the argument from patent owner that 'practical and economic necessity' compelled it to base the royalty on the price of the downstream product because the infringer did not track prices of individual components and that it purchased components for a 'mask price' which is 'nominal' and 'essentially accounting fiction that offers little evidence of the drive's actual value').

[24] J Putnam and T Williams, 'The Smallest Salable Patent-Practicing Unit (SSPPU): Theory and Evidence' (2016) Working Paper, available at: papers.ssrn.com/sol3/papers.cfm?abstract_id=2835617.

[25] ibid, 42.

[26] ibid, 43.

[27] See *Unwired Planet v Huawei* [2015] EWHC 3366 (Pat) (Claim 1 of EP 2 229 744: 'Method in a first node for requesting a status report from a second node, the first node and the second node both being comprised within a wireless communication network'; and *Unwired Planet v Huawei* [2016] EWHC 576 (Pat) (Claim 1 of EP 1 230 818: 'A method for conveying measurement information from a terminal in a first communication system to a second communication system').

[28] *Saint Lawrence v Deutsche Telekom* (EP1 125 276 B1 covering pitch analysis device and pitch codebook search device).

[29] *Philips v Archos*, 7 O 209/15 Mannheim Regional Court (1 July 2016) (EP 1 062 745 B1 covering radio communication system compromising primary stations and a plurality of secondary stations; EP 1 062 743 B1 covering a radio station for use in a radio communication system having a communications channel between the radio stations and a further radio station).

A final argument in favour of using end-devices as a royalty base is that it is the prevailing industry practice in ICT and the smartphone industry. Companies normally voluntarily enter into business transactions using end-devices as a royalty base. Publicly available information from litigated SEPs cases shows that licensing agreements are commonly based on the value of the end-products.[30] A study by Stasik gathered information on the terms under which several of the largest contributors to the 4G standard license their patents, showing that all companies stated their expected rate as a percentage of the price of the final end-product device.[31] The same is true for 5G, where Qualcomm, Nokia, Ericsson and Interdigital announced their royalties all based on the value of end-product devices.[32] Of course, just because everyone is doing it does not automatically make it right, but we have seen above how a standard's value is realised in end-devices and how cellular SEPs are not directly infringed by components. Licensing agreements using end-devices as a royalty base are typically entered with end-device makers, which is justified by the efficiencies of cross-licensing between vertically integrated SEP owners, the ease of monitoring and compliance with royalty payments and the transaction cost savings of negotiating a licensing agreement with only one group of companies.[33]

Therefore, end-devices best reflect the value of connectivity standards and would consequently be the most optimal royalty base. However, this does not mean that SEP owners should be able to obtain unrestricted royalties unrelated to the value of their technology or to capture the value of other patented or unpatented features or components. Quite the opposite. The question is only which royalty base best reflects the value made by the standardised technology. The proper valuation of the technology should come through adjustment of the royalty rate. The royalty rate should be adequately adjusted to reflect the value of SEPs. This can be achieved by applying appropriate per-unit royalty rates or using running royalties together with royalty caps. Publication of detailed royalty programmes, discussed in chapter five, would make terms and conditions for licensing of SEPs known in advance and would ensure that SEP owners would not be able to claim royalties associated with other features and components. Principally, it should be immaterial whether the end-device or component makers take a licence as long as the value of the standard and SEPs is based on the value the standard brings to end-devices and consumers. In this way, the amount of FRAND royalty should stay the

[30] *Microsoft v Motorola*, 2013 WL 2111217, 67–72 (WD Wash 2013) (all Motorola's licences based on the value of end-products); *In re Innovatio IP Ventures* (n 12) 31 (finding that all Innovation's licences calculated royalties on the basis of end-product prices); *Unwired Planet v Huawei* [2017] EWHC 2988 (Pat) 382–469 (all licences based on end-products); *TCL v Ericsson* 2017 WL 6611635, 76–89 (CD Cal 2017) (all licences based on end-products).

[31] E Stasik, 'Royalty Rates and Licensing Strategies for Essential Patents on LTE (4G) Telecommunications Standards' (2010) September *les Nouvelles* 114; also Putnam and Williams (n 24) 33–34 (analysing publicly available licensing agreements and finding that all are based on the value of end-products).

[32] See ch 2, section III.B.

[33] See discussion in ch 7 for efficiency argument of end-device licensing.

same regardless of which company in the supply chain takes a licence, as will be explained more in chapter seven.

III. The Legal Requirement to Use a Particular Royalty Base

Having considered the policy of which royalty base best reflects the value of the standard, this section analyses whether there is a legal requirement to use a particular royalty base in SEP licensing agreements. Such an obligation may primarily come from SDO IPR rules. However, as seen SDOs typically do not further elaborate on the details of a FRAND commitment and leave licensing issues to bilateral negotiations between the parties.[34] The only exception seems to be the IEEE which recommends, but does not require, the use of SSPPU in FRAND royalty determinations.[35]

The IEEE's IPR policy is an outlier. In addition to recommending the use of SSPPU as a royalty base, it introduced wide-ranging changes to licensing practice by providing a definition of a FRAND royalty rate as excluding all the value resulting from standardisation (discussed in chapter four), limiting the use of comparable licences in royalty determinations, and severely restricting the use of injunctions for infringement of SEPs. Such changes have not been received favourably and studies have shown that many companies are unwilling to license SEPs under the new IPR policy.[36] From January 2016 to June 2019, 77 per cent of letters

[34] See *HTC v Ericsson*, 2019 WL 126980 (ED Tex 2019) 6 (analysing whether ETSI's FRAND commitment and IPR policy require the use of SSPPU as a royalty base and finding that it does not: 'the FRAND commitment embodied in the ETSI IPR policy does not require a FRAND license to be based on the SSPPU. To be clear, the ETSI IPR policy neither *requires* nor *precludes* a license with a royalty based on the SSPPU. Rather, whether a license meets the requirements of FRAND will depend on the particular facts of the case, as there is no prescribed methodology for calculating a FRAND license') (emphasis added).

[35] IEEE-SA, 'Standards Board Bylaws' (August 2020), available at: standards.ieee.org/content/dam/ieee-standards/standards/web/documents/other/sb_bylaws.pdf, Clause 6.1, Definitions, definition of the 'Reasonable Rate' ('In addition, determination of such Reasonable Rates should include, but need not be limited to, the consideration of:

> 'The value that the functionality of the claimed invention or inventive feature within the Essential Patent Claim contributes to the *value of the relevant functionality of the smallest saleable Compliant Implementation that practices the Essential Patent Claim.*
>
> *The value that the Essential Patent Claim contributes to the smallest saleable Compliant Implementation that practices that claim,* in light of the value contributed by all Essential Patent Claims for the same IEEE Standard practiced in that Compliant Implementation') (emphasis added).

[36] See R Katznelson, 'The IEEE Controversial Policy on Standard Essential Patents – The Empirical Record Since Adoption' (September 2017), available at: works.bepress.com/rkatznelson/80/; K Mallinson, 'Development of Innovative New Standards Jeopardised by IEEE Patent Policy' (September 2017), available at: www.4ipcouncil.com/application/files/6015/0479/2147/Mallinson_IEEE_LOA_report.pdf, but on the contrary that IEEE's new IPR policy had no impact on standardisation activities, see T Pohlmann, 'Empirical Study on Patenting and Standardization Activities at IEEE' (March 2017), available at: www.iplytics.com/wp-content/uploads/2018/01/IPlytics_2017_Patenting-and-standardization-activities-at-IEEE.pdf.

of assurance for Wi-Fi standard were negative, meaning that the SEP owner refused to license under the new policy,[37] and the overall number of new positive letters of assurance accepting licensing under the new IPR policy has dropped by 90 per cent since the adoption.[38] The opposition comes from major SEP owners such as Qualcomm, Nokia, Ericsson, IBM, Panasonic, Orange, Fraunhofer, General Electric and Huawei.[39] In 2020, the Department of Justice revoked its initial positive business review letter of the IEEE's IPR policy of 2015 and encouraged the IEEE to consider changing the policy in light of the effects of policy on innovation and ensuring the balance of interests of both patent holders and implementers.[40] Therefore, it remains to be seen what will be the final destiny of the IEEE's IPR policy and whether it will revert to the practices of other SDOs.

Even if SDOs do not specify the royalty base, it is often argued that US patent damages law requires the use of components (SSPPU) as a royalty base.[41] If this is the case, then any damages for infringement of SEPs in the US would be based on the price of components, regardless of whether licensing agreements are based on end-devices. The result of a court-imposed royalty base would then be expected to feed into future licensing agreements. The next section will analyse US patent damages law, tracing the evolution of the SSPPU doctrine, and the rationale behind its introduction and application in practice.

A. Origins and Evolution of the SSPPU Theory

i. US Patent Damages System and the Emergence of the SSPPU Theory

In the US, patent damages are calculated either as lost profits or, if they cannot be proven, a reasonable royalty.[42] A long-standing rule in the case of multi-component products is that patent damages should be *apportioned* to the value of the patented technology. The rule of apportionment is supposed to prevent the patentee from being overcompensated by receiving damages that go beyond the value of the patented technology. The rule was established by the US Supreme Court in *Garretson v Clark* in 1884 concerning damages of lost profits.[43]

[37] D Cohen, 'The IEEE 2015 Patent Policy – A Natural Experiment in Devaluing Technology' (12 August 2019), available at: www.kidonip.com/standard-essential-patents/the-ieee-2015-patent-policy-a-natural-experiment-in-devaluing-technology/.

[38] K Gupta and G Effraimidis, 'IEEE Patent Policy Revisions: An Empirical Examination of Impact' (2019) 64 *Antitrust Bulletin* 151, 156.

[39] Mallinson (n 36) 7.

[40] IEEE III Business Review Letter (n 7).

[41] Kattan, Ordover and Shampine (n 1).

[42] US Patent Act 35 USC § 284 ('the court shall award the claimant damages adequate to compensate for the infringement but in no event less than a reasonable royalty for the use made of the invention by the infringer').

[43] *Garretson v Clark*, 111 US 120, 121 (1884).

The patent covered an improvement in mop head, and the lower court rejected the patent holder's damages claim on the ground that the patent holder had not shown that the entire value of the mop could be attributed to the patent. The US Supreme Court agreed and held that:

> The patentee … must in every case give evidence tending to separate or apportion the defendant's profits and the patentee's damages between the patented feature and the unpatented features, and such evidence must be reliable and tangible, and not conjectural or speculative; or he must show, by equally reliable and satisfactory evidence, that the profits and damages are to be calculated on the whole machine, for the reason that the entire value of the whole machine, as a marketable article, is properly and legally attributable to the patented feature.[44]

The apportionment principle in lost profits cases is that the patent holder may rely on the entire market value of the patented product ('the entire market value rule' or EMVR) only if it is properly attributed to the patented feature. The subsequent case law clarified that the EMVR in lost profits cases applies when: (i) the patented feature is 'the basis for customer demand' of the infringing product; and (ii) the patented and unpatented components together 'constitute a functional unit'.[45] If this is not the case, lost profits must be awarded on a smaller component that is properly attributable to the patented feature.

On the other hand, the apportionment in reasonable royalty cases is generally done by the proper combination of a royalty base and a royalty rate which should reflect the value attributable to the patented feature in multi-component products. From an economic perspective, adjusting the royalty rate and the royalty base can lead to identical results. For example, a royalty rate of 1 per cent applied to a royalty base of $10 million is the same as the royalty rate of 10 per cent applied to a royalty base of $1 million. Both result in total royalties of $100,000. The point of apportionment in reasonable royalty cases is that the ultimate combination of royalty rate and royalty base should reflect the value of the patented technology and no more.[46]

However, the US Federal Circuit introduced the EMVR rule from lost profits damages into reasonable royalty calculation.[47] In *Rite-Hite Corp v Kelley Co* it held that the EMVR is applicable to reasonable royalties damages cases when selecting the appropriate royalty base.[48] Since then, courts in the US looked

[44] ibid.

[45] For an overview see FTC, 'The Evolving IP Marketplace' (n 4) 154–56.

[46] See: *Ericsson v D-Link*, 773 F.3d 1201, 1226 (Fed Cir 2014); also *Lucent Technologies, Inc v Gateway, Inc*, 580 F.3d 1301, 1338–39 (Fed Cir 2009) ('the base used in a running royalty calculation can always be the value of the entire commercial embodiment, as long as the magnitude of the rate is within an acceptable range (as determined by the evidence). Thus, even when the patented invention is a small component of a much larger commercial product, awarding a reasonable royalty based on either sale price or a number of units sold can be economically justified').

[47] M Greene, 'All Your Base Are Belong to Us: Towards an Appropriate Usage and Definition of the "Entire Market Value Rule" in Reasonably Royalty Calculations' (2012) 53 *Boston College Law Review* 233 (explaining the US patent damages law and tracing the EMVR from lost profits to reasonably royalty damages calculations).

[48] *Rite-Hite Corp v Kelley Co*, 56 F.3d 1538, 1549 (Fed Cir 1995).

at the EMVR and considered whether the patented feature was the basis for consumer demand in deciding whether to use a broader or narrower royalty base.[49] The application of the EMVR rule in reasonable royalty cases, however, is under heavy criticism for belonging naturally in the lost profits category, for mischaracterising the apportionment in reasonable royalty calculations and, importantly, for not corresponding to real-world licensing where parties do not choose the royalty base solely on the requirement that the patented feature drives consumer demand.[50]

Against this background, the term 'smallest saleable patent-practicing unit' was first introduced in 2009 by Judge Rader in *Cornell University v Hewlett-Packard*.[51] The case concerned one patent that read on one component that was a part of a larger multi-component product. The patent at issue read on an instruction reorder buffer (IRB), which is a part of the computer processor, which itself is a part of a CPU module, which is a part of a 'CPU brick', and which is ultimately a part of a larger computer server.[52] Cornell's damages expert initially calculated reasonable royalty damages by using Hewlett-Packard's revenues from its sales of servers and workstations as the royalty base – final downstream products. Judge Rader excluded the expert's damages testimony on the grounds that it did not offer 'sufficient economic proof that the patented invention drove demand for Hewlett–Packard's entire server and workstation market'.[53] He noted that the computer servers and systems include 'vast amounts of technology beyond the infringing part of the processors'[54] and, in this factual scenario, basing damages on the value of servers and systems would 'mislead the jury to award damages far in excess of their compensatory purpose'.[55]

[49] S Amundson, 'Apportionment and the Entire Market Value Rule Have Presented Problems in Practice When Determining the Value of a Patented Invention' (2014) 23 *Texas Intellectual Property Law Journal* 1 (analysis of how district courts applied EMVR in deciding whether the royalty base should be the whole product or a smaller component).

[50] A Landers, 'Let the Games Begin: Incentives to Innovation in the New Economy of Intellectual Property Law' (2006) 46 *Santa Clara Law Review* 307, 362 (holding that the EMVR is inconsistent with the US Patent Act's statutory language); B Love, 'Patentee Overcompensation and the Entire Market Value Rule' (2007) 60 *Stanford Law Review* 263, 265 ('the application of the entire market value rule routinely overcompensates patentees and thereby exacerbates many problems inherent in the current system for awarding patent infringement damages'); M Lemley, 'Distinguishing Lost Profits from Reasonable Royalties' (2009) 51 *William & Mary Law Review* 655 (explaining that EMVR's natural place is in the lost profits damages category); FTC, 'The Evolving IP Marketplace' (n 4) 211 (recommending the elimination of the EMVR and the question of whether the patented feature was the 'basis for customer demand' from the determination of the appropriate base in a reasonable royalty damages calculation); T Cotter, 'Patent Damages Heuristics' (2018) 25 *Texas Intellectual Property Law Journal* 159 (arguing that parties in real-world licensing often use the entire product as a royalty base and do not follow the EMVR rule).

[51] *Cornell University v Hewlett-Packard Co* (n 23).

[52] ibid, 283.

[53] ibid, 284.

[54] ibid, 283.

[55] ibid, 284.

Cornell's expert came back with a revised damages testimony that was based on a CPU brick – one component down the ladder from the servers and workstations. The jury found Cornell's patent valid and infringed an awarded damages of $184 million by applying a 0.8 per cent royalty rate on a royalty base on $23 billion from the sales of CPU bricks.[56] Judge Rader was not impressed and excluded Cornell's revised expert testimony. He held that CPU bricks contained numerous non-patented components in addition to the infringing processors and that Cornell's revised royalty base was still 'beyond the scope of the claimed invention'.[57] He criticised Cornell from not providing any evidence that its patented feature drove demand for CPU bricks, and for the fact that CPU bricks are not sold separately on the market. Judge Rader then held that 'the logical and readily available alternative [for royalty base] was the smallest salable infringing unit with close relation to the claimed invention – namely the processor itself'.[58] He then used processors as a royalty base and reduced damages to $53.5 million by multiplying the jury's 0.8 per cent royalty rate by a royalty base of $6.7 billion from processor revenues (instead of $23 billion from CPU bricks).[59] Thus, the SSPPU was born.

Judge Rader's opinion should be understood in the context of the case. The key point is that Judge Rader was driven mostly by the concern that the jury would award excessive damages for infringement of one patented feature that read on a computer processor. Indeed, it may appear that initially awarded jury damages of $184 million for one patented feature may be exaggerated. However, Judge Rader did not explain why, instead of reducing the royalty base, the same outcome could not have been realised by simply lowering the royalty rate.

ii. Reception and Expansion of the SSPPU Doctrine by the Federal Circuit

The Federal Circuit picked up Judge Rader's 'smallest salable patent practicing unit' notion in 2012 in *Laser Dynamics v Quanta*.[60] The case concerned a patent that enabled an optical disk drive to automatically identify the type of optical disk – a CD or a DVD – that is inserted into the optical disk drive.[61] Quanta Computers manufactured laptops that included optical disk drives that infringed Laser Dynamics' patent. Laser Dynamics' damages expert proposed the royalty base to be the final downstream product – a laptop. He applied a 2 per cent royalty on total revenues from the sales of laptops – $2.53 billion – to arrive at total reasonable royalty damages of $52.1 million, the amount which jury awarded.[62]

[56] ibid, 282.
[57] ibid, 285.
[58] ibid, 288.
[59] ibid, 292.
[60] *LaserDynamics, Inc v Quanta Computer, Inc* (n 23).
[61] ibid, 56.
[62] ibid, 60–61.

The district court judge, however, held that Laser Dynamics improperly applied the EMVR because Laser Dynamics presented no evidence that its patented technology drove the demand for whole laptops.[63] In a new damages trial, Laser Dynamics proposed a 6 per cent royalty over a smaller royalty base – a stand-alone optical disk drive. The jury ultimately awarded reasonable royalty damages in the amount of $8.5 million. On appeal, the Federal Circuit confirmed the district court's ruling that Laser Dynamics should not have used the price of the whole laptop as the royalty base and, by referring to Judge Rader's opinion in *Cornell University v Hewlett-Packard*, held that in a case where small elements of multi-component products are accused of infringement, royalties should generally be based on the 'smallest salable patent-practicing unit'.[64] Consequently, the SSPPU was endorsed by the Federal Circuit.

It would seem that the Federal Circuit established that a default royalty base in multi-component products should be the SSPPU.[65] The Court held that

> the entire market value rule is a narrow exception to this general rule. If it can be shown that the patented feature drives the demand for an entire multi-component product, a patentee may be awarded damages as a percentage of revenues or profits attributable to the entire product.[66]

It continued that a very small royalty rate may not offset the use of a downstream product as a royalty base,[67] and that the patent holder's use of the value of the downstream product would simply shift the difficulty from the apportionment of the royalty base to the apportionment of the royalty rate.[68]

The Federal Circuit also rejected Laser Dynamics' argument that 'practical and economic necessity' compelled it to base the royalty on the price of an entire laptop.[69] Laser Dynamics argued that Quanta Computers sells laptops, not independent optical disk drives and does not track prices of individual components. It further emphasised that usually parties structure licensing agreements on the prices of the downstream products, to address such accounting difficulties.[70] The Federal Circuit's solution was recommending using lump-sum royalties instead – which are not calculated as a percentage of any component or product.[71]

[63] ibid, 63.

[64] ibid, 67 ('Where small elements of multi-component products are accused of infringement, calculating a royalty on the entire product carries a considerable risk that the patentee will be improperly compensated for non-infringing components of that product. Thus, it is generally required that royalties be based not on the entire product, but instead on the 'smallest salable patent-practicing unit').

[65] ibid ('We reaffirm that in any case involving multi-component products, patentees may not calculate damages based on sales of the entire product, as opposed to the smallest salable patent-practicing unit, without showing that the demand for the entire product is attributable to the patented feature').

[66] ibid.

[67] ibid, 68 ('the requirement to prove that the patented feature drives demand for the entire product may not be avoided by the use of a very small royalty rate').

[68] ibid, 70.

[69] ibid, 69.

[70] ibid, 69–70.

[71] ibid, 70.

The Federal Circuit indicated why it preferred using the SSPPU as a default rule for royalty base – the risk of jury confusion.[72] It was concerned that the use of revenues from a downstream product 'only serve to make a patentee's proffered damages amount appear modest by comparison, and to artificially inflate the jury's damages calculation beyond that which is adequate to compensate for the infringement'.[73] A broad royalty base would allegedly 'skew the damages horizon for the jury, regardless of the contribution of the patented component'.[74]

In 2014 *VirnetX v Cisco and Apple*,[75] the Federal Circuit further expanded the SSPPU doctrine by holding that if the SSPPU itself is a multi-component product, further apportionment is required below the SSPPU. The case concerned VirnetX patents that related to FaceTime and VPN on Demand features of Apple's products (iPhones, iPads, iPods). VirnetX's damages expert presented three damages models, all based on the value of Apple's products. The jury found all patents valid, infringed and awarded reasonable royalty damages of $368 million. Apple appealed because, among other reasons, it considered that the district court's jury instructions were erroneous. The jury was instructed to consider the value of the final product as a royalty base only if (i) the patented feature drives demand for the entire product, or (ii) if the product constitutes the smallest saleable patent-practicing unit.[76] The Federal Circuit agreed that the second condition mistakenly implies that there is no need to apportion the royalty base further if the final product is the SSPPU.[77] It held that 'the SSPPU approach was intended to produce a royalty base much more closely tied to the claimed invention' and that where the SSPPU is itself a multi-component product, 'the patentee must do more to estimate what portion of the value of that product is attributable to the patented technology'. In other words, apportionment should go below the SSPPU if the unit itself is a multi-component product. That said, the Federal Circuit offered no guidance on what should be the royalty base if the unit 'closely tied to patented technology' is never sold individually on the market.[78]

Again, the fear of jury bias was the main reason behind the Federal Circuit's opinion. The court said that the 'fundamental concern' is that the reliance on the value of the final downstream products would 'skew the damages horizon for the jury',[79] and that the 'patentee may not balance out an unreasonably high royalty base simply by asserting a low enough royalty rate'.[80] 'Although the result of that equation would be mathematically sound if properly applied by the jury, there is

[72] ibid, 68.
[73] ibid.
[74] ibid.
[75] *VirnetX, Inc v Cisco Systems, Inc*, 767 F.3d 1308 (Fed Cir 2014).
[76] ibid, 1327.
[77] ibid.
[78] ibid, 1328.
[79] ibid, 1327.
[80] ibid, 1333, referring to *Uniloc USA, Inc v Microsoft Corp*, 632 F.3d 1292, 1320 (Fed Cir 2011) ('the Supreme Court and this court's precedents do not allow consideration of the entire market value of accused products for minor patent improvements simply by asserting a low enough royalty rate').

concern that the high royalty base would cause the jury to deviate upward from the proper outcome'.[81]

It would appear the Federal Circuit in these two cases established a general rule in jury trials that patent damages for multi-component products must be based on the SSPPU, or even less if the SSPPU itself is a multi-component product. The principal reason behind this is the fear of jury bias – a concern that juries would award excessive damages if presented with the large royalty base.

iii. Clarification and Backtracking of the SSPPU Doctrine by the Federal Circuit

However, the Federal Circuit in subsequent cases clarified and narrowed down the applicability of the SSPPU doctrine. In *Ericsson v D-Link*,[82] Ericsson sued the manufacturers of laptops and routers for infringement of SEPs relating to Wi-Fi standard. The jury found that three of Ericsson's SEPs were valid and infringed and awarded reasonable royalty damages of $10 million, or approximately 15 cents per end-product device.[83] Manufacturers appealed arguing, among other things, that the district court should have excluded Ericsson's damages testimony because it used Ericsson's prior licences that were based on the value of end-products. In their view, Wi-Fi technology related to only one component of end-products, a Wi-Fi chip, and damages testimony based on the value of end-product devices should not have been allowed.[84]

The Federal Circuit disagreed and clarified that the SSPPU doctrine has two parts – a substantive legal rule and an evidentiary principle. A substantive legal rule is the requirement of apportionment, namely that 'the ultimate combination of royalty base and royalty rate must reflect the value attributable to the infringing features of the product, and no more'.[85] The Federal Circuit further recognised that apportionment could be done in various ways,

> by careful selection of the royalty base to reflect the value added by the patented feature, where that differentiation is possible; by adjustment of the royalty rate so as to discount the value of a product's non-patented features; or by a combination thereof. The essential requirement is that the ultimate reasonable royalty award must be based on the incremental value that the patented invention adds to the end-product.[86]

On the other hand, the evidentiary principle behind the SSPPU is the fear of jury bias. According to the Court,

> the point of the evidentiary principle is to help our jury system reliably implement the substantive statutory requirement of apportionment … The principle, applicable

[81] ibid.
[82] *Ericsson v D-Link* (n 46).
[83] ibid, 1207.
[84] ibid, 1225.
[85] ibid, 1226.
[86] ibid.

> specifically to the choice of a royalty base, is that, where a multi-component product is at issue, and the patented feature is not the item which imbues the combination of the other features with value, care must be taken to avoid misleading the jury by placing undue emphasis on the value of the entire product. It is not that an appropriately apportioned royalty award could never be fashioned by starting with the entire market value of a multi-component product – by, for instance, dramatically reducing the royalty rate to be applied in those cases – it is that reliance on the entire market value might mislead the jury, who may be less equipped to understand the extent to which the royalty rate would need to do the work in such instance.[87]

After stating these principles, the Federal Circuit held that the SSPPU does not apply when damages are based on real-world comparable licensing agreements. It recognised that 'licenses are generally negotiated without consideration of the EMVR' and that 'making real world, relevant licenses inadmissible … would often make it impossible for a patentee to resort to license-based evidence'.[88] The Court thus rejected the argument that the district court should have excluded expert damages testimony that was based on prior licences.

In *CSIRO v Cisco*, another SEP case, the Federal Circuit held that is wrong to require that all damages calculations must use the SSPPU.[89] Unlike other cases that were decided by juries, this case was a bench trial for damages for infringement of CSIRO's one Wi-Fi SEP. Judge Davis based the damages calculation on the parties' failed licensing negotiations that referred to Cisco's end-products. Cisco appealed arguing that the district court should have started its damages analysis with the wireless chip, which is the SSPPU. The Federal Circuit disagreed, holding that 'the rule Cisco advances – which would require all damages models to begin with the smallest salable patent-practicing unit – is untenable. It conflicts with our prior approvals of a methodology that values the asserted patent based on comparable licenses'.[90]

The Court reaffirmed that actual market valuations are the most reliable method of apportionment, regardless of the royalty base used:

> Where the licenses employed are sufficiently comparable this method is typically reliable because the parties are constrained by the market's actual valuation of the patent. Moreover, otherwise comparable licenses are not inadmissible solely because they express the royalty rate as a percentage of total revenues, rather than in terms of the smallest salable unit. Therefore, adopting Cisco's position would necessitate the exclusion of comparable license valuations that may be the most effective method of estimating the asserted patent's value.'[91]

The Federal Circuit also reiterated that the SSPPU is an evidentiary principle created to avoid confusing juries and helping them in apportionment analysis.[92]

[87] ibid, 1226–27.
[88] ibid, 1228.
[89] *CSIRO v Cisco*, 809 F.3d 1295 (Fed Cir 2015).
[90] ibid, 1303.
[91] ibid.
[92] ibid, 1302.

Even in non-SEP cases the Federal Circuit confirmed that the SSPPU is not fixed, a substantive rule that must be followed in each case. In *Exmark v Briggs*,[93] it held that damages calculations only require apportionment, which can be done by a

> careful selection of the royalty base, or adjustment of the royalty rate or by a combination of both.[94] So long as Exmark adequately and reliably apportions between the improved and conventional features of [the final product], using the [final product] as a royalty base and apportioning through the royalty rate is an acceptable methodology.[95]

The Federal Circuit also clarified that if a patent's claim covers the whole product and not just a single component, then apportionment through the royalty rate would be appropriate.[96] Using the end-product as the royalty base 'is consistent with the realities of a hypothetical negotiation and accurately reflects the real-world bargaining that occurs, particularly in licensing'.[97]

Therefore, the Federal Circuit clarified that the SSPPU is not a substantive rule of law that requires all patent damages to start with the SSPPU. Instead, what is required is apportionment – a combination of royalty base and royalty rate must reflect the value of the patent. The SSPPU only applies in jury trials and was introduced as an evidentiary principle because of the fear that juries may award excessively large damages if presented with a large royalty base. Nevertheless, even in jury trials, the SSPPU is inapplicable if there is real market-based evidence such as comparable licences, or where patents claim the whole product.

iv. *Jury Bias as a Reason for the Introduction of the SSPPU*

Therefore, the primary reason behind the introduction of the SSPPU royalty base in US patent damages law is the fear of juries awarding disproportionately high damages. Indeed, one study showed that juries award 15 times higher damages than when the case is decided by a judge.[98]

The concern about jury bias may be explained by behavioural economics and the notions of 'framing' and 'anchoring' that describe how people make decisions under uncertainty.[99] Framing refers to the tendency of people to respond to a particular choice in different ways depending on how that choice is presented,[100]

[93] *Exmark Manufacturing Company Inc v Briggs & Stratton Power Products Group*, 879 F.3d 1332 (Fed Cir 2018).

[94] ibid, 1348.

[95] ibid.

[96] ibid.

[97] ibid, 1349.

[98] PWC, '2017 Patent Litigation Study: Change on the Horizon?' (2017) 10, available at: www.pwc.com/us/en/forensic-services/publications/assets/2017-patent-litigation-study.pdf (finding that from 2012 to 2016 the median bench damages award was $0.6 million, while the median jury damages award was $9.5 million).

[99] D Kahneman, *Thinking, Fast and Slow* (Penguin Books, 2011).

[100] ibid, 363–74 (discussing framing).

while anchoring refers to the tendency of people to rely too heavily on the first piece of information they receive (the anchor) when making decisions.[101] The concern is that juries may use the large royalty base as an anchor and award excessive damages for infringement of one or a few patents that read on multi-component products. Similarly, if a question is framed to the jury as a low royalty applied on a large royalty base, this may make a difference than if the question is framed as a higher royalty applied on a smaller royalty base. Consequently, juries may frame and anchor damages on an infringer's overall revenues and award damages of more than any reasonable value of the patents in suit.

However, anchoring and framing go in both directions.[102] If a jury can be biased upwards towards excessive damages that overcompensate patent holders, so too can it be biased downwards towards low damages that effectively leave patent holders undercompensated. Having a small component as a royalty base would require a correspondingly larger royalty rate, but precisely because framing and anchoring matters juries may decline to adjust the royalty rate upwards, leading to under-valuation of patented technology. For example, a royalty rate of 1 per cent applied on the royalty base of \$10 million and a royalty rate of 20 per cent applied on the royalty base of \$500,000 lead to the same result (\$100,000). However, juries may find a 20 per cent royalty rate to be disproportionate and decline to make proper adjustments, leaving patent holders undercompensated.

Therefore, recognising that framing and anchoring biases matter does not lead to support of an automatic application of the SSPPU. They may lead juries to err on both sides by awarding excessively high, as well as excessively low damages. A solution may be to educate jurors, not to craft specific legal rules applicable to them.

B. Conclusion

In conclusion, there is currently no legal requirement mandating the use of a particular royalty base in SEP licensing. SDOs typically leave licensing issues to bilateral negotiations between the parties and do not prescribe the use of a precise royalty base, with the only exception of the IEEE but the future of its IPR policy is uncertain after the Department of Justice's withdrawal of its favourable business review letter. US patent damages law also does not require the use of the SSPPU in all cases. As seen, the SSPPU emerged from US jury trials because of the fear that juries may award excessively high royalties if presented with a large royalty base. However, the SSPPU is not a substantive rule of law applicable in all cases; it applies only in jury trials and even then, it does not apply if: (i) damages are based on comparable licences or prior negotiations of the parties; (ii) the patent claims

[101] ibid, 119–28 (discussing anchoring).

[102] Teece and Sherry (n 5) 8–10; Froeb and Shor (n 5) 7.

cover the whole product; (iii) damages are based on lump-sum royalties; and (iv) if the patent is the basis for consumer demand.

IV. The Royalty Base in Standard Essential Patent Litigation

It would be interesting to see how courts decide when presented with arguments about the royalty base in SEP litigation. In a large majority of cases the issue is not even raised as parties voluntarily decide to use end-devices, with the dispute being only about the royalty amount.[103] When the question is raised, we have seen how the US Federal Circuit explained that the SSPPU cannot overrule market-based evidence and is a not substantive rule for all damages calculations.[104]

In just two SEP cases in the US the SSPPU was used as a royalty base, but they did not establish binding precedents or rules for the future. We have seen how in *Innovatio* Judge Holderman calculated FRAND royalties for 19 Wi-Fi SEPs based on the average profit of chip manufacturers.[105] However, this was done because of the failure of proof from Innovatio to apportion the value of the patented feature from the value of the end-product, and not as an endorsement of the SSPPU principle. In Judge Holderman's words: 'in light of that failure of proof, the court has no choice … but to calculate a royalty based on the Wi-Fi chip'.[106] In *GPNE v Apple*, Judge Koh examined damages testimonies for 3G and 4G SEPs, one proposed using a baseband processor and the other based on end-devices – tablets. Judge Koh interpreted patent damages law as requiring the use of the SSPPU in all cases of multi-component products and held that a baseband processor, as an SSPPU, should be used in a damages calculation.[107] However, this case was limited to jury trial where the SSPPU may apply, and was given before the Federal Circuit's clarification in *CSIRO v Cisco* and *Ericsson v D-Link*. It was later overruled by the Ninth Circuit in *FTC v Qualcomm*, discussed below.

However, there are instances where parties may voluntarily choose to use the price of components, as evidenced by *Realtek v LSI* concerning the Wi-Fi standard where the SEP owner voluntarily decided to licence to a component manufacturer.[108] The jury ruled in the SEP owner's favour and ordered running royalties of 0.12 per cent and 0.07 per cent per infringing SEP based on the implementer's products. Here the royalty base was not contested as the SEP owner itself decided to approach and sue the component manufacturer. The case shows that

[103] *Microsoft v Motorola* (n 30) 67–72; *TCL v Ericsson* (n 30); *Unwired Planet v Huawei* [2017] EWHC 2988 (Pat).

[104] *Ericsson v D-Link* (n 46); *CSIRO v Cisco*, 809 F.3d 1295 (Fed Cir 2015).

[105] *In re Innovatio IP Ventures* (n 12).

[106] ibid, 14.

[107] *GPNE v Apple*, 2014 WL 1494247 (ND Cal 2014) 13.

[108] *Realtek v LSI*, 2014 WL 2738216 (ND Cal 2014).

it might be possible to use the value of a component as a royalty base, at least with respect to non-cellular standards, but it should not be capped at the profit margins of component manufacturers. As mentioned, the apportionment can come through the proper adjustment of the royalty rate, although it remains questionable whether prices of unlicensed components are high enough to provide an adequate value of SEPs.

US courts in two recent cases may have finally put to rest the notion that the SSPPU as a royalty base is required in all SEPs cases. The *FTC v Qualcomm* litigation concerned allegations of the anti-competitive licensing practices of Qualcomm, which included refusal to license at a component level, a 'no licence no chip' policy where Qualcomm refused to sell chips without a licence for its SEP portfolio, and basing SEP royalties on the value of end-products. The district court found such practices a violation of antitrust laws, but on appeal the Ninth Circuit reversed.[109] Related to the allegation that Qualcomm's royalty rates are unreasonable and anti-competitive because they are based on handset prices and not the SSPPU, the Ninth Circuit disagreed and reiterated that the SSPPU is not a *per se* rule for reasonable royalty calculations and, instead, the concept is used as a tool in jury cases to minimise potential jury confusion when the jury is weighing complex expert testimony about patent damages.[110] It also recognised that parties routinely enter into licence agreements that base the value of patented inventions as a percentage of the commercial products' sales price, and thus there is nothing inherently wrong with using the market value of the entire product.[111] The Ninth Circuit concluded that the law and industry practice runs 'counter to the district court's conclusion that patent royalties cannot be based on total handset price and that doing so exposes a firm to potential antitrust liability'.[112]

In *HTC v Ericsson*, HTC argued that Ericsson breached its FRAND commitment by not basing its royalties on the SSPPU, ie, the baseband processor.[113] HTC proposed to use a profit margin of a baseband processor as the maximum aggregate royalty for 4G SEPs, which is between $0.19 and $1.22. Apportioned to Ericson's share of 4G SEPs this should produce a royalty of between $0.01 and $0.08 per processor. The court rejected HTC's arguments. It first observed that a profit margin of a component maker is not necessarily reflective of the value of the standardised technology, especially when the component maker does not pay IP royalties.[114] In baseband processor markets some manufacturers sell their chips at a net loss, but that does not mean the value of the technology contained in the components has no value. It also observed that HTC sells tablets with cellular connectivity $120 higher than tablets with only Wi-Fi connectivity. The fact that

[109] *Federal Trade Commission v Qualcomm*, 411 F.Supp.3d 658 (ND Cal 2019); *Federal Trade Commission v Qualcomm*, 969 F.3d 974 (9th Cir 2020).

[110] *Federal Trade Commission v Qualcomm*, 969 F.3d 974 (9th Cir 2020) 37.

[111] ibid.

[112] ibid.

[113] *HTC v Ericsson*, 407 F.Supp.3d 631 (ED Tex 2019).

[114] ibid, 637.

consumers are willing to pay $120 more for cellular connectivity is taken to speak to its value. The court also examined Ericsson's SEPs and found they are not limited in scope only to a baseband processor but encompass mobile terminals or user equipment.[115] Since SEPs are not infringed by a baseband processor alone, it was held not to be an adequate royalty base. Finally, the court found that parties in the industry routinely and voluntarily choose to enter into licences based on the value of end-devices and there were no examples, not even presented by HTC's expert, of licences based on profit margin or costs of baseband processors.[116] Therefore, these cases demonstrate that a US court recognised that there is no requirement mandating the use of the SSPPU as a royalty base.

In the EU, the question of the royalty base did not arise until recently. In the *Nokia v Daimler* litigation in Germany, Nokia offered a licence for its 4G SEPs to Daimler based on the price of a connected car, while Daimler first refused to take a licence arguing that licensing should be done by its suppliers, but later accepted taking a licence only if it was based on the price of a component – a telematic control unit (TCU). Mannheim Regional Court found that the use of a TCU as a base for the calculation of FRAND royalties was not appropriate, as it did not adequately reflect the value that the technology brings to the end-product.[117] It held that patent holders in principle must be given a share in the economic benefits that the technology realises in end-products and, accordingly, the selling price of TCUs do not sufficiently represent the value that SEPs bring to car manufacturers. A TCU's selling price represents only Daimler's costs while, on the other hand, connectivity allows Daimler to generate income from other services and provides cost savings by optimising R&D.[118] Thus, the Court rejected the use of a component as a base for FRAND royalty rates.

V. Conclusion

The chapter addressed the question of a royalty base used in SEP royalty calculations. In principle, a royalty base should be the one that best reflects the value that standardised technology brings to end-products. For connectivity standards this is normally the end-device since the value of connectivity is fully realised at end-devices. Moreover, claims of SEPs are not limited only to baseband chips but cover devices and networks, and the prevailing practice in ICT and smartphone markets is to voluntarily enter into licensing agreements based on the value of end-devices. However, this is not to say there is one-size-fits-all approach that can be applicable in all other cases; the appropriate royalty base may vary across different standards and different industries and a careful case-by-case assessment would

[115] ibid, 637–38.
[116] ibid, 638.
[117] *Nokia v Daimler*, 2 O 34/19 Mannheim Regional Court (18 August 2020) 169–72.
[118] ibid, 174–80.

need to be made. From a legal perspective, it was seen how SDOs typically do not define which royalty base to use and leave the determination to bilateral negotiations between the parties. Neither does the US patent damages law mandate the use of components (the SSPPU) as a royalty base in all cases. The SSPPU doctrine emerged from jury trials as an evidentiary tool to help juries properly assess patent damages. It is thus not a substantive rule of law and courts recognised that licensing agreements based on end-devices are reliable evidence of a SEP's value. Finally, a separate but related question is which company in the production chain should take a licence, which is covered in the next chapter.

7

FRAND and Value Chain Licensing

The question of where to license in the production chain is increasingly coming to attention given the advent of the IoT where many different industries with different degrees of complexity in the production chains will need to engage in SEP licensing. The issue boils down to whether a licence for SEPs should be taken by an end-device maker or some component manufacturer further upstream. Value chain licensing is closely related to the question of the appropriate royalty base discussed in chapter six, but it is a distinct issue. As seen, a royalty base is a factor in determining the amount of royalty, while a licensing level concerns with whom the licence should be concluded. However, in practice they often overlap since the argument that SEP licences should be concluded with component manufacturers is tied in with the request to use components as the royalty base and vice versa; the claim that end-device manufacturers should take SEP licences is because the value of end-devices should be used in determining FRAND royalties.

Chapter six analysed policy and legal questions concerning the appropriate royalty base in a SEP licensing context, while this chapter will address whether a FRAND commitment requires, or should require, SEP owners to licence at every level of the supply chain (including to component makers) or not. It will first explain the debate in the industry and literature about access to all (ATA) and licence to all (LTA) approaches to SEP licensing, and will then move on to analysing what legal obligations exist in SDO IPR rules, patent law and competition law. It will conclude with observations of what FRAND commitment requires and policy implications for the future. The principles for determining the appropriate licensing levels in the IoT will be discussed at the end of the chapter.

I. The Value Chain Licensing Debate

The debate in the industry and literature about where to license in the production chain effectively mirrors the one about the appropriate royalty base. On the one hand, the LTA approach argues that SEP owners are obliged to license to any company in the production chain that requests it, even to component manufacturers.[1] This is because of the underlying assumption that SEPs are largely

[1] For industry arguments, see: Fair Standards Alliance, 'Competitive and Industry Harms Related to Refusal to License SEPs and Other Forms of 'Level Discrimination' in SEP Licensing'

implemented in a component (typically a baseband chip) and thus components best reflect the value of standardised technology. Component manufacturers are then logical counterparts in licensing negotiations as they possess the necessary knowledge directly relating to the standardised technology, while basing royalties and concluding licensing on the end-product level has been likened to a 'tax on innovation' that inappropriately overcompensates SEP holders for the value of multiple inventions and components unrelated to the standardised technology Additionally, SEPs are seen as having one unique value independent of its downstream use, which would prohibit the SEP owner from price discriminating based on the use of SEPs.[2] Licensing only at component level would be efficient and bring transaction cost savings as SEP owners would negotiate only with a few chip manufacturers rather than numerous end-device makers.

On the other hand, the ATA approach submits that a FRAND commitment is open and flexible to accommodate the needs of different industries.[3] As seen, for some standards and some industries like smartphones, end-products most accurately reflect the true value of standardised technologies as the functionality of the standard is only fully realised in the end-product device. The ordinary industry practice for cellular standards in the mobile communication industry is to licence SEPs at final downstream devices. It allows the transaction costs savings achieved in negotiations with one group of licensees; the ease of monitoring the compliance with royalty payments and the use of products; the possibility to obtain mutual cross-licences between vertically integrated SEP owners; and ensures non-discrimination between similarly situated licensees.[4] The ATA approach works by SEP owners choosing the level of the supply chain at which they want to conclude licences, which is selected based on which level best reflects the added value of the standards to the end-products and consumers, transactions costs savings and efficiencies. Once this is done, firms located elsewhere in the value chain indirectly benefit by having access to a standard without the need to directly obtain a licence and are free to implement the standard. The ATA approach is currently applied in the mobile communications industry and it is submitted that no firm willing to take a licence was ever denied access to standardised technology, and no firm

(2 December 2020); Apple, 'A Statement on FRAND Licensing of SEPs' (2019); CEN-CENELEC, 'Core Principles and Approaches for Licensing of Standard Essential Patents' (June 2019), available at www.cencenelec.eu/news/workshops/Pages/WS-2019-014.aspx; Fair Standards Alliance, 'Position Paper – SEP Licences Available to All' (24 June 2016), available at: fair-standards.org/wp-content/uploads/2016/09/160624_FSA_Position_Paper_-_SEP_licenses_available_to_all.pdf. For academic literature, see: J Ordover and A Shampine, 'Implementing the FRAND Commitment' (2014) 10 *Antitrust Source* 1; R Grasso, 'Standard Essential Patents: Royalty Determination in the Supply Chain' (2017) 8 *Journal of Competition Law & Practice* 283.

[2] CEN-CENELEC, 'Core Principles and Approaches' (n 1) 14–15.

[3] CEN-CENELEC, 'Principles and Guidance for Licensing Standard Essential Patents in 5G and the Internet of Things (IoT), including the Industrial Internet' (June 2019) 7, available at: www.cencenelec.eu/news/workshops/pages/ws-2019-013.aspx.

[4] M Blecker, T Sanchez and E Stasik, 'An Experience-Based Look at the Licensing Practices that Drive the Cellular Communications Industry: Whole Portfolio/Whole Device Licensing' (2016) December *les Nouvelles* 221.

wishing to sell components to downstream manufacturers has been prevented from doing so.[5] A requirement to license simultaneously across the production chain may create adverse negative effects: it would effectively impose a revenue cap and drive the royalties downwards,[6] create legal uncertainty, raise transaction costs, lead to unintended discrimination, increase licensing disputes and prevent beneficial mutual cross-licensing.[7]

The question of where it is most appropriate to license in the production chain is becoming more pressing with the advent of 5G and the IoT when a large number of firms in diverse industries will be confronted with SEP licensing. The European Commission stressed that there is 'no one-size-fits-all' solution and that the approach differs 'from sector to sector and over time'.[8] We are seeing the first signs of disputes relating to connected cars,[9] where there is a clash between two different industry practices. While it is ordinary in the telecommunications industry to license cellular standards at the end-device level, in the automotive industry component suppliers are responsible for clearing relevant IP rights and providing indemnity clauses to compensate car manufacturers for any IP infringement. Therefore, it is crucial to understand the precise legal obligations of SEP owners regarding the question of where to license in the production chain under patent, contract and competition law.[10]

II. Patent Law and Value Chain Licensing

From a patent law perspective, a central question is whether SEPs are infringed by a component or end-device. If the claims of SEPs are limited only to specific component(s), then a natural choice for concluding licensing agreements would be with component manufacturers. However, if SEPs claims are broader – for example, they read on final downstream devices or networks – then the situation is more complicated. In this variant, it may be equally legitimate for patent holders to seek licences from downstream producers.

[5] IP Europe, 'Why "License to All" Could be a Licence to Kill Innovation in Europe' (May 2017).

[6] A Gautier and N Petit, 'Smallest Salable Patent Practicing Unit and Component Licensing: Why 1$ is not 1$' (2019) 15 *Journal of Competition Law & Economics* 690.

[7] J Martinez, 'FRAND as Access to All vs License to All' (2019) 14 *Journal of Intellectual Property Law & Practice* 642.

[8] Commission, 'Setting Out the EU Approach to Standard Essential Patents' (Communication) COM(2017) 712 final, 6.

[9] *Nokia v Daimler*, 2 0 34/19 Mannheim Regional Court (18 August 2020); *Sharp v Daimler*, 7 O 8818/19 Munich Regional Court (10 September 2020).

[10] For detailed analysis see J-S Borghetti, I Nikolic and N Petit, 'FRAND Licensing Levels Under EU Law' (2021) *European Competition Journal*, available at: doi.org/10.1080/17441056.2020.1862542; A Layne-Farrar and R Stark, 'License to All or Access to All? A Law and Economics Assessment of Standard Development Organizations' Licensing Rules' (2020) 88 *George Washington Law Review* 1307.

In chapter six, section II we saw a study and cases demonstrating that cellular standards for smartphones are claiming end-devices and whole networks and are not confined to a single component. This means that SEPs would be directly infringed only once the end-device is connected to a network. A component can only be said to indirectly infringe SEPs if it is supplied to a manufacturer that will make end-devices that will put SEPs into effect. A directly infringing end-device in this case would be more natural choice for licensing level. However, a case-by-case assessment would be required for each standard and SEPs in order to ascertain whether they are directly infringed by a component or end-device. While cellular standards are directly infringed by end-devices, a result may be different for other standards and other industries.

The doctrine of patent exhaustion also impacts the point of licensing in the production chain. The patent exhaustion provides that the first authorised sale of a patented item terminates all patent rights to that item.[11] From an economic standpoint, patent exhaustion seeks to limit intellectual property holders' control over the distribution of patented goods once they have lawfully sold them in a market. Under the patent exhaustion doctrine, a patent holder may collect royalties only once per patented article, the first licensed (or authorised) sale exhausts his patent rights.

The practical implication is that a patent holder may license only once in the production chain per patent, either to a component or end-device manufacturer. However, the problem with licensing to component manufactures is that SEP owner may not obtain adequate returns for its SEPs for the value that SEP brings to end-devices and the consumer.[12] Additionally, if a component maker were to receive a licence it would exhaust a subset of SEPs claiming only a component, but those SEPs that are infringed by end-devices would still need to be licensed to end-device manufacturers. This would lead to portfolio splitting and double licensing. A better approach is to have only one licence where most, or better all, the patents in a portfolio are infringed and exhausted by the sale of the licensed product. This is achieved in the telecommunications industry by licensing at end-device level. The exhaustion principle ensures that those downstream of the licensed party do not need a licence, while upstream parties (component makers) are protected by 'have made' rights or indirect licence, whereby the licence allows having or supplying components that may infringe licensed patents. Thus, as long as components

[11] For patent exhaustion in the US, see: *Quanta Computers v LG Elecs*, 128 S.Ct. 2109 (2008); *Impression Prods v Lexmark*, 137 S.Ct. 1523 (2017). For patent exhaustion in the EU, see: C Stothers, *Parallel Trade in Europe: Intellectual Property, Competition and Regulatory Law* (Hart Publishing, 2007) 40–44; Regulation (EU) 1257/2012 of 17 December 2012 Implementing Enhanced Cooperation in the Area of the Creation of Unitary Patent Protection [2012] OJ L 361/1, Article 6 (defining patent exhaustion: 'the rights conferred by a European patent with unitary effect *shall not extend to acts concerning a product covered by that patent … after that product has been placed on the market* in the Union by, or with the consent of, the patent proprietor, unless there are legitimate grounds for the patent proprietor to oppose further commercialisation of the product') (emphasis added).

[12] See ch 7, section V.

are supplied to licensed end-device makers, component manufacturers are operating within the licence. However, even without explicit 'have made' clauses or supplying components to unlicensed end-device makers, it is unlikely that component manufacturers would be exposed to infringement suits as that would exhaust SEPs at the component level and SEP owners would lose royalties from end-device manufacturers. In a case where the SEP owner nevertheless decided to assert some SEPs that read only on components against component manufactures, it would not be able to obtain injunctions without first offering a FRAND licence, as will be seen in chapter eight.

At this point it is also important to distinguish between a licence and access to a standard. Often the literature conflates a refusal to grant a licence with a refusal of access to the standard. However, not having a licence does not mean that others are automatically prevented from using and producing standardised products. As we can see from real life, SEP licensing agreements are often concluded *after* companies have started bringing a product to the market. The SEP owner can only prevent others from using the patent if it goes to court and successfully sues for an injunction. This is not a given fact; a SEP owner may decide not to enforce its patent for various reasons or, if it decides to go to court, injunctions are not an automatic outcome and it is in fact rare for SEP holders obtain one.[13] First, not all SEP owners are able to license and/or willing to sue, owing to the transaction costs of both licensing and litigation. Some SEP owners prefer not to monetise their IP portfolio and instead focus on downstream production. Any revenue return from a licence may not justify the costs of negotiating with all other similarly situated parties. Even if it decides to sue, a patent believed by the SEP holder as valid and essential may still be deemed invalid or non-essential by a court after lengthy and costly arguments from both sides. Moreover, even if the SEP owner prevails in patent litigation, an injunction may not be granted, granted on condition of onerous escrow deposits, only granted for a short period, not enforced, or overturned on appeal. With this background, a refusal to grant a licence by itself does not lead to an implementer's market exclusion.

Therefore, while patent law does not impose any direction obligations on SEP owners to license in the production chain, it provides a framework under which licensing operates. The doctrine of patent exhaustion effectively necessitates licensing only at one point in the production chain. Which level of the production chain to choose would depend on the contractual legal obligations of SEP owners (if any), the efficiencies associated with licensing at a particular level and claims where most SEPs are exhausted. Importantly, under patent law not having a licence does not necessarily mean that a company is excluded from the market as there are other ways to operate and obtain access to the standard.

[13] See ch 8 for injunctions for SEPs.

III. FRAND Commitments and Value Chain Licensing

The main source of obligation for SEP owners regarding where to license in the production chain is text of the relevant FRAND commitment and SDO IPR policies. The precise text of a FRAND commitment varies between SDOs, and it is thus important to analyse the exact wording of any contractual obligation given to different SDOs. As will be seen, apart from the IEEE, all other SDOs do not appear to require licensing at any particular point in the production chain and leave it to SEP owners to ensure effective access to the standard.

The ETSI IPR policy provides that the SEP owner will provide:

> [A]n irrevocable undertaking in writing that it is prepared to grant irrevocable licences on fair, reasonable and non-discriminatory ('FRAND') terms and conditions under such IPR to at least the following extent:
>
> - MANUFACTURE, including the right to make or have made customized components and sub-systems to the licensee's own design for use in MANUFACTURE;
> - sell, lease, or otherwise dispose of EQUIPMENT so MANUFACTURED;
> - repair, use, or operate EQUIPMENT; and
> - use METHODS.[14]

The term 'MANUFACTURE' is further defined as the 'production of 'EQUIPMENT', and 'EQUIPMENT' as 'any system, or device fully conforming to a STANDARD'.[15] The central question in the interpretation of ETSI's FRAND commitment is whether the term 'equipment' covers all types of devices, including components, or only end-user devices.

The text of Article 6.1 at first glance does not provide a clear answer and was subject to different interpretations.[16] Since ETSI's IPR policy is governed by French law, the principles of French contract law must be used in interpreting unclear contractual terms. The interpretation of unclear contractual terms first looks at the intention of the parties and, if intention is not possible to establish, it then examines a meaning that a reasonable person would give to disputed terms.[17]

[14] ETSI, 'Intellectual Property Rights Policy' (3 September 2020) Clause 6.1, available at: www.etsi.org/images/files/IPR/etsi-ipr-policy.pdf.

[15] ibid, Clause 15.

[16] See KH Rosenbrock, 'Why the ETSI IPR Policy Requires Licensing to All' (2017), available at: fair-standards.org/wp-content/uploads/2017/08/Why-the-ETSI-IPR-Policy-Requires-Licensing-to-All_Karl-Heinz-Rosenbrock_2017.pdf; KH Rosenbrock, 'Licensing At All Levels is The Rule Under The ETSI IPR Policy: A Response to Dr Bertram Huber' (2017), available at: papers.ssrn.com/sol3/papers.cfm?abstract_id=3064894 (former ETSI director general reading the clause as benefiting any third party, including upstream component manufacturers); B Huber, 'Why the ETSI IPR Policy Does Not and Has Never Required Compulsory "License to All": A Rebuttal to Karl Heinz Rosenbrock' (2017), available at: papers.ssrn.com/sol3/papers.cfm?abstract_id=3038447 (former member of ETSI IPR committee arguing that the drafter's of ETSI IPR policy only intended to confirm the industry practice at the time when the policy was adopted which was to grant licences only at the end-device level).

[17] Borghetti, Nikolic and Petit (n 10).

The contractual interpretation of ETSI's FRAND commitment appears not to require licensing at all levels in the production. While it is difficult to obtain direct evidence of the intention of the parties during the creation and approval of ETSI's first IPR policy between 1990 and 1994, and we have two conflicting views of direct participants,[18] elements after the conclusion of the contract, such as the behaviour of the parties, can be used to shed light on the parties' intentions. The fact that ETSI resisted proposals to modify its IPR policy in order to explicitly acknowledge that SEP owners should be ready to also grant licences to component-makers – whereas the IEEE has recently officially endorsed the LTA approach – would suggest that the initial intent of ETSI members was indeed to grant a right to be granted a licence only at the end-user device level. Additionally, the common licensing practice in the telecommunications industry at the time of the adoption of ETSI's IPR policy was, and remains, to grant licences at the end-user device level.[19] Absent a clear indication that the ETSI IPR policy intended to depart from this practice, a reasonable person familiar with the industry would have interpreted the policy as simply confirming this practice. The IPR policy also uses the word 'device', and avoids words such as 'element', 'component', 'part', or 'unit', which further suggests that it should be interpreted as being aimed at the end-user device level.

Finally, the definition of 'equipment' in Article 15 requires licensing only for 'any system, or device fully conforming to a standard'. It is typically only the end-devices that can fully conform to the standard, since ETSI standards are intended to enable interoperability and connection between different user devices and a network and do not focus on the components themselves.[20] Components alone cannot implement all functionalities of cellular standards and cannot carry out a method conforming to the standard, as discussed in chapter six, section II.

Therefore, ETSI's FRAND commitment bounds SEP owners only to negotiate in good faith towards a licence on FRAND terms with manufacturers of end-user devices when they intend to assert the patent. Of course, this does not mean that SEP owners are not *allowed* to license their SEPs to component makers under the ETSI IPR policy if they voluntarily decide to do so, but there is no positive obligation compelling them to do so. This conclusion was confirmed in *HTC v Ericsson*, where the court examined the text of ETSI's FRAND commitment and found that it does not require SEP owners to licence to component makers.[21]

[18] Rosenbrock, 'Why the ETSI IPR Policy Requires Licensing to All' (n 16); Huber (n 16).

[19] Borghetti, Nikolic and Petit (n 10).

[20] J Padilla and K Wong-Ervin, 'Portfolio Licensing to Makers of Downstream End-User Devices: Analyzing Refusals to License FRAND-Assured Standard-Essential Patents at the Component Level' (2017) *Antitrust Bulletin*, 494, 500–01; R Vary, 'A Review of SDO IPR Policies: Do They Require Component Level Licensing?' (16 November 2020).

[21] *HTC v Ericsson*, 2019 WL 126980 (ED Tex 2019).

The IEEE, on the other hand, imposes a direct obligation on SEP owners to license at a component level. The IEEE's FRAND commitment provides that

> the Submitter will make available a license for Essential Patent Claims to an unrestricted number of Applicants … to make, have made, use, sell, offer to sell, or import *any Compliant Implementation* that practices the Essential Patent Claims for use in conforming with the IEEE Standard.[22]

Compliant Implementation is further defined as '*any product (eg, component, sub-assembly, or end-product)* or service that conforms to *any mandatory or optional portion* of a normative clause of an IEEE Standard'.[23] While a component alone might not fully implement a standard, depending on the circumstances it might implement a portion of a standard. By explicitly defining 'Compliant Implementation' to include components and specifying that the obligation applies to any portion of a standard, the SEP owner giving FRAND commitment at the IEEE is required to license its patents at all levels in the production chain, including to component manufacturers.

Other SDOs have more ambiguous wording. A common version of such FRAND commitments is to require licences to be available to an 'unrestricted number of applicants' or to 'all applicants'. This is the case with the ITU-T, ISO and IEC's FRAND commitment which provides that the 'Patent Holder is prepared to grant a licence to an *unrestricted number of applicants* on a worldwide, non-discriminatory basis and on reasonable terms and conditions to make, use and sell implementations of the above document'.[24] TIA's FRAND commitment similarly provides that

> the license rights which are held by the undersigned Patent Holder, will be made available to *all applicants* under terms and conditions that are reasonable and non-discriminatory, which may include monetary compensation, and only to the extent necessary for the practice of any or all of the Normative portions for the field of use of practice of the Standard.[25]

ANSI requires

> assurance that a license to such essential patent claim(s)will be made available to *applicants* desiring to utilize the license for the purpose of implementing the standard … under reasonable terms and conditions that are demonstrably free of any unfair discrimination.[26]

[22] IEEE-SA, 'Standards Board Bylaws' (August 2020) Clause 6.2. Policy, available at: standards.ieee.org/content/dam/ieee-standards/standards/web/documents/other/sb_bylaws.pdf.

[23] ibid.

[24] ITU-ISO-IEC, 'Patent Statement and Licensing Declaration Form for ITU-T, ITU-R Recommendation, ISO or IEC Deliverable' (2 November 2018), available at: www.itu.int/dms_pub/itu-t/oth/04/04/T04040000020005PDFE.pdf.

[25] TIA, 'Intellectual Property Rights Policy' (21 October 2016) 8, available at: www.tiaonline.org/wp-content/uploads/2018/05/TIA_Intellectual_Property_Rights_Policy.pdf.

[26] ANSI, 'Essential Requirements: Due Process Requirements for American National Standards' (January 2021) 11, available at: www.ansi.org/american-national-standards/ans-introduction/essential-requirements.

Who can be considered as an 'applicant' is open for interpretation. On the one hand, such broad wording could arguably encompass companies at all levels of the production chain, and SEP owners giving such commitments would be required to offer licences to component manufacturers should they request so. On the other hand, as explained, not all SEPs claim one single component, meaning that a component might not be fully implementing all features of the standard. It can thus be argued that 'applicants' are only fully complying downstream producers, and component manufacturers will therefore not need a licence if they are selling to licensed end-device manufacturers. An argument in favour of such interpretation can be found in the wording of FRAND commitments providing that licences will be given for the 'implementation of a standard'. ITU-T, ISO and IEC, as noted above, require FRAND licences for the 'implementation' of standards, and define essential patents as those that would be required to 'implement' a specific Recommendation or Deliverable.[27] ANSI also further qualifies that licences will be made available only to applicants 'for the purpose of implementing the standard',[28] while TIA provides that licences shall be made available 'only to the extent necessary for the practice of any or all of the Normative portions for the field of use of practice of the Standard'.[29] Such limitations arguably restrain the availability of licences only to fully compliant implementations of a standard, which are often only end-devices, and not necessarily chips. Of course, an assessment will have to be carried out for each standard and relevant SEPs to see whether it is fully implanted by a component or end-device.

There are several cases in the US where courts interpreted the text of the FRAND commitment in assessing whether there exists the duty to license to component manufacturers. Cases mostly related to disputes between end-device manufacturers and courts recognised that such practice is consistent with a FRAND commitment. To date it seems that no court has definitively interpreted FRAND commitment as imposing a duty to license at any level of the production chain.

In *Microsoft v Motorola*, the court was deciding whether to grant an antisuit injunction prohibiting Motorola from enforcing an injunction in Germany until the case was resolved by the US court.[30] Interpreting ITU's FRAND commitment the court held that the 'language admits of no limitations as to who or how many applicants could receive a license ("unrestricted number of applicants") or as to which country's patents would be included ("worldwide", "the patented material necessary")'.[31] However, such a sentence should not be interpreted as endorsing an LTA approach. The court did not rule on whether ITU's FRAND commitment requires licensing at a component or end-device level but was deciding whether

[27] ITU-ISO-IEC, 'Patent Statement and Licensing Declaration Form' (n 24).
[28] ANSI, 'Essential Requirements' (n 26) 11.
[29] TIA, 'Intellectual Property Rights Policy' (n 25) 8.
[30] *Microsoft v Motorola*, 696 F.3d 872 (9th Cir 2012).
[31] ibid, 884.

injunction for infringement of SEPs is allowed, and the case itself related to two end-device manufacturers. Thus, the sentence in this context could be read only to indicate that a FRAND commitment does not restrict the number of licensees at the end-device level and requires licensing of a worldwide portfolio. The Ninth Circuit similarly in *Microsoft v Motorola II*, an appeal from the breach of contract action where the court determined FRAND terms for Motorola's SEP portfolio, held that under FRAND commitments 'an SEP holder cannot refuse a license to a manufacturer who commits to paying the RAND rate'.[32] Again, the court was not deciding on the level chain licensing question. The case, in fact, related to two end-device manufacturers and could be read only in that context.

In *Ericsson v D-Link*, the district court was interpreting the IEEE's FRAND commitment given under the previous IPR policy.[33] Ericsson adopted a policy of offering FRAND licenses only to 'fully compliant' products. By licensing end-product manufacturers, Ericsson believed it was indirectly licensing chip manufacturers as well. The court said that there is nothing inherently wrong or unfair with Ericsson's policy of licensing only fully compliant products; other large companies have adopted similar policies and that there is nothing in the previous IEEE IPR policy that would require otherwise.[34] Therefore, companies are free to restrict or limit the production chain where they want to license.

In *FTC v Qualcomm*, the district court interpreted FRAND commitments given at TIA and ATIS as requiring licensing at any level of the production chain, including to component manufacturers.[35] It held that the plain wording of FRAND commitments to make licences available to 'all applicants' is unambiguous and rejected arguments that a FRAND obligation applies only to device manufacturers that fully implement or practise the standard.[36] The court observed that TIA's IPR policy 'expressly contemplates that a TIA standard may have 'portions' or 'elements', and that an applicant may receive a license as necessary to practise 'any' portion of a TIA standard, and the ATIS IPR policy states that a licence must be '*for the purpose* of implementing a standard'.[37] It held that a modem chip has the purpose of practising or implementing cellular standards, meaning that a FRAND commitment applies to chip manufacturers and requires them to have a licence. In reaching that conclusion, the court relied on Qualcomm's public statement and annual report that modem chips are at the 'heart of a cellphone'.[38] However, a proper analysis would have to look at which portions of the standard are implemented solely by a component, and which by the end-device, and whether Qualcomm holds those SEPs that claim only a component. On appeal the district court's judgment was vacated without reaching the merits because the

[32] *Microsoft v Motorola* 795 F.3d 1024, 1031 (9th Cir 2015).
[33] *Ericsson v D-Link*, 2013 WL 4046225 (ED Tex 2013) 23–24.
[34] ibid, 24.
[35] *Federal Trade Commission v Qualcomm*, WL 5848999 (ND Cal 2018).
[36] ibid, 14.
[37] ibid.
[38] ibid.

main claim that Qualcomm's practices were anti-competitive was dismissed.[39] Thus the district court's judgment remains unenforced and does not represent a binding precedent.

In conclusion, most SDOs, including ETSI, do not appear to impose an obligation to license at a particular level of the production chain and leave the decision to SEP owners. On the other hand, the IEEE explicitly provides that SEP owners are required to license to all interested companies at any level of the production chain. Therefore, unless an IPR policy makes it clear and explicit that the SEP owner is required to grant licences to any company so requesting, regardless of its position in the production chain, SEP owners are legally free to decide on the precise level of the production chain to license their SEPs. That said, in the IoT it might be more appropriate in some circumstances to license at a component level and the FRAND commitment is flexible enough to allow such a possibility. A case-by-case approach would have to be undertaken in the IoT to find the most appropriate licensing level that ensures licensing efficiencies, lowers transactions costs and secures adequate pricing of standardised technology.

IV. Competition Law and Value Chain Licensing

The final argument to consider is whether there is a competition law duty to license SEPs at all levels in the production chain. It will be seen that EU and US competition law is unlikely to apply in this context, although it appears that some Asian jurisdictions used domestic competition law to impose a duty on vertically integrated SEP owners to license to component manufacturers as well.[40]

[39] *Federal Trade Commission v Qualcomm*, 969 F.3d 974, 987 (9th Cir 2020).

[40] See in India, G Sidak, 'FRAND in India' in J Contreras (ed), *The Cambridge Handbook of Technical Standardization Law: Competition, Antitrust, and Patents* (Cambridge University Press, 2018) (showing how the Competition Commission of India in cases brought against Ericsson based on the complaints of Indian handsets manufacturers considers licensing on the end-product devices as anti-competitive). In South Korea, Qualcomm was found to have abused its dominant position by refusing to license its SEPs to chipset manufacturers, see S Young Lee and S Nellis, 'South Korea fines Qualcomm $854 million for violating competition laws' *Reuters* (28 December 2016), available at: www.reuters.com/article/us-qualcomm-antitrust/south-korea-fines-qualcomm-854-million-for-violating-competition-laws-idUSKBN14H062; H Yang, 'Qualcomm to Appeal Record South Korea Anti-Trust Fine' *Reuters* (4 December 2019), available at: www.reuters.com/article/us-qualcomm-southkorea-idUSKBN1Y807J. In Taiwan, Qualcomm was also found to have abused its dominant position by refusing to license its SEPs to chipset manufacturers, however, the case settled without definite ruling liability, see: T Bradshaw and E White, 'Qualcomm Settles $774 Million Antitrust Dispute in Taiwan' *Financial Times* (10 August 2018), available at: www.ft.com/content/a785787e-9c41-11e8-9702-5946bae86e6d. In Japan, the Japan Fair Trade Commission in 2016 issued Guidelines which appear to consider as an unfair trading practice a refusal to license SEPs to any party willing to take a licence, presumably also including component manufacturers. See Japan Fair Trade Commission, 'Guidelines for the Use of Intellectual Property under the Antimonopoly Act' (2016) part 4 (2) (iv), available at: www.jftc.go.jp/en/legislation_gls/imonopoly_guidelines_files/IPGL_Frand.pdf.

A. Refusal to License and EU Competition Law

EU competition law recognises that a firm has the right to choose its trading partners and to dispose freely of its property.[41] Any competition law limitation on the freedom to contract and the right to private property can only be imposed after careful considerations, and should not impinge on the existence of such rights.[42] This applies equally to intellectual property, whose protection is guaranteed by the EU Charter of Fundamental Rights.[43] The practical implication is that compulsory licensing has remained more the exception than the rule in EU competition law.

EU competition law nonetheless provides for a limited derogation to the right to freely exercise intellectual property rights. In 'exceptional circumstances', a refusal to license intellectual property rights may be deemed an abuse of dominant position.[44] In *Magill*, *IMS Health* and *Microsoft*, the EU courts have held that the following criteria have to be met to impose a duty to license IPRs on a dominant firm: (i) a refusal to license IPRs relates to a product or service that is indispensable to the exercise of a particular activity on a neighbouring market; (ii) the refusal to license IPRs is of such kind as to exclude any effective competition on that neighbouring market; and (iii) the refusal to license IPRs prevents the appearance of a new product for which there is potential consumer demand.[45]

It would be difficult to establish the abusive refusal to license when the SEP holder has adopted the policy of licensing its SEPs only at the end-device level and thus indirectly licensing component manufacturers. To start, observed empirical realities are inconsistent with the idea that refusal to license to component manufacturers leads to elimination of competition on the downstream market and prevents the appearance of new products. In the smartphone industry, we have witnessed a rapid entry of new market players, vigorous downstream competition, and an overall decrease in consumer prices.[46] Licensing directly to component manufacturers is also hardly indispensable under the first condition. As mentioned, having a direct licence from the SEP owner is only one way of having access to the standard. Other methods include indirectly benefiting from a licence by selling components to licensed downstream manufacturers, concluding non-assertion

[41] Commission, 'Guidance on the Commission's Enforcement Priorities in Applying Article 82 of the EC Treaty to Abusive Exclusionary Conduct by Dominant Undertakings' (Communication) [2009] OJ C 45/7; Opinion of AG Jacobs in *Oscar Bronner* C-7/97 EU:C:1998:264, 56–57.

[42] Opinion of AG Jacobs in *Oscar Bronner* C-7/97 EU:C:1998:264, 62.

[43] Charter of Fundamental Rights of the European Union [2012] OJ C 326, Article 17(2).

[44] C/241/91 P *RTE and ITP v Commission* EU:C:1995:98; C-7/97 *Oscar Bronner v Media Print* EU:C:1998:569; C-418/01 *IMS Health v NDC Health* EU:C:2004:257; T-201/04 *Microsoft v Commission* EU:T:2007:289.

[45] T-201/04 *Microsoft v Commission* EU:T:2007:289, 332; see also Commission, 'Enforcement Priorities Guidelines' (n 41) 81 (the European Commission will consider the following legal tests in deciding to bring the case in refusal to license cases: (i) the refusal to license relates to a product or service that is objectively necessary to be able to compete effectively on a downstream market; (ii) the refusal to license is likely to lead to the elimination of effective competition on the downstream market; and (iii) the refusal to license is likely to lead to consumer harm).

[46] See ch 2, section III.A.

agreements, or even not having any licence at all if the patent owner has a policy of not monetising its patents and thus not having a licensing programme. Therefore, with or without a licence, component manufacturers are not precluded from selling their products to downstream manufacturers when the SEP owners implement a policy of licensing only at end-device level.

A successful refusal to license case would require an extreme set of facts. For example, a SEP holder refuses to license all and any third party, and reserves for itself the manufacture of standard-compliant products. In such a scenario, the three conditions defined in the case law are prima facie fulfilled. The scenario is extreme in the sense that no SEP holder to date appears to have taken such a radical position. Such a position would not only risk competition law liability but is also a breach of contractual FRAND commitment and a SEP owner would likely be punished by exclusion from most standardisation organisations.

Recognising the limitations of the refusal to license doctrine, some authors suggests that a competition law duty to license component manufacturers may arise out of *Huawei v ZTE*, a case which concerned the use of injunctions for the infringement of SEPs.[47] There the CJEU held that the particular circumstances of the case involving SEPs that are encumbered by the FRAND commitment justify restricting the use of injunctions.[48] By way of analogy, it was suggested that the CJEU's reasoning should be extended to impose a special competition law duty to license SEPs to component manufacturers.[49] The argument relies on the passage from the *Huawei v ZTE* judgment where the court held that

> FRAND terms creates legitimate expectations on the part of third parties that the proprietor of the SEP will in fact grant licences on such terms, a refusal by the proprietor of the SEP to grant a licence on those terms may, in principle, constitute an abuse within the meaning of Article 102 TFEU.[50]

By way of extension it was claimed that since

> SEP is as essential to component manufacturers to produce and sell components as it is to end-product manufacturers … a FRAND commitment … gives rise to a legitimate expectation of any party who needs a licence in order to produce and sell standard-compliant products, including, therefore, undertakings producing components.[51]

It concludes that

> if a dominant SEP holder cannot enforce its SEP against an infringing undertaking which is a willing licensee because of the FRAND commitment that it made, it must follow that the SEP holder has a duty to grant a licence to that undertaking on FRAND terms.[52]

[47] R Nazzini, 'Level Discrimination and FRAND Commitments Under EU Competition Law' (2017) 40 *World Competition* 213.

[48] C-170/13 *Huawei v ZTE*, EU:C:2015:477, 48–50. See ch 8 for discussion.

[49] Nazzini (n 47) 231.

[50] C-170/13 *Huawei v ZTE* (n 48) 53.

[51] Nazzini (n 47) 231.

[52] ibid.

However, the reasoning found in *Huawei v ZTE* in no way provides a legal basis for an additional doctrine leading to a competition law duty to license. *Huawei v ZTE* concerned the general conditions under which SEP holders can seek injunctions against unlicensed implementers, and it says nothing about a duty to license *specifically* to component suppliers. The case itself concerned two end-device manufacturers, and it would be difficult to think that the court also had in mind component manufacturers when deciding on the issue of availability of injunctions between end-device manufacturers. While it is true that the court discussed legitimate expectations in the context of bilateral negotiations between a SEP owner and a prospective licensee that the SEP owner decided to license, it cannot be said that this reference also implies a competition law duty to license to any party, including component manufacturers the SEP owner never licensed in the past and which may not infringe all SEPs in the portfolio. A well-established, and demanding, competition law refusal to licence doctrine already exists. It is, of course, right to point out that if the SEP holder decides to sue component manufacturers for infringement, it may not be able to obtain an injunction unless it offers them a FRAND licence. But the same is true if the SEP holder decides to sue end-product manufacturers for infringement. Finally, the argument misreads the legitimate expectations requirement of the FRAND commitment.[53] Component suppliers can only be said to entertain legitimate expectations to obtain FRAND licences if such an obligation is included in the text of the FRAND commitment itself or in the SDO policy documents underpinning such commitments. However, as seen above the wording of the FRAND commitment differs among SDOs. Some specifically seek to impose a duty to license at any level of the production chain while most others do not. The takeaway from *Huawei v ZTE* is that the CJEU refrained from getting directly involved in FRAND price- setting and instead provided a general framework for parties to voluntarily reach an agreement. It in no way regulated sensitive commercial issues between the parties, including the question of where to license in the production chain.

The role of EU competition law has been invoked in SEP automotive litigation in Germany. In *Nokia v Daimler*, Mannheim Regional Court held that the SEP owner is free to choose the level of the supply chain to assert its rights and did not find that the assertion of SEPs against end-device manufacturers only could lead to consumer harm.[54] In *Sharp v Daimler*, Munich Regional Court also found that it is not abusive for SEP owners to seek licences only from end-device manufacturers.[55] It recognised that a FRAND commitment given at ETSI creates an obligation to enable access to the standards, but does not create a duty to grant licences at all levels of the production chain.[56] Access to the standard can be obtained by a licence given at the last level in the production chain from which suppliers can

[53] For discussion on the legitimate expectations, see Borghetti, Nikolic and Petit (n 10).
[54] *Nokia v Daimler* (n 9) 202, 213.
[55] *Sharp v Daimler* (n 9).
[56] ibid, 165.

benefit from have-made rights.[57] The Court also viewed that the legitimate expectations reference in *Huawei v ZTE* cannot be extended to impose an obligation to license at every level of the supply chain, since effective access to the standard can also be achieved by other means.[58] However, in another *Nokia v Daimler* case before Düsseldorf Regional Court, the Court decided to make a preliminary reference to the CJEU about whether Article 102 of TFEU imposes an obligation on SEP owners to license to component manufacturers.[59] However, the parties settled the case before the CJEU could decide, leaving the question open and it could possibly emerge again in another reference in a dispute between SEP owners and car manufacturers.[60] Nevertheless, the CJEU should leave the level chain licensing issue to commercial negotiations and policy-making where it rightfully belongs.

B. Article 101 TFEU and the Horizontal Cooperation Guidelines

An argument is also made that Article 101 TFEU and the Commission's Horizontal Cooperation Guidelines require SDOs to implement an obligation to license to any company at any level of the production chain.[61] In the part discussing standardisation agreements, the HCG provides that

> in order to ensure effective access to the standard, the IPR policy would need to require participants wishing to have their IPR included in the standard to provide an irrevocable commitment in writing to offer to license their essential IPR to *all third parties* on fair, reasonable and non-discriminatory terms.[62]

The reference to 'all third parties' is said to require SDOs to impose an obligation to license at every level of the supply chain to any manufacturer that requests it.

However, a careful examination of the HCG calls into question such a claim. The HCG do not prescribe a positive competition law obligation. Its function is to provide a safe harbour that specifies which competitors' agreements can be deemed presumptively lawful. Outside this safe harbour, there is no competition law presumption of liability.[63] Any reading of the HCG as a source of a positive competition law obligation to license at any level of the production chain would

[57] ibid, 171.
[58] ibid.
[59] C-182/21 *Nokia Technologies* (23 March 2021).
[60] M Kloss, 'Nokia and Daimler Settle all Global Litigation in Connected Cars Dispute' (1 June 2021) *JUVE Patent*, available at: www.juve-patent.com/news-and-stories/cases/nokia-and-daimler-settle-all-global-litigation-in-connected-cars-dispute/.
[61] Commission,' Guidelines on the Applicability of Article 101 of the Treaty on the Functioning of the European Union to Horizontal Co-operation Agreements' (Communication) [2011] OJ C 11/01 (Horizontal Cooperation Guidelines).
[62] ibid, 285.
[63] ibid, 279 ('the non-fulfilment of any or all of the principles set out in this section will not lead to any presumption of a restriction of competition within Article 101 TFEU').

ignore the fact that the HCG acknowledges the impossibility of an unconditional Article 101 TFEU application and stresses the importance of SDOs' IPR policies being 'adapted to the particular industry and the needs of the standard-setting organisation in question'.[64] Lastly, the term 'all third parties' in the HCG is not further defined. As seen, SEPs include wide claims and often the full implementation of a standard's functionality is provided by the end-device. Accordingly, 'all third parties' could then only be those that fully implement the standard ie, end-devices. This question will often be sector specific and depend on each industry.

Instead, the goal of the HCG is to ensure effective *access* to the standard, which is mentioned throughout the text. For instance, paragraph 283 of the HCG provides that 'the standard-setting organisation's rules would need to ensure effective access to the standard on fair, reasonable and non-discriminatory terms'.[65] In paragraph 287 the HCG continue to explain that FRAND commitments 'are designed to ensure that essential IPR protected technology incorporated in a standard is *accessible* to the users of that standard'.[66] Finally, the assessment of whether the SDO IPR policies restrict competition will focus on 'access to the standard'.[67] As already explained, access to a standard does not equate with having a direct licence, but can be provided by other means, such as by indirectly benefiting from a licence by supplying licensed end-device makers, by having non-assertion agreements, or by the decision of the patent owner not to enforce its patents and not having a licensing programme.

C. Refusal to License and US Antitrust Law

US antitrust law would also be difficult to interpret as imposing an antitrust duty to license to all companies across the production chain. The Sherman Act does not restrict the right of a company to decide with whom it wants to deal.[68] The US Supreme Court explained that compelling companies to enter into a business relationship 'may lessen the incentive for the monopolist, the rival, or both to invest in … economically beneficial facilities',[69] and would require 'antitrust courts to act as central planners, identifying the proper price, quantity, and other terms of dealing – a role for which they are ill-suited'.[70] In the context of intellectual property rights, the essence of patents rights is the right to exclude others from using the patented invention as well as to decide whom to license. Thus, US antitrust agencies have stated that antitrust 'liability for mere unilateral, unconditional refusals to license

[64] ibid, 284.
[65] ibid, 283.
[66] ibid, 287.
[67] ibid, 294.
[68] *Verizon Communications Inc v Law Offices of Curtis v Trinko*, 540 US 398, 408 (2004).
[69] ibid.
[70] ibid.

will not play a meaningful part' in their enforcement efforts.[71] The Assistant Attorney General Makan Delrahim noted that, in his view, 'a unilateral and unconditional refusal to license a patent should be considered as *per se* legal'.[72]

Against this background, the US Supreme Court accepted only a limited exception to the general right of companies to freely decide on their business partners. In *Aspen Skiing* and later in *Verizon v Trinko*, the US Supreme Court held that, under certain circumstances, a refusal to cooperate with rivals could constitute anti-competitive conduct.[73] An antitrust duty to deal would arise only if the plaintiff can satisfy the following legal tests: (i) unilateral termination of a voluntary and profitable course of dealing; (ii) a refusal to deal even if compensated at retail price, which suggested that the conduct was anticompetitive; and (iii) a refusal to provide its competitor with a product that was already sold in a retail market to other customers.[74] If the plaintiff succeeds, a defendant could then try to provide an objective justification for the conduct.

It would be very difficult to establish an antitrust duty to deal with component manufacturers under the present US antitrust refusal to deal doctrine.[75] Namely, when SEP owners are already licensing at the end-device level and are not asserting their SEPs at the component level, it seems unlikely that the first and third requirements are present. There could be no unilateral termination of a voluntary and profitable business dealing when the SEP holder is not licensing on the component level in the first place, and by licensing only at the end-device level component manufacturers are effectively indirectly licensed. Also, it seems unlikely that component manufacturers would accept paying the same amount of royalties as end-device manufacturers, which would make the second condition also not fulfilled. Even if the plaintiff could somehow satisfy the refusal to deal legal test, the SEP holder could adduce procompetitive business justifications for such conduct, such as receiving the appropriate valuation for SEPs, avoiding

[71] US Department of Justice and the Federal Trade Commission, *Antitrust Enforcement and Intellectual Property Right: Promoting Innovation and Competition* (2007) 30.

[72] M Delrahim, Assistant Attorney General US Department of Justice, 'The "New Madison" Approach to Antitrust and Intellectual Property Law' (16 March 2018) 5, available at: www.justice.gov/opa/speech/file/1044316/download.

[73] *Aspen Skiing Co v Aspen Highlands Skiing Corp*, 472 US 585 (1985); *Verizon Communications Inc v Law Offices of Curtis v Trinko* (n 67) 408.

[74] *Aspen Skiing Co v Aspen Highlands Skiing* Corp (n 72); *Verizon Communications Inc v Law Offices of Curtis v Trinko* (n 67) 408–11; also *MetroNet Services Corp v Qwest Corp*, 383 F.3d 1124, 1131 (9th Cir 2004).

[75] See T Cotter, 'Comparative Law and Economics of Standard-Essential Patents and FRAND Royalties' (2014) 22 *Texas Intellectual Property Law Journal* 311, 333–35 (discussing the application of refusal to license and essential facilities doctrines to refusal to license SEPs); E Hovenkamp, 'Tying, Exclusivity, and Standard-Essential Patents' (2017) 19 *Columbia Science & Technology Law Review* 79, 120–25 (analysing US antitrust law and finding that a SEP holder's refusal to license rivals is unlikely to support a viable antitrust claim); Padilla and Wong-Ervin (n 20) 502–03, 504 ('To sum up, antitrust liability for refusals to license is highly disfavored under US law. In addition … the existence of a legitimate business justification is likely to preclude liability at least in the United States under a refusal to deal theory').

patent exhaustion, or the efficiencies of cross-licensing with other vertically integrated companies.

The *FTC v Qualcomm* case tested whether US antitrust law can impose an antitrust duty to deal with all companies in the production chain. In the first instance, the Northern District Court of California upheld the Federal Trade Commission's (FTC) complaint whereby Qualcomm's licensing practices towards competing chip manufacturers constituted cognisable violations of section 2 of the Sherman Act.[76] One of the contested practices was Qualcomm's policy of licensing SEPs only to final downstream manufacturers and refusing to license SEPs to competing chip manufacturers.[77] According to the FTC, 'Qualcomm's refusal to license competing manufacturers of [modem chips], in contravention of its FRAND commitments, contributes to [Qualcomm's] ability to tax its competitors' [modem chip] sales, and thus maintain Qualcomm's modem chip monopoly'.[78] Following the plaintiff, the district court ruled that Qualcomm had an antitrust duty to license to all.[79] The district court judge considered that all three *Aspen Skiing* criteria had been fulfilled as Qualcomm historically used to license component manufacturers, which it terminated in order to extract unreasonably high royalties from end-device manufacturers.[80]

The case was reversed on appeal. The Ninth Circuit criticised the district court for misapplying *Aspen Skiing* and erred in holding that Qualcomm was under an antitrust duty to license rival chip manufacturers.[81] The Ninth Circuit reiterated the Supreme Court's holding that an antitrust duty to deal in *Aspen Skiing* should be applied only in rare circumstances and that this doctrine is 'is at or near the outer boundary of Section 2 liability'.[82] In contrast to the district court, it did not find persuasive evidence that Qualcomm in the past gave exhaustive licences to chip manufacturers. Qualcomm gave only non-exhaustive licences but ceased licensing to chip manufacturers when the US patent exhaustion doctrine was changed that might potentially lead to exhaustion of its SEPs on a chip level.[83] The second criteria of refusal to deal even if compensated at a retail price was also found not to be met. Qualcomm responded to the change in patent exhaustion law by choosing a more lucrative option both in the short and the long term. However, the goal of antitrust law is not to force companies to forego profits and choosing a more profitable licensing level in itself is not prohibited.[84] Finally, the Ninth Circuit found no evidence that Qualcomm singled out any specific chip

[76] *Federal Trade Commission v Qualcomm*, 411 F.Supp.3d 658 (ND Cal 2019).

[77] Other allegedly anti-competitive practices included 'no licence to chip', whereby Qualcomm sold its chips only to downstream product manufacturers under the conditions that they also take a licence for Qualcomm's SEPs, and entering an exclusive dealing arrangement with Apple.

[78] *FTC v Qualcomm*, Case 5:17-CV-00220 (Complaint) 115.

[79] *FTC v Qualcomm*, 411 F.Supp.3d 658 (ND Cal 2019).

[80] ibid.

[81] *Federal Trade Commission v Qualcomm*, 969 F.3d 974 (9th Cir 2020).

[82] *Verizon Communications Inc v Law Offices of Curtis v Trinko* (n 67).

[83] *Federal Trade Commission v Qualcomm*, 969 F.3d 974, 994 (9th Cir 2020).

[84] ibid.

suppler for anti-competitive treatment. Instead, it applied device level licensing equally and declined to enforce its patents against rival chipmakers. The Court thus described Qualcomm's licensing policy as 'no license, no problem'.[85]

The Court noted that a situation would be different if Qualcomm were to refuse to license its SEPs to end-device manufacturers unless they first agreed to purchase its chips, characterised as 'no chips, no license' policy.[86] Under this scenario chip manufacturers might have an antitrust claim, because end-device makers would be forced to purchase either Qualcomm's chips or pay for both Qualcomm's and the competitor's chips. However, this is not what occurred and Qualcomm's practice was held to be chip-supplier neutral since, regardless of which chip is purchased, Qualcomm collects royalties only at the end-device level.

The Ninth Circuit also examined an additional argument by the FTC that Qualcomm's conduct was nevertheless anticompetitive since Qualcomm breached its FRAND commitments requiring it to license to all companies in the production chain. Without going into the merits of whether the text of relevant FRAND commitments imposes a contractual duty to license to all, the Court rejected the FTC's claim as it was not persuaded that the alleged breach of a contractual commitments *itself* impaired the opportunities of rivals.[87] On the facts of the case, the Court held that not enforcing SEPs against rival chip manufacturers under a 'no license, no problem' policy is equivalent to a de facto licence that allows chip manufacturers to practise Qualcomm's SEPs royalty-free.[88] Moreover, Qualcomm's licensing policy was consistent with existing industry practice. Thus, the Ninth Circuit concluded that the appropriate remedy for breach of FRAND commitments lies in contract or patent law, not competition law.[89]

V. Policy Outlook for the Internet of Things

As seen, most FRAND commitments and SDO IPR policies do not impose an obligation on SEP owners to license to any company in the production chain but leave it to SEP owners to ensure effective access to the standard. Competition law also does not specify the level of the production chain at which licensing must be conducted. Thus, the legal flexibility grants parties the freedom to efficiently tailor licensing agreements in accordance with their needs and the peculiarities of each industry.

What FRAND commitments, patent and competition law do require is effective *access* to the standard. They prevent SEP owners from reserving the use of

[85] ibid, 995.
[86] ibid, 1002.
[87] ibid, 995
[88] ibid, 996.
[89] ibid, 1005.

SEPs just for themselves and excluding all others from using the standard. Anyone wishing to implement a standard should have access to it.[90] Having a direct licence from the SEP owner is not the only way of accessing the standard. Other methods include indirectly benefiting from a licence by selling components to licensed downstream manufacturers, concluding non-assertion agreements, or even not having any licence at all if the patent owner has a policy of not monetising its patents and thus not having a licensing programme. Nothing prevents component manufacturers from supplying end-device makers that will ultimately take a licence, as evidenced by the empirical success of the smartphone industry.

Requiring SEP owners to license at every level of the supply chain could lead to burdensome portfolio splitting, where those SEPs that read only on components will be licensed to component manufacturers, while all other SEPs that have wider claims will continue to be licensed to end-device manufacturers. Instead of simplifying and easing licensing, this approach would result in considerable complexity and increased transaction costs. It would increase instead of reducing the number of companies needing to take a licence, which would be unattractive to all participants in standardisation. SEP owners would also need to conduct expensive patent searches and analyse which claims read only on components in order split their portfolio, imposing significant search costs.

The IoT, however, will bring challenges to SEP licensing and will require careful selection of the most appropriate licensing level. The factors associated with the telecommunications industry, a relatively small number of SEP owners and implementers, and the use of cross-licensing between vertically integrated companies, will not be present in the IoT. The IoT environment is characterised by countless companies from diverse industries – from consumer electronics, automotive, utilities, health to manufacturing – needing to license SEPs and already having their own unique IP licensing practice. The automotive industry, for example, clears all IP rights at a component level and provides indemnity clauses to car manufacturers.[91] Moreover, many IoT implementers will be SMEs with little experience of SEP licensing and the resources for expensive patent licensing negotiations. Finally, the importance of cross-licensing will be reduced as IoT companies will not hold corresponding SEP portfolios. Thus, while end-device licensing was the most efficient option in the telecommunications industry, it may not be for other IoT industries.

The European Commission's SEP Expert Group recently proposed three principles for finding a satisfactory solution for the most appropriate licensing level in the IoT: (i) licensing at a single level in the value chain for a particular licensed product; (ii) a uniform FRAND royalty for a particular product irrespective of

[90] See M Heim and I Nikolic, 'A FRAND Regime for Dominant Digital Platforms' (2019) 10 *JIPITEC* 38 (analysing how a FRAND regime has enabled efficient access across various industries and sectors).

[91] J Baron et al, 'Group of Experts on Licensing and Valuation of Standard Essential Patents – Contribution to the Debate on SEPs' (January 2021) 82, available at: ec.europa.eu/docsroom/documents/45217.

the level of licensing; and (iii) FRAND royalty is a cost element in the price of a component and should be passed on downstream.[92] These are sound principles that recognise the efficiency of licensing only at one level of the production chain and the fact that the value of the standard is reflected in its downstream use and not on the price or profit margins of unlicensed component manufacturers, as discussed in chapter six. This is an important recognition that may unlock component level licensing in the future. As explained, a standard's functionality, bandwidth and use are different in a smartphone, smart car, or a smart utility. Some IoT industries like connected cars would use the full extent of functionality and bandwidth of 5G standards, while other industries, like smart meters, would use only limited functionality of 5G and only occasionally. Thus, a price for the standard needs to be differentiated based on the downstream use. The principles recognise this distinction, making the amount of royalties irrespective of whether they are borne by end-device makers or component manufacturers as they represent a cost that should be passed on further downstream.

Once the price of SEPs is set in relation to its downstream use, then the only question remains is which level of the production chain is more efficient to license. The optimal licensing level in the IoT would depend on the extent it can generate licensing efficiencies such as transaction costs savings, licensing experience, the possibility to price differently depending on the downstream use, the ease of monitoring the compliance with royalty payments and the possibility of cross-licensing.[93] In many instances the efficiencies would lead to licensing at a downstream level, but not necessarily, sometimes licensing at a component level may be viable. For example, in the IoT the number of firms supplying connectivity components is smaller than the number of downstream firms, suggesting lower transaction costs of licensing only to a few component manufacturers.[94] Component manufacturers may also be in a better position to negotiate licences as they have more experience with standardised technology which they directly implement in their components, than IoT end-device manufacturers, many of them SMEs, that may only assemble products acquired from different suppliers and do not expect to be involved with IP licensing for each component.[95] On the other hand, component manufactures may be reluctant to pay the full price of the standard based on its downstream value, which might exceed their current profit margins and would necessitate the increase in the price of components. That may lead to a collective action problem where no firm is willing to take a licence until all other competitors are also licensed, otherwise a company that takes a licence would be significantly price disadvantaged in relation to its unlicensed component competitors. The SEP

[92] ibid, 83–84; see also, T Kuhnen, 'FRAND Licensing and Implementation Chains' (2019) 14 *Journal of Intellectual Property Law & Practice* 964; B Heiden, J Padilla and R Peters, 'The Value of Standard Essential Patents and the Level of Licensing' (2020), available at: papers.ssrn.com/sol3/papers.cfm?abstract_id=3717570.

[93] Baron et al (n 90) 84.

[94] J Henkel, 'How to License SEPs to Promote Innovation and Entrepreneurship in the IoT' (2021) 14–17, available at: papers.ssrn.com/sol3/papers.cfm?abstract_id=3808987.

[95] Baron et al (n 90) 83.

Expert Group thus recommends joint negotiations between SEP owners on the optimal licensing level for each IoT industry and, once they agree, joint consultations with implementers and among implementers on the ways to pass on the costs of licensing further downstream.[96] If consensus could be reached voluntarily that would be the optimal outcome. Finally, a component licensing model would need to ensure an efficient tracking system to monitor which chips go to which downstream product in order to price differently based on downstream use. The more industries the component maker supplies, the more complex the monitoring and tracking system becomes. The SEP Expert Group recommends investigating whether a tracking mechanism in the form of a software code could be implemented indicating the type of end-product for which a component is intended.[97] Additionally, it might be possible that chips with different connectivity rates may be more complex than chips with lower connectivity rates, ie, a connectivity chip for a smart car will likely be more complex than a connectivity chip for a smart meter. If that is so, then SEP owners could license at a chip level and charge different royalties for different chips depending on connectivity rates.[98]

An example of the possible component level licensing in IoT is reported in the automotive industry, where Sharp signed an exhaustive licence with Huawei for the supply of chips to connected cars.[99] The licence relates to the most upstream Tier 1 baseband chip, which goes to connectivity modules (Tier 2) that are then incorporated in telecommunication control units (Tier 3) which are then supplied to connected cars. While the precise terms of the licence are confidential, assuming that Huawei agreed to pay royalties based on the downstream value that SEPs bring to connected cars, then licensing at component level would bring significant transaction cost savings as there are far fewer Tier 1 manufacturers than car makers. Additionally, cross-licensing did not play a role in the automotive sector as Sharp is not active in vehicle manufacturing, making component level licensing more attractive.

In conclusion, SDOs' IPR policies and FRAND commitments are legally flexible enough to allow the selection of the optimal licensing level that may be adjusted to the specific circumstances of each IoT industry. Thus, the openness of FRAND commitments and a requirement to ensure access to the standard allows adopting the optimal licensing level for each IoT industry.

VI. Conclusion

The FRAND commitment is an open and flexible concept that generally requires SEP owners to ensure effective access to the standard. Access to the standard can

[96] ibid, 86–89.

[97] ibid, 93–94

[98] ibid, 94; also Henkel (n 93) 20–21.

[99] J Schindler, 'Sharp Grants Huawei SEP Licence for Auto Components' (*IAM*, 14 July 2020), available at: www.iam-media.com/frandseps/sharp-huawei-license-deal-could-shake-the-car-wars-in-germany.

be achieved by having a direct licence, or indirectly benefiting from a licence by selling components to licensed downstream manufacturers, concluding non-assertion agreements, or even not having a licence at all if the patent owner has a policy of not monetising its patents. Competition and patent law do not restrict SEP owners from choosing the level of the production chain for licensing. The only exception are those SDOs, like the IEEE, that directly impose component level licensing obligations in their FRAND commitments and IPR policies by requiring licences only for portions of standards implemented by components. However, the unrestricted level licensing obligation risks negative consequences and inefficient SEP licensing.

The openness and flexibility of FRAND commitments enables adopting different licensing levels for different IoT industries. Which licensing level is optimal would depend on the specifics of each IoT industry and the choice should be based on the three principles suggested by the Commission's SEP Expert Group: there should be one level in the value chain for a particular licensed product, with a uniform royalty irrespective of the level of licensing, and a FRAND royalty is a cost element in the price of a component that should be passed on further downstream. Once FRAND royalties are determined based on the value that SEPs bring to end-devices and consumers, then the question is which licensing level generates more efficiencies for the parties and to the industry, such as transaction costs savings, the ease of monitoring of downstream use and compliance with royalty payments and the possibility of cross-licensing. There is no one-size-fits-all solution, and the flexibly of a FRAND commitment is a feature that allows adopting different licensing levels for each particular IoT industry.

8

Remedies

This chapter addresses the remedies available for infringement of SEPs. If licensing negotiations fail, the SEP owner can sue for patent infringement and request remedies from courts. However, the availability and the scope of remedies available for SEPs remains contested. The chapter will analyse injunctions for infringement of SEPs, the scope of the FRAND licence that a court can set (global or territorial), the grant of antisuit (ASI) and anti-antisuit injunctions (AASI) to consolidate all litigation within one court, the amount of past damages and some procedural remedies to facilitate licensing.

I. Injunctions

The use of injunctions for SEPs has been highly controversial. An injunction is a remedy for the infringement of a valid patent which prevents the sale of infringing products until the infringer can secure a licence or designs around the patent. Injunctions have been seen as the most powerful tool for opportunistic holdup strategies by SEP owners, as even if one SEP is found to be valid and infringed it may stop the sale of the whole product.[1] SEP holders are said to be able to use injunctions, or even the threat of injunctions, to force implementers to accept excessive licensing terms. Accordingly, many have argued that injunctions are inconsistent with FRAND commitments and should, in principle, not be available or granted only in extreme circumstances.[2] The only remedy available for SEP owners should be the award of FRAND damages.[3]

[1] See ch 2, section II on patent holdup.

[2] M Dolmans, 'Standards for Standards' (2002) 26 *Fordham International Law Journal* 163; J Farrell et al, 'Standard Setting, Patents and Hold-up' (2007) 74 *Antitrust Law Journal* 603; J Miller, 'Standard Setting, Patents and Access Lock-in: RAND Licensing and the Theory of the Firm' (2007) 40 *Indiana Law Review* 351; D Lichtman, 'Understanding the RAND Commitment' (2010) 47 *Houston Law Review* 1023, 1043; M Lemley and C Shapiro, 'A Simple Approach to Setting Reasonable Royalties for Standard-Essential Patents' (2013) 28 *Berkeley Technology Law Journal* 1135, 1144; T Cotter, 'Comparative Law and Economics of Standard-Essential Patents and FRAND Royalties' (2014) 22 *Texas Intellectual Property Law Journal*. 311, 342–43; IEEE-SA, 'Standards Board Bylaws' (August 2020) Clause 6.1 Definitions, available at: standards.ieee.org/content/dam/ieee-standards/standards/web/documents/other/sb_bylaws.pdf (obligation on SEP owners not to seek or enforce injunctions unless the implementer fails to comply with appellate court judgment).

[3] S Michel, 'Bargaining for FRAND Royalties in the Shadow of Patent Remedies Law' (2011) 77 *Antitrust Law Journal* 889, 908; D Carlton and A Shampine, 'An Economic Interpretation of FRAND' (2013) 9 *Journal of Competition Law & Economics* 531, 550; J Ordover and A Shampine, 'Implementing the FRAND Commitment' (2014) 10 *Antitrust Source* 7.

However, as seen in chapter two, section IV, restricting injunctions may lead to the opposite effect – opportunistic holdout by standard implementers. Namely, there would be no incentive for implementers to take a licence if the only consequence of the infringement was the payment of a court awarded FRAND royalty. Indeed, it may be more efficient to infringe SEPs and wait to be sued than to take a licence in advance. The SEP owner may not have the resources to pursue expensive patent litigation across the world and against many implementers. If the implementer has financial resources it can draw out litigation, using it as leverage to impose below FRAND rates or bankrupt SEP owners. Even if the SEP owner legitimately asks for a FRAND rate it will not be able to enforce the deal before spending years in litigation and millions in litigation expenses. The worst-case scenario – payment of FRAND terms – does not incentivise early and voluntary licensing. The prospect of an injunction is thus the only tool to bring recalcitrant implementers back to the negotiating table.

Nevertheless, concerns about the opportunistic use of injunctions to extract excessive royalties have dominated early SEPs cases and alerted competition authorities. Both the US and EU have placed restrictions on their use and availability, although by different means. As will be seen, the US relied on patent law while the EU used competition law. Over time, however, the position has gradually changed to a more balanced view where injunctions are not automatically removed in SEP cases; their grant depends on the specific circumstances of each case and the behaviour of both the SEP owner and a potential licensee is taken into account. In other words, the award of an injunction revolves around the concept of 'willing licensor' and 'willing licensee'. If the implementer is found to be unwilling to take a licence by intentionally delaying negotiations and negotiating in bad faith, an injunction may be justified to sanction holdout. Conversely, if the SEP owner is perceived as an unwilling licensor by insisting on excessive non-FRAND terms, an injunction may be refused.

The next section will describe the evolution of the position on injunctions in the US and EU. In practice, courts and competition authorities constrained the availability of injunctions for SEPs by seeing them as: (i) contrary to the principles of equity; (ii) contrary to public policy; (iii) an unfair method of competition; and (iv) an infringement of competition law.

A. Principles of Equity (US Courts)

In the US, the Patent Act provides that a permanent injunction 'may' be granted 'in accordance with the principles of equity, on such terms as the court deems reasonable'.[4] The decision to grant or deny an injunction is thus at the discretion of US district courts, reviewable on appeal only for abuse of discretion.

[4] Patent Act 35 USC § 283.

Traditionally, injunctions were almost automatically granted in patent cases after a finding of infringement and validity.[5] The Federal Circuit established a general rule that courts would grant permanent injunctions absent 'exceptional circumstances'. However, this all changed in 2006 when the Supreme Court in *eBay v MercExchange* held that to obtain an injunction a patent holder must prove the following four requirements: (i) that it has suffered irreparable injury; (ii) that remedies available at law, such as monetary damages, are inadequate to compensate for that injury; (iii) that, considering the balance of hardships between the plaintiff and defendant, a remedy in equity is warranted; and (iv) that the public interest would not be disserved by a permanent injunction.[6]

After *eBay*, it has become more difficult to obtain injunctions in patent cases.[7] In practice, it is extremely difficult for a SEP holder to satisfy *eBay* criteria and no permanent injunction has been granted for the infringement of a FRAND committed SEP.[8] Injunctions were typically denied because it could not be established that the patentee would suffer irreparable harm and that damages would not provide sufficient compensation.[9] For example, in *Apple v Motorola* the Federal Circuit held that: 'Considering the large number of industry participants that are already using [Motorola's patent], including competitors, Motorola has not provided any evidence that adding one more user would create [irreparable] harm'.[10] The court also noted that many other licences that Motorola concluded regarding the SEP in question, 'strongly suggest that money damages are adequate to fully Motorola compensate for any infringement'.[11] Similarly in *Microsoft v Motorola*,[12] the court held that Motorola failed to demonstrate that it would suffer irreparable harm absent an injunction because Microsoft committed to accept a licence on FRAND terms for Motorola's SEP portfolio, the litigation was continuing to determine the details of such a licence, and at some point in the future, either by agreement of the parties or by court adjudication, a licence agreement would become a reality.[13]

[5] *Smith International, Inc v Hughes Tool Co*, 718 F.2d 1573, 1581 (Fed Cir 1983), *WL Gore & Assocs, Inc v Garlock, Inc*, 842 F.2d 1275, 1281 (Fed Cir 1988).

[6] *eBay Inc v MercExchange, LLC*, 547 US 388, 391 (2006).

[7] C Seaman, 'Permanent Injunctions in Patent Litigation After *eBay*: An Empirical Study' (2016) 101 *Iowa Law Review* 1949 (finding that after *eBay*, injunctions are available only to practising companies that compete against the infringer, while non-competitors and other non-practising entities are generally denied injunctive relief); *eBay* also applies to SEPs see *Apple v Motorola*, 757 F.3d 1286, 1331–32 (Fed Cir 2014) ('the framework laid out by the Supreme Court in *eBay* … provides ample strength and flexibility for addressing the unique aspects of FRAND committed patents and industry standards in general').

[8] K Gupta and M Snyder, 'Smartphone Litigation and Standard Essential Patents' (2014) Hoover IP2 Working Paper Series No 14006 (finding that in litigation between smartphone manufacturers from 2001 to 2013 no injunction was granted for any patent determined to be SEP). It seems that no permanent injunction for SEPs has been awarded in the period after 2013 either.

[9] *Apple v Motorola*, 757 F.3d 1286 (Fed Cir 2014); *Apple v Motorola*, 869 F.Supp.2d 901 (ND Ill 2012); *Microsoft v Motorola*, 2012 WL 5993202 (WD Wash 2012).

[10] *Apple v Motorola*, 757 F.3d 1286, 1331–32 (Fed Cir 2014).

[11] ibid.

[12] *Microsoft v Motorola*, 2012 WL 5993202 (WD Wash 2012).

[13] ibid.

The impending licence agreement would also provide an adequate remedy to Motorola as a matter of law, instead of an injunction.[14]

Nevertheless, this does not mean that SEP holders will always be denied injunctions. The Federal Circuit has confirmed that there is no per se rule that injunctions are unavailable for SEPs.[15] Rather, it would be generally problematic for SEP holders to prove irreparable harm and that money damages would not be an adequate remedy. However, Judge Rader noted in his dissent in *Apple v Motorola* that an injunction may be available in case of a holdout.[16] This might be the case if the infringer refused to negotiate, negotiates in bad faith, or refuses to take a licence that was determined to be FRAND.[17] The US Patent and Trademark Office, the Department of Justice and the National Institute of Standards and Technology at the end of 2019 issued a Policy Statement on Remedies for SEPs holding that 'all remedies available under national law, including injunctive relief and adequate damages, should be available' for infringement of FRAND committed SEPs if the facts of a given case warrant them.[18] They consider that a FRAND commitment is a factor in determining appropriate remedies but does not act as a bar to any remedy. These statements make a balanced approach focusing on the conduct of both parties and specific circumstances of each case. Nevertheless, no court has yet entered a final permanent injunction in the US for the infringement of SEPs.

B. Public Policy (International Trade Commission)

The US International Trade Commission (ITC) is another venue where an injunction might be obtained in the US. The ITC is a federal agency that enforces the US Tariff Act and protects from importation goods that infringe upon a valid US patent. The ITC has the possibility to grant only two types of remedy: exclusion,[19]

[14] ibid.

[15] *Apple v Motorola*, 757 F.3d 1286 (Fed Cir 2014) 49. However, see *Apple v Motorola*, 869 F.Supp.2d 901 (ND Ill 2012) (Judge Posner came close to a *per se* prohibition by saying: 'I don't see how, given FRAND, I would be justified in enjoining Apple from infringing unless Apple refuses to pay a royalty that meets the FRAND requirement. By committing to license its patents on FRAND terms, Motorola committed to license to anyone willing to pay a FRAND royalty and thus implicitly acknowledged that a royalty is adequate compensation for a license to use that patent. How could it do otherwise? How could it be permitted to enjoin Apple from using an invention that it contends Apple *must* use if it wants to make a cell phone with UMTS telecommunications capability – without which it would not be a cell *phone*?' (emphasis added).

[16] *Apple v Motorola*, 757 F.3d 1286 (Fed Cir 2014) (Judge Rader considered that Apple was behaving as an unwilling licensee).

[17] See also, US Department of Justice and US Patent & Trademark Office, 'Policy Statement on Remedies for Standard Essential Patents Subject to Voluntary F/RAND Commitments' (8 January 2013).

[18] US Patent and Trademark Office, the Department of Justice and National Institute of Standards and Technology, 'Policy Statement on Remedies for Standard-Essential Patents Subject to Voluntary F/RAND Commitments' (19 December 2019) 4–5.

[19] 19 Inc C § 1337(d)(2); 19 Inc C § 1337 (d)(1).

and cease-and-desist orders,[20] prohibiting further importation and sale of infringing products. It is not authorised to grant monetary damages, which is reserved for district courts.

The procedure before the ITC is unique. It is not bound by the *eBay* ruling;[21] the Federal Circuit noted that the legislative history shows that Congress intended exclusion orders to be the normal remedy when the ITC finds patent infringement.[22] However, the ITC may deny exclusion orders if the effects would be against the public interest factors provided in the Tariff Act, namely: (i) public health and welfare; (ii) competitive conditions in the economy; (iii) the production of competitive articles in the US; and (iv) consumers' interests.[23] Nevertheless, it is exceptional for the ITC to use this provision and exclusion orders are rarely denied.[24] After an exclusion order is issued, the US Trade Representative acting on behalf of the President may disapprove the exclusion order for policy reasons within 60 days.[25] Such disapprovals are also very rare, and after a finding of infringement exclusion orders follow almost automatically. This characteristic made the a ITC more attractive venue for patent litigation, as it is more likely that injunctions will be obtained at the ITC than before district courts.[26]

The ITC has to date issued only one exclusion order for the infringement of FRAND SEPs against Apple in its dispute with Samsung.[27] However, this exclusion order was ultimately disapproved by the US Trade Representative because of public policy interest and remained unenforced.[28]

The case concerned Samsung's complaint that certain models of Apple's iPhones and iPads infringed Samsung's FRAND-committed SEPs. During the proceedings, Apple argued that exclusion orders are incompatible with a FRAND commitment, would facilitate patent holdup and are contrary to public interest considerations. The ITC held that there is no per se prohibition from granting

[20] 19 Inc C § 1337 (f)(1). The remaining text will use the term 'exclusion orders' as referring to both types of remedy.

[21] *Spansion, Inc v ITC*, 629 F.3d 1331, 1358 (Fed Cir 2010).

[22] ibid, 1358–59.

[23] 19 Inc C § 1337 (d)(1).

[24] *Certain Fluidized Supporting Apparatus and Components*, USITC Inv No 337-TA-182/188, Pub 1667 (1 October 1984); *Certain Inclined-Field Acceleration Tubes and Components Thereof*, USITC Inv No 337-TA-67, Pub 1119 (1 December 1980); *Certain Automatic Crankpin Grinders*, USITC Inv No 337-TA-60, Pub 1022 (1 December 1979).

[25] 19 Inc C § 1337 (j)2.

[26] See: Federal Trade Commission, 'The Evolving IP Marketplace: Aligning Patent Notice and Remedies with Competition' (2011) 239–40; C Chien and M Lemley, 'Patent Holdup, the ITC and the Public Interest' (2012) 98 *Cornell Law Review* 1, 15–16 (finding that after *eBay* the overall injunction rate in the district court has declined to 75%, while the injunction rate at the ITC remained at 100%).

[27] Letter from Michael BG Froman, Executive Office of the President, the US Trade Representative, to Hon Irving A Williamson, Chairman, US International Trade Commission (3 August 2013), available at: ustr.gov/sites/default/files/08032013%20Letter_1.PDF (US Trade Representative Letter).

[28] *Certain Electronic Devices, Including Wireless Communications Devices, Portable Music and Date Processing Devices, and Tablet Computers*, USITC Inv No 337-TA-794 (4 June 2013) (Commission Opinion).

exclusion orders on FRAND committed SEPs.[29] It found that Apple had not presented empirical evidence that patent holdup occurred in practice and 'absent empirical evidence of actual harm to consumers or innovation, what remains are policy arguments that the risk of hold-up occurring is sufficiently great to warrant denying an exclusion order to Samsung in this investigation'.[30] The ITC held that it is not a policymaking body and is not empowered to make that decision.[31] The ITC also reviewed the history of negotiations between the parties and found that Apple had not proved a failure by Samsung to negotiate in good faith.[32] On the other hand, the ITC was concerned that Apple engaged in holdout, by using SEPs without compensation to the patent owner and refusing to pay any royalties until after the full litigation and appeal on the patent's infringement, validity and enforceability, forcing the patent holder to defend its rights through expensive litigation.[33] After finding that one SEP was infringed, the ITC entered a limited exclusion order against Apple. The US Trade Representative, however, disapproved the exclusion order on the ground that the relevant public policy considerations concerning holdup generally weigh against permitting exclusion orders in cases involving SEPs subject to FRAND obligations.[34] He instructed the ITC to make 'explicit findings' of holdup and holdout to 'the maximum extent possible' in future cases involving FRAND SEPs.[35] Thus, the exclusion order never came into effect.

In the following case, the ITC examined the actual evidence of holdup and holdout. In *Certain 3G Mobile Handsets and Components* InterDigital sought an exclusion order against Nokia and Microsoft's mobile phones that infringed on Interdigital's SEPs.[36] After examining all the arguments of the parties, the administrative law Judge Essex concluded that there was no evidence of patent holdup and that InterDigital did not act in bad faith in licensing negotiations.[37] He noted that the infringer bears the burden of providing evidence of patent holdup and that Nokia and Microsoft failed to carry that burden.[38] The ITC could not adopt a policy that favours 'speculative and unproven positions' and assume that the remedy of an exclusion order should be removed in cases of FRAND committed SEPs.[39] Even if Interdigital had used the exclusion order to negotiate above FRAND licensing terms, the judge noted that Nokia and Microsoft would have the option to go to

[29] ibid, 112.
[30] ibid, 114.
[31] ibid.
[32] ibid, 54.
[33] ibid, 62–63.
[34] US Trade Representative Letter (n 27).
[35] ibid, 3.
[36] *Certain 3G Mobile Handsets and Components Thereof*, USITC Inv No 337-TA-613 (27 April 2015) (Initial Determination on Remand).
[37] ibid, 40–42.
[38] ibid, 43–44; 30: 'the respondents simply restate the possibility of a hold-up, without providing or citing to any evidence that has been presented in this case'.
[39] ibid, 59–60.

court and sue Interdigital for breach of a FRAND commitment.[40] He also noted that many courts and government agencies have been analysing SEPs and that patent holdup is 'unlikely because too many hostile eyes are watching'.[41] In the end, the judge held that if injunctions and exclusion orders are so problematic, SDOs always have the option to change their IPR policies restricting their use.[42]

Judge Essex, however, found that Microsoft and Nokia engaged in holdout. He found Microsoft and Nokia were on notice of the infringement after the Federal Circuit's decision, but they did not seek a licence and rejected all the patent holder's offers.[43] He held that an infringer's failure to negotiate in a meaningful way and refusal to take a licence while continuing to make standard-compliant devices is an evidence of holdout.[44] However, the ITC did not issue an exclusion order because the full Commission found that SEPs were not infringed and, consequently, did not address the FRAND issues.[45]

Therefore, exclusion orders for SEPs before the ITC are not precluded and the ITC will consider allegations of holdup and holdout and the behaviour of both parties when deciding on exclusion orders. The burden of proof is on the defendant to provide evidence of opportunistic behaviour on the part of the SEP owner. To date, however, there is no enforceable exclusion order for the infringement of SEPs.

C. Unfair Competition (Federal Trade Commission)

The FTC considered the use of injunctions for SEPs in two cases.[46] It took the view that the mere seeking of injunctions and exclusion orders against willing licensees represents an unfair method of competition and unfair acts or practices, which are broader than traditional antitrust prohibitions. Unfair methods of competition cover acts and practices that contravene the spirit of the antitrust laws and those that, if allowed to mature, could violate the Sherman Act,[47] while unfair or deceptive acts or practices typically cover consumer protection issues and other conduct that directly affects consumers. The first FTC case concerned Bosch's proposed

[40] ibid, 62–63.

[41] ibid, 62.

[42] ibid, 66. In March 2015, IEEE became the first SDO to expressly regulate the use of injunctions for FRAND-committed SEPs. See IEEE, 'Standards Board Bylaws' (August 2020) 18.

[43] *Certain 3G Mobile Handsets and Components Thereof*, Initial Determination on Remand (n 36) 51–52.

[44] ibid, 54.

[45] *Certain 3G Mobile Handsets and Components Thereof*, USITC Inv No 337-TA-613 (28 August 2015) (Notice of Commission Determination Finding no Violation of Section 337; Termination of Investigation).

[46] *In the Matter of Robert Bosch GmbH*, Docket No C-4377 (2013); *In the Matter of Motorola Mobility LLC and Google Inc*, Docket No C-4410 (2013).

[47] FTC, 'Statement of Enforcement Principles Regarding "Unfair Methods of Competition" Under Section 5 of the FTC Act' (13 August 2015).

merger with a company, SPX Services, that held certain SEPs relating to air conditioning equipment standards, which it committed to license on FRAND terms and was pursuing injunctions against implementers of air conditioning equipment.[48] The second case concerned Motorola's request for injunctions and exclusion orders against Microsoft and Apple.[49]

The FTC reasoned that injunctions for SEPs should be limited and available only under strict circumstances. In the FTC's view, seeking injunctions against a willing licensee is incompatible with a FRAND commitment as it may allow the SEP holder to obtain unreasonable licensing terms.[50] It held that 'negotiation that occurs under threat of an injunction may be weighted heavily in favour of the patentee in a way that is in tension with the [F]RAND commitment'.[51] Accordingly, the SEP owner may only seek injunctions if the implementer: (i) is outside US jurisdiction; (ii) has stated in writing or in sworn testimony that it will not accept a licence on any terms; (iii) refuses to enter a licence agreement determined by a court or arbitration; (iv) files a claim for injunctive relief against a SEP holder for its own FRAND SEPs; (v) fails to assure that it is willing to accept a licence on FRAND terms; or (vi) a court determined that the implementer used SEPs for purposes other than implementing the standard.[52]

The conditions under which seeking an injunction for a SEP that would be allowed by the FTC appear very restrictive. It is unlikely that the infringer will state in writing or in sworn testimony that it will not accept a licence under any terms. Waiting to sue for an injunction only after a court ruled on FRAND terms would incentivise delaying tactics on the part of implementers. The only realistic option is if the implementer fails to assure that it is willing to take a licence, but the conditions for determined willingness remain open. In any event, it is unclear how the FTC's position relates to already existing *eBay* factors which, as we have seen, would not allow an injunction against a willing licensee and courts have already refused injunctions in a few SEP cases that examined them. It seems that the FTC's factors mirror the already existing assessment performed by courts under *eBay*, making the additional layer of unfair methods of competition liability for the seeking of an injunction for SEPs seem redundant.

Both the *Bosch* and *Motorola* cases were concluded with consent orders without definitive establishment of liability, and the position of the FTC remains untested in court. Given that US courts are reluctant to grant injunctions under

[48] *In the Matter of Robert Bosch GmbH*, Docket No C-4377 (2013).

[49] *In the Matter of Motorola Mobility LLC and Google Inc*, Docket No C-4410 (2013).

[50] *In the* Matter *of Robert Bosch GmbH*, Docket No C-4377 (2013) (Analysis of Agreement Containing Consent Orders to Aid Public Comments) 4; *In the Matter of Motorola Mobility LLC and Google Inc*, Docket No C-4410 (2013) (Analysis of Proposed Consent Order to Aid Public Comment) 2.

[51] *In the Matter of Motorola Mobility LLC and Google Inc*, Docket No C-4410 (2013) (Analysis of Proposed Consent Order to Aid Public Comment) 3–4.

[52] See: *In the Matter of Robert Bosch GmbH*, Docket No C-4377 (2013) (Decision and Order), IV E; *In the Matter of Motorola Mobility LLC and Google Inc*, Docket no C-4410 (2013) (Decision and Order) II E.

eBay criteria and, in any event, must carefully examine the conduct of both parties before reaching a decision, the precise influence of the FTC's decisions for the future remains unsettled. It does signal, however, that the FTC is carefully watching the conduct of SEP owners.

D. Competition Law (EU)

In the EU, injunctions for SEPs are constrained by the application of competition law. In 2014, the European Commission adopted two decisions holding that seeking injunctions for infringement of FRAND committed SEPs against willing licensees constitutes an abuse of dominant position.[53] The cases emerged from Motorola and Samsung's disputes with Apple, where they sought injunctions against Apple's products for the infringement of 3G and 4G SEPs. The Commission adopted an infringement decision against Motorola and a commitments decision with Samsung, where Samsung committed to approach and negotiate with prospective licensees for up to 12 months and, if no agreement is reached, to seek the determination of FRAND terms by the court or arbitration.

The Commission took the view that seeking injunctions for a FRAND commitment SEPs represents an automatic abuse of dominance *unless* the SEP holder can show that the infringer is behaving as an unwilling licensee. Like the FTC it held that SEP owners may seek injunctions only under strict conditions if the infringer: (i) is in financial distress and unable to pay its debts; (ii) has assets that are located in jurisdictions that do not provide for adequate means of enforcement of damages; (iii) is unwilling to enter into a licence agreement on FRAND terms;[54] or (iv) is seeking injunctive relief for its own SEPs.[55] The Commission placed the analysis in the objective justifications part of the decision, meaning that merely seeking injunctions is automatically considered as abusive with the burden of proof shifting to the SEP owner to justify its conduct by proving the unwillingness of the infringer. According to the Commission, the infringer can always escape injunction, and prove it willingness to license, if it agrees for FRAND terms to be set by a court or arbitration and accepts to be bound by such determination.[56] Challenging the validity, essentiality and infringement of SEPs, however, is not considered as unwillingness to license on the part of the implementer.[57]

[53] *Motorola – Enforcement of GPRS standard essential patents* (Case AT.39985) Commission Decision C(2014) 2892 (29 April 2014); *Samsung – Enforcement of UMTS standard essential patents* (Case AT.39939), Commission Decision C(2014) 2891 (29 April 2014).

[54] *Motorola*, Case AT.39985 (n 53) 427; *Samsung*, Case AT.39939 (n 53) 67.

[55] *Samsung*, Case AT.39939 (n 53) 79.

[56] *Motorola*, Case AT.39985 (n 53) 437; *Samsung*, Case AT.39939 (n 53) 98.

[57] *Motorola*, Case AT.39985 (n 53) 439–40; Commission, 'Antitrust decisions on standard essential patents (SEPs) – Motorola Mobility and Samsung Electronics – Frequently asked questions' MEMO (29 April 2014).

The *Motorola* decision is significant because it introduced a new type of abuse that did not exist before – asking a court for a remedy for patent infringement.[58] However, the problem with this approach is that it does not recognise that the mere seeking of an injunction does not necessarily lead to the granting of one. A patentee would need to prove infringement and validity of SEP and, even if it does so, courts may not automatically issue an injunction. The decision on granting an injunction lies with the judge and not only on the will of the SEP owner. The Commission nevertheless relied on past cases concerning the relationship between intellectual property rights and competition law under which the exercise of an intellectual property right may, in exceptional circumstances, amount to abuse,[59] and held that the exceptional circumstances in SEPs cases are participation in the standard-development process and the obligation to license on FRAND terms justifying the limitation on the right to seek and enforce injunctions.[60]

The motives for the Commission's intervention were concerns about opportunistic holdup strategies by SEP owners and diverging and still nascent practices of national courts in FRAND disputes. In *Motorola*, the Commission said that the decision 'promotes the proper functioning of standard-setting by ensuring the accessibility of the technology … and by preventing hold-up'.[61] However, the real reason for intervention was the different practices of national courts for assessing SEP injunctions and the lack of an EU-wide framework. At that time, it was not yet entirely clear whether a FRAND commitment is of a contractual nature and what rights and obligations it entails. The Commission was primarily concerned with the situation in Germany, which adopted a lenient pro-patentee approach and was prepared to grant injunctions more freely.[62] Another characteristic of Germany is bifurcation, where actions for infringement and validity are split

[58] For extensive discussions on the appropriate legal test for the application of Article 102 TFEU to seeking injunctions for SEPs, see: N Petit, 'Injunctions for FRAND-Pledged SEPs: The Quest for an Appropriate Test of Abuse Under Article 102 TFEU' (2013) 9 *European Competition Journal* 677 (warning against antitrust intervention and the introduction of a new type of abuse); U Petrovcic, 'Patent Holdup and the Limits of Competition Law: A Trans-Atlantic Perspective' (2013) 50 *Common Market Law Review* 1363; A Jones, 'Standard-Essential Patents: FRAND Commitments, Injunctions and the Smartphone Wars' (2014) 10 *European Competition Journal* 1 (supporting the competition law prohibition of injunctions); P Larouche and N Zingales, 'Injunctive Relief in Disputes Related to Standard-Essential Patents: Time for the CJEU to Set Fair and Reasonable Presumptions' (2014) 10 *European Competition Journal* 551; for the US perspective see D Ginsburg, T Owings and J Wright, 'Enjoining Injunctions: The Case Against Antitrust Liability for Standard Essential Patent Holders Who Seek Injunctions' (2014) 10 *Antitrust Source* 1.

[59] *Motorola*, Case AT.39985 (n 53) 278, referring to Case 238/87 *Volvo v Veng*, ECLI:EU:C:1988:477, 9; C-241/91 P and C-242/91 P *RTE and ITP* v *Commission*, ECLI:EU:C:1995:98, 50 (*Magill*); Case C-7/97 *Oscar Bronner v Media Print*, ECLI:EU:C:1998:569, 39; C-418/01 *IMS Health v NDC Health*, ECLI:EU:C:2004:257, 35; T-201/04 *Microsoft v Commission*, ECLI:EU:T:2007:289, 331.

[60] *Motorola*, Case AT.39985 (n 53) 279–300.

[61] ibid, 418.

[62] In Germany injunctions generally follow almost automatically in cases of infringement and, due to bifurcation where one court decides on infringement and the other on validity, it is possible to obtain an injunction while validity proceedings are ongoing and where a patent may latter be invalidated. The Federal Supreme Court in the *Orange-Book Standard* case established a special competition law exception to SEP injunctions. The *Orange-Book Standard* requires that the infringer must have made, and

between two different courts and it is possible to obtain an injunction while validity proceedings are pending. In these circumstances, the Commission wanted to establish an EU-wide framework for SEP injunctions rooted in competition law, but in doing so it adopted a very pro-infringer approach by reversing the burden of proof to SEP owners and viewing the mere seeking of injunctions as an automatic abuse of dominance.

A middle ground was reached in the CJEU's preliminary reference in *Huawei v ZTE*. During the *Motorola* and *Samsung* investigations, a dispute arose in Germany between Huawei and ZTE. Huawei held SEPs for the 4G LTE standard which it committed to license on FRAND terms. It offered a licence to ZTE, and after several months of unsuccessful negotiations, Huawei initiated infringement proceedings seeking, among other things, an injunction prohibiting infringement and the recall of products.[63] Düsseldorf Regional Court noted that there was a discrepancy between the German approach to SEP injunctions and the Commission's approach in *Motorola* and *Samsung*, and decided to stay proceedings and refer questions to the CJEU on whether, and under what conditions, seeking injunctions for SEPs could represent an abuse of dominant position.

The CJEU provided a framework for SEP injunctions under competition law. It confirmed that they may, in exceptional circumstances, represent an abuse of dominant position. The fact that the patent is a SEP and a FRAND commitment exists are held to be exceptional circumstances justifying limitation on the exercise of patent rights.[64] The CJEU, however, did not say in the affirmative when the seeking of injunction infringes Article 102. Instead, it couched the terms in the negative: it would *not* be an abuse of dominant position if the SEP holder complies with the following steps:

i. Before seeking an injunction, the SEP holder must approach and notify the implementer about infringement and designate specific SEPs that are infringed and the way they are infringed.[65]
ii. The infringer should express its willingness to conclude the licensing agreement.[66]
iii. The SEP holder should then provide the specific, written offer for a licence on FRAND terms, specifying, in particular, the amount of the royalty and the way in which is to be calculated.[67]

should remain bound by, an unconditional offer to conclude a licence agreement, not limited exclusively to patents in infringement proceedings, which cannot be rejected by the patentee without abusing its dominant position. The infringer also must already be behaving as if the licence had been granted, which includes either the payment of a reasonable licence fee or the guarantee of such payment by putting a sufficient amount in escrow for the time of use of the patented technology. The infringer must also render regular accounts with respect to the use and pay the patent holder the resulting licence fees. Only under these circumstances would seeking of injunctions be abusive. See *Orange-Book Standard*, KZR 39/06 Federal Court of Justice (6 May 2009).

[63] C-170/13 *Huawei Technologies v ZTE*, ECLI:EU:C:2015:477.

[64] ibid, 49–51.

[65] ibid, 60–61.

[66] ibid, 63.

[67] ibid.

iv. The infringer must then diligently and in good faith respond to the offer, without any delaying tactics. If the infringer does not accept, it must submit promptly and in writing his FRAND counter-offer.[68]
v. If the SEP holder rejects the counter-offer, the infringer must provide appropriate security (for example, by providing a bank guarantee or placing necessary amounts on deposit) and render accounts.[69]
vi. At that point, the parties may by common agreement request the FRAND royalty to be determined by an independent third party (presumably court or arbitration).[70]

Also, the licensee should be allowed to challenge the validity, essentiality and infringement of SEPs both during the negotiations and after the conclusion of a licensing agreement.[71]

Overall, the *Huawei v ZTE* judgment provides a balanced framework for assessing the conduct of both parties. It ensures that injunctions will not be granted before the SEP owner has indeed been offered a FRAND licence and against implementers who are willing to enter a licence on FRAND terms, and establishes criteria for the assessment 'willingness' of licensees. It is thus more balanced than the Commission's initial approach in the *Motorol*a and *Samsung* decisions.

i. *The Interpretation of* Huawei v ZTE *by National Courts*

Further application of the *Huawei v ZTE* framework lies with national courts which have been very active in hearing SEP disputes. The majority of cases come from Germany where courts examined each criterion in particular detail. For example, regarding the first requirement of the notification of infringement by the SEP owner, courts held that it should come before litigation and the SEP owner must describe infringed patents and specific infringing use.[72] The presentation of claim charts is a sufficient, but not mandatory condition, and detailed technical or legal explanation of infringement are not required.[73]

On many occasions courts found that implementers did not express a willingness to conclude licensing agreements, often using delaying tactics and not responding diligently and in good faith to a SEP owner's licensing offer. In *Sisvel v Haier*, the Federal Court of Justice (FCJ) said that the implementer must clearly and unequivocally declare his willingness to conclude a licence on FRAND terms and must participate in negotiations in a target-oriented manner.[74] The FCJ

[68] ibid, 65–66.
[69] ibid, 67.
[70] ibid, 68.
[71] ibid, 69.
[72] *Sisvel v Haier*, KZR 36/17 Federal Court of Justice (5 May 2020) 85; *Saint Lawrence v Vodafone*, 4a O 73/14 Düsseldorf Regional Court (31 March 2016); *NTT DoCoMo v HTC*, 7 O 66/15 Mannheim Regional Court (29 January 2016); *Philips v Archos*, 7 O 2019/15 Mannheim Regional Court (1 July 2016).
[73] *Sisvel v Haier*, KZR 36/17 (n 72) 85.
[74] ibid, 83.

found the infringer to be an unwilling licensee because it waited more than a year to respond to the first notification of infringement and, moreover, the response was deficient. It did not demonstrate serious and unconditional willingness to take a licence on FRAND terms, but merely expressed the hope that they will enter into formal negotiations.[75] In later correspondence, the infringer made signing a licence conditional on a prior confirmation of the validity and infringement of patents in suit in Germany and insisted taking a licence only under the terms it proposed. According to the FCJ, a willingness to license cannot be conditional, although the implementer remains free to challenge patents even after the conclusion of the agreement. Finally, the FCJ held that the implementer engaged in delaying tactics by insisting, after more than three years from the notification of infringement, on the production of claim charts for all patents in the portfolio. This was not motivated by a genuine willingness to conclude a licence but served to delay negotiations until the expiry of the patent in suit.[76] Having found the implementer unwilling to take a licence, the FCJ allowed an injunction. *Unwired Planet v Huawei* in the UK also clarified that a willingness to conclude a licence must be unqualified. In other words, a willing licensee must be the one willing to take a FRAND licence on whatever terms are in fact FRAND, whether settled by negotiation, by a court or an arbitrator, and cannot insist only on its own terms.[77] Otherwise this would amount to a 'contingent willingness'.[78]

Other cases also found implementers as unwilling to license or engaging in delaying tactics. In *Saint Lawrence v Vodafone*, the implementer waited more than five months to reply to the notification of infringement, which was considered as belated and an insufficient expression of willingness to conclude a FRAND licence.[79] The precise time needed for response will vary from case to case depending on the content of the infringement notification; in general the more detailed the notification of infringement the less time the implementer has to reply and express its willingness to license. In *Saint Lawrence v Deutsche Telekom*, the court held that three months to reply was too long.[80] Therefore it seems that German courts require a quicker initial response by implementers when approached with a notification of infringement. A prompt response must also follow if the implementer rejects a SEP owner's offer and makes its own counter-offer. In *NTT DoCoMo v HTC*, a delaying tactic was found because the implementer made its counter-offer a year and a half after the SEP owner's offer and six months after litigation was initiated.[81]

[75] ibid, 95.
[76] ibid, 98.
[77] *Unwired Planet v Huawei* [2017] EWHC 2988 (Pat) 708.
[78] ibid.
[79] *Saint Lawrence v Vodafone*, 4a O 73/14 (n 72); *Saint Lawrence v Vodafone*, I-15 U 36/16 Düsseldorf Higher Regional Court (9 May 2016).
[80] *Saint Lawrence v Deutsche Telekom*, 2 O 106/14 Mannheim Regional Court (27 November 2015).
[81] *NTT v HTC* (n 72).

A question where German and UK courts appear to diverge is whether *Huawei v ZTE* criteria are mandatory or represent only a safe harbour. Mandatory interpretation considers any deviation from *Huawei v ZTE* criteria as an automatic abuse of dominance, while a safe harbour approach does not consider a departure from the *Huawei v ZTE* framework as an automatic abuse but looks at all circumstances of the case in order to decide whether there is an infringement of Article 102 TFEU.

UK courts interpret *Huawei v ZTE* criteria as constituting a safe harbour. In *Unwired Planet v Huawei*, the SEP owner brought lawsuit before making a FRAND offer to the implementer. On the face of it, *Huawei v ZTE* requirements were clearly not complied with before an injunction was sought. If *Huawei v ZTE* criteria are mandatory, then a consequence would be an automatic finding of abuse of dominance and refusal of injunction. The court, however, interpreted *Huawei v ZTE* as not setting out a series of rigid predefined rules.[82] Instead, three main principles were interpreted. First, *Huawei v ZTE* provides a safe harbour, meaning that if the SEP owner complies with the scheme prior to seeking an injunction, then bringing a claim for injunction will not be abusive under Article 102.[83] Second, only if the SEP owner seeks an injunction without prior notice of infringement of any kind will there be an automatic abuse of dominance.[84] Thus, only the first requirement – notification of infringement – was held to be a mandatory condition, its non-fulfilment triggering an automatic abuse of dominance. A third principle considered that if the SEP owner sought an injunction after sufficient notice of infringement, but other *Huawei v ZTE* requirements are not complied with, then the finding of abuse would depend on the assessment of all the circumstances of the case.[85] Such interpretation was supported by the Court of Appeal and the Supreme Court.[86] On the facts of the case, it was found that the SEP owner contacted the implementer before initiating proceedings, provided the implementer with a licence offer a few weeks after commencing proceedings and

[82] *Unwired Planet v Huawei* [2017] EWHC 2988 (Pat) 741.

[83] ibid, 744.

[84] ibid.

[85] ibid ('the scheme sets out standard of behaviour against which both parties behaviour can be measured to decide in all the circumstances if an abuse has taken place').

[86] *Unwired Planet v Huawei* [2018] EWCA Civ 2344, 282 ('compliance with the protocol laid down by the CJEU affords the SEP owner safe harbour protection against a finding of breach of a dominant position arising from the commencement of proceedings for an injunction. If the SEP owner steps outside the protocol, the question whether its behaviour has been abusive must be assessed in light of all of the circumstances'); *Unwired Planet v Huawei; Huawei and ZTE v Conversant* [2020] UKSC 37, 157 ('It [*Hauwei v ZTE* requirements] prevents an organisation which is unwittingly using a SEP without a licence from being ambushed by injunction proceedings without any prior notification of the problem, provides the SEP owner with a route map which, if followed precisely, will ensure it can seek an injunction without risking infringing article 102, and otherwise provides a number of points of reference to assist in assessing the all-important question of whether each of the parties is willing to enter into a licence on FRAND terms').

the parties exchanged offers and continued negotiating. Thus, the first requirement of the notification of infringement was met. Having found that both the SEP owner's and implementers' offers were non-FRAND, therefore falling outside the *Huawei v ZTE* safe harbour, the Court examined all other circumstances of the case to determine whether the seeking of an injunction was abusive. It held that the insistence of the implementer to accept only its own interpretation of licensing terms and never making an unqualified offer to accept whatever terms were FRAND made it an unwilling licensee. Consequently, the Court determined that the SEP owner did not abuse the dominant position and granted an injunction which would come into effect if the implementer did not accept adjudicated FRAND terms.[87]

On the other hand, it seems that German courts consider the *Huawei v ZTE* requirements as mandatory and sequential, meaning that they should follow one after another and the fulfilment of each step must be assessed. Any deviation on the side of the SEP owner would result in refusal of an injunction, while non-compliance by the implementer would result in the granting of an injunction. For example, in *Sisvel v Haier* the Federal Supreme Court examined in detail only the first two requirements: the notification of infringement and an expression of willingness to license.[88] It held that the SEP owner fulfilled its obligation to notify infringement by specifying an infringing patent and the way it is infringed by manufacturing and selling mobile phones implementing the SEP. On the other hand, the implementer did not fulfil its obligation to express a willingness to license in an unconditional and target-oriented manner. Due to the deficiency on the side of the implementer, no other *Huawei v ZTE* criteria were assessed and an injunction was granted. In *Pioneer v Acer* and *Philips v Wiko*, courts similarly stopped at the third step by finding that the SEP owner's offer was not FRAND and denied an injunction.[89] They did not continue to assess whether the implementer's counter-offer was FRAND and submitted in a timely manner. However, in *Sisvel v Haier II*, the FCJ appeared to hint that *Huawei v ZTE* requirements should not be interpreted so strictly and are, in fact, only a safe harbour.[90] The FCJ adopted a conduct-oriented view of FRAND where balanced and reasonable terms can only be determined as the result of a negotiation process leading to a mutually consented balance of interests. Thus, if the SEP owner makes an initial non-FRAND offer that does not in itself constitute an abuse of dominant position, all other circumstances of the case need to be taken into account, including

[87] *Unwired Planet v Huawei* [2017] EWHC 1304 (Pat).

[88] *Sisvel v Haier*, KZR 36/17 (n 72).

[89] *Pioneer v Acer*, 6 U 55/16 Karlsruhe Higher Regional Court (31 May 2016); *Philips v Wiko*, 6 U 183/16 Karlsruhe Higher Regional Court (30 October 2019); also *Sisvel v Haier*, I-15 U 66/15 Düsseldorf Higher Regional Court (30 March 2017).

[90] *Sisvel v Haier II*, KZR 35/17 Federal Court of Justice (24 November 2020) 59–60.

the behaviour of the implementer.[91] It remains to be seen how the practice of German courts will further evolve, especially with first instance courts that see the bulk of SEP litigation. A safe-harbour approach to *Huawei v ZTE* requirements would be preferable as it allows flexibility for the parties to reach a mutually acceptable solution, rather than courts micro-managing complex commercial negotiations under the mandatory–sequential approach.

A resolution on the nature of *Huawei v ZTE* requirements may ultimately be answered by the CJEU itself. In a preliminary reference from *Nokia v Daimler*,[92] Düsseldorf Regional Court raised several questions on the interpretation of the *Huawe v ZTE* framework in addition to the production chain licensing issues discussed in chapter seven. It essentially asked whether *Huawei v ZTE* criteria are mandatory steps that need to be followed sequentially or if they represent a safe harbour, and what is the time frame for the infringer to respond and express willingness to license after the notification of infringement. However, given that the parties settled, the question will likely arise again before the CJEU in another case.

Another difference between the UK and Germany is the depth of the examination of the FRANDness of offers and counter-offers. UK courts are ready to specify the actual content of a FRAND licence by determining the exact royalty rates and terms. As seen in chapter four, they conducted an elaborate analysis by unpacking comparable licences, performing versions of a top-down approach, and determining the actual number of truly essential patents. On the other hand, German courts are reluctant to set by themselves the precise FRAND terms and tend to rely more indirect methods for the estimation of FRAND terms, such as the fairness of the negotiation process, the balance of interests of both parties, the relevant commercial practice in a particular industry and some structural elements that must be included in all FRAND offers. For example, the FCJ in *Sisvel v Haier II* held that reaching a FRAND licence requires a balance of conflicting interests of both parties that can only be achieved as a result of the negotiation process where these interests are articulated and discussed in order to achieve a fair and appropriate balance of interests.[93] Other courts have required that the SEP owner's offer must contain all necessary elements which the implementer only has to accept; it must provide the implementer with all information required for assessing whether the offer is FRAND; and must make transparent the calculation of a royalty by referencing the standard licensing programme implemented in the market or patent pool rates.[94] Prior licences play an important role in establishing whether an offer is FRAND. The more SEP owners' licences are accepted in the market the stronger the presumption that the same offer is FRAND. In *Tagivan (MPEG-LA) v Huawei* the court held that existing

[91] ibid, 75–76.
[92] C-182/21 *Nokia Technologies* (23 March 2021).
[93] ibid.
[94] *Pioneer v Acer*, 7 O 96/14 Mannheim Regional Court (8 January 2016); *Philips v Archos* (n 72); *IP Bridge v HTC*, 7 O 165/16 Mannheim Regional Court (28 September 2018).

licences could establish a presumption that the offered terms are FRAND.[95] In the case, the approximately 2,000 licensing agreements concluded by the MPEG LA patent pool provided a strong indication that the offer is FRAND, which the implementer failed to rebut. Courts also looked at the relevant industry practice of worldwide portfolio licensing and consequently held that the implementer cannot insist on a country-by-country or patent-by-patent licence.[96]

The German conduct-oriented approach appears to be quicker and more efficient than the more in-depth determination undertaken by UK courts. The conduct-oriented approach is strongly grounded in commercial practice and recognises that a more efficient outcome is to ensure that parties themselves reach an agreement on pricing. By focusing on other non-royalty aspects of a licence, courts avoid dragging themselves into directly regulating technology prices. However, there may come a time when neither the offer nor the counter-offer of a party is FRAND, in which case even German courts would have to delve into detailed FRAND royalty calculations.

E. Conclusion

As seen, injunctions for SEPs have been limited in the US and the EU but they are not entirely unavailable. Instead, a careful examination of the conduct of both parties and the assessment of all the circumstances of the case are required before reaching a decision. There may be cases where SEP owners are insisting on excessive non-FRAND terms when injunctions will not be granted, and conversely, there may be instances when implementers are refusing to take a licence, are negotiating in bad faith, and are holding out as much as possible which would justify granting an injunction. Another aspect of the injunction debate is that there is no practical way to force the implementer to enter into a court determined FRAND licence unless the failure to do so is sanctioned by an injunction. Thus, the only way to enforce a court's FRAND determination is to enter an injunction that will come into effect if the implementer refuses to accept a court determined FRAND licence.[97] Therefore, injunctions also have an important role in securing the compliance with FRAND royalty adjudications.

II. Global or Territorial Scope of a FRAND Licence?

In today's globalised world, large SEP owners hold a portfolio of patents spanning many jurisdictions while implementers likewise, like smartphone or car

[95] *Tagivan (MPEG-LA) v Huawei*, 4a O 17/15 Düsseldorf Regional Court (15 November 2018).
[96] *Pioneer v Acer*, 7 O 96/14 (n 94); *Saint Lawrence v Vodafone*, 4a O 73/14 (n 72).
[97] Mr Justice Birss called it a 'FRAND Injunction', see *Unwired Planet v Huawei* [2017] EWHC 1304 (Pat) 20.

manufacturers, often have a global presence. In these circumstances, companies would naturally negotiate licensing agreements that are global in scope in order to secure freedom to operate. However, tensions arise if disagreements over FRAND licensing terms escalate into litigation. Since patents are national rights, courts can only enforce national patents and grant remedies – damages and injunctions – only with respect to national patents. Thus, while a FRAND licensing dispute is global, patent litigation can only be local.

The question of the scope of a FRAND licence that a national court can set has become a contentious issue. On the one hand, argument in favour of courts setting worldwide FRAND licences is that global licensing is an ordinary commercial practice between global companies which recognise the need to ensure the freedom to operate and transact costs savings for negotiating and licensing the whole portfolio, rather than on a country-by-country and patent-by-patent basis.[98] The ease of monitoring and compliance with royalty payments also contributes to the general efficiency of global portfolio licensing. Consequently, global portfolio licensing represents a 'one-stop-shop' for multinational licensees. In contrast, it would be detrimental and inefficient for courts to set only national FRAND licences and it would result in a significant holdout risk. Namely, SEP owners would be forced to assert larger numbers of patents across multiple jurisdictions, further straining judicial recourses and increasing the costs of patent enforcement. Given that it is unrealistic to enforce SEPs in every jurisdiction, many patents would remain unenforced and unlicensed. Moreover, requiring licensing offers to be limited only to asserted national patents and calculating FRAND royalties only for those patents would deprive SEP owners of a large share of the value of their portfolios. Therefore, a strategy of insisting on patent-by-patent, territory-by-territory licensing would result in giving implementers free access to a large share and value of SEP portfolios.

On the other hand, arguments against courts deciding on global FRAND licences is that while voluntarily negotiated, FRAND licences are often global and they should not be set by courts without the consent of parties.[99] Namely, national courts lack the jurisdiction to do so since patents are national rights, and they could only grant national remedies and rule on national patents. However, by imposing a global licence a national court would be indirectly ruling on the validity and

[98] Lemley and Shapiro (n 2) 1151 ('the FRAND concept involves a reasonable rate for a party's entire portfolio of standard-essential patents. Establishing a FRAND rate for an entire standard-essential patent portfolio is simpler than – and matches more closely to – real-world licensing practices in the information technology sector, where implementers commonly negotiate portfolio licenses that give them the freedom to operate'); R Jacob and A Milner, 'Lessons from *Huawei v ZTE*' (2016) 4IP Council Research Paper 1; K Dasgupta and D Teece, 'The UK's Role as a Venue for FRAND Litigation: Have the UK Courts Gone Far Enough? (21 December 2020) *CPI Antitrust Chronicle* 1.

[99] See Fair Standards Alliance, 'Coerced Global SEP Portfolio Licences are Not FRAND' (26 October 2020); CEN-CENELEC, 'Core Principles and Approaches for Licensing of Standard Essential Patents' (June 2019), available at: www.cencenelec.eu/news/workshops/pages/ws-2019-013.aspx; D Geradin, 'SEP Licensing After two Decades of Legal Wrangling: Some Issues Solved, Many Still to Address' (24 March 2020), *CPI Antitrust Chronicle* 1.

infringement of foreign patents for which it is not competent. Additionally, licensees should not be coerced into taking a licence for patents that are non-essential, invalid and/or not infringed and should remain free to challenge the validity/infringement of patents and take a licence only for those SEPs they really need. A final argument is that if every national court is able to set global FRAND rates, it would lead to a 'race to the bottom' between countries to attract litigation to their jurisdictions. Namely, those jurisdictions that tend to determine high global FRAND rates would attract SEP owners, while jurisdictions with a reputation for setting low global FRAND rates may attract implementers seeking to challenge the rates of SEP owners.[100] Consequently, we may also expect a 'race to the courthouse' where parties are encouraged to be the first to litigate in the most favourable jurisdiction to foreclose a later suit in a less favourable jurisdiction.[101]

When addressing the scope of a FRAND licence that courts can grant, two interrelated but distinct legal issues must be recognised: one is the question of SEPs and patent law, and another is contractual obligation under a FRAND commitment and contract law. Due to the impracticality of enforcing the whole portfolio, the SEP owner often chooses only a few representative patents to enforce against infringers before national courts. For these SEPs it can ask for ordinary patent remedies: damages and injunctions. On the other hand, interpreting SEP owners' obligations under a FRAND commitment is a matter of contract law. SDOs typically provide that a SEP owner must make available *worldwide licences*. For example, ETSI's IPR policy expressly notes that a FRAND commitment given to a specific SEP shall apply to all existing and future SEPs of that patent family, unless there is explicit written exclusion.[102] The ITU-T, ISO, IEC and the IEEE clearly specify that the patent holder is prepared to grant licences on a worldwide basis.[103] An industry practice of portfolio licensing between global players is also important in determining what a willing licensor and a willing licensee would do. Therefore, a contractual obligation under a FRAND commitment would require offering a worldwide portfolio licence.

In practice, the assessment of the scope of a FRAND commitment may come via three routes: (i) a declaratory judgment that the SEP owner complied with FRAND obligations; (ii) an agreement of the parties to set FRAND terms; or (iii) in the process of assessing whether to grant an injunction for valid and infringed national SEP. These distinctions are important to keep in mind when discussing the competence of courts for determining the scope of a FRAND licence.

[100] J Contreras, 'The New Extraterritoriality: FRAND Royalties, Anti-Suit Injunctions and the Global Race to the Bottom in Disputes Over Standard-Essential Patents' (2019) 25 *Boston University Journal of Science & Technology Law* 253, 281–82.

[101] ibid, 283.

[102] ETSI, 'Intellectual Property Rights Policy' (3 September 2020) Clause 6.2, available at: www.etsi.org/images/files/IPR/etsi-ipr-policy.pdf.

[103] ITU/ISO/IEC, Patent Statement and Licensing Declaration Form (2 November 2018), available at: www.itu.int/dms_pub/itu-t/oth/04/04/T04040000020005PDFE.pdf; IEEE-SA, 'Standards Board Bylaws' (August 2020) 17.

In practice to date, courts in the UK and Germany have interpreted a FRAND commitment as being global in scope and set the terms of a global licence. Such a conclusion was reached by interpreting contractual obligation under ETSI's FRAND commitment and assessing what a willing licensor and a willing licensee would do under the *Huawei v ZTE* framework for injunctions. Therefore, their decisions were grounded in a contract law approach and the interpretation of a SEP owner's FRAND commitment, as well as being tied to the assessment of whether to grant an injunction after finding the infringement of a national SEP.

In the UK, in *Unwired Planet v Huawei* Mr Justice Briss concluded that a willing licensor and a willing licensee with global sales should agree on a worldwide licence. In his words, 'they would regard country by country licensing as madness' and 'a worldwide licence would be far more efficient'.[104] Parties may agree different rates for different regions, for example for China, major markets, and the rest of the world, but would not accept country-by-country licensing. He also noted that all licensing agreements disclosed in the litigation were worldwide,[105] and ETSI's FRAND commitment requires worldwide licensing as it applies to patent families in different jurisdictions.[106] Finally, he added that a global licence should not prevent the licensee from challenging the validity and essentiality of licensed patents and a licence agreement should provide a mechanism for the adjustment of royalties reflecting the outcome of patent trials.[107]

The approach was endorsed by the UK Court of Appeal and the Supreme Court. They both recognised the efficiency of portfolio licensing between a SEP owner with a global portfolio and an implementer with an international presence, a common and ordinary practice in the industry.[108] Requiring SEP owners to litigate country-by-country and patent-by-patent was deemed as a blueprint for holdout.[109] The SEP owner would not be able to secure payment of royalties for those jurisdictions in which it could not afford to bring proceedings and the implementer would have an incentive for holdout until compelled to pay only a national royalty.[110] The Supreme Court confirmed that the obligation of portfolio licensing stems from ETSI's FRAND commitment which applies not only to whole patent families but also to the whole company group.[111] Additionally, ETSI's IPR policy

[104] *Unwired Planet v Huawei* [2018] EWCA Civ 2344 543; also para 544 ('The real inefficiency of country by country licensing is the effort required to negotiate and agree so many different licences and then to keep track of so many different royalty calculations and payments. No rational business would do this if it could be avoided').

[105] ibid, 543.

[106] ibid, 546.

[107] ibid, 567.

[108] *Unwired Planet v Huawei*, [2018] EWCA Civ 2344, 34–35; *Unwired Planet v Huawei; Huawei and ZTE v Conversant* [2020] UKSC 37, 15.

[109] *Unwired Planet v Huawei*, [2018] EWCA Civ 2344, 88, 111.

[110] ibid.

[111] *Unwired Planet v Huawei; Huawei and ZTE v Conversant* [2020] UKSC 37, 62.

is said to be an attempt to mirror commercial practice in the telecommunications industry, which is licensing a global portfolio.[112] As to the argument that a licensee should take a licence only for patents that are verified to be valid and infringed, the Court noted that companies are taking global licences in order to gain access to the standard at a price which reflects the untested nature of many patents and in doing so implementers purchase certainty.[113] Implementers, however, should remain free to challenge patents or a sample of patents in relevant foreign courts and a licence should provide an adjustment mechanism to reflect the outcome of patent trials.[114] Regarding the risk of forum shopping, conflicting judgments and applications for antisuit injunctions, the Supreme Court placed the blame on SDOs that do not provide any international tribunal or mechanism to settle the terms of such licences.[115] SDOs could amend their IPR policies to provide for a SEP royalty tribunal or may identify existing national or international IP courts to resolve global FRAND determinations.

In Germany, courts also held that global portfolio licences are FRAND when assessing the conduct of parties under the *Huawei v ZTE* framework for injunctions, after finding the infringement of a national SEP. In *Sisvel v Haier*, the FCJ held that under *Huawei v ZTE* it is not anti-competitive to insist on a global FRAND licence as long as it does not tie non-SEPs and royalties do not disadvantage users developing products for a specific, geographically limited area.[116] Regional courts in *Saint Lawrence v Vodafone* and *Pioneer v Acer* also confirmed that worldwide portfolio licences are FRAND and in line with common commercial practice, unless the circumstances of an individual case require a different approach, for example if the implementer is active only in a single market, then a national licence would be appropriate.[117]

The approach of UK and German courts in deciding on global FRAND licences seems correct. From a legal perspective, FRAND commitments, as seen, require worldwide licensing between parties that operate globally. UK and German courts have avoided stepping out of their jurisdictions by tying the decision on the global FRAND licence with the assessment of whether to grant an injunction for an infringed national SEP. Therefore, a remedy for the infringement of a national SEP is for the implementer to enter into a global FRAND licence determined by the court. If it refuses, then an injunction for infringement of a national SEP will be granted and parties would remain free to litigate in other jurisdictions. On the other hand, if the implementer accepts a global FRAND licence determined by a national court, it remains free to challenge the validity and infringement of SEPs in other jurisdictions. As confirmed by the UK Supreme Court, an adjustment mechanism should be included in a licence to provide for the adjustment of

[112] ibid.
[113] ibid, 60.
[114] ibid, 64.
[115] ibid, 90.
[116] *Sisvel v Haier*, KZR 36/17 (n 72) 78.
[117] *Pioneer v Acer*, 7 O 96/14 (n 94); *Saint Lawrence v Vodafone*, 4a O 73/14 (n 72).

royalties following the outcome of patent trials in other jurisdictions. For example, if most of the patents in one jurisdiction or in one portfolio turn out to be invalid and non-infringed, that would bring a royalty downwards and vice versa; royalties could be adjusted upwards if most challenged patents are confirmed.

However, if an implementer's business is limited only to one country or region, it should be offered a national/regional licence. The terms of such a licence should be adjusted to reflect the value of the portfolio in that one country. In this case, it may be possible to litigate the whole or the majority of a national SEP portfolio, and the royalty should be set in accordance with the outcome of patent trials. Details from the *TCL v Ericsson* litigation show that local companies may secure a special local licence.[118]

An inevitable consequence of national courts deciding on the terms of a global FRAND licence, coupled with the granting of an antisuit injunction and an anti-antisuit injunction discussed below, is that we may indeed see a race to the most favourable court and jurisdiction. Besides European courts, Chinese courts have also expressed a willingness to set the terms of a global FRAND licence and assert exclusive jurisdiction via antisuit injunctions.[119] That, however, is an inevitable consequence of the tension between the global nature of technology markets and correspondingly no international court or tribunal. Thus, although disputes must be brought before national courts, they are not about specific national patents but about globally relevant portfolios of patents. In the future, international tribunals for resolving global FRAND royalty disputes may be set up,[120] but until that time comes, we remain with national litigation of global disputes.

That said, not all courts have accepted ruling on global FRAND terms. The Eastern District Court of Texas in *PanOptis v Huawei* and *PanOptis v Apple* refused to adopt a declaratory judgment that the SEP owner complied with its FRAND commitment by offering a worldwide licence for its SEP portfolio.[121] The Court noted that it would be required to decide whether the SEP owner breached a foreign FRAND obligation with respect to foreign patents and assuming jurisdiction over foreign patents is almost always an abuse of discretion.[122] However, the Court seems to have conflated the distinction between a contractual obligation under a FRAND commitment given to a relevant SDO, for which it is competent to interpret and set the terms, with a patent question of infringement and validity.

[118] *TCL v Ericsson*, 2017 WL 6611635 (CD Cal 2017) 59.

[119] Shenzhen Intermediate People's Court ruled in 2020 in a dispute between Oppo and Sharp that it can set a global FRAND portfolio rate, see M Renaud, J Wodarski and M Galica, 'Is this Seat Taken? A Chinese IP Court Proclaims its Authority to Declare Global FRAND Terms' *National Law Review* (7 December 2020), available at: www.natlawreview.com/article/seat-taken-chinese-ip-court-proclaims-its-authority-to-declare-global-frand-terms#:~:text=A%20Chinese%20IP%20Court%20Proclaims%20Its%20Authority%20to%20Declare%20Global%20FRAND%20Terms&text=In%20a%20dispute%20between%20Oppo,3G%2C%204G%20and%20WLAN%20technology.

[120] See ch 9.

[121] *Optis Wireless v Huawei* 2018 WL 3375192 (ED Tex 2018); *Optis Wireless v Apple* 2020 WL 999463 (ED Tex 2020).

[122] *Optis Wireless v Huawei* 2018 WL 3375192 (ED Tex 2018) 8.

By interpreting the obligation under a FRAND commitment the court will not be ruling on the infringement validity of foreign patents, and under the terms of the FRAND licence a licensee would remain free to challenge such patents and have the royalty correspondingly adjusted. Nevertheless, at this time there appears to be a split between European and Chinese courts willing to rule on the terms of a global FRAND licence, and US courts which refuse to do so without the express agreement of the parties.[123]

III. Antisuit Injunctions

Another consequence of having a global licensing dispute with national patents is that a patent litigation will often be worldwide, covering multiple jurisdictions in Europe, North America and Asia. For example, a SEP licensing dispute between Apple and Qualcomm involved litigation in the US, UK, Japan, China and Taiwan.[124] The SEP owner will typically litigate in a few key jurisdictions where parties will test the strength of the relevant national SEP portfolio and try to reach an agreement on a FRAND licence.

A mechanism to consolidate all litigation within one court is to use an ASI or AASI. An ASI is an order by the court in one jurisdiction restraining a party for initiating or continuing with proceedings in a foreign court.[125] On the other hand, an AASI is an order from a court in one jurisdiction restraining a party from seeking an ASI with a foreign court. ASIs are traditionally associated with common law jurisdictions, but in relation to SEPs they have started emerging in civil law countries as well.[126] They are a powerful tool in SEP disputes where one court can stop all other parallel patent litigation until it resolves FRAND issues.[127] The positive sides of an ASI injunction are lower litigation costs, the avoidance of duplicative and inconsistent judgements and the ultimate resolution of the dispute before one court. However, the downside of a wider use of ASIs is the potential for forum shopping and a race to the most favourable court. Coupled with the power of national courts to rule on the global FRAND licensing terms ASIs can be used to consolidate all litigation in the jurisdiction seen as the most favourable for the party that sues first. For example, courts that are perceived as granting lower

[123] See *TCL v Ericsson* (n 118) (parties agreed that court should determine the terms of a global portfolio licence).

[124] *Apple v Qualcomm*, 2017 WL 3966944 (SD Cal 2017).

[125] See G Bermann, 'The Use of Anti-Suit Injunction in International Litigation' (1990) 28 *Columbia Journal of Transnational Law* 589; G Fisher, 'Anti-Suit Injunction to Restrain Foreign Proceedings in Breach of an Arbitration Agreement' (2010) 22 *Bond Law Review* 1.

[126] J Contreras and M Eixenberger, 'The Anti-Suit Injunction – A Transnational Remedy for Multi-Jurisdictional SEP Litigation' in J Contreras (ed), *The Cambridge Handbook of Technical Standardization Law: Competition, Antitrust, and Patents* (Cambridge University Press, 2018) 452; Contreras, 'The New Extraterritoriality' (n 100) 265–67.

[127] Contreras, 'The New Extraterritoriality' (n 100) 266.

FRAND royalties would naturally attract implementers to sue first and request ASIs preventing the SEP owner from initiating or maintaining parallel patent litigation in other jurisdictions. Conversely, SEP owners may be quick to initiate litigation in a country seen as having stronger IP protection and determining higher FRAND royalties. Additionally, ASIs raises some fundamental questions: which, if any, national court is the proper forum to adjudicate on a global FRAND licensing dispute, and does any court have the right to decide that it is better placed than others to resolve the terms of a FRAND licence?

We are increasingly seeing global jurisdictional battles between courts in the US, Europe and China. The US and Chinese courts appear more willing to issue ASIs to consolidate a dispute in their jurisdiction, while European courts respond by granting AASIs to protect ongoing litigation at home. As will be shown, the effects of the mass use of ASIs and AASIs is increased uncertainty, litigation gamesmanship and a general stalemate as courts issuing ASIs are regularly retaliated with corresponding AASI in other jurisdictions.

In the US, the first ASI was issued in *Microsoft v Motorola* where Microsoft brought a breach of contract action against Motorola for the failure to offer a licence on FRAND terms.[128] As a response, Motorola sued Microsoft in Germany for patent infringement and the German court, finding infringement, enjoined Microsoft from selling its Xbox and software products (Windows 7 and Internet Explorer 9).[129] Microsoft then sought an ASI from the district court in Washington to prevent Motorola from enforcing the German injunction. The district court agreed, holding that 'pending contract action before it would be dispositive of the German patent action', because the patent at issue was included in Motorola's FRAND licensing offer and because Motorola entered into a contract with the ITU to license its SEPs, including German ones, on FRAND terms on a worldwide basis.[130] Additionally, German action 'raised concerns against inconsistent judgments and that the timing of the filing of the German action raises concerns of forum shopping and duplicative and vexatious litigation'.[131] The Appeal Court agreed.

In *Huawei v Samsung*, parties had been negotiating since 2011, then Huawei decided to sue in the US in 2016 for infringement of its SEPs and asked the court to set the terms and conditions for a global FRAND cross-licence.[132] One day later, Huawei filed 11 patent infringement actions in China asking the court to determine whether SEPs are infringed and, if so, to issue an injunction. Chinese actions proceeded faster that the US one, and Shenzhen Court found two of Huawei's Chinese SEPs infringed and enjoined Samsung from manufacturing and selling its 4G smartphones in China. When deciding on an injunction, the Shenzhen

[128] *Microsoft v Motorola*, 854 F.Supp.2d 993 (WD Wash 2012); *Microsoft v Motorola*, 696 F.3d 872 (9th Cir 2012).

[129] *Microsoft v Motorola*, 696 F.3d 872 (9th Cir 2012) 879.

[130] ibid, 880.

[131] ibid.

[132] *Huawei v Samsung*, 2018 WL 1784056 (ND Cal 2018).

Court evaluated evidence and found that 'Huawei's behaviours had complied with FRAND principles while Samsung's behaviours had not complied with FRAND principles'.[133] Samsung appealed the Chinese injunction and, at the same time, asked the US court to enter an ASI preventing Huawei from enforcing the Chinese injunction.

The US court decided to order an ASI against Huawei because the US action would dispose of the Chinese action as it concerned a breach of contract claim and determination of a global cross-licence between the parties.[134] The availability of injunctive relief depends on the breach of contract claims and the court held that it should have the opportunity to adjudicate that claim without Samsung facing the threat of injunction. Additionally, a risk of inconsistent judgments and a significant harm to Samsung would likely force it to accept Huawei's licensing terms before any court had an opportunity to adjudicate on FRAND terms.[135] Finally, the court took into account that Huawei first filed an action in the US, if only just by one day before the Chinese one, with the result that enjoining the foreign action would not be an 'intolerably impact comity'.[136]

A jurisdictional battle between Chinese and US courts played out again in *Ericsson v Samsung*.[137] After failed negotiations on the renewal of a global cross-licensing agreement Ericsson filed a complaint against Samsung before the US court alleging that Samsung breached its FRAND obligation. However, a few days before the US action, Samsung filed a suit before Wuhan Court in China asking the Court to determine the global FRAND licensing terms and to issue an ASI. Without hearing the other party, the Chinese court issued a very wide ASI preventing Ericsson from requesting from any court in the world to adjudicate on FRAND licensing terms with Samsung, prohibiting determination of whether Samsung breached its FRAND obligation, and barring Ericsson from seeking and enforcing injunctions for its SEPs against Samsung.[138] Ericsson quickly responded by seeking an AASI from the US court preventing Samsung from enforcing its Chinese ASI. The US court agreed, holding that the Chinese ASI would frustrate the policy interest in ensuring that litigation proceeds in the US and imposes an inequitable hardship on Ericsson as it unfairly deprives it of the right to bring claims under US laws.[139]

Courts in Europe have recently started experimenting with AASIs as a response to ASIs granted in the US and China in order to protect their right to

[133] ibid, 3.
[134] ibid, 8.
[135] ibid, 10.
[136] ibid, 12.
[137] *Ericsson v Samsung*, WL 89980 (ED Tex 2021).
[138] ibid, 2–3.
[139] ibid, 4–5. Interestingly, the court noted that Chinese and US actions are not duplicative; they involve similar facts but different legal question. In China the court is asked to determine the terms of a global FRAND licence, while in the US the court is asked to adjudicate whether the conduct of parties breached a FRAND commitment.

assess the validity and infringement of national SEPs. In *Conversant v Huawei and ZTE*, Conversant sued for infringement in the UK and requested the court to set FRAND terms for its global SEP portfolio.[140] However, ZTE initiated proceedings before Shenzhen Court in China asking it to determine a FRAND rate for Chinese SEPs in Conversant's portfolio and for an ASI restraining Conversant from pursuing UK proceedings.[141] In response, Conversant requested an AASI in the UK restricting ZTE from prosecuting conflicting claims in China. ZTE eventually agreed to remove an ASI request in China, which would have given rise to an AASI in the UK.[142] In *IPCom v Lenovo*, the parties were unsuccessfully negotiating for years overs a FRAND licence when Lenovo brought an action before the US court seeking an adjudication of FRAND terms for a global licence for IPCom's SEP portfolio.[143] As a response, IPCom initiated infringement litigation in the UK and France, while Lenovo asked the US court to enter an ASI barring IPCom from litigating its SEPs until the US action was resolved. However, IPCom obtained AASIs from UK and French courts prohibiting Lenovo from seeking and enforcing the US ASI as, in their view, the infringement and validity of a national patent can only be resolved by a national court.[144] Moreover, the Paris court viewed ASIs as against French public order except in limited circumstances when aimed at complying with arbitration or choice of jurisdiction contractual clauses. The US ASI would thus infringe IPCom's fundamental rights, such as the right to property, a fair trial and the right to be heard by a judge.[145] Similarly, the Munich court in *Continental v Nokia* issued an AASI requiring Continental to withdraw an ASI request in the US that would prevent Nokia from continuing with German SEP infringement proceedings.[146] The Munich court viewed potential US ASIs as unlawfully interfering with property rights as the SEP owner must have the right to enforce its national SEP before the German court.

Asian countries have also stepped into global FRAND jurisdictional battles. In *Conversant v Huawei*, Nanjing Court issued an ASI barring Conversant from enforcing an injunction against Huawei obtained in Germany until Chinese proceedings for the determination of FRAND terms were resolved.[147] In *InterDigital v Xiaomi*, Xiaomi requested Wuhan Court to determine FRAND royalty terms for

[140] *Conversant v Huawei and ZTE* [2018] EWHC 2549 (Ch).
[141] ibid, 10–12.
[142] ibid, 24.
[143] *IPCom v Lenovo* [2019] EWHC 3030 (Pat) 7–11.
[144] ibid, 46–48.
[145] E Bonadio and L McDonagh, 'Paris Court Grants an SEP Anti-Anti-Suit Injunction in *IPCom v Lenovo*: A Worrying Decision in Uncertain Times?' (2019) *Journal of Intellectual Property Law & Practice* 149.
[146] *Continental v Nokia*, 6 U 5042/19 Munich Higher Regional Court (12 December 2019).
[147] Y Yu and J Contreras, 'Will China's New Anti-Suit Injunction Shift the Balance of Global FRAND Litigation' (*PatentlyO*, 22 October 2020), available at: patentlyo.com/patent/2020/10/contreras-injunctions-litigation.html; B Li, L Li and C Xu, 'Recent Development on SEP Disputes in China – Anti-Suit Injunction' (*Kluwer Patent Blog*, 20 November 2020), available at: patentblog.kluweriplaw.com/2020/11/20/recent-development-on-sep-disputes-in-china-anti-suit-injunction/.

InterDigital's SEPs, while Interdigital retaliated by suing in India before Delhi High Court for infringement and seeking damages and an injunction.[148] Consequently, Wuhan Court entered a very wide ASI ordering Interdigital to withdraw its request for injunctions in India, prohibited InterDigital from seeking injunctions for its SEPs against Xiaomi anywhere in the world and from asking any other court to determine FRAND terms. InterDigital retaliated by asking for an AASI before Indian and German courts which granted the request and prohibited Xiaomi from enforcing its Chinese ASI.[149]

Therefore, global ASI and AASI litigation has not produced a clear winner but only led to an international fight between courts and additional expenses for the parties.[150] A degree of opportunism can be observed where parties try to consolidate litigation before what they believe is the most favourable court. However, there is no easy way out of this situation unless parties willingly concede the jurisdiction of one court or agree on arbitration of FRAND terms, or potentially even a global FRAND tribunal is set up that might be a venue for resolving FRAND licensing issues in one place.[151] In the meantime, courts could exercise restraint in issuing ASIs. A solution could be recognising the distinction between a contractual question of whether the SEP owner's global licensing offer is FRAND, which is suspectable to be resolved by one court, and the question of infringement and validity of SEPs that can only be decided by corresponding national courts. Thus, a contractual claim could be subject to an ASI which would prohibit parties from asking for declaratory judgments on compliance with FRAND terms in other jurisdictions, while patent issues of infringement, validity and injunctions for SEPs should not be subject to ASIs and must be examined by national courts. This way at least some degree of litigation certainty would be reached.

IV. Past Damages

Past damages are a remedy for a patent that is found valid and infringed in litigation. Normally, if during litigation the SEP owner offers a FRAND licence such licence will include provisions on royalties for the future use, as well as the amount of royalties for past use from the date of infringement that a licensee must pay.

[148] Yu and Contreras (n 147).

[149] R Lloyd, 'Indian Court Hands InterDigital Anti Anti-Suit Injunction in Xiaomi Fights' (*IAM*, 9 October 2020), available at: www.iam-media.com/frandseps/indian-court-hands-interdigital-anti-anti-suit-injunction-in-xiaomi-fight; *Interdigital v Xiaomi*, 7 0 14276/20 Munich Regional Court (28 January 2021).

[150] Although ASIs have not been given all the time when requested, at least in the US. See *Apple v Qualcomm* (n 124) (ASI denied as US judgment would not dispose of Apple's foreign claims, US and foreign actions were not functionally similar or duplicative); *Optis v Hauwei*, 2:17-cv-00123-JRG-RSP (ED Tex 2018) (ASI denied as Chinese action related only to Chinese patents, while US action related to US patents).

[151] See ch 9 for the discussion on the feasibility of such tribunals.

Past royalties are normally calculated in the same way as an ongoing royalty. However, it may be possible for the implementer to accept an injunction and exit the market rather than enter a global FRAND licence. The infringer may find it more profitable to exit a market where the value of its sales is not high, instead of paying for a global portfolio licence. In such case, the question is how to determine the amount of past damages for infringed SEPs. This occurred in *Philips v Asus* and *IPCom v HTC* where infringers chose to withdraw from the UK's market and accept an injunction instead of entering into a global FRAND licence set by the court.[152]

Past damages are to be resolved by the rules of national patent damages laws and can only be determined for litigated, valid and infringed SEPs.[153] Therefore, the interpretation of a FRAND commitment under contract law and the rules of national patent damages that apply for calculating damages only for litigated, valid and infringed SEPs, are two conceptually different exercises. The precise rules for patent damages can vary from jurisdiction to jurisdiction, but in general an infringer would be liable for loss which a SEP owner incurs by infringement. The amount would normally be what a willing licensor and a willing licensee agreed at the time of infringement.

Because past damages are calculated solely with respect to national SEPs they must consider only infringing national sales. In *Philips v Asus* and *IPCom v HTC*, SEP owners argued that what a willing licensee and a willing licensor would agree is a global portfolio licence and thus, damages for a SEP owner is a loss of revenue it would have earned pursuant to such a licence. Accordingly, they suggested damages should be calculated with respect to global sales. Courts correctly disagreed with such an approach. Patent damages are calculated only with respect to an infringement of national patents and cannot be based on non-infringing global sales.[154] Calculating past damages based on global sales risks overcompensating SEP owners and having an extraterritorial overreach. Namely, if the SEP owner claimed damages based on global sales in one jurisdiction, there is nothing to stop it from going to another jurisdiction, litigating a national SEP and obtaining global damages again.[155]

Some principles for determining past damages for infringed national SEPs can be identified. Comparable licences are not entirely reliable if they are all global in scope but could be used subject to adjustments. Namely, voluntarily concluded

[152] *Philips v Asus* [2020] EWHC 29 (Ch) (the question of past damages not susceptible of summary determination and must be determined at a trial); *IPCom v HTC* [2020] EWHC 2941 (Pat).

[153] See *Unwired Planet v Huawei* [2018] EWCA Civ 2344 52 and 80 ('the only relief to which UP would be entitled would be relief for infringement of the two UK SEPs the judge had found to be valid and essential'); *Unwired Planet v Huawei; Huawei and ZTE v Conversant* [2020] UKSC 37, 87 ('the award of damages is not to be equated with the royalties that are paid under a contractual licence. If an implementer agrees to enter into a FRAND licence which a SEP owner offers, it is entering into a voluntary obligation. If the court awards damages it does so on proof of the loss which the SEP owner has suffered through the infringement of its patent or patents').

[154] *IPCom v HTC* (n 152) (Pat) 30.

[155] *Philips v Asus* (n 152) 47.

global licences include a double discount – one for transaction costs savings for having only once licence with a blended worldwide rate, as opposed to country-by-country licensing, and another discount for uncertainty that some SEPs in the portfolio will be invalid or not infringed. These discounts should not be available in a damages enquiry, as transactions costs savings are lost in country-by-country licensing and the validity and infringement are established. To what extent a national rate should be adjusted depends on the initial perception of the strength of portfolio. If more patents are confirmed as valid and infringed, the royalty should be adjusted upwards and conversely, the royalty should be decreased if more SEPs are invalidated or not infringed than initially assessed. In *Unwired Planet v Huawei*, for example, Mr Justice Birss held that a rate for a UK-only licence would be double that of a worldwide rate.[156]

A final issue to consider is how to adjust past damages because the SEP is FRAND-committed. An argument could be made that if a willing licensor and a willing licensee were to accept a global FRAND licence, then a SEP owner has discharged its FRAND obligation by offering a worldwide FRAND licence. Thus, if an infringer refuses to enter a global FRAND licence it loses the benefit of receiving a FRAND royalty. Such an interpretation would protect against hold-out by making it costly to avoid taking a FRAND licence. It would also guard against paradoxical results in the US where damages awarded for non-SEPs are much higher than for SEPs. For instance, in a dispute between Ericsson and TCL, a jury awarded $75 million in damages for infringement of one non-SEP,[157] while a judge set a FRAND royalty for unlicensed past sales for the whole SEPs portfolio in the amount of $16 million.[158] Therefore, past damages for infringed national SEPs should not include a FRAND discount if a global portfolio licence is found to be FRAND.

V. Procedural Remedies to Facilitate Patent Licensing

The final points to consider are some procedural remedies that may accelerate patent licensing and settlement between the parties. Ordinarily, when negotiations break down a SEP owner must sue on a few selected SEPs from its portfolio and ask for an injunction, while the implementer typically responds with counterclaims of invalidity and non-infringement. Before moving on to the core of the dispute – whether the SEP owner offered a FRAND licence and whether the parties have negotiated in good faith as a willing licensor and a willing licensee – patent issues are resolved first which, together with appeals, may take several years. In order to focus on key issues promptly, the procedure could be reversed:

[156] *Unwired Planet v Huawei* [2017] EWHC 2988 (Pat) 602.
[157] *Ericsson v TCL*, 2018 WL 2149736 (ED Tex 2018) 1.
[158] *TCL v Ericsson* (n 118) 115.

have a FRAND trial first and, after that, order the implementer to make interim payments into escrow, followed later by a patent trial. This way the parties would know up front the court-determined FRAND terms and which party negotiated in good faith, facilitating settlement.

A. A FRAND Trial First

Whether the offer of the SEP owner and the counter-offer by the implementer are FRAND is at the core of any SEP licensing dispute. Where possible, courts could order a FRAND trial first before a patent trial where they would determine FRAND licensing terms between the parties in accordance with the principles explained in chapter four. An assessment would largely focus on comparable prior licences: the more prior licences the higher the likelihood that the SEP owner's offer is FRAND. The strength of the SEP portfolio should also be assessed by considering the rate of essentiality and validity of SEPs in the portfolio, which can be undertaking by sampling of key SEPs.

Court will have several options when setting FRAND terms. If the SEP owner's offer is found to be within the FRAND range, courts should accept this as appropriate FRAND terms. Namely, there is no contractual duty on the SEP owner to further negotiate once it is offered FRAND terms, otherwise it would discriminate against those implementers who promptly accepted a FRAND licence without years of negotiation and litigation. In other words, requiring the SEP owner to further negotiate once it is offered a FRAND licence would represent a holdout discount. On the other hand, if the SEP owner's offer was not FRAND, but the implementer's counter-offer was FRAND, then the court should accept the implementer's counter-offer. This would be a sanction for the SEP owner's non-compliance with its FRAND obligation. In case neither the SEP owner's offer nor implementer's counter-offer are FRAND, then the court should directly set FRAND terms.

Once the court has resolved FRAND issues it can move on to patent trials. Parties however will have an incentive to settle as the central issue is resolved. Only if the implementer believes that all or most of its SEPs are invalid would it have a reason to continue with patent litigation, as the court ruling in its favour would drive FRAND royalties downwards. However, such a scenario may be possible only in cases when the SEP owner holds a small portfolio, possibly acquired from an outside source, and has not directly participated and contributed to standardisation. The prospect of invalidity of the whole portfolio of large, well-established SEP owners that directly participated in standardisation efforts is improbable, as evidenced by regular settlements before cases reach merits.[159]

[159] See M Lemley and T Simcoe, 'How Essential Are Standard Essential Patents?' (2019) 104 *Cornell Law Review* 607, 623 (finding that 75.9% of US SEP cases settle and 16.1% were resolved on procedural grounds. Only 8% went to the merits. No case involved successful invalidation of the whole or large part of the SEP portfolio).

B. Interim Payments

Once a court has resolved FRAND issues, but the parties do not settle and choose to continue with patent litigation, the court can require the implementer to make interim payments into escrow. This secures the compliance with FRAND determination, incentivises settlements and deters unmeritorious litigation aimed solely at further delaying the conclusion of a licence. Thus, a patent litigation where the implanter strongly believes it has chances of success in invalidating a large part of a SEP owner's portfolio would still be allowed to proceed. Courts should generally have a discretion in deciding whether to grant this type of remedy,[160] and in several cases in India courts have ordered implementers to make interim payments to the SEP holder pending the final outcome of a trial.[161]

VI. Conclusion

SEP remedies have been contentious. From the initial hostility and almost outright ban of injunctions, we have moved to recognition that injunctions for SEPs should be available in circumstances when the implementer is not negotiating as a wiling licensee and refuses to accept court-determined FRAND terms. However, while patent litigation is inevitably national, licensing disputes in today's globalised world are global. The pursuance of ASIs and AASIs, as well as national courts setting the terms of a global FRAND licence, have raised the question of whether we may need a corresponding global solution to SEP licensing disputes. Fragmented litigation and piecemeal approaches do not seem adequate for the IoT with numerous companies from many different industries using SEPs and needing to take a licence. The potential for disputes and litigation is enormous. The next chapter will assess what needs to change for a more efficient, transparent and predictable SEP licensing environment in the IoT.

160 For the UK see CPR, Rules & Practice Directions, Part 25, Rule 25.7.

161 G Sidak, 'FRAND in India: The Delhi High Court's Emerging Jurisprudence on Royalties for Standard-Essential Patents' (2015) 10 *Journal of Intellectual Property Law & Practice* 609.

PART III

Standard Essential Patent Licensing in the Internet of Things

9

Standard Essential Patent Licensing in the Internet of Things

Parts I and II analysed the experience with SEP licensing in the telecommunications industry, they clarified the meaning and scope of FRAND licensing commitments and highlighted some issues that would need to be addressed in the future. This part will focus on what needs to be changed to create a smoother, transparent and more predictable licensing framework in the new environment of 5G and the IoT. Chapter nine will first describe the challenges of the current bilateral FRAND licensing model in the light of the digitalisation of other sectors of the economy which will require many new and inexperienced companies to use and take licences for SEPs. Various existing proposals will then be analysed that recommend improving some aspects of SEP licensing in the future. While some measures have their merits, it is unclear whether they offer comprehensive solutions or practical suitability in the IoT context. The chapter will lastly address the potential for wider applicability of collective licensing via patent pools which may provide a simple and efficient licensing model for the IoT environment.

I. Challenges of FRAND Licensing in the Internet of Things

The FRAND licensing framework for cellular standards was made primarily with the ICT industry in mind, where there are a certain number of identifiable technology developers and standard implementers. As seen in chapter two, in the early days of 1G, 2G and mid-3G cellular standards the telecommunications industry was dominated by a relatively few vertically integrated companies that held both SEPs and manufactured downstream products. The primary model of licensing was cross-licensing that offset the total royalty costs. When new companies entered the market during the period of mid-3G and 4G, despite tensions, the system generally worked as there was still a discernible number of entities that held SEPs and those that manufactured standard-implementing products. Moreover, companies that at first did not have any cellular SEPs quickly assembled a large SEP portfolio to use for cross-licensing.[1] Those licensing disputes that arose largely settled before final judgment on patent issues.[2]

However, the 5G cellular standard and the emergence of the IoT are expected to radically transform such a landscape. It is estimated that a large number of industries – cars, domestic appliances, buildings healthcare, utilities – will be powered by 5G connectivity. This means that billions of devices will be connected to the internet: already around 20 billion devices are estimated have connectivity, with an expected rise to as much as 41 billion by 2025.[3] As a result, many new companies coming from different industries will now have to take a licence for the use of SEPs. However, these companies generally have little experience with SEP licensing and hold no corresponding SEP portfolios of their own to use for cross-licensing, meaning they would be net licensees and often needing to take a licence on a cash basis. Many of new licensees would be SMEs with little knowledge of SEP matters and no budgets for expensive patent negotiations, further complicating successful licensing.

Moreover, the number of standards used in the IoT will become more complex. Besides connectivity standards, such as Wi-Fi, 5G, Bluetooth, IoT objects will also cover different quality and security standards; standards for cooperation between IoT devices and cloud services; standards within IoT devices and cyber security standards.[4] Some IoT devices may rely on certain standards more than others, and connectivity standards can be used to a different degree in different IoT objectives. For example, a connected car would use connectivity standards differently in terms of bandwidth and frequency from a smart meter that may use connectivity standards only occasionally and only to send simple consumption information.

[1] eg, Asian companies such as Samsung, LG, Huawei and ZTE at first did not own cellular SEPs but quickly caught up by taking part in the standard-development process. See T Pohlmann and K Blind, 'Landscaping Study on Standard Essential Patents (SEPs)' (2016) 26–28, available at: available at: ec.europa.eu; also, some new entrants in the ICT sectors acquired SEPs from previous incumbents, such as Google acquiring Motorola's SEP portfolio of about 15,000 patents and patent applications, and a consortium of Apple and Microsoft, among others, acquiring Nortel's 6,000 patents and patent applications. See: COMP/M.6381*Google/Motorola Mobility*, Commission Decision [2012] C(2012) 1068; US Department of Justice, 'Statement of the Department of Justice's Antitrust Division on its Decision to Close its Investigations of Google Inc's Acquisition of Motorola Mobility Holdings Inc. and the Acquisitions of Certain Patents by Apple Inc, Microsoft Corp' (Press Release, 13 February 2012).

[2] M Lemley and T Simcoe, 'How Essential Are Standard Essential Patents?' (2019) 104 *Cornell Law Review* 607, 623 (only 8% of US SEP cases reached a decision on the merits).

[3] M Hung (ed), 'Leading the IoT: Gartner Insights on How to Lead in a Connected World' (2017), available at: www.gartner.com/imagesrv/books/iot/iotEbook_digital.pdf; IDC, 'The Growth in Connected IoT Devices is Expected to Generate 79.4ZB of Data in 2025, According to a New IDC Forecast' (18 June 2019), available at: www.businesswire.com/news/home/20190618005012/en/The-Growth-in-Connected-IoT-Devices-is-Expected-to-Generate-79.4ZB-of-Data-in-2025-According-to-a-New-IDC-Forecast#:~:text=A%20new%20IDC%20forecast%20estimates,ZB)%20of%20data%20in%202025.&text=IDC%20projects%20that%20the%20amount,the%202018%2D2025%20forecast%20period; Ericsson Mobility Report (June 2020) 23, available at: www.ericsson.com/en/mobility-report/reports/november-2020 (providing a more conservative but still significant estimate of 10 billion IoT devices in 2020 with expected growth to 24.6 by 2025).

[4] J Baron et al, 'Group of Experts on Licensing and Valuation of Standard Essential Patents – Contribution to the Debate on SEPs' (January 2021) 9, available at: ec.europa.eu/docsroom/documents/45217.

The IoT thus creates new challenges for SEP licensing. The main obstacles relate to increased transaction costs, an unclear SEP landscape and the complexity of different industries and business models. Transactions costs are related to countless numbers of new companies needing to take a licence, making it unlikely that every SEP owner individually would be able to a conclude licences with each and every company in the IoT sector. However, if only a few companies take a licence, this would put them at a disadvantage against their unlicensed competitors, disincentivising them from taking a licence in the first place unless all competitors in one relevant market are licensed as well. For implementers, the additional problem is an untransparent SEP landscape – due to over-declaration the number of truly essential patents is unknown, SEP databases within SDOs are incomplete, making it difficult for them to know if and what SEPs they may be infringing. Additionally, because of the bilateral nature of licensing, implementers do not know the aggregate royalty for the standard that they could then factor in as an input cost in their business plans. Finally, different IoT industries may have different IP licensing business models that may be different from licensing practice in the telecommunications sector. For example, in the telecommunications industry a practice is to license on the final device level due to efficiencies and the possibility of cross-licensing, while in the automotive industry IP licensing is done by component suppliers who provide IP indemnities for their products supplied to car manufacturers.[5] Thus, it is not realistic to expect that a licensing model suited for telecommunications sector should be automatically applied or imposed on all other IoT industries.

Therefore, it is easy to see that the current model of individual and bilateral SEP licensing from the telecommunications sector strongly focused on cross-licensing is not well suited for the more complex environment of the IoT. A successful SEP licensing in the IoT would need to make the SEP landscape more transparent; adopt different licensing models that would lower transaction costs and make possible the conclusion of large number of licences covering the whole industry; and have the openness and flexibility to take into account the peculiarities of each IoT industry.

II. Current Proposals for Improving the Standard Essential Patent Licensing Framework

Over the years there have been many discussions on how to improve the SEP licensing framework. The main considerations relate to increasing the transparency of the SEP landscape, providing certainty on the overall price of the standard and, recently, how to consolidate global SEP litigation under one SEP tribunal.

[5] ibid, 42.

A. Transparency of the SEP Landscape

One of the main objectives of the European Commission from its 2017 Communication on SEPs is to increase the transparency on SEP exposure.[6] Current SDO databases of declared SEPs are seen as unreliable as they do not convey the full picture of the SEP landscape – many declared SEPs turn out to be non-essential due to widespread over-declaration;[7] the use of blanket disclosures conceals the true number of SEPs; and the lack of detail in SEP declarations makes it hard to verify their essentiality and use by implementers. The reason for this unclear SEP landscape is because SDO databases were primarily designed to facilitate standard development and assure SDOs and implementers that licences to SEPs will be available on FRAND terms, but were not intended to advance successful licensing negotiations. The current system therefore increases transaction costs both to SEP owners and implementers.

An idea considered by the Commission is to incentivise SEP owners to make more detailed specific SEP disclosures.[8] Specific declarations should identify individual patents, or preferably patent claims, that are believed to be essential, as well as an explanation of standards or parts or standards that SEPs read on. Banket disclosures would be reserved only for early stages in the standardisation process, while specific disclosure would be required at a later stage once the information on the scope of final standard and granted patents becomes available. The main benefit is that any interested party could validate whether or not a claimed patent is indeed essential and will provide more clarity on SEPs' essentiality. The use of blanket disclosures has been largely criticised for concealing the full existence and ownership of SEPs. Without the knowledge of the actual number of SEPs in a standard, it makes it impossible to use the top-down approach in royalty calculations as well as agreeing on the aggregate royalty cap for a standard. Thus, blanket disclosures would be permitted only initially during the development of the standard to ensure that any potential SEP will be licensed on FRAND terms, but then specific disclosures would be required once the final version of the standard is set.

SDO SEP databases could also be regularly updated with new information.[9] SEP owners could include information on whether they continue to believe that a patent is essential, the results of essentiality checks, court rulings regarding

[6] Commission, 'Setting out the EU Approach to Standard Essential Patents' COM(2017) 712 final, 3–5.

[7] See ch 1, section III.C for discussion of the problem of over-declaration.

[8] Commission, 'Patents and Standards: A Modern Framework for IPR-based Standardization' (2014) 144–46, available at: pure.tue.nl/ws/files/3916785/391736021255721.pdf; P Régibeau, R De Coninck and H Zenger, 'Transparency, Predictability and Efficiency of SSO-based Standardisation and SEP Licensing: A Report for the European Commission' (2016) 54–58, available at: ec.europa.eu/growth/content/study-transparency-predictability-and-efficiency-sso-based-standardization-and-sep-licensing_en; Commission, 'Setting Out the EU Approach to Standard Essential Patents' COM(2017) 712 final, 4; Baron et al (n 4) 50–52.

[9] Commission, 'Patents and Standards' (n 8) 141–44; Commission 'Setting Out the EU Approach to Standard Essential Patents' (n 8) 4; Baron et al (n 4) 52–54.

validity and essentiality, the information on the outcome of patent application and the information on a patent's expiry.[10] As discussed, there are various reasons why a patent disclosed at one point in time may not be essential at a later point. For instance, patents declared essential during the development of a standard may not end up in the finally approved version of the standard. Standards also evolve and change over time, and a patent essential to an earlier release may not be essential to a later version of a standard. Furthermore, patents expire, get invalidated in litigation, or opposed and, in case of patent applications, the scope of the finally issued patent may be narrowed or modified during the review by the patent office and may no longer contain claims that are essential. The patent application may also be rejected or abandoned. As SDOs do not require updates on disclosed patents all these changes are not reflected in a database of disclosed SEPs. Thus, requiring regular updates would increase the transparency on the true number of SEPs and SEP exposure of implementers.

Strengthening the chances of validity of SEPs is also considered. One proposal is to require SDOs to use the existing ETSI example of making draft standards, written contributions, studies and other submissions to SDOs in the standard-development process available to patent offices in order to be more easily identified as a prior act in patent examination.[11] This would be a simple and easy measure to implement that might strengthen the validity of granted SEPs.

While all these proposals will certainly make the SEP landscape more transparent and will be beneficial to future SEP licensing, the main obstacle is the costs of implementation that will primarily fall on SEP owners. They would have to initiate lengthy patent searches of their portfolios to identify individual patents and parts of a standard they relate to, and would have to continuously provide such information for different future releases of the standard. Also, further clarifications are required on the cut-off date to make specific disclosure and what happens if some SEPs are not disclosed in time. A study for the European Parliament recommends requiring undisclosed SEPs to be licensed royalty-free,[12] but such would be disproportionately punitive on SEP owners and clearly disincentivise participation in SDOs. Standard implementers are already protected by a blanket comment to license any SEPs on FRAND terms and adding an additional royalty-free penalty on SEP owners may tilt the balance too much in the opposite direction. Moreover, the additional SEP information would be available only late in the standardisation process, after a standard has been approved and possible licensing contract concluded, casting doubt on the usability of such additional databases.[13] There is also a concern that some SEP owners may submit biased and unreliable information. Therefore, a balancing exercise needs to be undertaken

[10] Baron et al (n 4) 52–53.

[11] ibid, 70.

[12] L McDonagh and E Bonadio, 'Standard Essential Patents and the Internet of Things' (2019) 7, available at: www.europarl.europa.eu/thinktank/en/document.html?reference=IPOL_IDA(2019)608854.

[13] Baron et al (n 4) 54.

before implementation to assess whether the costs do not outweigh the benefits and risk SDOs becoming less attractive, which might shift innovation and standardisation to SDOs or consortia with less stringent disclosure requirements or even to proprietary standards.

Another initiative by the Commission is to introduce a mechanism for essentiality checks.[14] Currently, there is no institutional mechanism to verify the essentiality of disclosed SEPs other than litigation. It is proposed that essentiality checks should be voluntary and only for those SEPs that a SEP owner intends to commercialise.[15] Ideally, essentiality checks should be done as quickly as possible after the approval of a standard and before a SEP owner starts licensing its SEPs. However, the costs of a full essentiality check represent a significant obstacle. Estimates are that a 'quick look' assessment of essentiality by a qualified expert costs approximately between €600 and €1,800 per patent, while a more thorough essentiality assessment ranges between €5,000 and €15,000 per patent.[16] Applying these figures to all 2G, 3G and 4G SEPs declared at ETSI, a thorough essentiality check would cost at least €427,5 million or even more.[17] To lower the costs, it is suggested that the SEP owner need not test its whole declared SEP portfolio but only those SEPs it believes are still essential at the time of the adoption of the final version of the standard (the estimate is that between 60 per cent and 75 per cent of declared SEPs would be filtered out by the SEP owner itself) and then only one patent per patent family in a major market country.[18] Patent offices are seen as the preferred bodies to perform essentiality checks or, in the alternative, a supervised network of certified European law firms could be used. If possible, essentiality checks could also indicate the type of invention that the SEP covers (ie, 'fundamental', 'key') which could be used to better assess the underlying value of SEPs. Finally, SEP owners could submit essentiality confirmation and relevant claim charts to be recorded in SDO SEP databases.[19]

Overall, the idea of having some form of voluntary essentiality test sounds reasonable and could be a valuable mechanism to increase the transparency of the SEP landscape, facilitating licensing negotiations. It remains to be seen how essentiality checks will be implanted by the European Commission. The success lies in the balance of not imposing unreasonably high costs to SEP owners and not providing recalcitrant implements with another venue to delay negotiations.

[14] Commission 'Setting Out the EU Approach to Standard Essential Patents' (n 8) 5; R Bekkers et al, 'Pilot Study for Essentiality Assessment of Standard Essential Patents' (2020), available at: publications.jrc.ec.europa.eu/repository/handle/JRC119894; Baron et al (n 4) 56.

[15] Bekkers et al (n 14) 18–20; Baron et al (n 4) 56–59.

[16] Commission, 'Patents and Standards' (n 8) 148; Bekkers et al (n 14) 15 (full essentiality assessment of patent pools €10,000 per patent); Baron et al (n 4) 61 (estimating average costs of €4,000–5,000 per patent).

[17] Régibeau, De Coninck and Zenger (n 8) 59; also Pohlmann and Blind (n 1) 50–51 (estimating costs of over €1 billion for a thorough essentiality assessment for ETSI's declared SEPs for 2G, 3G and 4G standards).

[18] Baron et al (n 4) 56, 59.

[19] ibid, 65.

Thus, any essentiality mechanism should remain strictly voluntary and available to those SEP owners that intend to monetise SEPs.

B. Unilateral Ex Ante Disclosure of Maximum Licensing Terms

One of the early proposals in the literature aimed at increasing the transparency of licensing terms is requiring patent holders to disclose, during the development of a standard, the maximum rates that they would charge for SEPs should their patented technology be incorporated into a standard.[20] In theory, this approach would enable companies during the development of a standard to assess the technology based not only on its technical merit but also on price. Standard developers could then choose alternative technologies if the one under consideration is priced too high. Implementers would also know in advance the price they would have to pay for the use of a standard. Recently, the Commission's SEP Expert Group also considered the possibility of mandating ex ante disclosures of maximum licensing terms together with views on the reasonable aggregate royalty for a standard.[21]

Some SDOs have already adopted policies permitting the disclosure of maximum licensing terms. For example, one SDO – VMEbus International Trade Association (VITA), requires a mandatory disclosure of maximum royalty rates by its members.[22] According to VITA's IPR policy, any member should disclose its SEPs and maximum licensing terms prior to voting for the inclusion of the relevant technology into a standard.[23] Failure to disclose patents or maximum licensing terms is sanctioned with an obligation to license SEPs royalty-free.[24] Because of potential competition law concerns, VITA sought and obtained a favourable business review letter from the US Department of Justice.[25] The IEEE,

[20] See G Ohana, M Hansen and O Shah, 'Disclosure and Negotiation of Licensing Terms Prior to Adoption of Industry Standards: Preventing Another Patent Ambush?' (2003) 24 *European Competition Law Review* 648; R Skitol, 'Concerted Buying Power: Its Potential for Addressing the Patent Hold-up Problem in Standard Setting' (2005) 72 *Antitrust Law Journal* 727; M Lemley, 'Ten Things to Do About Patent Holdup and Standards (and One Not To)' (2007) 48 *Boston College Law Review* 149; US Department of Justice and the Federal Trade Commission, 'Antitrust Enforcement and Intellectual Property Rights: Promoting Innovation and Competition' (2007) (US DOJ and FTC: Promoting Innovation and Competition) 49–50 (discussing ex ante disclosures); V Torti, *Intellectual Property Rights and Competition in Standard Setting: Objectives and Tensions* (Routledge, 2016) 197–209 (suggesting the implementation of ex ante disclosure policies as a method of increasing the price transparency in standard-setting).

[21] Baron et al (n 4) 101; also McDonagh and Bonadio (n 12) 7.

[22] VITA, VSO Policies and Procedures (1 September 2015) 10.3.2, available at: www.vita.com/resources/Documents/Policies/vso-pp-r2d8.pdf.

[23] ibid, Appendix 7: Implementation Plan for VITA's Revised Patent Policy.

[24] ibid, 10.4.

[25] Department of Justice, Letter from Thomas Barnett, Assistant Attorney General to Robert Skitol (30 October 2006) (VMEBus Business Review Letter) 9–10.

ETSI and IETF provide only for the voluntary ex ante disclosures of maximum licensing terms.[26]

However, unilateral ex ante disclosures of maximum licensing terms will hardly solve all the problems relating to SEP licensing and have proven to be an impractical solution.[27] It would be difficult to accurately set the price of the standard and individual SEPs when the future applications of the standard are unknown. To be on the safe side, companies would simply announce the maximum possible rate, but in practice these maximum prices will not be used, and concrete licensing offers will be made once more information on the standard and downstream products are known. Indeed, SEP owners are already posting their maximum prices,[28] and observed market prices are much lower than announced ones, as evidenced by the 4G LTE standard. For example, by looking only at the price announcements for the 4G standard of nine SEP owners an aggregate royalty rate would be 14.8 per cent of the end-product price,[29] but in practice the observed cumulative SEP royalty is only 3.4 per cent of the smartphone's average selling price.[30] This shows that SEP owners are concluding licensing agreements with much lower royalties that initially announced. Contreras also illustrates how the Next Generation Mobile Network consortium required members to disclose their maximum SEP royalty rates and for some standards the aggregate royalty rate was 130 per cent of the relevant product price.[31] Thus, the unilateral ex ante disclosures of maximum licensing terms would not add anything to the transparency and certainty of a standard's overall price. Additionally, requiring mandatory ex ante disclosures of maximum licensing terms may be used as a pretext for collusion between standard implementers in order to put pressure on

[26] See IEEE-SA, 'Standards Board Bylaws' (August 2020) Clause 6.1. Definitions, available at: standards.ieee.org/content/dam/ieee-standards/standards/web/documents/other/sb_bylaws.pdf; Department of Justice, Letter from Thomas Barnett, Assistant Attorney General to Michael Lindsay (30 April 2007) (IEEE I Business Review Letter); ETSI, Ex-ante Disclosure of Licensing Terms, available at: www.etsi.org/about/how-we-work/intellectual-property-rights-iprs/ex-ante-disclosures; IETF, 'Intellectual Property Rights in IETF Technology' (May 2017) Article 5.5, available at: www.rfc-editor.org/rfc/pdfrfc/rfc8179.txt.pdf.

[27] For criticism see: D Geradin and A Layne-Farrar, 'The Logic and Limits of Ex Ante Competition in a Standard-Setting Environment' (2007) 3 *Competition Policy International* 79; A Layne-Farrar, G Llobet and J Padilla, 'Preventing Patent Hold Up: An Economic Assessment of Ex Ante Licensing Negotiations in Standard Setting' (2009) 37 *AIPLA Quarterly Journal* 445; C Tapia, *Industrial Property Rights, Technical Standards and Licensing Practices (FRAND) in the Telecommunications Industry* (Carly Heymanns Verlag, 2010).

[28] eg, for 5G, Ericsson announced that it would license its 5G SEP portfolio at between $2.5 and $5 per device, Nokia up to €3 per device, up to $1.2 for Interdigital, 3.25 % of the end-device price by Qualcomm. See E Stasik and D Cohen, 'Royalty Rates and Licensing Strategies for Essential Patents on 5G Telecommunication Standards: What to Expect' [2020] *les Nouvelles* 176.

[29] E Stasik, 'Royalty Rates and Licensing Strategies for Essential Patents on LTE (4G) Telecommunications Standards' (2010) September *les Nouvelles* 114.

[30] A Galetovic, S Haber and L Zaretzki, 'An Estimate of the Average Cumulative Royalty Yield in the World Mobile Phone Industry: Theory, Measurement and Results' (2018) 42 *Telecommunications Policy* 263.

[31] J Contreras, 'Technical Standards and Ex Ante Disclosure: Results and Analysis of an Empirical Study' (2013) 53 *Jurimetrics* 163, 178–79.

SEP owners to lower royalties.[32] Such conduct raises competition law concerns and should be carefully assessed.[33]

In conclusion, the ex ante disclosures of most restrictive licensing terms do not provide reliable information on either the aggregate royalty rate for a standard or the precise licensing terms of individual SEP holders. A better approach, suggested in chapter five, would be for SEP owners to publish the precise standard licensing terms they would offer to any similarly situated licensee ex post, once the information on the final version of the standards and downstream applications are known. Such ex post declarations are more reliable and can be used immediately as a standard licensing offer, thus increasing the standard's price transparency on the market.

C. Collectively Setting an Aggregate Royalty for a Standard

Another proposal is to collectively set an aggregate royalty for a standard.[34] Determining the total price for the standard upfront would increase transparency and certainty in the market, and implementers could plan their business strategy with the full knowledge of the costs for the use of SEPs. It also effectively resolves royalty stacking and holdup concerns as the standard's aggregate royalty is known in advance and individual royalties will not exceed the maximum agreed amount. However, agreeing on a standard's aggregate royalty is a form of price fixing which is strongly prohibited by competition law.[35] Its application would require a more lenient interpretation of competition rules and endorsement from competition

[32] Geradin and Layne-Farrar (n 27) 103–04.

[33] See US DOJ and FTC: Promoting Innovation and Competition (n 20) 53–55 (assessing policies requiring ex ante disclosure of maximum royalty terms under rule of reason approach, but will condemn *per se* any hidden price-fixing or collusion among patent holders or standard implementers); Commission, 'Guidelines on the Applicability of Article 101 of the Treaty on the Functioning of the European Union to Horizontal Co-operation Agreements' [(Communication) [2011] OJ C 11/01 (Horizontal Cooperation Guidelines) 299 (holding that unilateral ex ante disclosures of most restrictive licensing terms as not, in principle, restricting of competition unless they serve as a cover to jointly fix prices either of downstream products or standardised technology – which is prohibited as a restriction of competition by object).

[34] See M Lemley and C Shapiro, 'Patent Holdup and Royalty Stacking' (2007) 85 *Texas Law Review* 1991, 2042–43; Lemley (n 20) 159–61; J Farrell et al, 'Standard Setting, Patents and Hold-up' (2007) 74 *Antitrust Law Journal* 603, 654–55; Régibeau, De Coninck and Zenger (n 8) 43–46; J Contreras, 'Aggregated Royalties for Top-Down FRAND Determination: Revisiting "Joint Negotiation"' (2017) 62 *Antitrust Bulletin* 690; Baron et al (n 4) 105–07.

[35] See US DOJ and FTC: Promoting Innovation and Competition (n 20) 54–55 (apply a rule of reason approach in assessing any SDO activity of determining ex ante licensing terms but also warning that 'If intellectual property holders turn joint ex-ante licensing discussions into a sham to cover up naked agreements on the licensing terms each IP holder will offer the SSO, *per se* condemnation of such agreements among "sellers" of IP rights may be warranted. Similarly, ex-ante discussion of licensing terms within the standard-setting process may provide an opportunity for SSO members to reach side price-fixing agreements that are per se illegal'); also Commission, Horizontal Cooperation Guidelines (n 33) 274 (any fixing of technology prices would constitute a restriction of competition by object).

authorities recognising the pro-competitive benefits of predictability and price transparency in standard-setting.[36]

One of the issues is who should decide on a standard's aggregate royalty. A decision could be left to joint negotiations between SEP owners and standard implementers,[37] or to SEP owners only.[38] Joint negotiations are said to provide a fairer outcome as endorsement by implementers would lead to less litigation and disputes over royalties. However, joint negotiations may result in sub-optimal outcomes,[39] as a large group of implementers negotiating licence rates with SEP holders may collectively exert anti-competitive pressure to depress royalties below a reasonable level.[40] In other words, implementers may behave as buyers' cartels and exercise downward pressure on royalty rates.[41] Economists have confirmed that it is likely that SEP royalties negotiated collectively will be lower than those set by SEP owners individually.[42]

Another, more practical problem with the implementation of joint negotiations between SEP holders and standard implementers would be reaching a consensus between entities with fundamentality diverging interests. It may lead to endless battles within SDOs. Moreover, if the decision on the aggregate royalty were to be made by a simple majority vote, it risks SEP owners being outvoted by implementers, alienating SEP holders from participating in standardisation activities.[43] Contreras argues that joint ex ante negotiations would be efficient as SEP holders would have the option to defect from SDOs if implementers exert too much

[36] Lemley (n 20) 161–62; Contreras, 'Aggregated Royalties' (n 34) 705–07; Régibeau, De Coninck and Zenger (n 8) 45. The Commission's SEP Experts Group recently also endorsed the possibility of collectively setting standard's aggregate royalty, see Baron et al (n 4) 105–07.

[37] Farrell et al (n 34) 655; Contreras, 'Aggregated Royalties' (n 34) 709.

[38] Régibeau, De Coninck and Zenger (n 8) 44–45.

[39] See Torti (n 20) 99–105 (discussing the shortcomings of joint ex ante negotiations between patent holders and implementers).

[40] G Sidak, 'Patent Holdup and Oligopsonistic Collusion in Standard-Setting Organizations' (2009) 5 *Journal of Competition Law & Economics* 123.

[41] ibid, 126.

[42] See R Gilbert, 'Deal or No Deal? Licensing Negotiations in Standard Setting Organizations' (2011) 77 *Antitrust Law Journal* 855, 866–68 ('ex-ante joint negotiations are likely to result in royalties per firm that are lower than the royalties that most, if not all, licensees would pay with bilateral bargaining'); Layne-Farrar, Llobet and Padilla (n 27) 461 ('with joint ex-ante negotiations the patent holder will generally be under-rewarded').

[43] eg, the IEEE in 2015 adopted a new IPR policy that materially changed licensing conditions, despite the opposition from large SEP holders. As a result, some studies report that a large number of companies are unwilling to license their SEP in accordance with the new IPR policy. See R Katznelson, 'The IEEE Controversial Policy on Standard Essential Patents – The Empirical Record Since Adoption' (September 2017), available at: works.bepress.com/rkatznelson/80/; K Mallinson, 'Development of Innovative New Standards Jeopardised by IEEE Patent Policy' (September 2017), available at: www.4ipcouncil.com/application/files/6015/0479/2147/Mallinson_IEEE_LOA_report.pdf; K Gupta and G Effraimidis, 'IEEE Patent Policy Revisions: An Empirical Examination of Impact' (2019) 64 *Antitrust Bulletin* 151; for contrary conclusions that the IEEE's new IPR policy had no impact on standardisation activities, see T Pohlmann, 'Empirical Study on Patenting and Standardization Activities at IEEE' (March 2017), available at: www.iplytics.com/wp-content/uploads/2018/01/IPlytics_2017_Patenting-and-standardization-activities-at-IEEE.pdf.

downward pressure on royalties, acting as a counterbalance to any potential harmful collective behaviour by standard implementers.[44] However, forcing technology developers to leave an SDO and establish proprietary solutions does not appear to be a socially desirable outcome. Permitting companies that have not developed and do not own technology to decide on its price would effectively resemble an expropriation of technology.

On the other hand, allowing SEP holders to decide on the aggregate royalty offers some benefits. Technology developers have the incentive to price reasonably, as the amount of collected royalties depends on a standard's successful adoption in the market. Also, it would generally be easier to reach a consensus among a more uniform group, although SEP owners themselves likewise have different business models depending on whether they are only upstream technology developers or are vertically integrated companies. The Commission's SEP Expert Group recommends that, as a first step, SEP owners should internally agree on a reasonable aggregate royalty for a standard for different product categories and then, as a second step, consult with implementers.[45] This seems a reasonable approach as the ultimate decision is on the SEP owners who should consider inputs from implementers in order to arrive at a widely accepted price.

Once the aggregate royalty for a standard is agreed, the second issue is how to distribute the overall royalty among SEP owners. Contreras proposes a 'pseudo-pool' approach where total royalties would be divided by a simple number of SEPs that each company holds (ie, numerical proportionality), subject to an over-declaration penalty.[46] Any person could challenge the essentiality of declared SEPs and, if it is successfully determined that a SEP is not essential, then the patent holder's share in the aggregate royalty would be reduced.[47] Under this approach, SEP holders would still need to bilaterally negotiate licences with all interested implementers and only SEP holders with concluded licences would be granted a share in the aggregate royalty.[48] On the other hand, Régibeau, De Coninck and Zenger suggest simply leaving the division of royalties to bilateral negotiations between patent holders and implementers.[49] An established aggregate royalty cap increases the transparency and predictability in licensing and would help the parties assess the reasonableness of individual licensing proposals.[50] An aggregate royalty cap would also assist courts in determining FRAND royalties, especially if they apply the top-down approach. As a supplement, they propose undertaking essentiality checks of a random sample of patents in a portfolio to determine

[44] Contreras, 'Aggregated Royalties' (n 34) 707.

[45] Baron et al (n 4) 105–07.

[46] J Contreras, 'Fixing FRAND: A Pseudo-Pool Approach to Standards-Based Patent Licensing' (2013) 79 *Antitrust Law Journal* 47, 78–83.

[47] ibid, 82.

[48] ibid, 80–81.

[49] Régibeau, De Coninck and Zenger (n 8) 85.

[50] ibid.

the proportion of truly essential patents.[51] Knowing the number of truly essential patents in a portfolio, together with knowing the aggregate royalty cap, would help both courts and parties in arriving at a FRAND royalty rate.

Individual valuations of the quality and strengths of SEP portfolios seems like a better approach, but shortcomings of individual bilateral licensing remain. In individual negotiations parties can evaluate the portfolio based on the estimated strength of SEPs, taking into account parts of the standard they claim (mandatory portions being more valuable than optional ones or key technologies in a standard being more valuable than others), estimates of a SEP's validity and essentiality, the number of forward citations and the number and quality of standard contributions made during the development of standard.[52] Each of these factors taken together can help approximate the value of an individual SEP portfolio. Numerical proportionality, while simpler to apply, does not adequately reflect the value of a SEP portfolio and may disincentivise participation in standard-development and contribution of the most valuable technologies in a standard.[53]

Nevertheless, individual bilateral negotiations in IoT with many new companies and industries needing to take a licence may not be a feasible solution. While transparency in a standard's aggregate price will indeed bring some clarity and allow predictability to implementers who could plan the costs of a standard's use in their business plans, individual disputes about reasonableness of SEP owner's offers would inevitably remain, as well as market distortions arising from the impossibility to individually license all implementers in different IoT markets.

D. Global Rate-Setting Tribunals

As seen in chapter eight, SEP disputes are global and are often litigated across many jurisdictions. National courts are increasingly willing to act as a sole venue for resolving all litigation by setting the terms of a global FRAND licence and consolidating jurisdiction by issuing anti-suit or anti-anti suit injunctions. The situation is leading to forum shopping and a race to the most favourable court. As a solution, the use of different alternative dispute resolution mechanisms is suggested to resolve a global dispute between the parties.

Arbitration is already at the disposal should parties wish to resolve their case that way. The World Intellectual Property Organization (WIPO) has a dedicated Arbitration and Mediation Centre for FRAND disputes and Munich IP Dispute Resolution Forum is also specialised in FRAND litigation.[54] Voluntary arbitration is encouraged by authorities and commentators alike because parties can resolve

[51] ibid, 60–61.
[52] See ch 4, section II on SEP valuation techniques.
[53] ibid.
[54] WIPO, 'Guidance on WIPO FRAND Alternative Dispute Resolution' (2017).

their disputes faster and with fewer costs than with a global national litigation.[55] Indeed, many SEP disputes are already resolved through arbitration, although because of the confidential nature of arbitration there is no reliable statistical evidence of its use.[56] However, for various reasons parties may disagree on arbitration – conflicts may arise on the selection of arbitration rules, the appointment of arbitrators, the choice of applicable law and issues to be arbitrated. Because of the inability to agree on precise issues to be arbitrated, national litigation may be inevitable. Some SDOs have imposed mandatory arbitration,[57] but this option appears not to be widely supported by the industry,[58] and opens important questions regarding a fundamental right to access to court since a patent's validity can only be ultimately decided by a court, entails a loss of freedom over licensing and raises concerns over potential gamesmanship before arbitral tribunals, all of which would negatively impact standardisation.[59] Thus, arbitration should remain strictly voluntary and its speed and cost-effectiveness may often incentivise parties to confer the resolution of their FRAND licensing dispute to international arbitration institutions.

In the alternative, it is suggested that it might be better to set up a specialised international FRAND tribunal tasked with determining the terms of a global FRAND licence.[60] Contreras proposes the introduction of a FRAND rate-setting tribunal before SDOs that would be tasked with setting the aggregate royalty rate for the standard and apportioning royalties among all SEP owners.[61] In this version, a FRAND tribunal would not be limited only to parties initiating the proceedings. Arbitrators would be determining both an aggregate rate for a standard as well as an individual allocation of that aggregate royalty to each SEP owner.[62] While this approach in one step resolves all SEP pricing issues within the industry, such wide powers vested into one tribunal open an important question about its usability

[55] Commission 'Setting Out the EU Approach to Standard Essential Patents' (n 8) 11; Japan Patent Office, 'Guide to Licensing Negotiations Involving Standard Essential Patents' (5 June 2018) 19–20, available at: www.jpo.go.jp/e/support/general/sep_portal/document/index/guide-seps-en.pdf; J Contreras and D Newman, 'Developing a Framework for Arbitrating Standard-Essential Patent Disputes' (2014) 1 *Journal of Dispute Resolution* 23; M Lemley and C Shapiro, 'A Simple Approach to Setting Reasonable Royalties for Standard-Essential Patents' (2013) 28 *Berkeley Technology Law Journal* 1135.

[56] D Geradin, 'FRAND Arbitration: The Determination of Fair, Reasonable and Non-discriminatory Rates for SEPs by Arbitral Tribunals' (15 September 2016) *CPI Antitrust Chronicle* 1.

[57] VITA, VSO Policies and Procedures (n 22) 10.5.

[58] Régibeau, De Coninck and Zenger (n 8) 74 ('While the majority of respondents seem to be favourable to the introduction of arbitration mechanisms, few appear ready to support making them mandatory').

[59] Geradin (n 56) 5; P Larouche, J Padilla and R Taffet, 'Settling FRAND Disputes: Is Mandatory Arbitration a Reasonable and Nondiscriminatory Alternative? (2014) 10 *Journal of Competition Law & Economics* 581, 584; G Sidak, 'Mandating Final-Offer Arbitration of FRAND Royalties for Standard-Essential Patents' (2014) 18 *Stanford Technology Law Review* 1.

[60] J Contreras, 'Global Rate Setting: A Solution for Standards-Essential Patents?' (2019) 94 *Washington Law Review* 701; R Ghafele, 'Global Licensing on FRAND Terms in Light of *Unwired Planet v Huawei*' (2020) 24 *UCLA Journal of Law & Technology* 1.

[61] Contreras, 'Global Rate Setting' (n 60) 738.

[62] ibid, 741.

and acceptance. SDO members would be unlikely to accept a tribunal with *erga omnes* powers reaching beyond the parties to the dispute. Additionally, with no right to appeal and no universally accepted methodology for determining FRAND rates its reception by the industry is questionable. Moreover, the validity and infringement of patents can only be determined by courts and it's unclear how the result of patent litigation would feed into a tribunal's rate setting. Such a wide-ranging FRAND rate-setting tribunal would effectively leave SEP owners with no control over licensing.

Another suggestion by Ghafele is to set up an international tribunal by an international treaty tasked with determining a global FRAND rate.[63] Such a tribunal would determine a global FRAND rate only between the parties and would gather information on patents' validity, essentiality and infringement from national courts to be used in royalty calculations. This is a more elegant approach, where we would have one global system for determining a FRAND rate with a dialogue with national courts over patent matters. However, waiting for an international treaty may take too long to provide a viable solution to present IoT SEP disputes.

If and until international FRAND rate-setting systems are established, a short-term solution is for parties to aim to agree to arbitration for resolving the terms of a global FRAND licence. In the meantime, a more efficient private ordering solution should be sought as, arguably, leaving the decision on royalty rates to courts or arbitrators should be the last resort. Collective licensing models via patent pools would provide more efficient licensing, greater price transparency and certainty, and consequently fewer individual disputes over licensing terms. The formation and suitability of collective licensing of SEPs for IoT will be examined below.

III. Collective Licensing Models for the Internet of Things

The complex IoT environment calls into question current bilateral SEP licensing models used in the ICT industry. Many companies from different IoT industries will need to take a licence not only for cellular but many other IoT-related standards. It would be impossible for SEP owners to individually conclude licences with all IoT implementers across many different industries. Transactions costs would be prohibitively high as SEP owners would need to have a special licensing programme for each industry or product, must identify and negotiate licences with each implementer and monitor the compliance. Implementers would be

[63] Ghafele (n 60).

rightfully reluctant to take licences if they are not assured that their competitors will be licensed as well. Measures described above, such as making SEP disclosures more specific, introducing essentiality checks and agreements on the aggregate price of a standard will make the SEP landscape more transparent but will not make SEP licensing more efficient. If bilateral licensing was the norm in the ICT, a solution to the challenges and changed environment of the IoT can be collective licensing. Namely, SEP owners could converge to form patent pools which would simplify and smooth out licensing. The next section describes the possibility of using collective licensing in the IoT and makes suggestions for overcoming some of the obstacles in their formation.

A. Patent Pools for the IoT

A standard-based patent pool is an arrangement among SEP owners to assemble a package of SEPs and jointly license them under common terms and condition to themselves and to third parties.[64] Historically, patent pools have been around since the nineteenth century as a private ordering solution to patent thickets caused by mutually blocking patents and were a way to overcome expensive patent litigation.[65] The first documented patent pool from 1856 related to sewing machines and was formed after protracted 'sewing machine patent wars' between four sewing machine patentees, which agreed to cross-license each other's patents and offered a joint licence to their patent portfolio to third parties.[66] In 1917, a patent pool in the aviation industry was formed under explicit US government influence to facilitate the production of military aircraft during the First World War.[67] Before its formation, a patent war was raging between the Wright Brothers and the Curtis Company effectively blocking the building of new aeroplanes. Other pools soon followed, ranging from steel-making, farming tools, automobiles, radio and oil refining, to name a few.[68] Thus, patent pools have a long history of being used as a mechanism to clear blocking patent rights, reduce litigation and secure freedom to operate.

[64] See Baron et al (n 4) 150; Commission, 'Guidelines on the Application of Article 101 of the Treaty on the Functioning of the European Union to Technology Transfer Agreements' (Communication) [2014] OJ C 89/03 (Technology Transfer Guidelines) 244; US DOJ and FTC: Promoting Innovation and Competition (n 20) 64.

[65] C Shapiro, 'Navigating the Patent Thicket: Cross Licensing, Patent Pools, and Standard Setting' (2000) 1 *Innovation Policy and the Economy* 119.

[66] A Mossoff, 'The Rise and Fall of the First American Patent Thicket: The Sewing Machine War of the 1850s' (2011) 53 *Arizona Law Review* 165.

[67] M Mattioli, 'Power and Governance in Patent Pools' (2014) 27 *Harvard Journal of Law & Technology* 421, 449.

[68] ibid 463–65.

The positive side of patent pools is their efficiency in patent licensing. They reduce transaction costs by offering a 'one-stop-shop' to implementers who need to conclude only one licence for a patent portfolio, instead of bilaterally negotiating and paying royalties separately to each patent owner. Merges and Mattioli estimate that the transaction cost savings of pool licensing are significant.[69] With an average estimated cost of negotiating a patent licence of at least $50,000, and often higher especially if there is litigation, they calculate that patent pools for MPEG and HEVC standards have saved approximately $600 million and $400 million respectively in transaction costs.[70] Another positive aspect of standard-related pools is the transparency and predictability they bring to SEP licensing – a pool's royalty provides an estimate of the aggregate royalty for a standard; the mandatory essentiality checks of patents included in a pool weeds out non-essential patents; the publication of SEPs included in a pool enables licensees to verify whether they are infringing patents; and the publication of uniform licensing terms promotes non-discriminatory licensing.[71] Moreover, pools are also said to reduce litigation and encourage research and development.[72]

Having said that, patent pools may also have negative effects. If pools include substitute patents, ie, patents covering technologies that are competing alternatives, it will lead to a loss of competition and amount to a price-fixing cartel.[73] However, this is rarely a concern in standard-related pools as SEPs are by definition complementary patents, and pools of complementary patents are shown to resolve royalty stacking and double-marginalisation, leading to overall lower royalties than when complementary patents are priced separately.[74] With standard-related pools, the primary concern is of potential collusion between SEP owners who may use patent pools as a vehicle for price restrictions and outpost limitations.[75] Exclusivity arrangements in pool licences may also be used to strengthen a pool's market power and reduce innovation incentives by licensees. Indeed, it seems that early patent pools were thinly disguised cartels consisting of substitute patents,

[69] R Merges and M Mattioli, 'Measuring the Costs and Benefits of Patent Pools' (2017) 78 *Ohio State Law Journal* 281.

[70] ibid, 322.

[71] Baron et al (n 4) 153.

[72] Shapiro, 'Navigating the Patent Thicket' (n 65).

[73] R Gilbert, 'Antitrust for Patent Pools: A Century of Policy Evolution' (2004) *Stanford Technology Law Review* 3 (describing the history of US antitrust policy towards patent pools); E Hovenkamp and H Hovenkamp, 'Patent Pools and Related Technology Sharing' in R Blair, D Sokol (eds), *The Cambridge Handbook of Antitrust, Intellectual Property, and High Tech* (Cambridge University Press 2017).

[74] J Lerner and J Tirole, 'Efficient Patent Pools' (2014) 94 *The American Economic Review* 691, 706; R Gilbert, 'Collective Rights Organizations: A Guide to Benefits, Costs and Antitrust Safeguards' in J Contreras (ed) *The Cambridge Handbook of Technical Standardization Law: Competition, Antitrust and Patents* (Cambridge University Press 2018) 133.

[75] Hovenkamp and Hovenkamp (n 73); US Department of Justice and the Federal Trade Commission, 'Antitrust Guidelines for the Licensing of Intellectual Property' (2017) 30 ('when cross-licensing or pooling arrangements are mechanisms to accomplish naked price-fixing or market division, they are subject to challenge under the per se rule').

harming innovation.[76] Thus, safeguards should be included to prevent sharing of sensitive information, screening exclusivity clauses for potential anti-competitive effects and promoting independent licensing by pool members.[77]

Another argument against pools is that they shield weak patents from challenges as potential licensees have reduced incentives to test their validity.[78] While this may be a problem in smaller non-standard related pools, in ICT standard pools consisting of thousands of patents it is quite possible that some are invalid, which is reflected in the royalty rate that accounts for the probability of the invalidity of some patents. Therefore, challenging only a few patents from a portfolio of thousands would have no impact on overall royalties.[79] To have an impact, a prospective licensee would have to invalidate a large number of patents in a portfolio, which may make sense only in a smaller patent pool. For example, in a patent pool with only 10 patents, invalidating seven might indeed impact royalties downwards. However, as an alternative to costly patent litigation parties may simply negotiate the probability of invalidity into the royalty rate. Thus, Hovenkamp and Hovenkamp compared pool licensing to a restaurant buffet.[80] For a single price, parties gain access to the whole portfolio of pooled patents: some are used by one licensee and some are not. In other words, the price of a pool's licence does not reflect the value of all pooled patents.[81] This is true especially in relation to standards where a pool would determine the aggregate royalty based on the value the standard brings to end products, regardless of the value of individual SEPs. Thus, identifying the number of truly valid patents is more of a concern for licensors in their internal division of a pool's licensing revenues than to licensees, as will be explained below.

Overall, standard-related pools consisting of complementary patents are seen in a positive light. The US and EU competition authorities produced guidelines for assessing the conditions for pool formation that will not raise competition

[76] R Lampe and P Moser, 'Do Patent Pools Encourage Innovation? Evidence from the Nineteenth-Century Sewing Machine Industry' (2010) 70 *Journal of Economic History* 898 (finding that following the formation of a sewing machine pool, patenting relating to lockstitch sewing methods fell relative to patenting on alternative swing technologies); R Lampe and P Moser, 'Do Patent Pools Encourage Innovation? Evidence from 20 US Industries Under the New Deal' (2012) NBER Working Paper 18316 (examining the effects of pools on innovation in 20 industries from 1921 to 1948 and finding a decline in patenting after the creation of a pool compared with the rate of patenting in similar industries that did not participate in the pool. The negative effects are explained by pools combining substitute patents, which would now be challenged as cartels).

[77] J Lerner and J Tirole, 'The Design of Patent Pools: The Determinants of Licensing Rules' (2007) 38 *RAND Journal of Economics* 610; Commission, Technology Transfer Guidelines (n 64) 248–61.

[78] J-P Choi, 'Patent Pools and Cross Licensing in the Shadow of Patent Litigation' (2010) 51 *International Economic Review* 441; J-P Choi and H Gerlach, 'Patent Pools, Litigation and Innovation' (2015) 46 *RAND Journal of Economics* 499.

[79] R Gilbert, 'The Essentiality Test for Patent Pools' in R Dreyfuss, D Zimmerman and H First (eds), *Working Within the Boundaries of Intellectual Property* (Oxford University Press, 2010); Hovenkamp and Hovenkamp (n 73).

[80] Hovenkamp and Hovenkamp (n 73) 367.

[81] ibid.

concerns.[82] Common principles include: (i) that patents included in a pool must be essential and an independent mechanism for verification of essentiality must be established; (ii) safeguards must be included to ensure that exchange of sensitive information is restricted; (iii) pooled patents should be licensed into the pool on a non-exclusive basis and licensed out of the pool on FRAND terms; (iv) independent licensing by pool members must be allowed; (v) grant-back clauses should be limited only to essential patents and parties must remain free to develop competing technologies; and (vi) licensors and licensees should remain free to challenge the validity and essentiality of pooled patents. Patent pools formed in accordance with these criteria will normally not be challenged by the competition authorities.

Many successful patent pools have been formed for consumer electronic standards in accordance with the above competition requirements. Baron and Pohlmann document 50 patent pools relating to CD, DVD and Blue Ray standards, audio-visual standards (AVC), MPEG, MP3, H.264 and DVB digital video standards.[83] Most standard pools are run by a few independent administrators, such as Via Licensing, MPEG LA and Sisvel. While these pools often do not cover the totality of SEP owners and SEPs,[84] they have generally been regarded as successful in facilitating licensing and ensuring smoother use of standards in downstream products.

Nevertheless, patent pools to date have not been widely used in relation to connectivity standards and the majority of ITC-related standards are not licensed in a pool. One study found that only 9 per cent of worldwide declared SEPs are licensed in a pool,[85] while another established that only 3 per cent of interoperability standards in an average laptop are pooled.[86] Some initiatives to establish wider pools for cellular standards did not gain sufficient tracking. Back in 2002, 3GPP aimed to establish a licensing platform for five competing 3G standards designed to provide a voluntary, cost-effective mechanism for evaluating,

[82] Commission, Technology Transfer Guidelines (n 64) 248–61; Department of Justice, Letter from Joel Klein, Assistant Attorney General to Gerrard Beeney (26 June 1997) (MPEG-LA Business Review Letter); Department of Justice, Letter from Joel Klein, Assistant Attorney General to Gerrard Beeney (16 December 1998) (DVD3 Business Review Letter); Department of Justice, Letter from Joel Klein, Assistant Attorney General to Carey Ramos (10 June 1999) (DVD6 Business Review Letter); Department of Justice, Letter from Charles James, Assistant Attorney General to Ky Ewing (12 November 2002) (3GPP Partnership Business Review Letter); Department of Justice, Letter from Makan Delrahim, Assistant Attorney General to Mark Hamer (28 July 2020) (Avanci Business Review Letter); Department of Justice and the Federal Trade Commission, 'Antitrust Guidelines for the Licensing of Intellectual Property' (2017) 30.

[83] J Baron and T Pohlmann, 'The Effect of Patent Pools on Patenting and Innovation – Evidence from Contemporary Technology Standards' (2015) Working Paper 4–5.

[84] A Layne-Farrar and J Lerner, 'To Join or Not to Join: Examining Patent Pool Participation and Rent Sharing Rules' (2011) 29 *International Journal of Industrial Organization* 294 (finding that between 30% and 60% participation in surveyed pools).

[85] Pohlmann and Blind (n 1) 36–37.

[86] B Biddle, A White and S Woods, 'How Many Patents in a Laptop (and other empirical questions)?' (2010), available at: papers.ssrn.com/sol3/papers.cfm?abstract-id=1619440.

certifying and licensing SEPs.[87] There would be five separate platforms for five distinct 3G standards that would identify, evaluate and certify the essentiality of SEPs and would provide a mechanism for licensors and licensees to enter into bilateral licences. It was thus not a pool in a sense that it would aggregate SEPs and license them collectively in a package, as SEPs would still be licensed bilaterally, but it aimed to facilitate and ease SEP licensing. However, the 3GPP licensing platform failed to gain much traction among SEP owners and licensees and ultimately only two versions of 3G standard prevailed. Other pools also failed to attract a sufficient number of SEP owners and SEPs. For example, Sisvel and Via Licensing both manage pools for IEEE's 802.11 (Wi-Fi) and 4G LTE standards, but they include only a fraction of the overall SEP coverage. More recently, Avanci is a pool that gathers 2G, 3G and 4G SEPs for licensing specifically in the IoT. It currently provides a licensing programme for connected vehicles with more programmes for different IoT uses and 5G SEPs expected in the future. It offers a per-unit royalty rate of $15 for 2G/3G/4G SEPs which has been guaranteed to stay the same no matter how many SEP owners join the pool. Avanci is precisely a pool that would fit the IoT environment, but it remains to be seen how it will be received by the market.

What are the reasons for the failure of pools to take off for connectivity and wider ICT standards? It contradicts the theory predicting that strong patent rights and high transaction costs would lead individual patent owners to form collective licensing organisations.[88] The lack of interest in pool licensing can be explained by several factors. First, in the smartphone industry there was relatively small number of market players consisting of many vertically integrated companies that cross-licensed each other's portfolios. Thus, the licensing costs did not outweigh the benefits of cross-licensing and individually negotiated transactions. Second, setting up a patent pool is costly. As seen, independent essentiality checks are necessary to filter out truly essential patents to be included in a pool. A full essentiality check would cost approx. €10,000 per patent and one study estimated that a thorough essentiality check of 2G, 3G and 4G SEPs declared at ETSI would cost at least €27.5 million.[89] Merges and Mattioli calculate that the costs of an essentiality test for an MPEG pool operated by Via Licensing amounted to $5,25 million.[90] Thus, the high upfront costs act as a barrier to wider pool formation. Finally, the heterogenous interests of SEP owners are the major reason for the failure to agree on pool licensing. Generally, we can distinguish between two

[87] D Choumelova, 'Competition Law Analysis of Patent Licensing Arrangements – The Particular Case of 3G3P' (2003) 1 *Competition Policy Newsletter*; 3GPP Partnership Business Review Letter (n 82).

[88] R Merges, 'Contracting Into Liability Rules: Intellectual Property Rights and Collective Rights Organizations' (1996) 84 *California Law Review* 1293.

[89] Bekkers et al (n 14) 15; Régibeau, De Coninck and Zenger (n 8) 59; Pohlmann and Blind (n 1) 50–51 (estimating costs of over €1 billion for a thorough essentiality assessment for ETSI's declared SEPs for 2G, 3G and 4G standards).

[90] Merges and Mattioli (n 69) 307.

groups of SEPs owners: vertically integrated companies that derive most of their profits from manufacturing of downstream products, and pure upstream companies engaging mainly in R&D and relying on licensing revenues.[91] Vertically integrated companies have an incentive to keep royalties as low as possible in order to reduce their own production costs, while upstream companies would tend to price higher as they rely on royalties as their primary source of income, although not too high since it would reduce demand. Thus, the two conflicting business models jeopardise successful pool creation. Layne-Farrar and Lerner show that formed pools are largely compromised of vertically integrated companies, while the majority of upstream companies stayed outside the pool.[92] The division of a pool's royalty also affects participation as treating all patents as having the same value discourages firms with more valuable patents from joining and incentivises firms to inflate the number of patents in order to receive a larger share in the overall royalty.[93] Therefore, more creative rules would have to be devised to appreciate the difference in the value of patents and persuade upstream firms to join.

However, the environment in the IoT will bring changes that may facilitate the greater use of pool licensing. With many diverse IoT sectors using standards and needing to take a licence, the majority of SEP owners from the ICT sector will find themselves being only upstream companies. It would simply be impossible for ICT SEP owners to be present in all IoT sectors. For example, a SEP owner that is also a smartphone manufacturer may, perhaps, produce smart TVs or connected refrigerators, but it is unlikely that it would also be producing connected cars, connected medical equipment or smart industrial manufacturing machines. The importance of cross-licensing will consequently diminish. Thus, the interests of SEP owners can converge as in the IoT they will all, to a certain degree, be upstream companies. This could make it easier to reach an agreement on the level of royalty and the appropriate royalty allocation mechanism. The next section will describe in more detail the ways to overcome the difficulties in pool formation.

i. Overcoming the Obstacles in Pool Formation

This section provides some suggestions in facilitating pool formations in the IoT. A pool can either be formed for specific standards, for example 5G, Wi-Fi, or it can be formed for a specific product covering all or many standards used by such products.[94] A pool for one standard could be easier to set up and negotiate than a pool consisting of many different standards, although only the latter creates a true

[91] R Aoki and S Nagaoka, 'The Consortium Standards and Patent Pools' (2004) 55 *Economic Review* 345; also ch 1, section II.B.

[92] Layne-Farrar and Lerner (n 84).

[93] Aoki and Nagaoka (n 91) 353 ('requiring all members of the pool to be treated equally could be a source of patent pool's failure').

[94] Baron et al (n 4) 171.

'one-stop-shop' for implementers who would need to transact with just one pool to clear all standard-related IP rights for the production of a particular product. Whichever model is chosen, the following guiding principles could be used to facilitate pool creation.

a. Assembling a Critical Number of Upstream Companies is Sufficient

A pool does not necessarily need to include all SEP owners and SEPs in order to be successful. Only a critical mass of upstream SEP owners is required to reap the benefits of transaction cost savings, predictability and transparency of SEP licensing. Mattioli, for instance, shows that slightly fragmentary patent markets are preferable to 'grand coalitions' of all patent owners.[95] This is because a unified pool would need to induce outsiders to join by offering them royalties equal or greater than the royalties outsiders already collected independently. To do that, a unified pool would need to raise royalty across the board for all other members as well. In other words, a unified pool would charge a higher rate than the sum of individual rates that a licensee would pay to a partially complete pool and to outsiders.[96] The ability of pool outsiders to free ride on the pool and demand higher royalties than they otherwise would as members of the pool, upsetting the transaction cost savings that the pool provides, is mitigated by the fact that licensing takes place 'in the shadow' of the pool.[97] Namely, the pool's royalty creates a powerful signal to the market on the value of patents inside the pool as well as to patents outside the pool.[98] Thus, licensees may resist an outsider's demands that deviate too much from a pool and courts may use a pool's royalty in their FRAND determinations.

Mattioli illustrates with examples from MPEG-2 and DVD pools. When the MPEG-2 pool was created under the management of MPEG LA, two companies, Alcatel-Lucent and Thomson, decided to remain outside the pool.[99] Their reason for staying out of the pool was the fact that they had already developed independent licensing programmes and believed they had more valuable patents, thus hoping to generate higher royalty income by staying outside the pool. However, while MPEG LA achieved wide success with licensees, Alcatel-Lucent and Thomson failed to convince prospective licensees that they had more valuable portfolios than MPEG LA's and later rejoined the pool.[100] Licensing of the DVD standard was also split between two pools – DVD3C consisting of Sony, Philips and Pioneer, and DVD6C including Hitachi, Matsushita, Mitsubishi, Time Warner, Toshiba and the Victor Company – and one outsider, Thomson.[101] The division of royalties was the

[95] M Mattioli, 'Patent Pool Outsiders' (2018) 33 *Berkeley Technology Law Journal* 233.
[96] ibid, 240.
[97] ibid, 233.
[98] ibid, 238.
[99] ibid, 266–67.
[100] ibid, 266–71.
[101] ibid, 275.

main obstacle for forming a unified pool: SEP owners were split whether to treat each SEP equally and adopt a numerical proportionality method or devise a more complex value-based mechanism for division of royalties.[102] However, despite fragmentation, Mattioli found that three licensors requested royalties that resulted in roughly comparable rates relative to the number of licensed patent-families.[103] He explains this result by the mutual awareness of SEP owners that the aggregate licensing costs could not be too high, and licensors set their royalties in relation to one another.[104]

The takeaway is that a unified pool of all SEP owners is not a necessary precondition for successful licensing in the IoT. It may actually be damaging to implementers as such a pool would have to charge the highest possible rate in order to attract all SEP owners. Imposing mandatory pool participation would also not be desirable as voluntary participation is the best guarantee of a pool's pro-competitive effects. Making pool participation mandatory may lead to internal gamesmanship and coalitions of pool members imposing rules in their favour, from decisions on the aggregate royalty rate, the formula for division of royalties, to a pool's licensing terms. A large number of vertically integrated SEP owners could outvote upstream companies and impose terms that fail to adequately compensate for R&D and which harm future innovation incentives. Preventing anti-competitive outcomes of mandatory pool participation would require carefully designing internal pool rules together with government authorities, requiring even more regulatory involvement in technology markets.

A successful IoT standard pool requires only a sufficient number of upstream SEP owners. Since upstream SEP owners are primarily interested in actively monetising SEPs and relying on licensing income, only by having a critical number of them could a pool achieve a market-signalling function and provide transaction costs savings to licensees. Licensees would be protected as companies that are mostly interested in enforcing SEPs will be aggregated in one pool. Some vertically integrated companies may stay outside the pool, but that would not be damaging to the overall success of the pool, as such companies may not be interested in actively enforcing SEPs in the first place and may rather keep them for defensive purposes or cross-licensing. In case they do decide to enforce SEPs, a pool's royalty would present a strong signal to the market and courts on the aggregate value of the standard and individual value of a SEP owner's portfolio.

We may be seeing a move in this direction already. The Avanci pool appears to have gathered all major upstream SEP owners and has wide enough coverage It has about 50–75 per cent of SEPs.[105] Although some important vertically integrated SEP owners are currently outside the pool, they have not yet been active in

[102] ibid.
[103] ibid, 276.
[104] ibid, 279.
[105] Avanci Business Review Letter (n 82) 3.

licensing SEPs in the IoT. Thus, given the large number of upstream SEP owners, Avanci's aggregate rate for cellular standards can be expected to have an important signalling effect on the market.

b. Pool Royalty to Induce Pool Participation and Prevent Free Riding

A pool's royalty should be set high enough to discourage independent licensing and facilitate upstream SEP owners to join the pool. Setting a low royalty is shown to discourage participation of upstream SEP owners,[106] preventing the pool from reaching a critical level of upstream SEP owners necessary for successful market acceptance. Low royalty, in fact, encourages independent licensing outside the pool which Gilbert refers to as 'headroom holdup'.[107] Namely, pool outsiders could charge a higher royalty because the pool has lowered the royalty or reduced transaction costs for other SEPs, leaving more value available to outsiders.[108] Therefore, we should allow the pool to set the royalty higher on the level that would encourage participation of upstream SEP owners and disincentivise free riding.

Just how 'high' royalty should be and whether it is too high is naturally subjective, but some guiding principles can be provided. The overall royalty should still be FRAND, meaning that the principles of FRAND royalty from chapter four can be used. In any case, the royalty should be determined in relation to the value that the standard brings to end products and consumers. Since there will be many different IoT devices and uses of the standard, different royalties should be set for different IoT uses. SEP owners may engage in consultations with implementers to better understand a particular industry and get a sense of how the standard is being used by different devices and the distinct value it generates. A wider market acceptance of licensing terms by implementers would signal that terms are indeed FRAND.[109] Finally, whether the royalty is too high should be compared with the alternative of having disaggregated licensing, an unknown aggregate price of the standard and the transaction costs of bilateral licensing. As shown, transaction costs savings and the ease of one-stop-shop licensing from pools are significant.[110]

[106] Layne-Farrar and Lerner (n 84).

[107] R Gilbert, 'Ties that Bind: Policies to Promote (Good) Patent Pools' (2011) 77 *Antitrust Law Journal* 1, 31.

[108] ibid.

[109] German courts ruled that terms offered by patent pools MPEG LA and HEVC Advance for video coding standards, AVC/H.264 and HEVC respectively are FRAND because standard pool licensing terms have been accepted by a large number of licensees. See *Tagivan (MPEG-LA) v Huawei*, 4a O 17/15 Düsseldorf Regional Court (15 November 2018); *HEVC (Dolby) v MAS Elektronik*, 4c 0 44/18 Düsseldorf Regional Court (7 May 2020).

[110] Merges and Mattioli (n 69).

c. Division of Royalties

The most important and contentions issue in pool formation is how to a divide pool's royalty among members. The reason why many pools failed to take off is related to difficulties in reaching an agreement between members on the precise formula for the allocation of royalties.[111] The simplest method is to use numerical proportionality which treats every patent equally and divides royalty based on the proportional share of SEPs the company owns. Layne-Farrar and Lerner show that six out of nine pools in their study adopted a numerical proportionality method, covering standards such as MPEG, WCDMA, ACV, DVB and 1394.[112] The advantage is the simplicity in application: it lowers transaction costs of negotiating and applying more complex formulas and is generally useful for vertically integrated companies and companies with symmetrical portfolios.[113] Another argument is that, by definition, if a patent is truly essential it must be used by all licensees and treating every SEP equally prevents discrimination among SEP owners. Moreover, in the eyes of a licensee every SEP is equal as the infringement of any one can prevent standard-implementing products being sold on the market.

However, there are serious disadvantages to the numerical proportionality method. As explained above, not all patents have the same value.[114] SEPs that read on core (mandatory) features of a standard contribute more to the value of the standard than SEPs that read on optional or peripheral features. Economists have long found that only a relatively small number of patents provide the most value. The numerical proportionality rule creates perverse incentives for members to 'game the system' by patenting aggressively for narrower and more incremental patents in order to increase their share in the overall royalty. For instance, Baron and Delcamp have found that after formation, pool members introduce patents that are increasingly narrow, incremental and insignificant over time,[115] meaning that pool members are aware that the number of patents impacts their royalty distribution and are actively seeking to inflate their share. Members can also try to increase their share by filing as many divisional or continuation patents as possible. Consequently, a pool with numerical proportionality rules would be more likely to attract narrow and incremental SEPs rather than more valuable or breakthrough innovation. The numerical proportionality method would also not be attractive to upstream firms and companies believing they have more valuable portfolios.[116] Finally, the system of allocating pool royalties according to the simple number of patents may also be detrimental to innovation as companies may under-invest in the quality of the standard if they are unable to obtain an appropriate return on R&D efforts.[117]

[111] Mattioli, 'Patent Pool Outsiders' (n 95).
[112] Layne-Farrar and Lerner (n 84) 296.
[113] ibid, 295.
[114] See ch 4, section II.B.
[115] J Baron and H Delcamp, 'The Strategies of Patent Introduction into Patent Pools' (2015) 24 *Economics of Innovation and New Technology* 776, 777.
[116] Layne-Farrar and Lerner (n 84) 299.
[117] Aoki and Nagaoka (n 91) 353.

Another option is to adopt value proportionality rules that specify a formula for the division of royalties that seeks to award a larger share to members with more valuable contributions. This method is generally fairer as it assigns a large share to more valuable patents, providing adequate innovation incentives and is, thus, more attractive to upstream companies. However, the main problem is the higher costs of agreeing on and implementing more complex royalty-sharing rules. Parties would need to reach an agreement on the factors to include in the royalty-division formula, which may not be a straightforward task, and also undertake an assessment of the quality of pooled patents in addition to already expensive essentiality tests. However, as examples below will show it is not impossible to create and apply such rules.

Some pools have adopted different value proportionality rules in the division of a pool's royalties. For example, the DVD6 pool which gathered six licensors for the DVD standard had a royalty allocation formula that took into account not only the number of patents, but also how often SEPs are infringed by a licensee's products, the age of patents and whether SEPs relate to optional or mandatory features of the standard.[118] The formula also took into account the fluctuations in the number of SEPs owned by a licensor; some SEPs will be removed from the portfolio due to expiration or if an independent expert determines that a patent is no longer essential, while new SEPs can also be added into a portfolio.[119] One Blue patent pool for Blue Ray technology also adopted the value proportionality formula. It recognised that some patents are more valuable than others and wanted to ensure that members do not skew the royalty distribution by filing as many divisional or continuation patents as possible.[120] Consequently, it introduced a cap for divisional or continuation patents for royalty-sharing purposes and adopted a rule under which the total weighting of all divisionals and continuations could not exceed the weighting of parent patents.[121] Additionally, it distinguished between SEPs that read on different parts of the standard. A physical format invention represents the core of Blue Ray technology, requires more costly research, and is used all the time in a product other than an application of format technology which is often used only incidentally.[122] Thus, One Blue pool gives more weight to physical format patents than to application format patents. Finally, Avanci, a patent pool for licensing SEPs in the IoT also has a unique royalty distribution formula. Avanci takes four factors into account: the first is the number of confirmed SEPs with a cap on the maximum number of points in this category.[123] A cap is intended to incentivise companies to submit as many SEPs as possible but also encourages small licensors to join as they would be able to realise a meaningful

[118] DVD6 Business Review Letter (n 82) 7.

[119] ibid.

[120] R Peters, 'One-Blue: A Blueprint for Patent Pools in High-Tech' (2011) (September/October) *Intellectual Asset Management* 38, 40.

[121] ibid, 41.

[122] ibid.

[123] Avanci Business Review Letter (n 82) 6.

share in royalty distribution and would not be overrun by large SEP owners. The cap also discourages 'gaming the system' tactics of filing as many divisional and continuation patents as possible to increase the number of patents in a portfolio. The second factor is historical licensing revenue earned outside the pool which is intended to ensure that upstream SEP owners with developed independent licensing programmes also join the pool.[124] Next, the formula takes into account contributions made during the development of the standard as one of the proxies for the value of a SEP portfolio.[125] Lastly, a limited number of points are awarded to licensors that enforce SEPs on behalf of the pool.[126] The idea is to reward those SEP owners that incur litigation costs on behalf of all pool members.

Therefore, some form of value proportionality method can be expected to be used in IoT-related pools. Pool members should agree on what weight to give to different SEPs by, for example, assigning different values to SEPs that read on mandatory or optional parts of the standards, making a distinction between parent patents and continuation or divisional patents, considering contributions during the development of the standard or some other factors. The more complex the value proportionality formula, the higher the start-up costs for setting up a pool, but it is arguably the only way to ensure the widest possible participation from all SEP owners. The unique position and business interests of each group of licensors should be taken into account in the royalty distribution formula. The experience of existing pools that use different value proportionality formulas is valuable in designing future IoT pools.

d. Essentiality Checks

Pools must ensure that they include only truly essential patents, but the high costs of essentiality checks are an obstacle to pool formation. The European Commission is currently considering initiatives to introduce an independent system of third-party essentiality checks, which may also be used for pools and could be a way of bringing the total costs of essentiality checks to manageable levels.[127] A study commissioned by the Commission recommended establishing a small and independent supervisory body that would define procedure, oversee the implementation and ensure the quality of essentiality tests.[128] Such a body should be self-financing and all benefiting stakeholders would contribute. If such an initiative takes off, it would provide a mechanism for essentiality checks that would split the total costs of essentiality to all users of the system.

[124] ibid.
[125] ibid.
[126] ibid.
[127] Commission, 'Making the Most of the EU's Innovative Potential: An Intellectual Property Action Plan to Support the EU's Recovery and Resilience' COM(2020) 760 final, 13; Commission 'Setting Out the EU Approach to Standard Essential Patents' (n 8) 5; Bekkers et al (n 14); Baron et al (n 4) 56.
[128] Bekkers et al (n 14) 20.

SEP owners may already use some instruments to lower the costs of essentiality checks for inclusion of patents in a pool. For example, only one patent per family can be tested and, if essentiality is confirmed, there could be a presumption of essentiality appliable to all other members of the family.[129] Since only certified SEPs are included in a pool and count in the royalty allocation formula, it would be expected that SEP owners would only test patents they are reasonably certain to be essential. In other words, many declared SEPs would be self-filtered by SEP owners. It would be expected that SEP owners will not submit patents to expensive third-party essentiality assessment unless they have first internally checked and assured that the patent is truly essential. Finally, pool members and third parties must be free to challenge the essentiality and validity of a SEP included in a pool. Pool members may actually have a bigger incentive to challenge pooled patents since the number of pooled patents influences their share of the overall royalty. Thus, while for licensees it may make no difference if only a few patents out of hundreds or thousands are invalidated or essentiality challenged, for pool members it can make a difference if the patents of an individual SEP owner are invalidated or turn out to be non-essential as that will impact the internal division of royalties. A pool may even consider setting up an internal mechanism for validity and essentiality challenges that would provide a faster resolution than courts, although a final decision would still have to be reserved for courts.

e. IoT Industry-Specific Licensing Terms

Some specific licensing features will need to apply in IoT-related pools. Namely, a pool should determine different royalty programmes for different IoT industries and product categories. In other words, price discrimination between different IoT industries and uses should be permitted. As discussed, connectivity standards will bring different values to different downstream uses.[130] For example, a connected car would use the full extent of the functionality of the 5G standard and would require uninterrupted high speeds and latency while in use, whereas, on the other hand, a smart meter will use limited functionalities of the 5G standard only to occasionally send and receive data. Consequently, connectivity chips may be designed differently for different IoT uses.[131] A chip that provides higher connectivity rates may be more complex and expensive than a chip with lower connectivity rates. This also impacts the use of SEPs, since a chip that is designed to provide only limited 5G functionality and connectivity rates may only need to implement a small subset of all the normative parts of the standard and would therefore infringe a smaller number of SEPs.[132] Therefore, pools should be free to set up different royalty programmes for different IoT industries depending on the

[129] Baron et al (n 4).
[130] See ch 5; also Baron et al (n 4) 84–94.
[131] Baron et al (n 4) 94.
[132] Bekkers et al (n 14) 112.

value that a standard brings to end-products and the extent of the use of functionalities of a standard by end-products.

Examples of such differentiated treatment already exist in practice. DVD3 and DVD6 pools had different royalty rates for DVD disks and DVD players,[133] One Blue pool maintains separate licensing programmes for Blue Ray players, PC Driver, Blue Ray software and disks.[134] In relation to cellular standard, Via Licensing has a separate 4G licensing programme for mobile devices and cars with different royalty rates,[135] and Avanci offers 2G/3G/4G portfolios for connected vehicles with the expectation of launching other IoT licensing programmes in the future.

Next, an IoT pool should decide the level of production chain for where to license a particular IoT industry or use.[136] As seen in chapter seven, licensing only at one level of the production chain is much more efficient than disbursed licensing across multiple levels. It reduces transaction costs by negotiating only with only one group of licensees and is easier to apply and monitor the compliance with licensing agreements. The precise level to choose would depend on the specifics of each IoT industry and it is possible to envisage that for some uses licensing could be done at the end-product level, while for some other industries it would be efficient to license only at a component level.[137] Some factors to take into account are the level at which most or all SEPs are implemented and the number of potential licensees, as it would be more efficient to license at a level that would exhaust all or most SEPs and where the number of licensees is lower in order to reduce transaction costs. Also, the existing business practice in a particular IoT industry should be considered since it is possible that it has already adopted the most efficient licensing model tailored to its specific circumstances. The ease of applying use-based licensing is another factor to be considered. For example, if a component maker supplies different IoT industries with connectivity chips, some tracking mechanism would be needed in order to monitor which chips goes to which use and be priced differently. If implementing a component tracking mechanism is too expensive, it might be more efficient to license at the end-device level. Conversely, if a component maker supplies connectivity chips only to one specific IoT industry it might be more efficient to license at the component level as there are generally fewer chip manufacturers, thus lowering transaction costs.

Pool members may also consider consulting with implementers in order to better understand the circumstances of each IoT industry and arrive at the most efficient and widely accepted licensing level.[138] Reaching an understanding on the

[133] DVD3 Business Review Letter (n 82) 6; DVD6 Business Review Letter (n 82) 6–7.

[134] One Blue, Royalty Rates, available at: www.one-blue.com/royalty-rates/royalty_rates.html.

[135] Via Licensing, Multi-Generational (MG) Wireless, available at: www.via-corp.com/licensing/mg-multi-generational-wireless/.

[136] Baron et al (n 4) 84.

[137] See generally, Baron et al (n 4) 80–83.

[138] ibid 86–88 (exploring possible collective negotiations frameworks).

appropriate licensing level for each IoT industry between licensors and prospective licensees would greatly reduce future licensing friction. Nevertheless, in the absence of an agreement, a pool should proceed to select the most appropriate level.

One Blue pool is an example of having different licensing levels for different uses in one pool. One Blue licenses the Blue Ray standard for different uses. For Blue Ray players and recorders, it licenses at the end-device level because they implement most of the SEP from a portfolio, which is more efficient than splitting the portfolio and licensing different parts of the SEP portfolio to various component manufacturers.[139] The end-device level licensing reduces royalty stacking as the aggregate royalty paid by Blue Ray players is lower than the aggregate royalty that component manufacturers would have to pay in case they have to conclude separate licences for different standards used in Blue Ray players.[140] On the other hand, a component-level approach was adopted for drive manufacturers and software providers in the PC industry, and disk pressers for the content industry.[141] In this case, it was more efficient to transact further up in the production chain as there were only a relative few drive makers and software producers compared with PC makers, and it was easier for them to report and pay royalties.[142] For similar reasons, a disk presser supplying Blue Ray disks to the content industry were selected. The experience of One Blue is valuable in the IoT context and demonstrates the possibility of adopting the most efficient licensing levels depending on the characteristics of a particular industry.

f. Transparency of Terms and Patents

Patent pools should be transparent on pooled SEPs and licensing terms. Transparency increases the confidence of prospective licensees in the system: it assures them that pooled SEPs are in fact being used by their products, enables planning IP costs in advance; and guarantees that the same terms will be offered to all other competitors. A pool should make public the list of pooled SEPs and summary claims charts including information on what part of the standard the SEP relates to. This would not entail additional costs as such information is already available and was submitted for the pool's essentiality check. Licensing terms should also be made public and standardised for different IoT product categories. If each prospective licensee is being offered the same terms from a publicly announced licensing programme, that would resolve many of the concerns about compliance with the non-discrimination obligation of a FRAND commitment.[143]

[139] B Heiden, J Padilla and R Peters, 'The Value of Standard Essential Patents and the Level of Licensing' (2020) 1, 26, available at: papers.ssrn.com/sol3/papers.cfm?abstract_id=3717570.

[140] ibid.

[141] ibid, 26–27.

[142] ibid.

[143] See ch 5.

Indeed, pools are typically providing such information and such a practice should be carried over into the IoT.

B. Implementers' Collective Licensing Associations

Besides SEP owners coming together and forming a pool for collective licensing of SEPs, it has been suggested that implementers could similarly form their own associations for the purpose of collectively negotiating licences with SEP owners. This would arguably additionally reduce transaction costs as SEP owners would be negotiating with a group of implementers instead of every single company from the specific IoT sector.

The European Commission's SEP Expert Group examined in depth how such collective licensing negotiation groups (LNGs) could work.[144] Members of an LNG would have to first agree among themselves about the licensed product, the licensing level and the maximum acceptable royalty.[145] Then, LNG members should authorise the LNG representative to negotiate a licence with SEP owners in accordance with the pre-agreed conditions, and LNG members should additionally commit to accepting the negotiated outcome between the LNG representative and the SEP owners and sign a licence agreement without delay.[146] However, in case they do not accept the outcome of the deal negotiated by the LNG representative, implementers should without delay enter into subsequent bilateral negotiations with SEP owners. Thus, a two-step negotiation process is envisaged: SEP owners would first negotiate with the LNG representative (after LNG members have agreed among themselves) and, if the agreement is not reached within a certain time frame, then SEP owners could approach LNG members individually.

However, the proposal for implementers coming together in LNGs and negotiating royalties with SEP owners raises serious competition and practical concerns. Namely, there is a danger of LNGs becoming a façade for buyers' cartels that would depreciate SEP royalties and, second, that LNGs would be a venue for collective holdout of implementers. As already seen in section II.C a large group of implementers negotiating licence rates with SEP holders has an incentive to collectively exert anti-competitive pressure to depress royalties below a reasonable level and refuse licensing even at most reasonable rates unless SEP owners agree on their proposals. It is plausible to envisage that the maximum acceptable royalty for LNG members could be lower than the minimum acceptable royalty for SEP owners. If such a proposal is to be adopted, then there is nothing left to negotiate with SEP owners who would be faced with a take-it-or-leave-it offer. Even if there was room for negotiation on royalty rates, there is nothing to prevent LNGs from insisting on

[144] Baron et al (n 4) 168–71.
[145] ibid, 169.
[146] ibid.

the lowest amount of royalties as possible, raising questions about the appropriate returns to innovation and incentives to innovate.

Moreover, the proposal of the SEP Expert Group would possibly allow the exchange of sensitive commercial information and anti-competitive collusion. As seen, it suggests that LNG members agree, before the start of negotiations, on the licensed product, the level in the value chain at which to license and the maximum amount of acceptable royalty. In order to reach an agreement on these points, implementers would have to exchange between themselves sensitive commercial information, such as the revenues following the incorporation of connectivity in the products, costs, actual and forecast sales and price projections. Such exchanges can lead to anti-competitive price coordination among competitors.

Another practical concern is that LNG members would have a conflict of interests as they would simultaneously be using the technology and negotiating on its price. Namely, 3G, 4G and 5G standards are already developed and IoT companies are expected to first use 3G and 4G connectivity in their products, followed by the next generation 5G products. Thus, implementers will already be using the technology while, at the same time, negotiating on its price. The main incentive for implementers would then be to cut their licensing costs as much as possible rather than to appropriately evaluate the technology. As a matter of principle, permitting companies that have not developed and are already using the technology to decide on its price would effectively resemble an expropriation of technology.[147]

The second related problem is that LNGs may be used as another venue for collective holdout, delaying the conclusion of licences unless all their demands are met. We have seen in chapter two how many litigated cases consisted of implementers avoiding or delaying taking a licence. According to the SEP Expert Group proposal, during both the LNG and individual negotiations, the SEP owner should not sue for an injunction. It is therefore reasonable to assume that implementers would use the additional venue for negotiations within the LNG, even if they genuinely do not want to take a licence, in order to be shielded from injunctions and to buy the extra time to avoid licensing, or until SEP holders agree on terms below FRAND. Furthermore, even in bilateral negotiations, implementers have a reason to insist on favourable licensing terms coordinated within LNG in order not to be disadvantaged against their competitors. Thus, LNGs could effectively represent another option to delay the efficient conclusion of a licensing agreement.

Consequently, while in theory LNGs of implementers might reduce transaction costs even more, they raise serious competition and holdout concerns in their practical application. The use of patent pools instead can greatly facilitate the efficiency, transparency and predictability of SEP licensing without the corresponding anti-competitive effects.

[147] I Nikolic and N Galli, 'SEP Expert Group Report: A Look into the IoT Future of SEP Licensing' (May 2021) *CPI Columns* 1, 6.

IV. Conclusion

The IoT brings new challenges to existing SEP licensing models. The experience from the ICT industry cannot be automatically replicated to a diverse universe of connected objects. The countless number of potential licensees, many different uses of standards and the diminished role of cross-licensing requires creating a new SEP licensing framework. If the ICT was characterised by bilateral licensing, the IoT would need more collective licensing models. The benefits are a significant reduction in transaction costs for every side, as well as transparency and predictability for implementers who would know the overall price of SEPs which they can factor into their business plans and thus benefit from a clearer SEP landscape. Collective licensing also ensures the level playing field between implementers as all competitors would be offered the same standard licensing terms. Thus, patent pools are expected to play larger role in the IoT. Their formation requires some upfront costs, and implementation in practice needs antitrust safeguards, but they represent an overall direction for the future.

BIBLIOGRAPHY

Books

American Bar Association, *Standards Development Patent Policy Manual* (ed J Contreras) (2007)
—— Section of the Antitrust Laws, *Handbook on the Antitrust Aspects of Standard Setting*, 2nd edn (ABA, 2011)
Aplin, T and Davies J, *Intellectual Property Law: Text, Cases, and Materials*, 2nd edn (Oxford University Press, 2013)
Bently, L and Sherman, B, *Intellectual Property Law*, 4th edn (Oxford University Press, 2014)
Biddle, B et al, *Patent Remedies and Complex Products* (Cambridge University Press, 2019)
Bishop, S and Walker, M, *The Economics of EC Competition Law: Concepts, Application and Measurement*, 3rd edn (Sweet & Maxwell, 2010)
Cournout, A, *Researches Into the Mathematical Principles of the Theory of Wealth* (Nathaniel Bacon trans) (MacMillan Company, 1897)
Elhauge, E and Geradin, D, *Global Competition Law and Economics*, 2nd edn (Hart Publishing, 2011)
Jacob, R, *IP and Other Things: A Collection of Essays and Speeches* (Hart Publishing, 2015)
Jones, A and Sufrin, B, *EU Competition Law: Text, Cases, and Materials*, 6th edn (Oxford University Press, 2016)
Kahneman, D, *Thinking, Fast and Slow* (Penguin Books, 2011)
Lundqvist, B, *Standardisation Under EU Competition Rules and US Antitrust Law* (Edward Elgar, 2014)
Niels, G, Jenkins, H and Kavanagh, J, *Economics for Competition Lawyers*, 2nd edn (Oxford University Press, 2016)
O'Donoghue, R and Padilla, J, *The Law and Economics of Article 102 TFEU*, 2nd edn (Hart Publishing, 2013)
Petrovcic, U, *Competition Law and Standard Essential Patents: A Transatlantic Perspective* (Kluwer Law International, 2014)
Shapiro, C and Varian, H, *Information Rules: A Strategic Guide to the Network Economy* (Harvard Business School Press, 1999)
Stothers, C, *Parallel Trade in Europe: Intellectual Property, Competition and Regulatory Law* (Hart Publishing, 2007)
Tapia, C, *Industrial Property Rights, Technical Standards and Licensing Practices (FRAND) in the Telecommunications Industry* (Carly Heymanns Verlag, 2010)
Teylas, D, *The Interface Between Competition Law, Patents and Technical Standards* (Kluwer Law International, 2014)
Torti, V, *Intellectual Property Rights and Competition in Standard Setting: Objectives and Tensions* (Routledge, 2016)
Whish, R and Bailey, D, *Competition Law*, 9th edn (Oxford University Press, 2018)
Zhang, L, *Standardization and Patent Licensing in the European Union* (Oy Nord print Ab, 2012)

Chapters in Edited Volumes

Biddle, B, 'No Standards for Standards: Understanding the ICT Standards-Development Ecosystem' in J Contreras (ed), *The Cambridge Handbook of Technical Standardization Law: Competition, Antitrust, and Patents* (Cambridge University Press, 2018)

Contreras, J, 'Assertion of Standard Essential Patents by Non-Practicing Entities' in D Sokol (ed), *Patent Assertion Entities and Competition Law* (Cambridge University Press, 2017)

—— 'Essentiality and Standard-Essential Patents' in J Contreras (ed), *The Cambridge Handbook of Technical Standardization Law: Competition, Antitrust, and Patents* (Cambridge University Press, 2018)

Contreras, J et al, 'The Effect of FRAND Commitments on Patent Remedies' in B Biddle et al (eds), *Patent Remedies and Complex Products* (Cambridge University Press, 2019)

Contreras, J and Eixenberger, M, 'The Anti-Suit Injunction – A Transnational Remedy for Multi-Jurisdictional SEP Litigation' in J Contreras (ed), *The Cambridge Handbook of Technical Standardization Law: Competition, Antitrust, and Patents* (Cambridge University Press, 2018)

Contreras, J and Layne-Farrar, A, 'Non-Discrimination and FRAND Commitments' in J Contreras (ed), *The Cambridge Handbook of Technical Standardization Law: Competition, Antitrust, and Patents* (Cambridge University Press, 2018)

Crane, D, 'Patent Pools, RAND Commitments, and the Problematics of Price Discrimination' in R Dreyfuss, H First and D Zimmerman (eds), *Working Within the Boundaries of Intellectual Property* (Oxford University Press, 2010)

Gandal, N and Regibeau, P, 'Standard-Setting Organisations: Current Policy Issues and Empirical Evidence' in P Delimatsis (ed), *The Law, Economics and Politics of Standardization* (Cambridge University Press, 2015)

Gilbert, R, 'The Essentiality Test for Patent Pools' in R Dreyfuss, D Zimmerman and H First (eds), *Working Within the Boundaries of Intellectual Property* (Oxford University Press, 2010)

—— 'Collective Rights Organizations: A Guide to Benefits, Costs and Antitrust Safeguards' in J Contreras (ed), *The Cambridge Handbook of Technical Standardization Law: Competition, Antitrust, and Patents* (Cambridge University Press, 2018)

Gupta, K, 'How SSOs Work: Unpacking the Mobile Industry's 3GPP Standards' in J Contreras (ed), *The Cambridge Handbook of Technical Standardization Law: Competition, Antitrust, and Patents* (Cambridge University Press, 2018)

Goddar, H and Moser, U, 'Traditional Valuation Methods: Cost, Market and Income Approach' in F Munari and R (eds), *The Economic Valuation of Patents: Methods and Applications* (Edward Elgar, 2011)

Ohana, G and Biddle, B, 'The Disclosure of Patents and Licensing Terms in Standards Development' in J Contreras (ed), *The Cambridge Handbook of Technical Standardization Law: Competition, Antitrust, and Patents* (Cambridge University Press, 2018)

Scott Morton, F and Shapiro, C, 'Patent Assertion: Are We Any Closer to Aligning Reward to Contribution?' in J Lerner and S Stern (eds), *Innovation Policy and the Economy, vol 16* (National Bureau of Economic Research, 2016)

Sidak, G, 'FRAND in India' in J Contreras (ed), *The Cambridge Handbook of Technical Standardization Law: Competition, Antitrust, and Patents* (Cambridge University Press, 2018)

Journal Articles

Abrams, D, Akcigit, U and Grennan, J, 'Patent Value and Citations: Creative Destruction or Strategic Disruption?' (2018) NBER Working Paper 19647

Akemann, M, Blair, J and Teece, D, 'Patent Enforcement in an Uncertain World: Widespread Infringement and the Paradox of Value for Patented Technologies' (2016) 1 *Criterion Journal on Innovation* 861

Allison, J et al, 'Valuable Patents' (2004) 92 *Georgetown Law Journal* 435

Amundson, S, 'Apportionment and the Entire Market Value Rule Have Presented Problems in Practice When Determining the Value of a Patented Invention' (2014) 23 *Texas Intellectual Property Law Journal* 1

Aoki, R and Nagaoka, S, 'The Consortium Standards and Patent Pools' (2004) 55 *Economic Review* 345

Armstrong, A, Mueller, J and Syrett, T, 'The Smartphone Royalty Stack: Surveying Royalty Demands for the Components Within Modern Smartphones' (2014), available at: papers.ssrn.com/sol3/papers.cfm?abstract_id=2443848

Arya, S, 'The Value of Standardized Technology to Connected Cars' (2020) 69 *GRUR International* 365

Atik, J, 'The FRAND Ceremony and the Engagement of Article 102 TFEU in the Licensing of Standard Essential Patents' (2019) 42 *Fordham International Law Journal* 949

Barazza, S, 'Licensing Standard Essential Patents Part One: The Definition of FRAND Commitments, the Determination of Royalty Rates' (2014) 9 *Journal of Intellectual Property Law & Practice* 465

Barnett, J, 'Has the Academy Led Patent Law Astray?' (2018) 32 *Berkeley Technology Law Journal* 1313

Baron, J, 'Counting Standard Contributions to Measure the Value of Patent Portfolios: A Tale of Apples and Oranges' (2020) 44 *Telecommunications Policy* 1

Baron, J and Delcamp, H 'The Strategies of Patent Introduction into Patent Pools' (2015) 24 *Economics of Innovation and New Technology* 776

Baron, J and Gupta, K, 'Unpacking 3GPP Standards' (2018) 27 *Journal of Economics & Management Strategy* 433

Baron, J, Meniere, Y and Pohlmann T, 'Standards, Consortia, and Innovation' (2014) 36 *International Journal of Industrial Organization* 22

Baron, J and Pohlmann, T, 'Who Cooperates in Standards Consortia – Rivals or Complementors?' (2013) 9 *Journal of Competition Law & Economics* 905

—— 'The Effect of Patent Pools on Patenting and Innovation – Evidence from Contemporary Technology Standards' (2015) Working Paper

—— 'Mapping Standards to Patents Using Databases of Declared Standard-Essential Patents and Systems of Technological Classification' (2018) 27 *Journal of Economics & Management Strategy* 504

Baron, J and Spulber, D, 'Technology Standards and Standard Setting Organisations: Introduction to the Searle Center Database' (2018) 27 *Journal of Economics & Management Strategy* 462

Bekkers, R et al, 'Disclosure Rules and Declared Essential Patents' (2019) NBER Working Paper 23627

Bekkers, R and Martinelli A, 'Knowledge Positions in High-Tech Markets: Trajectories, Standards, Strategies and True Innovators' (2012) 79 *Technological Forecasting & Social Change* 1192

Bekkers R and Upgedrowe, A, 'A Study of IPR Policies and Practices of a Representative Group of Standards Setting Organizations Worldwide', Commissioned by the US National Academies of Science, Board of Science, Technology, and Economic Policy (17 September 2012)

Bekkers R, Verspagen, B and Smits, J, 'Intellectual Property Rights and Standardization: The case of GSM' (2002) 26 *Telecommunications Policy* 171

Bermann, G, 'The Use of Anti-Suit Injunction in International Litigation' (1990) 28 *Columbia Journal of Transnational Law* 589

Biddle, B, 'Five Reasons Why Patent Disclosure in Standard Setting Organization's Doesn't Work (And What to Do Instead) (2015), available at: papers.ssrn.com/sol3/papers.cfm?abstract_id=2669893

Biddle, B et al, 'The Expanding Role and Importance of Standards in Information and Communications Technology Industry' (2012) 53 *Jurimetrics* 177

Biddle, B, White, A and Woods, S, 'How Many Patents in a Laptop (and other empirical questions)?' (2010), available at: papers.ssrn.com/sol3/papers.cfm?abstract-id=161944

Blecker, M, Sanchez, T and Stasik, E, 'An Experience-Based Look at the Licensing Practices that Drive the Cellular Communications Industry: Whole Portfolio/Whole Device Licensing' (December 2016) *les Nouvelles* 221

Bonadio, E and McDonagh, L, 'Paris Court Grants an SEP Anti-Anti-Suit Injunction in *IPCom v Lenovo*: A Worrying Decision in Uncertain Times?' (2019) *Journal of Intellectual Property Law & Practice* 149

Borghetti, J-S, Nikolic, I and Petit, N, 'FRAND Licensing Levels Under EU Law' (2021) *European Competition Journal*, available at: doi.org/10.1080/17441056.2020.1862542

Botta, M, 'The Challenge of Sanctioning Unfair Royalty Rates by the SEP Holder: "When", "How" and "What"' (2021) 44 *World Competition* 3

—— 'Non-Discrimination in Standard Essential Patents: ND Prong v Art 102(c) TFEU' (2021) *Journal of Competition Law & Economics* (forthcoming)

Brooks, R, 'SSO Rules, Standardization, and SEP Licensing: Economic Questions from the Trenches' (2013) 9 *Journal of Competition Law & Economics* 859

Brooks, R and Geradin, D, 'Interpreting and Enforcing the Voluntary FRAND Commitment' (2011) 9 *International Journal of IT Standards and Standardization Research* 1

Caffarra, C and Régibeau, P, 'Patent Explosion and Patent Wars: Holdup, Royalties and Misunderstandings over "Market Value" (2014), available at: ecp.crai.com/wp-content/uploads/2017/11/Caffarra_et_al_SEP_and_market_value_revised_clean.pdf

Camasasca, P et al, 'Injunctions for Standard-Essential Patents: Justice is Not Blind' (2013) 9 *Journal of Competition Law & Economics* 285

Carlton, D and Shampine, A, 'An Economic Interpretation of FRAND' (2013) 9 *Journal of Competition Law & Economics* 531

Cary, G et al, 'The Case for Antitrust to Police the Patent Holdup Problem in Standard Setting' (2011) 77 *Antitrust Law Journal* 913

Caviggioli, F et al, 'Patenting Strategies and Characteristics of Declared Inventions in the Long Term Evolution Standard' (2015) 46 *R&D Management* 664

Cawley, D and Leavitt, L, 'The Federal Circuit Disavows Mandatory Smallest Salable Patent Practicing Unit "Rule"' (2017) 36 *Review of Litigation* 52

Chappatte, P, 'FRAND Commitments – The Case for Antitrust Intervention' (2009) 5 *European Competition Journal* 319

Chien, C, 'Holding Up and Holding Out' (2014) 21 *Michigan Telecommunications & Technology Law Review* 1

Chien, C and Lemley, M, 'Patent Holdup, the ITC and the Public Interest' (2012) 98 *Cornell Law Review* 1

Chien, C and Schulman, E, 'Patent Semi-Comparables' (2018) 25 *Texas Intellectual Property Journal* 215

Choi, J-P, 'Patent Pools and Cross Licensing in the Shadow of Patent Litigation' (2010) 51 *International Economic Review* 441

Choi, J-P and Gerlach, H, 'Patent Pools, Litigation and Innovation' (2015) 46 *RAND Journal of Economics* 499

Contreras, J, 'Fixing FRAND: A Pseudo-Pool Approach to Standards Based Patent Licensing' (2013) 79 *Antitrust Law Journal* 47

—— 'Technical Standards and Ex Ante Disclosure: Results and Analysis of an Empirical Study' (2013) 53 *Jurimetrics* 163

—— 'A Brief History of FRAND: Analysing Current Debates in Standard Setting and Antitrust Through a Historical Lens' (2015) 80 *Antitrust Law Journal* 39

—— 'A Market Reliance Theory for FRAND Commitments and Other Patent Pledges' (2015) 2 *Utah Law Review* 479

—— 'A Tale of Two Layers: Patents, Standardization and the Internet' (2016) 93 *Denver Law Review* 853

—— 'Aggregated Royalties for Top-Down FRAND Determination: Revisiting "Joint Negotiation"' (2017) 62 *Antitrust Bulletin* 690

—— 'Global Markets, Competition and FRAND Royalties: The Many Implication of *Unwired Planet v Huawei*' (2017) 8 *Antitrust Source* 1

—— 'Global Rate Setting: A Solution for Standards-Essential Patents?' (2019) 94 *Washington Law Review* 701

—— 'Much Ado About Holdup' (2019) 3 *University of Illinois Law Review* 875

—— 'The New Extraterritoriality: FRAND Royalties, Anti-Suit Injunctions and the Global Race to the Bottom in Disputes Over Standard-Essential Patents' (2019) 25 *Boston University Journal of Science & Technology Law* 253

Contreras, J et al, 'Litigation of Standard-Essential Patents in Europe: A Comparative Analysis' (2018) 32 *Berkeley Technology Law Review* 1457

Contreras, J and Gilbert, R, 'A Unified Framework for RAND and Other Reasonable Royalties' (2015) 30 *Berkeley Technology Law Review* 1451

—— 'Non-Discrimination – FRAND's Last Stand? (21 December 2020) *CPI Antitrust Chronicle* 2

Contreras, J and Newman, D, 'Developing a Framework for Arbitrating Standard-Essential Patent Disputes' (2014) 1 *Journal of Dispute Resolution* 23

Cotter, T, 'Patent Holdup, Patent Remedies and Antitrust Response' (2009) 34 *Journal of Corporation Law* 1151

—— 'Comparative Law and Economics of Standard Essential Patents and FRAND Royalties' (2014) 22 *Texas Intellectual Property Law Journal* 311

—— 'Patent Damages Heuristics' (2018) 25 *Texas Intellectual Property Law Journal* 159

Cotter, T et al, 'Reasonable Royalties' in B Biddle et al (eds), *Patent Remedies and Complex Products* (Cambridge University Press, 2019)

Cotter, T, Hovenkamp, E and Siebrasse, N, 'Demystifying Patent Holdup' (2019) 76 *Washington & Lee Law Review* 1501

Dasgupta, K and Teece, D, 'The UK's Role as a Venue for FRAND Litigation: Have the UK Courts Gone Far Enough? (21 December 2020) *CPI Antitrust Chronicle* 1

Denicolo, V et al, 'Revisiting Injunctive Relief: Interpreting eBay in High-Tech Industries With Non-Practicing Patent Holders' (2008) 4 *Journal of Competition Law & Economics* 571

Dolmans, M, 'Standards for Standards' (2002) 26 *Fordham International Law Journal* 163

—— 'A Tale of Two Tragedies – A Plea for Open Standards' (2010) 2 *International Free and Open Source Software Law Review* 115

Elhauge, E, 'Do Patent Holdup and Royalty Stacking Lead to Systematically Excessive Royalties?' (2008) 4 *Journal of Competition Law & Economics* 535

Epstein, R and Noroozi, K, 'Why Incentives for "Patent Holdout" Threaten to Dismantle FRAND, and Why it Matters' (2018) 32 *Berkeley Technology Law Journal* 1381

Epstein, R, Scott Kieff, F and Spulber, D, 'The FTC, IP, and SSOs: Government Hold-Up Replacing Private Coordination' (2012) 8 *Journal of Competition Law & Economics* 1

Ernst, D, 'America's Voluntary Standards System – A "Best Practice Model" for Innovation Policy?' (2012) East–West Center Working Papers No 128

Farrell, J et al, 'Standard Setting, Patents and Hold-up' (2007) 74 *Antitrust Law Journal* 603

Fisher, G, 'Anti-Suit Injunction to Restrain Foreign Proceedings in Breach of an Arbitration Agreement' (2010) 22 *Bond Law Review* 1

Froeb, L, Ganglmair, B and Werden, G, 'Patent Hold-Up and Antitrust: How a Well-Intentioned Rule Could Retard Innovation' (2012) 60 *Journal of Industrial Economics* 249

Froeb, L and Shor, M, 'Innovators, Implementers and Two-Sided Holdup' (2015) 8 *Antitrust Source* 1

Galetovic, A and Gupta, K, 'Royalty Stacking and Standard Essential Patents: Theory and Evidence from the World Mobile Wireless Industry' (2017) available at: papers.ssrn.com/sol3/papers.cfm?abstract_id=2790347

—— 'The Case of the Missing Royalty Stacking in the World Mobile Wireless Industry' (2020) 29 *Industrial and Corporate Change* 827

Galetovic, A and Haber, S, 'The Fallacies of Patent Holdup Theory' (2017) 13 *Journal of Competition Law & Economics* 1

—— 'SEP Royalties: What Theory of Value and Distribution Should Courts Apply?' (2019) Hoover IP2 Working Paper Series 19001

Galetovic, A, Haber, S and Levine, R, 'An Empirical Examination of Patent Holdup' (2015) 11 *Journal of Competition Law & Economics* 549

Galetovic, A, Haber, S and Zaretzki, L, 'A New Dataset on Mobile Phone Patent License Royalties' (2017) Hoover IP2 Working Paper Series No 16011

—— 'An Estimate of the Average Cumulative Royalty Yield in the World Mobile Phone Industry: Theory, Measurement and Results' (2018) 42 *Telecommunications Policy* 263

—— 'Is there an Anti-Commons Tragedy in the Smartphone Industry?' (2018) 32 *Berkeley Technology Law Journal* 1527

Gautier, A and Petit, N, 'Smallest Salable Patent Practicing Unit and Component Licensing: Why 1$ is not $1' (2019) 15 *Journal of Competition Law & Economics* 690

Geradin, D, 'Pricing Abuses by Essential Patent Holders in a Standard-Setting Context: A View From Europe' (2009) 76 *Antitrust Law Journal* 329

—— 'Reverse Hold-ups: The (Often Ignored) Risks Faced by Innovators in Standardised Areas' (2010) paper prepared for the Swedish Competition Authority on the Pros and Cons of Standard-Setting, available at: papers.ssrn.com/sol3/papers.cfm?abstract_id=1711744

—— 'The European Commission's Policy Towards the Licensing of Standard-Essential Patents: Where do We Stand?' (2013) 9 *Journal of Competition Law & Economics* 1125

—— 'Moving Away from High Level Theories: A Market Driven Analysis of FRAND' (2014) 59 *Antitrust Bulletin* 327

—— 'The Meaning of "Fair and Reasonable" in the Context of Third-Party Determination of FRAND Terms' (2014) 21 *George Mason Law Review* 919

—— 'FRAND Arbitration: The Determination of Fair, Reasonable and Non-discriminatory Rates for SEPs by Arbitral Tribunals' (15 September 2016) *CPI Antitrust Chronicle* 1

—— 'SEP Licensing After two Decades of Legal Wrangling: Some Issues Solved, Many Still to Address' (24 March 2020) *CPI Antitrust Chronicle* 1.

Geradin, D and Layne-Farrar, A, 'The Logic and Limits of Ex Ante Competition in a Standard-Setting Environment' (2007) 3 *Competition Policy International* 79

—— 'Patent Value Apportionment Rule for Complex, Multi-Component Products' (2011) 27 *Santa Clara High Technology Law Journal* 763

Geradin, D, Layne-Farrar, A and Padilla J, 'The Complements Problem Within Standard Setting: Assessing the Evidence on Royalty Stacking' (2008) 14 *Boston University Journal of Science and Technology Law* 144

Geradin, D and Rato, M, 'Can Standard-Setting Lead to Exploitative Abuse? A Dissonant View on Patent Holdup, Royalty Stacking and the Meaning of FRAND' (2007) 3 *European Competition Journal* 101

—— 'FRAND Commitments and EC Competition Law: A Reply to Phillippe Chappatte' (2010) 6 *European Competition Journal* 129

Ghafele, R, 'Global Licensing on FRAND Terms in Light of *Unwired Planet v Huawei*' (2020) 24 *UCLA Journal of Law & Technology* 1

Ghafele, R and Schmitz, J, 'Economic Perspectives on FRAND' (2020) 11 *Journal of European Competition Law & Practice* 90

Gilbert, R, 'Antitrust for Patent Pools: A Century of Policy Evolution' (2004) *Stanford Technology Law Review* 3

—— 'Deal or No Deal? Licensing Negotiations in Standard Setting Organizations' (2011) 77 *Antitrust Law Journal* 855

—— 'Ties that Bind: Policies to Promote (Good) Patent Pools' (2011) 77 *Antitrust Law Journal* 1

Ginsburg, D, Owings, T and Wright, J, 'Enjoining Injunctions: The Case Against Antitrust Liability for Standard Essential Patent Holders Who Seek Injunctions' (2014) 10 *Antitrust Source* 1

Ginsburg, D, Wong-Ervin, K and Wright, J, 'The Troubling Use of Antitrust to Regulate FRAND Licensing' (2015) 10 *CPI Antitrust Chronicle* 2

Golden, J, 'Patent Trolls and Patent Remedies' (2007) 85 *Texas Law Review* 2111

Goodman, D and Myers, R, '3G Cellular Standards and Patents' (2005) 13 *IEEE WirelessCom* 1

Grasso, R, 'Standard Essential Patents: Royalty Determination in the Supply Chain' (2017) 8 *Journal of European Competition Law & Practice* 283

Greene, M, 'All Your Base Are Belong to Us: Towards an Appropriate Usage and Definition of the "Entire Market Value Rule" in Reasonably Royalty Calculations' (2012) 53 *Boston College Law Review* 233

Gupta, K, 'The Patent Policy Debate in the High-Tech World' (2013) 9 *Journal of Competition Law & Economics* 827

Gupta, K and Effraimidis, G, 'IEEE Patent Policy Revisions: An Empirical Examination of Impact' (2019) 64 *Antitrust Bulletin* 151

Gupta, K and Snyder, M, 'Smartphone Litigation and Standard Essential Patents' (2014) Hoover IP2 Working Paper Series No 14006

Hall, B, Jaffe, A and Trajtenberg, M, 'Market Value and Patent Citations' (2005) 36 *RAND Journal of Economics* 16

Harhoff, D et al, 'Citations Frequency and the Value of Patented Inventions' (1999) 81 *Review of Economics and Statistics* 511

Heiden, B, 'The Value of Connectivity in the Automotive Sector – A First Look' (2019) available at: papers.ssrn.com/sol3/papers.cfm?abstract_id=3521488

Heiden, B and Andreasson, J, 'Reevaluating Patent Damages in the Knowledge Economy: The Intellectual Value Chain in the Royalty Base for Standard-Essential Patents' (2016) 1 *Criterion Journal on Innovation* 229

Heiden, B, Padilla, J and Peters, R, 'The Value of Standard Essential Patents and the Level of Licensing' (2020), available at: papers.ssrn.com/sol3/papers.cfm?abstract_id=3717570

Heiden, B and Petit, N, 'Patent "Trespass" and the Royalty Gap: Exploring the Nature and Impact of Patent Holdout' (2018) 34 *Santa Clara High Technology Journal* 179

Heim, M and Nikolic, I, 'A FRAND Regime for Dominant Digital Platforms' (2019) 10 *JIPITEC* 38

Henkel, J, 'How to License SEPs to Promote Innovation and Entrepreneurship in the IoT' (2021), available at: papers.ssrn.com/sol3/papers.cfm?abstract_id=3808987

Hovenkamp, E, 'Tying, Exclusivity, and Standard-Essential Patents' (2017) 19 *Columbia Science & Technology Law Review* 79

Hovenkamp, E and Hovenkamp, H, 'Patent Pools and Related Technology Sharing' in R Blair and D Sokol (eds), *The Cambridge Handbook of Antitrust, Intellectual Property, and High Tech* (Cambridge University Press, 2017)

Hovenkamp, E and Mansur, J, 'How Patent Damages Skew Licensing Markets' (2018) 36 *Review of Litigation* 379

Hovenkamp, H, 'Standards Ownership and Competition Policy' (2007) 48 *Boston College Law Review* 87

—— 'Competition in Information Technologies: Standard-Essential Patents, Non-Practicing Entities and FRAND Bidding' (2012) 12–32 University of Iowa Legal Studies Research Paper 13

—— 'FRAND and Antitrust' (2020) 105 *Cornell Law Review* 101

Huber, B, 'Why the ETSI IPR Policy Does Not and Has Never Required Compulsory 'License to All': A Rebuttal to Karl Heinz Rosenbrock' (2017), available at: papers.ssrn.com/sol3/papers.cfm?abstract_id=3038447

Jacob, R, 'Competition Authorities Support Grasshoppers: Competition Law as a Threat to Innovation' (2013) 9 *Competition Policy International* 15

Jacob, R and Milner, A, 'Lessons from *Huawei v ZTE*' (2016) 4IP Council Research Paper 1

Jones, A, 'Standard-Essential Patents: FRAND Commitments, Injunctions and the Smartphone Wars' (2014) 10 *European Competition Journal* 1

Kang, B and Bekkers, R, 'Just-in-time patents and the development of standards' (2015) 44 *Research Policy* 1948

Kappos, D and Michel, P, 'The Smallest Salable Patent-Practicing Unit: Observations of its Origin, Development and Future' (2018) 32 *Berkeley Technology Law Journal* 1433

Kattan, J, 'FRAND Wars and Section 2' (2013) 27 *Antitrust* 30

—— 'The Next FRAND Battle: Why the Royalty Base Matters?' (31 March 2015) *CPI Antitrust Chronicle* 1

Kattan, J, Ordover, J and Shampine, A, 'FRAND and the Smallest Saleable Unit' (2016) 9 *Competition Policy International* 1

Katz, M and Shapiro, C, 'Systems Competition and Network Effects' (1994) 8 *Journal of Economics Perspectives* 93

Kesan, J and Hayes, C, 'FRAND's Forever: Standards, Patent Transfers and Licensing Commitments' (2014) 89 *Indiana Law Journal* 231

Kobayashi, B and Wright, J, 'Federalism, Substantive Preemption, and Limits on Antitrust: An Application to Patent Holdup' (2009) 5 *Journal of Competition Law & Economics* 469

—— 'The Limits of Antitrust and Patent Holdup: A Reply to Cary et al' (2012) 78 *Antitrust Law Journal* 701

Krechmer, K, 'Open Standards: A Call for Action' (2009) 47 *IEEE Communications Magazine* 88

Kuhnen, T, 'FRAND Licensing and Implementation Chains' (2019) 14 *Journal of Intellectual Property Law & Practice* 964

Lampe, R and Moser, P, 'Do Patent Pools Encourage Innovation? Evidence from the Nineteenth-Century Sewing Machine Industry' (2010) 70 *Journal of Economic History* 898

—— 'Do Patent Pools Encourage Innovation? Evidence from 20 US Industries Under the New Deal' (2012) NBER Working Paper 18316

Landers, A, 'Let the Games Begin: Incentives to Innovation in the New Economy of Intellectual Property Law' (2006) 46 *Santa Clara Law Review* 307

Langus, G, Lipatov, V and Neven N, 'Standard-Essential Patents: Who Is Really Holding Up (and When)?' (2013) 9 *Journal of Competition Law & Economics* 253

Larouche, P, Padilla, J and Taffet, R, 'Settling FRAND Disputes: Is Mandatory Arbitration a Reasonable and Non-discriminatory Alternative?' (2014) 10 *Journal of Competition Law & Economics* 581

Larouche, P and Schuett, F, 'Repeated Interaction in Standard Setting' (2018) *Journal of Economics & Management Strategy* 1

Larouche, P and Zingales, N, 'Injunctive Relief in Disputes Related to Standard-Essential Patents: Time for the CJEU to Set Fair and Reasonable Presumptions' (2014) 10 *European Competition Journal* 551

Layne-Farrar, A, 'Nondiscriminatory Pricing: Is Standard Setting Different?' (2010) 6 *Journal of Competition Law & Economics* 811

—— 'Innovative or Indefensible? An Empirical Assessment of Patenting within Standard Setting' (2011) 9 *International Journal of IT Standards and Standardization Research* 1

—— 'Patent Holdup and Royalty Stacking Theory and Evidence: Where Do We Stand After 15 Years of History?' (2014) OECD, DAF/COMP/WD(2014)84

—— 'Proactive or Reactive? An Empirical Assessment of IPR Policy Revisions in the Wake of Antitrust Actions' (2014) 59 *Antitrust Bulletin* 373

—— 'The Patent Damages Gap: An Economist's Review of US Statutory Patent Damages Apportionment Rules' (2018) 26 *Texas Intellectual Property Law Journal* 31

Layne-Farrar, A and Lerner, J, 'To Join or Not to Join: Examining Patent Pool Participation and Rent Sharing Rules' (2011) 29 *International Journal of Industrial Organization* 294

Layne-Farrar, A and Llobet, G, 'Moving Beyond Simple Examples: Assessing the Incremental Value Rule Within Standards' (2014) 36 *International Journal of Industrial Organization* 57

Layne-Farrar, A, Llobet, G and Padilla, J, 'Preventing Patent Hold Up: An Economic Assessment of Ex Ante Licensing Negotiations in Standard Setting' (2009) 37 *AIPLA Quarterly Journal* 445

—— 'Patent Licensing in Vertically Disaggregated Industries: The Royalty Allocation Neutrality Principle' (2014) 95 *Communications & Strategies* 61

—— 'Payments and Participation: The Incentives to Joint Cooperative Standard Setting Effort' (2014) 23 *Journal of Economics & Management Strategy* 24

Layne-Farrar, A, Padilla, J and Schmalensee, R, 'Pricing Patents for Licensing in Standard-Setting Organizations: Making Sense of FRAND Commitments' (2007) 74 *Antitrust Law Journal* 671

Layne-Farrar, A and Stark, R, 'License to All or Access to All? A Law and Economics Assessment of Standard Development Organizations' Licensing Rules' (2020) 88 *George Washington Law Review* 1307

Layne-Farrar, A and Wong-Ervin, K, 'Methodologies for Calculating FRAND Damages: An Economic and Comparative Analysis of the Case Law from China, the European Union, India, and the United States' (2017) 8 *Jindal Global Law Review* 127

Lee, W and Melamed, D, 'Breaking the Vicious Cycle of Patent Damages' (2016) 101 *Cornell Law Review* 385

Lemley, M, 'Intellectual Property Rights and Standard-Setting Organisations' (2002) 90 *California Law Review* 1889

—— 'Ten Things to do About Patent Holdup of Standards (And One Not To)' (2007) 48 *Boston College Law Review* 149

—— 'Distinguishing Lost Profits from Reasonable Royalties' (2009) 51 *William & Mary Law Review* 655

Lemley, M and Shapiro, C, 'Probabilistic Patents' (2005) 19 *Journal of Economic Perspectives* 75

—— 'Patent Holdup and Royalty Stacking' (2007) 85 *Texas Law Review* 1991

—— 'A Simple Approach to Setting Reasonable Royalties for Standard-Essential Patents' (2013) 28 *Berkeley Technology Law Journal* 1135

Lemley, M and Simcoe, T, 'How Essential Are Standard Essential Patents?' (2019) 104 *Cornell Law Review* 607

Leonard, G and Lopez, M, 'Determining RAND Royalty Rates for Standard-Essential Patents' (2014) 29 *Antitrust* 86

Lerner, J and Tirole, J, 'The Design of Patent Pools: The Determinants of Licensing Rules' (2007) 38 *RAND Journal of Economics* 610

—— 'Efficient Patent Pools' (2014) 94 *American Economic Review* 691

Lichtman, D, 'Understanding the RAND Commitment' (2010) 47 *Houston Law Review* 1023

Llobet, G and Padilla, J, 'The Inverse Cournot Effect in Royalty Negotiations with Complementary Patents' (2017), available at: papers.ssrn.com/sol3/papers.cfm?abstract_id=2866389

Lo Bue, M, 'Are these Cartels? Price Guidelines Adopted by Standard Setting Organisations (US, Institute of Electrical and Electronics Engineers)' (2016) 7 *Journal of European Competition Law & Practice* 537

Love, B, 'Patentee Overcompensation and the Entire Market Value Rule' (2007) 60 *Stanford Law Review* 263

Lundel, B, Gamalielsson, J and Katz, A, 'On Implementation of Open Standards in Software: To What Extent can ISO Standards be Implemented in Open Source Software?' (2015) 13 *International Journal of Standardization Research* 47

Makris, S and Tapia, C, 'Confidentiality in FRAND Licensing After *Huawei v ZTE*: National Courts in Europe Searching for Balance' (April 2019) *les Nouvelles* 210

Mallinson, K, 'Don't Fix What Isn't Broken: The Extraordinary Record of Innovation and Success in the Cellular Industry Under Existing Licensing Practices' (2016) 23 *George Mason Law Review* 967

Masur, J, 'The Use and Misuse of Patent Licenses' (2015) 110 *Northwestern University Law Review* 115

—— 'How Patent Damages Skew Licensing Markets' (2018) 36 *The Review of Litigation* 379

Mariniello, M, 'Fair, Reasonable and Non-Discriminatory (FRAND) Terms: A Challenge to Competition Authorities' (2011) 7 *Journal of Competition Law & Economics* 523

Martin, D and de Meyer, C, 'Patent Counting, a Misleading Index of Patent Value: A Critique of Goodman & Myers and its Uses' (2006), available at: papers.ssrn.com/sol3/papers.cfm?abstract_id=949439

Martinez, J, 'FRAND as Access to All vs License to All' (2019) 14 *Journal of Intellectual Property Law & Practice* 642

Mattioli, M, 'Power and Governance in Patent Pools' (2014) 27 *Harvard Journal of Law & Technology* 421

—— 'Patent Pool Outsiders' (2018) 33 *Berkeley Technology Law Journal* 233

Melamed, D and Shapiro, C, 'How Antitrust Law Can Make FRAND Commitments More Effective' (2018) 128 *Yale Law Journal* 2110

Merges, R, 'Contracting into Liability Rules: Intellectual Property Rights and Collective Rights Organizations' (1996) 84 *California Law Review* 1293

Merges, R and Mattioli, M, 'Measuring the Costs and Benefits of Patent Pools' (2017) 78 *Ohio State Law Journal* 281

Michel, S, 'Bargaining for RAND Royalties in the Shadow of Patent Remedies Law' (2011) 77 *Antitrust Law Journal* 889

Miller, J, 'Standard Setting, Patents and Access Lock-in: RAND Licensing and the Theory of the Firm' (2007) 40 *Indiana Law Review* 351

Mossoff, A, 'The Rise and Fall of the First American Patent Thicket: The Sewing Machine War of the 1850s' (2011) 53 *Arizona Law Review* 165

Nazzini, R, 'Level Discrimination and FRAND Commitments Under EU Competition Law' (2017) 40 *World Competition* 213

Neurohr, B, 'Dynamically Efficient Royalties for Standard-Essential Patents' (2020) 16 *Journal of Competition Law & Economics* 298

Nikolic, I and Galli, N, 'SEP Expert Group Report: A Look into the IoT Future of SEP Licensing' (May 2021) *CPI Columns* 1

Ohana, G, Hansen, M and Shah, O, 'Disclosure and Negotiation of Licensing Terms Prior to Adoption of Industry Standards: Preventing Another Patent Ambush?' (2003) 24 *European Competition Law Review* 648

Ohlhausen, M, 'The Elusive Role of Competition in the Standard-Setting Antitrust Debate' (2017) 20 *Stanford Technology Law Review* 93

Ordover, J and Shampine, A, 'Implementing the FRAND Commitment' (2014) 10 *Antitrust Source* 1

Padilla, J, Ginsburg, D and Wong-Ervin, K, 'Antitrust Analysis Involving Intellectual Property and Standards: Implications from Economics' (2019) 33 *Harvard Journal of Law & Technology* 1

Padilla, J and Wong-Ervin, K, 'Portfolio Licensing to Makers of Downstream End-User Devices: Analyzing Refusals to License FRAND-Assured Standard-Essential Patents at the Component Level' (2017) 62 *Antitrust Bulletin* 494

Peters, R, 'One-Blue: A Blueprint for Patent Pools in High-Tech' (2011) (September/October) *Intellectual Asset Management* 38

Petit, N, 'Injunctions for FRAND-Pledged SEPs: The Quest for an Appropriate Test of Abuse Under Article 102 TFEU' (2013) 9 *European Competition Journal* 677

—— 'The Smallest Salable Patent-Practicing Unit Experiment, General Purpose Technologies and Coase Theorem' (2016) 4IP Council, available at: www.4ipcouncil.com/application/files/8914/5554/8353/SSPPU_rule_GPTs_and_the_Coase_Theorem_-_N_Petit_15_02_16.pdf

—— 'The IEEE-SA Revised Patent Policy and its Definition of "Reasonable" Rates: A Transatlantic Antitrust Divide?' (2017) 27 *Fordham Intellectual Property, Media & Entertainment Law Journal* 211

Petrovcic, U, 'Patent Hold-up and the Limits of Competition Law: A Transatlantic Perspective' (2013) 50 *Common Market Law Review* 1363

Picht, P, 'FRAND Determination in *TCL v Ericsson* and *Unwired Planet v Huawei*: Same but Different? (2018) Max Planck Institute for Innovation and Competition Research Paper No 18-07

Pohlmann, T, 'The Evolution of ICT Standards Consortia' (2014) 95 *Communication & Strategies* 17

Putnam, J and Williams, T, 'The Smallest Salable Patent-Practicing Unit (SSPPU): Theory and Evidence' (2016) Working Paper, available at: papers.ssrn.com/sol3/papers.cfm?abstract_id=2835617

Ramsey, F, 'A Contribution to the Theory of Taxation' (1927) 37 *Economic Journal* 47

Ratlif, J and Rubinfeld, D, 'The Use and Threat of Injunctions in the RAND Context' (2012) 9 *Journal of Competition Law & Economics* 1

Rosenbrock, KH, 'Licensing At All Levels is The Rule Under The ETSI IPR Policy: A Response to Dr Bertram Huber' (2017) available at: papers.ssrn.com/sol3/papers.cfm?abstract_id=3064894

Rosenbrock, KH, 'Why the ETSI IPR Policy Requires Licensing to All' (2017), available at: fair-standards.org/wp-content/uploads/2017/08/Why-the-ETSI-IPR-Policy-Requires-Licensing-to-All_Karl-Heinz-Rosenbrock_2017.pdf

Rysman, M and Simcoe, T, 'Patents and the Performance of Voluntary Standard-Setting Organizations' (2008) 54 *Management Science* 1920

Salop, S and Scott Morton, F, 'Developing and Administrable MFN Enforcement Policy' (2013) 27 *Antitrust* 15

Schankerman, M, 'How Valuable is Patent Protection? Estimates by Technology Field' (1998) 29 *RAND Journal of Economics* 77

Scott Kieff, F and Layne-Farrar, A, 'Incentive Effects from Different Approaches to Holdup Mitigation Surrounding Patent Remedies and Standard-Setting Organisations' (2013) 9 *Journal of Competition Law & Economics* 1091

Scott Morton, F and Shapiro, C, 'Strategic Patent Acquisitions' (2014) 79 *Antitrust Law Journal* 463

Seaman, C, 'Permanent Injunctions in Patent Litigation After eBay: An Empirical Study' (2016) 101 *Iowa Law Review* 1949

Shah, R and Kesan, J, 'Lost in Translation: Interoperability Issues for Open Standards' (2012) 8 *I/S: A Journal of Law and Policy for the Information Society* 114

Shampine, A, 'Applying the Non-Discrimination Requirement of FRAND when Rates Change' (2016) 8 *Antitrust Source* 1

Shapiro, C, 'Navigating the Patent Thicket: Cross Licensing, Patent Pools, and Standard Setting' (2000) 1 *Innovation Policy and the Economy* 119

—— 'Injunctions, Hold-up, and Patent Royalties' (2010) 12 *American Law and Economics Review* 280

Shapiro, C and Lemley, M, 'The Role of Antitrust in Preventing Patent Holdup' (2020) 168 *University of Pennsylvania Law Review* 1

Sidak, G, 'Holdup, Royalty Stacking, and the Presumption of Injunctive Relief for Patent Infringement: A Reply to Lemley and Shapiro' (2008) 92 *Minnesota Law Review* 714

—— 'Patent Holdup and Oligopsonistic Collusion in Standard-Setting Organizations' (2009) 5 *Journal of Competition Law & Economics* 123

—— 'The Meaning of FRAND, Part I: Royalties' (2013) 9 *Journal of Competition Law & Economics* 931

—— 'Mandating Final-Offer Arbitration of FRAND Royalties for Standard-Essential Patents' (2014) 18 *Stanford Technology Law Review* 1

—— 'The Proper Royalty Base for Patent Damages' (2014) 10 *Journal of Competition Law & Economics* 989

—— 'Antitrust Division's Devaluation of Standard Essential Patents' (2015) 104 *Georgetown Law Journal Online* 48

—— 'FRAND in India: The Delhi High Court's Emerging Jurisprudence on Royalties for Standard-Essential Patents' (2015) 10 *Journal of Intellectual Property Law & Practice* 609

—— 'The Meaning of FRAND, Part II: Injunctions' (2015) 11 *Journal of Competition Law & Economics* 201

—— 'Apportionment, FRAND Royalties and Comparable Licenses after *Ericsson v D-Link*' (2016) 4 *University of Illinois Law Review* 1811

—— 'Converting Royalty Payment Structures for Patent Licenses' (2016) 1 *Criterion Journal on Innovation* 901

—— 'The Value of Standard vs the Value of Standardisation' (2016) 68 *Baylor Law Review* 59

—— 'What Aggregate Royalty Do Manufacturers of Mobile Phones Pay to License Standard-Essential Patents?' (2016) 1 *Criterion Journal on Innovation* 701

—— 'Fair and Unfair Discrimination in Royalties for Standard-Essential Patents Encumbered by a FRAND or RAND Commitment' (2017) 2 *Criterion Journal on Innovation* 301

—— 'The FRAND Contract' (2018) 3 *Criterion Journal on Innovation* 1

—— 'Is Patent Holdup a Hoax?' (2018) 3 *Criterion Journal on Innovation* 401

Sidak, G and Skog, J, 'Citation Weighting, Patent Ranking, and Apportionment of Value for Standard-Essential Patents' (2018) 3 *Criterion Journal on Innovation* 201

—— 'Hedonic Prices and Patent Royalties' (2017) 2 *Criterion Journal on Innovation* 601

—— 'Hedonic Prices for Multicomponent Products' (2019) 4 *Criterion Journal on Innovation* 301

Siebrasse, N and Cotter, T, 'The Value of the Standard' (2017) 101 *Minnesota Law Review* 1159

Skitol, R, 'Concerted Buying Power: Its Potential for Addressing the Patent Hold-up Problem in Standard Setting' (2005) 72 *Antitrust Law Journal* 727

Spulber, D, 'Finding Reasonable Royalty Damages: A Contract Approach to Patent Infringement' (2019) 2 *University of Illinois Law Review* 616

—— 'Licensing Standard Essential Patents with FRAND Commitments: Preparing for 5G Mobile Telecommunications' (2020) 18 *Colorado Technology Law Journal* 79

Stasik, E, 'Royalty Rates and Licensing Strategies for Essential Patents on LTE (4G) Telecommunications Standards' (September 2010) *les Nouvelles* 114

Stasik E and Cohen, D, 'Royalty Rates and Licensing Strategies for Essential Patents on 5G Telecommunication Standards: What to Expect' (September 2020) *les Nouvelles* 176

Stern, R, 'Who Should Own the Benefits of Standardization and the Value it Creates?' (2018) 19 *Minnesota Journal of Law, Science & Technology* 108

Swanson, D and Baumol, W, 'Reasonable and Non-discriminatory (RAND) Royalties, Standards Selection, and Control of Market Power' (2005) 73 *Antitrust Law Journal* 1

Teece, D, 'The "Tragedy of the Anticommons" Fallacy: A Law and Economics Analysis of Patent Thickets and FRAND Licensing' (2017) 32 *Berkeley Technology Law Journal* 1490

—— 'Profiting from Innovation in the Digital Economy' (2018) 47 *Research Policy* 1367

—— 'Patent Counting and the "Top-Down" Approach to Patent Valuations: An Economic and Public Policy Appraisal of Reasonable Royalties' (2020) 5 *Criterion Journal on Innovation* 157

Teece, D et al, 'Maintaining Ecosystem Innovation by Rewarding Technology Developers: FRAND, Ex Ante Rates and Inherent Value' (2017) Tusher Center for the Management of Intellectual Capital Working Paper Series No 2

Teece, D and Sherry, E, 'On the "Smallest Salable Patent-Practicing Unit" Doctrine: An Economic and Public Policy Analysis' (2016) Tushner Center for the Management of Intellectual Capital Working Paper No 11

—— 'Standard Setting, Standard Development and Division of Gains from Standardisation' (2016) *Competition Policy International* 1

Teffet, R and Wellford, H, 'Questioning the FTC's Incremental Value Test and Claims of Widespread Hold-up in Technology Standards' (2012) 57 *Antitrust Bulletin* 161

Tsai, J and Wright, J, 'Standard Setting, Intellectual Property Rights, and the Role of Antitrust in Regulating Incomplete Contracts' (2015) 80 *Antitrust Law Journal* 157

Uwe-Kuhn, K-W, Scott Morton, F and Shelanski, H, 'Standard Setting Organisations Can Help Solve the Standard Essential Patents Licensing Problem' (March 2013) *CPI Antitrust Chronicle* 1

Vary, R, 'Smartphone Patent Wars: A Phantom Menace' (November 2017) *CPI Antitrust Chronicle* 1

Werden, G and Froeb, L, 'Why Patent Hold-up Does Not Violate Antitrust Law' (2019) 27 *Texas Intellectual Property Law Journal* 1

Zingales, N and Kanevskaia, O, 'The IEEE-SA Patent Policy Update Under the Lens of EU Competition Law' (2016) 12 *European Competition Journal* 195

SDO Materials

3GPP, 'Technical Specification Group Working Methods', TR 21.900, V14.0.0 (2017), available at: www.etsi.org/deliver/etsi_tr/121900_121999/121900/14.00.00_60/tr_121900v140000p.pdf

—— 'Release 15' (3 March 2017), available at: www.3gpp.org/release-15

—— 'Releases', available at: www.3gpp.org/specifications/67-releases

—— 'Working Procedures' (20 October 2016), available at: www.3gpp.org/ftp/Information/Working_Procedures/3GPP_WP.pdf

5GPPP, '5G Innovations for New Business Opportunities' (March 2017), available at: 5g-ppp.eu/wp-content/uploads/2017/01/5GPPP-brochure-MWC17.pdf

ANSI, 'ANSI Essential Requirements: Due Process Requirements for American National Standards' (January 2021), available at: www.ansi.org/american-national-standards/ans-introduction/essential-requirements

—— 'Introduction to ANSI', available at: www.ansi.org/about_ansi/introduction/introduction?menuid=1

Bluetooth SIG, 'About Us', available at: www.bluetooth.com/about-us/our-history

Consortium Info, 'Standard Setting Organizations and Standards List', available at: www.consortiuminfo.org/links/#.WOz-j_67rMA

CEN-CENELEC, 'Standard Essential Patents and Fair, Reasonable and Non-Discriminatory (FRAND) Commitments' (2016), available at: www.cencenelec.eu/News/Policy_Opinions/PolicyOpinions/EssentialPatents.pdf

ETSI, Ex-ante Disclosure of Licensing Terms, available at: www.etsi.org/about/how-we-work/intellectual-property-rights-iprs/ex-ante-disclosures

—— 'Guide on Intellectual Property Rights' (19 September 2013), available at: www.etsi.org/images/files/ipr/etsi-guide-on-ipr.pdf

—— IPR Information Statement and Licensing Declaration Form (3 September 2020), available at: www.etsi.org/images/files/IPR/etsi-ipr-policy.pdf

—— 'Intellectual Property Rights Policy' (3 September 2020), available at: www.etsi.org/images/files/IPR/etsi-ipr-policy.pdf

—— Membership, available at: www.etsi.org/membership

IEEE-SA, Letters of Assurance for Essential Patents (1 June 2019), available at: mentor.ieee.org/myproject/Public//mytools/mob/loa.pdf

—— 'Standards Board Bylaws' (August 2020), available at: standards.ieee.org/content/dam/ieee-standards/standards/web/documents/other/sb_bylaws.pdf

IETF, 'About', available at: www.ietf.org

—— 'Intellectual Property Rights in IETF Technology' (May 2017), available at: www.rfc-editor.org/rfc/pdfrfc/rfc8179.txt.pdf

ISO, 'About', available at: www.iso.org/home.html

—— 'ISO 32000-1:2008 Document Management – Portable Document Format', available at: www.iso.org/standard/51502.html

ISO/IEC Guide 2:2004, 'Standardization and Related Activities – General Vocabulary', 4th edn (2004), available at: isotc.iso.org/livelink/livelink/fetch/2000/2122/4230450/8389141/ISO_IEC_Guide_2_2004_%28Multilingual%29_-_Standardization_and_related_activities_--_General_vocabulary.pdf?nodeid=8387841&vernum=-2

—— 'JTC 1 PAS Submitters', available at: jtc1info.org/page-3/page-4/jtc-1-pas-submitters/

ITU, 'About', available at: www.itu.int/en/Pages/default.aspx

—— 'Understanding Patents, 'Competition & Standardization in an Interconnected World' (ITU, 2014), available at: www.itu.int/en/ITU-T/Documents/Manual_Patents_Final_E.pdf

ITU-ISO-IEC, 'Patent Statement and Licensing Declaration Form for ITU-T, ITU-R Recommendation, ISO or IEC Deliverable' (2 November 2018), available at: www.itu.int/dms_pub/itu-t/oth/04/04/T04040000020005PDFE.pdf

ITU-T, 'Definition of Open Standards', available at: www.itu.int/en/ITU-T/ipr/Pages/open.aspx

ITU-T/ITU-R/ISO/IEC, Common Patent Policy, available at: www.itu.int/en/ITU-T/ipr/Pages/policy.aspx

Open Source Initiative, 'Open Standards Requirements for Software', available at: opensource.org/osr

Open Standards, 'Principles', available at: open-stand.org/about-us/principles/

Raising Standards, 'Comprehensive List of Consortia', 17th edn (August 2012), available at: www.raisingstandards.eu/new-page-1/

TIA, 'Guidelines to the Telecommunications Industry Association Intellectual Property Rights Policy' (1 May 2014), available at: www.tiaonline.org/wp-content/uploads/2018/05/Guidelines_to_the_Intellectual_Rights_Policy_of_the_Telecommunications_Industry_Association.pdf

—— Intellectual Property Rights Policy (21 October 2016)

USB Implementers Forum, 'About USB-IF', available at: www.usb.org/about

VITA, VSO Policies and Procedures (1 September 2015), available at: www.vita.com/resources/Documents/Policies/vso-pp-r2d8.pdf

W3C, 'About', available at: w3.org

Wi-Fi Alliance, 'Who We Are', available at: www.wi-fi.org/who-we-are

WIPO, 'Guidance on WIPO FRAND Alternative Dispute Resolution' (2017)

Wireless Power Consortium, 'About the WPC', available at: www.wirelesspowerconsortium.com/about/about-wpc

Reports and Studies

4IP Council, 'National Courts Guidance', available at: caselaw.4ipcouncil.com/guidance-national-courts

Amplified, GreyB, 'Exploration of 5G Standards and Preliminary Findings on Essentiality' (2020), available at: static1.squarespace.com/static/59fa01a118b27d1bfef7f050/t/5ecc8c109259ee3d45ecda99/1590463526894/5G+SEP+Preliminary+Report.pdf

Baron, J et al, 'Making the Rules: The Governance of Standard Development Organizations and their Policies on Intellectual Property Rights' (EUR 29655 EN, Publication Office of the European Union, 2019), available at: ec.europa.eu/jrc/sites/jrcsh/files/sdo_governance_final_electronic_version.pdf

—— 'Group of Experts on Licensing and Valuation of Standard Essential Patents – Contribution to the Debate on SEPs' (January 2021), available at: ec.europa.eu/docsroom/documents/45217

Bekkers, R and Upgedrowe, A, 'A Study of IPR Policies and Practices of a Representative Group of Standards Setting Organizations Worldwide', Commissioned by the US National Academies of Science, Board of Science, Technology, and Economic Policy' (17 September 2012), available at: www.nap.edu/resource/18510/Bekkers-Updegrove%20Paper_092013.pdf

Bekkers, R et al, 'Landscape Study of Potentially Essential Patents Disclosed to ETSI' (Publication Office of the European Union, 2020), available at: publications.jrc.ec.europa.eu/repository/handle/JRC121411

—— 'Pilot Study for Essentiality Assessment of Standard Essential Patents'(Publication office of the European Union, 2020), available at: publications.jrc.ec.europa.eu/repository/handle/JRC119894

Bezerra, J et al, 'The Mobile Revolution: How Mobile Technologies Drive a Trillion Dollar Impact' (Boston Consulting Group, 2015), available at: www.bcg.com/publications/2015/telecommunications-technology-industries-the-mobile-revolution

Blind, K, Jundgmittag, A and Mangelsdorf, A, 'The Economic Benefits of Standardisation' (DIN German Institute for Standardisation, 2011), available at: www.din.de/blob/89552/68849fab0eeeaaf b56c5a3ffee9959c5/economic-benefits-of-standardization-en-data.pdf

CEN-CENELEC, 'Core Principles and Approaches for Licensing of Standard Essential Patents' (June 2019), available at: www.cencenelec.eu/news/workshops/Pages/WS-2019-014.aspx

—— 'Principles and Guidance for Licensing Standard Essential Patents in 5G and the Internet of Things (IoT), Including the Industrial Internet' (June 2019), available at: www.cencenelec.eu/news/workshops/pages/ws-2019-013.aspx

—— 'Standard Essential Patents and Fair, Reasonable and Non-Discriminatory (FRAND) Commitments' (2016), available at: www.cencenelec.eu/news/policy_opinions/PolicyOpinions/EssentialPatents.pdf

Centre for Economics and Business Research, 'The Economic Contribution of Standards to the UK Economy' (British Standards Institution, 2015), available at: www.bsigroup.com/LocalFiles/en-GB/standards/BSI-standards-research-report-The-Economic-Contribution-of-Standards-to-the-UK-Economy-UK-EN.pdf

Cohen, D, 'The IEEE 2015 Patent Policy – A Natural Experiment in Devaluing Technology' (12 August 2019), available at: www.kidonip.com/standard-essential-patents/the-ieee-2015-patent-policy-a-natural-experiment-in-devaluing-technology/

Cyber Creative Institute, 'Evaluation of LTE Essential Patents Declared at ETSI' (2013), available at: www.cybersoken.com/file/lte03EN.pdf

Dot Econ and Axon Partners Group, 'Study on the Implication of 5G Deployment on Future Business Models' (14 March 2018), available at: berec.europa.eu/eng/document_register/subject_matter/berec/reports/8008-study-on-implications-of-5g-deployment-on-future-business-models

Ericsson Mobility Report (June 2020), available at: www.ericsson.com/en/mobility-report/reports/november-2020

European Commission, 'Patents and Standards: A Modern Framework for IPR Based Standardisation' (2014), available at: pure.tue.nl/ws/files/3916785/391736021255721.pdf

Fair Standards Alliance, 'Transparently FRAND: The Use (and Misuse) of Confidentiality Obligations in FRAND Licensing Negotiations' (13 February 2017), available at: www.ftc.gov/reports/patent-assertion-entity-activity-ftc-study

Fairfield Resources International, 'Analysis of Patents Declared Essential to GSM as of 6 June 2007' (2008), available at: fair-standards.org/wp-content/uploads/2017/02/170213-FSA-Position-PaperTransparency-FRAND-1.pdf

—— 'Review of Patents Declared Essential to WCDMA Through December 2008' (2009), available at: www.frlicense.com/wcdma1.pdf

—— 'Review of Patents Declared Essential to LTE and SAE (4G Wireless Standards) Through June 30, 2009' (2010), available at: frlicense.com/GSM_FINAL.pdf

Federal Trade Commission, 'Internet of Things: Privacy & Security in a Connected World' (2015), available at: www.ftc.gov/system/files/documents/reports/federal-trade-commission-staff-report-november-2013-workshop-entitled-internet-things-privacy/150127iotrpt.pdf

Fraunhofer Institute, 'Study on the Interplay Between Standards and Intellectual Property Rights' (2011), available at: ec.europa.eu/growth/content/study-interplay-between-standards-and-intellectual-property-rights-ipr-0_en

GSA, 'LTE Ecosystem Report: Status Update July 2020' (2020), available at: gsacom.com/paper/lte-ecosystem-july-2020-global-status-report/

GSMA, 'The Mobile Economy 2020' (2020), available at: www.gsma.com/mobileeconomy/wp-content/uploads/2020/03/GSMA_MobileEconomy2020_Global.pdf

Hung, M (ed), 'Leading the IoT: Gartner Insights on How to Lead in a Connected World' (2017), available at: www.gartner.com/imagesrv/books/iot/iotEbook_digital.pdf

IDC, 'The Growth in Connected IoT Devices is Expected to Generate 79.4ZB of Data in 2025, According to a New IDC Forecast' (18 June 2019), available at: www.businesswire.com/news/home/20190618005012/en/The-Growth-in-Connected-IoT-Devices-is-Expected-to-Generate-79.4ZB-of-Data-in-2025-According-to-a-New-IDC-Forecast#:~:text=A%20new%20IDC%20forecast%20estimates,ZB)%20of%20data%20in%202025.&text=IDC%20projects%20that%20the%20amount,the%202018%2D2025%20forecast%20period.

Japan Fair Trade Commission, 'Guidelines for the Use of Intellectual Property under the Antimonopoly Act' (2016), available at: www.jftc.go.jp/en/legislation_gls/imonopoly_guidelines_files/IPGL_Frand.pdf

Japan Patent Office, 'Guide to Licensing Negotiations Involving Standard Essential Patents' (5 June 2018), available at: www.jpo.go.jp/e/support/general/sep_portal/document/index/guide-seps-en.pdf

—— 'Manual of 'Hantei' (Advisory Opinion) for Essentiality Check' (revised June 2019)

Katznelson, R, 'The IEEE Controversial Policy on Standard Essential Patents – The Empirical Record Since Adoption' (September 2017), available at: works.bepress.com/rkatznelson/80/

IHS Economics & HIS Technology, 'The 5G Economy: How 5G Technology Will Contribute to the Global Economy' (January 2017), available at: cdn.ihs.com/www/pdf/IHS-Technology-5G-Economic-Impact-Study.pdf

Love, B, Lefouili, Y and Helmers, C, 'Do Standard-Essential Patent Owners Behave Opportunistically? Evidence from US District Court Dockets' (2020), available at: papers.ssrn.com/sol3/papers.cfm?abstract_id=3727085

Maskus, K and Merrill, S (eds), 'Patent Challenges for Standard-Setting in the Global Economy: Lessons from Information and Communication Technology' (National Research Council, 2013), available at: www.nap.edu/catalog/18510/patent-challenges-for-standard-setting-in-the-global-economy-lessons

Mallinson, K, 'Cumulative Mobile SEP Royalties' (19 August 2015), available at: www.wiseharbor.com/pdfs/Mallinson%20on%20cumulative%20mobile%20SEP%20royalties%20for%20IP%20Finance%202015Aug19.pdf

—— 'Development of Innovative New Standards Jeopardised by IEEE Patent Policy' (September 2017), available at: www.4ipcouncil.com/application/files/6015/0479/2147/Mallinson_IEEE_LOA_report.pdf

McDonagh, L and Bonadio E, 'Standard Essential Patents and the Internet of Things' (2019), available at: www.europarl.europa.eu/thinktank/en/document.html?reference=IPOL_IDA(2019)608854

McKinsey Global Institute, 'The Internet of Things: Mapping the Value Beyond the Hype' (June 2015), available at: www.mckinsey.com/~/media/McKinsey/Industries/Technology%20Media%20and%20Telecommunications/High%20Tech/Our%20Insights/The%20Internet%20of%20Things%20The%20value%20of%20digitizing%20the%20physical%20world/The-Internet-of-things-Mapping-the-value-beyond-the-hype.pdf

Noble, M, Mutimear, J and Vary, R, 'Determining Which Companies are Leading the 5G Race' (July/August 2019) *IAM Media* 35, available at: www.twobirds.com/~/media/pdfs/news/articles/2019/determining-which-companies-are-leading-the-5g-race.pdf

OECD, 'Price Discrimination' (2016) DAF/COMP (2016)15
—— 'Standard Setting' (2011) DAF/COMP(2010)33, available at: www.oecd.org/daf/competition/47381304.pdf
Padilla, J, Davies, J and Boutin, A, 'Economic Impact of Technology Standards' (Compass Lexecon, 2017), available at: www.compasslexecon.com/wp-content/uploads/2018/04/CL_Economic_Impact_of_Technology_Standards_Report_FINAL.pdf
—— 'Economic Impact of Technology Standards: Annexes to the Report' (Compass Lexecon, 2017), available at: www.compasslexecon.com/wp-content/uploads/2018/04/CL_Economic_Impact_of_Technology_Standards_Annexes.pdf
Pentheroudakis, C and Baron, J, 'Licensing Terms of Standard Essential Patents: A Comprehensive Analysis of Cases' (Joint Research Centre, Science for Policy Report, EUR 28302, 2017), available at: publications.jrc.ec.europa.eu/repository/handle/JRC104068
Pohlmann, T, 'Empirical Study on Patenting and Standardization Activities at IEEE' (March 2017), available at: www.iplytics.com/wp-content/uploads/2018/01/IPlytics_2017_Patenting-and-standardization-activities-at-IEEE.pdf
Pohlmann, T and Blind, K, 'Landscaping Study on Standard Essential Patents (SEPs)' (2016), available at: ec.europa.eu
—— 'Fact Finding Study on Patents Declared to the 5G Standard' (January 2020), available at: ipforbusiness.org/wp-content/uploads/2020/02/5G-patent-study_TU-Berlin_IPlytics-2020.pdf
PWC, '2017 Patent Litigation Study: Change on the Horizon?' (2017), available at: www.pwc.com/us/en/forensic-services/publications/assets/2017-patent-litigation-study.pdf
Régibeau, P, De Coninck, R and Zenger, H, 'Transparency, Predictability and Efficiency of SSO-based Standardisation and SEP Licensing: A Report for the European Commission' (2016), available at: ec.europa.eu/growth/content/study-transparency-predictability-and-efficiency-sso-based-standardization-and-sep-licensing_en
RPX Corporation, 'Standard Essential Patents: How do They Fare?' (2014), available at: www.rpxcorp.com/wp-content/uploads/2014/01/Standard-Essential-Patents-How-Do-They-Fare.pdf
Signals Research Group, 'The Essentials of Intellectual property, From 3G Through LTE Release 12. Quantifying Technology Leadership in the Development of the 3G and LTE Standards from their Inception Through December 2014' (May 2015), available at: signalsresearch.com/issue/the-essentials-of-intellectual-property-from-3g-to-lte-release-12-5/
UK Policy Paper: 'Open Standards Principles' (April 2018), available at: www.gov.uk/government/publications/open-standards-principles/open-standards-principles
Vary, R, 'A Review of SDO IPR Policies Do They Require Component Level Licensing?' (16 November 2020)

Speeches and Open Letters

77 US Professors' Letter to Assistant Attorney General Delrahim, 'Speeches on Patents and Holdups' (17 May 2018), available at: law.rutgers.edu/f/mc-05-18-2018.pdf
ACT | The App Association, Alliance of Automobile Manufacturers, Computer & Communications Industry Association (CCIA), High Tech Inventors Alliance (HTIA), National Retail Federation and Software & Information Industry Association (SIIA), 'Standards, Licensing, and Innovation: A Response to DOJ AAG's Comments on Antitrust Law and Standard-Setting' (2018), available at www.ccianet.org/wp-content/uploads/2018/05/Multi-Assn-DOJ-White-Paper-053018.pdf
Baer, B, Assistant Attorney General US Department of Justice, 'Remarks as Prepared for Delivery at the 19th Annual International Bar Association Competition Conference, Reflections on the Role of Competition Agencies When Patents Become Essential' (2015), available at: www.justice.gov/opa/speech/assistant-attorney-general-bill-baer-delivers-remarks-19th-annual-international-bar
Delrahim, M, Assistant Attorney General US Department of Justice, 'Take It to the Limit: Respecting Innovation Incentives in the Application of Antitrust Law' (10 November 2017), available at: www.justice.gov/opa/speech/file/1010746/download

—— 'The "New Madison" Approach to Antitrust and Intellectual Property Law' (16 March 2018), available at: www.justice.gov/opa/speech/file/1044316/download

—— 'Antitrust Law and Patent Licensing in the New Wild West' (18 September 2018), available at: www.justice.gov/opa/speech/assistant-attorney-general-makan-delrahim-delivers-remarks-iam-s-patent-licensing

—— 'Broke … but Not No More: Opening Remarks – Innovation Policy and the Role of Standards, IP and Antitrust' (10 September 2020), available at: www.justice.gov/opa/speech/assistant-attorney-general-makan-delrahim-delivers-remarks-leadership-virtual-series

Hesse, R, Deputy Assistant Attorney General US Department of Justice, Remarks as Prepared for the ITU-T Patent Roundtable, 'Six "Small" Proposals for SSOs Before Lunch' (10 October 2012), available at: www.justice.gov/atr/file/518951/download

—— Deputy Assistant Attorney General US Department of Justice, 'Remarks Presented at the Global Competition Review: 2nd Annual Antitrust Law Leaders Forum, IP, Antitrust and Looking Back on the Last Four Years' (2013), available at: www.justice.gov/atr/file/518951/download

—— Deputy Assistant Attorney General US Department of Justice, 'Remarks Presented at the Washington State Bar Association, 'The Art of Persuasion: Competition Advocacy at the Intersection of Antitrust and Intellectual Property' (2013), available at: www.justice.gov/atr/file/518356/download

—— Deputy Assistant Attorney General, Antitrust Division, US Department of Justice, 'Remarks as Prepared for the Global Competition Review: GCR Live IP & Antitrust USA Conference, A Year in the Life of the Joint DOJ-PTO Policy Statement on Remedies for F/RAND Encumbered Standards-Essential Patents' (2014), available at: www.justice.gov/atr/file/517771/download

Industry Letter to US Department of Justice Regarding Standards, Innovation and Licensing (24 January 2018), available at: www.ccianet.org/wp-content/uploads/2018/01/Industry-Letter-to-DOJ-AAG.pdf

Italianer, A, Director General for Competition, European Commission, 'Shaken not Stirred. Competition Law Enforcement and Standard Essential Patents' (2015), available at: ec.europa.eu/competition/speeches/text/sp2015_03_en.pdf

McSweeney, T, Federal Trade Commission, 'Holding the Line on Patent Holdup: Why Antitrust Enforcement Matters' (2018), available at: www.ftc.gov/system/files/documents/public_statements/1350033/mcsweeny_-_the_reality_of_patent_hold-up_3-21-18.pdf

Ohlhausen, M and Wright, J, 'Reply Submission on the Public Interest of Federal Trade Commissioners' In the Matter of Certain 3G Mobile Handsets and Components Thereof, ITC Case No 337-TA-613 (on remand) (2015), available at: www.ftc.gov/public-statements/2015/07/reply-submission-public-interest-federal-trade-commissioners-maureen-k

Ramirez, E, Chairwoman, Federal Trade Commission, 'Address at the 8th Annual Global Antitrust Enforcement Symposium, Standard-Essential Patents and Licensing: An Antitrust Enforcement Perspective' (2014), available at: www.ftc.gov/system/files/documents/public_statements/582451/140915georgetownlaw.pdf

Vestager, M, Commissioner for Competition, European Commission, 'Protecting Consumers from Exploitation' (2016), available at: wayback.archive-it.org/12090/20191129221154/https://ec.europa.eu/commission/commissioners/2014-2019/vestager/announcements/protecting-consumers-exploitation_en

US Professors' Letter to Assistant Attorney General Delrahim, 'Support of Evidence Based Antitrust Enforcement' (13 February 2018), available at: cpip.gmu.edu/wp-content/uploads/sites/31/2018/02/Letter-to-DOJ-Supporting-Evidence-Based-Approach-to-Antitrust-Enforcement-of-IP.pdf

News and Press Releases

Adobe, 'PDF Reference and Adobe Extensions to the PDF Specification', available at: www.adobe.com/devnet/pdf/pdf_reference.html

Bradshaw, T and White, E, 'Qualcomm Settles $774 Million Antitrust Dispute in Taiwan' *Financial Times* (10 August 2018), available at: www.ft.com/content/a785787e-9c41-11e8-9702-5946bae86e6d

Brittain, B, 'Tesla, Dell Sued Over Wireless Tech by European Patent Licensor' *Bloomberg* (15 May 2020), available at: news.bloomberglaw.com/tech-and-telecom-law/tesla-dell-sued-over-wireless-tech-by-european-patent-licensor?context=search&index=4

Business Dictionary, De Facto Standard Definition, available at: www.businessdictionary.com/definition/de-facto-standard.html

Duhigg, C and Lohr, S, 'Fighters in a Patent War' *New York Times* (7 October 2012), available at: archive.nytimes.com/www.nytimes.com/interactive/2012/10/08/business/Fighters-in-a-Patent-War.html

Ericsson, 'Ericsson's FRAND Licensing Terms for 5G/NR in 3GPP Release 15' (3 March 2017), available at: www.ericsson.com/assets/local/tech-innovation/patents/doc/frand-licensing-terms-for-5g-nr-in-3gpp-release-15.pdf

Fair Standards Alliance, 'Position Paper – SEP Licenses Available to All' (24 June 2016), available at: fair-standards.org/wp-content/uploads/2016/09/160624_FSA_Position_Paper_-_SEP_licenses_available_to_all.pdf

—— 'Competitive and Industry Harms Related to Refusal to License SEPs and Other Forms of 'Level Discrimination' in SEP Licensing' (2 December 2020)

—— 'Coerced Global SEP Portfolio Licences are Not FRAND' (26 October 2020)

Heitzner, C, 'Mercedes Touts New A Class as "Smartphone on Wheels" *Automotive News Europe* (2 February 2018), available at: europe.autonews.com/article/20180202/ANE/180209932/mercedes-touts-new-a-class-as-smartphone-on-wheels

Huawei, 'Huawei Releases White Paper on Innovation and Intellectual Property 2020' (16 March 2021), available at: www.huawei.com/en/news/2021/3/huawei-releases-whitepaper-innovation-intellectual-property-2020

IP Europe, 'Why "License to All" Could be a License to Kill Innovation in Europe' (May 2017)

Klos, M, 'Setback for Daimler in Connected Cars Dispute Against Avanci Pool Members' *JUVE Patent* (11 September 2020), available at: www.juve-patent.com/news-and-stories/cases/setback-for-daimler-in-connected-cars-dispute-against-avanci-pool-members/

—— 'Nokia and Daimler Settle all Global Litigation in Connected Cars Dispute' (1 June 2021) *JUVE Patent*, available at: www.juve-patent.com/news-and-stories/cases/nokia-and-daimler-settle-all-global-litigation-in-connected-cars-dispute/

Li, B, Li, L and Xu, C, 'Recent Development on SEP Disputes in China – Anti-Suit Injunction' (*Kluwer Patent Blog*, 20 November 2020), available at: www.reuters.com/article/us-qualcomm-antitrust/south-korea-fines-qualcomm-854-million-for-violating-competition-laws-idUSKBN14H062

Lloyd, R, 'Indian Court Hands InterDigital Anti Anti-Suit Injunction in Xiaomi Fights' (*IAM*, 9 October 2020), available at: www.iam-media.com/frandseps/indian-court-hands-interdigital-anti-anti-suit-injunction-in-xiaomi-fight

—— 'Tesla Targeted Again – this time by Conversant' (*IAM*, 27 April 2020), available at: www.iam-media.com/frandseps/tesla-targeted-again-in-new-infringement-suits-conversant

Nokia, 'Nokia Licensing Rate Expectations for 5G NR Mobile Phones' (21 August 2018), available at: www.nokia.com/en_int/news/releases/2018/08/21/nokia-licensing-rate-expectations-for-5gnr-mobile-phones

O'Brien, K, 'Nokia Settles 2-Year Fight With Apple on Patents' *New York Times* (14 June 2011), available at: www.nytimes.com/2011/06/15/technology/15nokia.html

Qualcomm, '5G NR Royalty Terms Statement' (19 November 2017), available at: www.qualcomm.com/media/documents/files/qualcomm-5g-nr-royalty-terms-statement.pdf

—— 'Examples of Royalties for Mobile Price Points' (1 April 2018), available at: www.qualcomm.com/media/documents/files/examples-of-royalties-for-smartphone-price-points.pdf

Renaud, M, Wodarski, J and Galica, M, 'Is this Seat Taken? A Chinese IP Court Proclaims its Authority to Declare Global FRAND Terms' *National Law Review* (7 December 2020), available at: www.natlawreview.com/article/seat-taken-chinese-ip-court-proclaims-its-authority-to-declare-global-frand-terms#:~:text=A%20Chinese%20IP%20Court%20Proclaims%20Its%20Authority%20 to%20Declare%20Global%20FRAND%20Terms&text=In%20a%20dispute%20between%20O-ppo,3G%2C%204G%20and%20WLAN%20technology

Richter, L, 'Daimler Loses to Conversant Over Connected Cars SEP' *JUVE Patent* (28 October 2020), available at: www.juve-patent.com/news-and-stories/cases/daimler-loses-to-conversant-over-connected-cars-sep/

Schindler, J, 'Sharp Grants Huawei SEP Licence for Auto Components' (*IAM*, 14 July 2020), available at: www.iam-media.com/frandseps/sharp-huawei-license-deal-could-shake-the-car-wars-in-germany

Schwab, K, 'The Fourth Industrial Revolution: What it Means, How to Respond' (World Economic Forum, 14 January 2016), available at: www.weforum.org/agenda/2016/01/the-fourth-industrial-revolution-what-it-means-and-how-to-respond/

Segan, S, 'Infographic: Smartphone Patent Wars Explained' *PC Magazine* (19 January 2012), available at: www.pcmag.com/article2/0,2817,2399098,00.asp and www.pcmag.com/image_popup/0,1740,iid=325524,00.asp

Sisvel, Wireless Program License Terms, available at: www.sisvel.com/licensing-programs/wireless-communications/wireless/license-terms

US Legal, 'Standard Setting Organizations Law & Legal Definitions', available at: definitions.uslegal.com/s/standard-setting-organization-sso/

Via Licensing, Connected Motor Vehicles & Component, License Fees, available at: www.via-corp.com/licensing/mg-multi-generational-wireless/connected-motor-vehicles/mg-connected-motor-vehicles-license-fees/

—— LTE License Fees, available at: www.via-corp.com/us/en/licensing/lte/licensefees.html

—— Mobile Devices & General Products Sub-Program, License Fees, available at: www.via-corp.com/licensing/mg-multi-generational-wireless/mobile-devices-general-products/mg-mobile-patent-license-fees/

—— Multi-Generational (MG) Wireless, available at: www.via-corp.com/licensing/mg-multi-generational-wireless/

Waters, R and Dye, J, 'Apple and Nokia Reboot Patent Wars' *Financial Times* (21 December 2016), available at: www.ft.com/content/04959354-c7b0-11e6-9043-7e34c07b46ef

Weintraub, S, 'Steve Jobs: "I'm going to destroy Android, because it's a stolen product. I'm willing to go thermonuclear war on this."', (20 October 2011) *9to5Mac*, available at: 9to5mac.com/2011/10/20/steve-jobs-im-going-to-destroy-android-because-its-a-stolen-product-im-willing-to-go-thermonuclear-war-on-this/

Yang, H, 'Qualcomm to Appeal Record South Korea Anti-Trust Fine' *Reuters* (4 December 2019), available at: www.reuters.com/article/us-qualcomm-southkorea-idUSKBN1Y807J

Young Lee, S and Nellis, S, 'South Korea fines Qualcomm $854 million for violating competition laws' *Reuters* (28 December 2016), available at: www.reuters.com/article/us-qualcomm-antitrust/south-korea-fines-qualcomm-854-million-for-violating-competition-laws-idUSKBN14H062

Yu, Y and Contreras, J, 'Will China's New Anti-Suit Injunction Shift the Balance of Global FRAND Litigation' (*PatentlyO*, 22 October 2020), available at: patentlyo.com/patent/2020/10/contreras-injunctions-litigation.html

INDEX

Introductory Note

References such as '178–79' indicate (not necessarily continuous) discussion of a topic across a range of pages. Wherever possible in the case of topics with many references, these have either been divided into sub-topics or only the most significant discussions of the topic are listed. Because the entire work is about 'standard essential patents', the use of this term (and certain others which occur constantly throughout the book) as an entry point has been restricted. Information will be found under the corresponding detailed topics.

Milton Keynes UK
Ingram Content Group UK Ltd.
UKHW020212300324
440271UK00004B/92

9 781509 947553